STALIN'S NIÑOS

Educating Spanish Civil War Refugee Children in the Soviet Union, 1937–1951

Stalin's Niños examines how the Soviet Union raised and educated nearly three thousand child refugees of the Spanish Civil War. An analysis of the archival record and numerous letters, oral histories, and memoirs uncovers a little-known story that describes the Soviet transformation of children into future builders of communism and reveals the educational techniques shared with other modern states. Classroom education taught patriotism for the two homelands and the importance of emulating Spanish and Soviet heroes, scientists, soldiers, and artists. Extra-curricular clubs and activities reinforced classroom experiences and helped discipline the mind, body, and behaviours. Adult mentors, like the heroes studied in the classroom, provided models to emulate and became the tangible expression of the ideal Spaniard and Soviet. The Basque and Spanish children thus were transformed into hybrid Hispano-Soviets fully engaged with their native language, culture, and traditions while also imbued with Russian language and culture and Soviet ideals of hard work, comradery, internationalism, and sacrifice for ideals and others.

Throughout their fourteen-year existence and even during the horrific relocation to the Soviet interior during the Second World War, the twenty-two Soviet boarding schools designed specifically for the Spanish refugee children – and better provisioned than those for Soviet children – transformed displaced niños into Red Army heroes, award-winning Soviet athletes and artists, successful educators and workers, and in some cases valuable resources helping to rebuild Cuba after the revolution. *Stalin's Niños* also sheds new light on the education of non-Russian Soviet and international students and the process of constructing a supranational Soviet identity.

KARL D. QUALLS is the John B. Parsons Chair in Liberal Arts and Sciences and a professor of History at Dickinson College.

KARL D. QUALLS

STALIN'S NIÑOS

Educating Spanish Civil War Refugee Children in the Soviet Union, 1937–1951

UNIVERSITY OF TORONTO PRESS
Toronto Buffalo London

© University of Toronto Press 2020
Toronto Buffalo London
utorontopress.com

ISBN 978-1-4875-0358-1 (cloth) ISBN 978-1-4875-1829-5 (EPUB)
ISBN 978-1-4875-2275-9 (paper) ISBN 978-1-4875-1828-8 (PDF)

Library and Archives Canada Cataloguing in Publication

Title: Stalin's niños: Educating Spanish Civil War refugee children in the Soviet Union, 1937–1951 / Karl D. Qualls.
Names: Qualls, Karl D., author.
Description: Includes bibliographical references and index.
Identifiers: Canadiana (print) 20190206063 | Canadiana (ebook) 20190206152 | ISBN 9781487522759 (softcover) | ISBN 9781487503581 (hardcover) | ISBN 9781487518295 (EPUB) | ISBN 9781487518288 (PDF)
Subjects: LCSH: Refugee children – Education – Soviet Union. | LCSH: Refugee children – Soviet Union – Social conditions. | LCSH: Refugee children – Spain – Social conditions. | LCSH: Spain – History – Civil War, 1936–1939 – Refugees – Education – Soviet Union. | LCSH: Spain – History – Civil War, 1936–1939 – Refugees – Soviet Union – Social conditions. | LCSH: Communist education – Soviet Union.
Classification: LCC LA831.8.Q35 2020 | DDC 371.826/9140947–dc23

University of Toronto Press acknowledges the financial assistance to its publishing program of the Canada Council for the Arts and the Ontario Arts Council, an agency of the Government of Ontario.

 Canada Council for the Arts Conseil des Arts du Canada

 ONTARIO ARTS COUNCIL
CONSEIL DES ARTS DE L'ONTARIO
an Ontario government agency
un organisme du gouvernement de l'Ontario

Funded by the Government of Canada Financé par le gouvernement du Canada | Canadä

To my parents, Samuel and Marilyn

Contents

List of Illustrations, Maps, and Tables ix

Acknowledgments xi

List of Abbreviations xiii

Introduction   3

1 "Like Reaching Paradise after Being in Hell": The Turbulent Transition from Spain to the USSR   16

2 "We, the Spanish, Were like an Island": Boarding Schools and Personnel as Loci and Models of Care and Soviet Values   39

3 *Obuchenie*: Classroom Instruction, Patriotism, and the Instilling of Soviet Values   63

4 *Vospitanie*: *Kul'turnost'* and *Kruzhki* as Techniques of Normative Behaviour Training   78

5 Becoming Soviet in Traumatic Times: Life in War, 1939–1944   101

6 No Longer Children: Transitioning to Adulthood during War and Reconstruction   132

Conclusion: Life after Stalin   155

Glossary   167

Notes   169

Bibliography   217

Index   237

Illustrations, Maps, and Tables

Illustrations

1.1 To the Pioneers of Heroic Spain from the Pioneers of the City of Lenin 23
1.2 Soviet Pioneers greeting the "little heroes" from Spain 29
3.1 Children in a Leningrad home, meeting hero aviator Valery Chkalov 71
4.1 Spanish Pioneers with the *puño* salute at Artek 86
4.2 Celebrating their first New Year's holiday in the USSR 88
5.1 Niños familiarizing themselves with rifles and a compass 114

Maps

Spain with regions xiv
The Soviet Union xv

Tables

1.1 Place of origin of Spanish children evacuated to the USSR 18
5.1 Relocation of homes for Spanish children in 1944 124

Additional maps, photographs, tables, and more are available at https://scholar.dickinson.edu/StalinsNinos/

Acknowledgments

If it takes a village to raise a child, then it must take a metropolis to write a historical monograph. Every historian knows that even though there is one name on the cover, there are many more names who deserve credit. *Stalin's Niños* has benefited from the professionalism and support of countless people and institutions, including staff in the European Reading Room of the Library of Congress, all the archives listed in the bibliography, and the superb interlibrary loan staff at Dickinson College (a small but mighty group that acquired books across the seas so I could work in central Pennsylvania when I could not go abroad). Photographs are reproduced courtesy of Spain's Ministerio de Cultura y Deporte and Centro Documental de la Memoria Histórica.

I teach at a small liberal arts college where there are no graduate students. However, because we are an internationalized campus, I have wonderful undergraduates with language skills who were invaluable in helping with early bibliographical work and with skimming sources in Russian (Evan Sparling) and Spanish (Andrea Dominguez, Azul Mertnoff, and Madeline Chandler) to help me prioritize. Hiring them was made possible through funding from Dickinson College. My colleagues also provided much needed assistance. Ryan Burke helped me think through possibilities for the e-book material, and Jess Howard designed and populated the website for the book. Thanks go also to colleagues Marcelo Borges and Elise Bartosik-Vélez for assisting me with some of the trickier Spanish translations. The Howard Foundation and Kennan Institute saw the promise of this book long before chapters had been written, and I thank them for their financial support and vision.

I had just started research when I moved to the United Kingdom for two years (2009–11). This new home allowed me to share initial ideas and gain feedback from talks at the universities of East Anglia, Sheffield, London (Birkbeck College), and Cambridge. Presentations in Prague, Salzburg, and Paris further sharpened my ideas. Thanks go to all who facilitated those talks. Other early supporters included Glennys Young, Lisa Kirschenbaum, Larry Holmes, Margaret

Peacock, Julie DeGraffenried, Jackie Olich, and panellists and discussants at the British Association for Slavonic and East European Studies (BASEEES); the Association for Slavic, East European, and Eurasian Studies (ASEEES); the International Oral History Workshop; and Social Science History Association. The work of Daniel Kowalsky, Olga Kucherenko, and Peter Gatrell helped me think through numerous ideas about Spanish-Soviet relations, children and war, and refugees. The remarkable "War and Childhood" workshop at the German History Institute, led by James Marten and Mischa Honeck, was invaluable for pushing me to consider international connections more deeply. The anonymous readers encouraged me to reorganize the text in ways that have made it better. I must also commend to my readers the staff at University of Toronto Press. Every person with whom I have interacted, in particular Stephen Shapiro, has been a first-degree professional, been helpful with suggestions and comments, and kept the process moving at a good pace.

I am grateful to the publishers of the following for their permission to reprint my ideas that originated elsewhere.

An elaboration on the reportage of Elena Kononenko can be found in "Defining the Ideal Soviet Childhood: Reportage about Child Evacuees from Spain as Didactic Literature," in *War and Childhood in the Era of the Two World Wars*, edited by Mischa Honeck and James Marten (Cambridge University Press, 2019), 71–86; reproduced with permission.

My first attempt to understand the importance of role modelling began as "From Hooligans to Disciplined Students: Displacement, Resettlement, and Role Modelling of Spanish Civil War Children in the Soviet Union, 1937–1951," in *Displaced Children in Russia and Eastern Europe, 1915–1953: Ideologies, Identities, Experiences*, edited by Nick Baron (Leiden: Brill, 2017), 131–54; reprinted with the permission of Koninklijke Brill NV.

The first case study of Spanish boarding schools in the USSR, which now looks rather naive, appeared as "From Niños to Soviets? Raising Spanish Refugee Children in House No. 1, 1937–51," *Canadian-American Slavic Studies* 48 (2014): 288–307; reprinted with the permission of Koninklijke Brill NV.

A final and abundant thanks go to my parents, to whom this book is dedicated. Neither had the opportunity to obtain a college education, but they instilled in me a solid work ethic and a love of reading, both of which have made this book (and my career) possible.

Abbreviations

ANC	Arxiu Nacional de Catalunya
ASSR	Autonomous Soviet Socialist Republic
BCC	Basque Children's Committee
CDMH	Centro Documental de la Memoria Histórica
Comintern	Communist International
GARF	State Archive of the Russian Federation
JSU	Spanish Unified Socialist Youth
Komsomol	Communist Youth League
MOPR	International Organization for Aid to Revolutionary Fighters
Narkompros	People's Commissariat of Enlightenment
NKVD	People's Commissariat for Internal Affairs
PCE	Spanish Communist Party
RGASPI	Russian State Archive of Socio-political History
RGVA	Russian State Military Archive
RSFSR	Russian Soviet Federative Socialist Republic
Sovnarkom	Council of People's Commissars
USSR	Union of Soviet Socialist Republics
VOKS	All-Union Society for Cultural Relations with Foreign Countries
VTsSPS	All-Union Central Council of Trade Unions

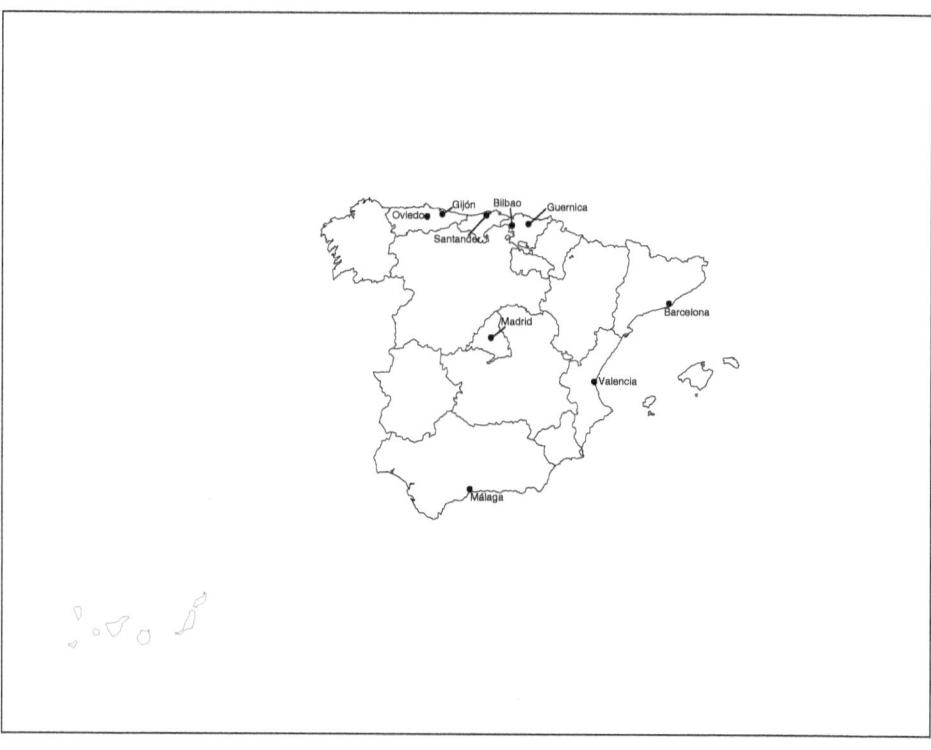

Spain with regions (an outline by FreeVectorMaps.com, modified by Amelia Deering and Karl Qualls)

The Soviet Union (By Hellerick – Own work, based on Natural Earth data, CC BY-SA 3.0, and modified by Amelia Deering and Karl Qualls)

STALIN'S NIÑOS

Educating Spanish Civil War Refugee Children
in the Soviet Union, 1937–1951

Introduction

Ripped apart by the war
from the one I was, two I became:
half remained in my village,
half arrived with the dawn.

Julio Mateu, "Dos patrias"

Julio Mateu, a Spanish poet exiled in the Soviet Union and a recipient of the Order of the Red Star, published "Dos patrias" decades after nearly three thousand Spanish children had fled their country's violent civil war and found refuge in the USSR.[1] For Mateu, Spain was a land of "martyred people, pain"; the Soviet Union provided "love of country, a new world, better." The Spanish children who arrived before Mateu were among approximately thirty-thousand children and 400,000 adults who fled aerial bombardment and the brutal advance of Nationalist forces. Even before the horrific 26 April 1937 Nazi bombing of Guernica – the Basque capital and a market town with no military value – parents feared for the lives of their children and sought refuge abroad. France's nearby border made a logical destination for nearly twenty-thousand children in the war zone, and smaller contingents resided temporarily in Belgium, Great Britain, the Soviet Union, Mexico, Switzerland, and Denmark. The Soviet Union, as the only country to aid the elected Spanish Republic, saw in the war and the rescue of the *niños* (children) the first campaign against the spread of fascism that threatened international socialism. Both Spanish and Soviet communists believed that, after being raised under the watchful eye of their Soviet comrades, the refugee children could then return as adults to build a modern Spain with socialism and communism. Soviet international engagement in the 1930s led to the Popular Front among fascism's foes and was part of broader humanitarian efforts from groups like the Red Cross, International Red Aid, Basque Children's Committee, Spanish Refugee Aid, and many civic and religious organizations in the countries hosting the children. Soviet authorities housed the Spanish children – the oldest in the centre of cities like Moscow, Leningrad, and Kiev and the youngest in the outskirts – and protected them as a humanitarian gesture, as an internationalist project to advance socialism, and as propaganda to differentiate the USSR from capitalist countries that either refused to accept refugees or left them dependent on non-state aid.

Mateu's poem captures the fluid identifications of the Spanish children who, during fourteen years (1937–51) in twenty-two Soviet boarding schools designed specifically for them,[2] learned Soviet values while at the same time retained an attachment to their Spanish language and culture and gained an internationalist world view. There was no one unified experience and therefore no one static or homogenous identification for these children. Unlike Americans and the assumptions prevalent in their Indigenous industrial schools, for example, the Soviets did not view the Spanish children as "blank slates" but rather as transformable children who could learn to adapt to Soviet mores.[3] Throughout their time in Soviet institutions the Spaniards, who on arrival were between three and fifteen years old, lived in liminal spaces that were both Soviet and Spanish, yet not fully either. Soviet teachers carefully designed – and, with Spanish adults, implemented – their education and upbringing to prepare them to contribute to the USSR and Spanish-speaking countries; however, Soviet institutions also unintentionally restricted the children's abilities to feel completely part of any one country. Their identifications remained fractured and shifted between Spanish and Soviet selves, yet were tied together by an internationalist ethos that often elided such differences. Soviet boarding schools protected, nurtured, and educated a vulnerable refugee population and presented them with possibilities they could not have imagined had they remained in Spain. These schools began a process of amalgamation, blending and mixing Spanish and Soviet cultures while not eliminating either. The start of war in the USSR shifted the relative weight of Spanish to Soviet instruction, and it also varied by person as circumstances changed. Trying to uncover one unifying Hispano-Soviet identity is foolhardy.[4] We are best served by trying instead to understand the process of construction.

The arc of the young Spanish refugees' experiences in the USSR is rather remarkable. Many of the 2,895 children who arrived in 1937–8 came from impoverished homes, and few of the children, particularly the girls, had had the opportunity for a quality education in Spain. Many of the refugee children reported fleeing violence in their homeland. Remedios Molinas recalled walking from Málaga to Valencia – trying to avoid attacks from air, land, and sea – with her four young siblings.[5] When children arrived in the Soviet Union, they were greeted by warm embraces, bountiful food, and palatial residences. José and Pilar Fernández, who had also experienced violence in Spain, wrote to their parents about the flag-waving crowds in Leningrad who showered them with songs and gifts before they moved to their new accommodations in a former palace and had the most food they had seen in their lives.[6] They soon settled into special boarding schools that sought to educate them as well as protect their health and well-being. However, after only a few years of something like normalcy the Nazi invasion forced them to flee violence again. The dreadful evacuation placed the children in temporary locations beyond the Ural Mountains without electricity, water, or food. As one person remembered, they endured "a winter of 50 degrees below zero, without knowing the language, without having relatives, without anyone to give a caress."[7] For the first time since arriving in the USSR the children feared for their lives and began to understand that they had been leading a privileged existence in their boarding schools. Now, living more like Soviet children, the Spaniards had to learn to behave like their counterparts. Manual labour helped put food in their mouths, military training helped prepare them for defence, and theft became a strategy of survival for some. The war began to teach them about sacrifice and self-discipline. It also forced their schools to confront the need to prepare them for long-term residence in the Soviet Union, which necessitated better job-skills training and more focused Russian-language learning. The Second World War shattered the privileged, protected environment created for the niños and thrust the older ones, poorly prepared, into Soviet society for the first time as they tried to navigate how to become Soviet.

During the war the older Spaniards entered labour training schools and factories. Some became shock workers; others struggled to adapt to their new world. The criminal behaviour of a few and the dangerous living conditions of many caused the Spanish Communist Party (PCE) to insist on the Spaniards' return to Moscow, where party members could accommodate and supervise them better. On their return to Moscow, "everything ... was all very good,"[8] and the new Chkalov Club allowed the now adolescent and adult Spaniards to socialize, stage Spanish plays, and perform Spanish music and dances, while speaking in their native tongue. In 1946 Spain and the USSR started secret negotiations about repatriation, and eventually refugees were allowed to return to Spain in large numbers, which 1,200 to 1,500 did in 1956–9.[9] However, many of those returnees realized that they had fewer opportunities in Franco's Spain and quickly returned to the USSR. Others returned because they missed spouses, children, and friends who were not allowed to follow them to Spain. Spaniards who remained in the Soviet Union often entered higher education, established families, and contributed to the society of which they had become a part. In this sense the Soviet experiment worked for many.

Most research about the 2,895 Spanish children seeks to understand their experiences based largely on oral histories, memoirs, and Spanish archives and far less on research in the Russian archival records of the institutions tasked with their upbringing. If we are to understand the adults they became, we need to study the ways in which Soviet institutions raised and cared for them, the values and world views that the adults tried to teach them, and how the children responded. *Stalin's Niños* differs from previous studies because, by placing the Spanish boarding schools in the context of the Soviet notions of childhood, the educational policy, and the place of non-Russians in the USSR, we can not only learn about Spanish experiences but also contribute to our understanding of Soviet education and nationality policies.

Several pioneering Spanish scholars have collected oral testimonies and examined letters in an attempt to understand the social and cultural anthropology of collective experience and thus give voice to the Spaniards.[10] Despite these important contributions we have no history of the children's education, and what we know of their experiences in the boarding schools comes largely from two years of letters (1937–9), oral histories conducted a half century after the fact, and a small number of memoirs written in advanced age. Verónica Sierra has suggested rightly that adult supervision of letter writing should make scholars question more this relatively small source base, and historians also must be cognizant of the limits of oral histories and memoirs published decades after events.[11] Spaniards who arrived in the USSR between the ages of three and fifteen years in 1937–8 could not understand the Soviet intentions for and methods of their upbringing and education. To allow memories to guide our investigation of the Soviet boarding schools for Spaniards sets us up for misunderstandings.

Therefore, *Stalin's Niños* comprehensively probes school reports in Russian archives to understand better the Soviet state's intent and practice in the education and raising of this population.[12] No scholar has attempted to investigate the boarding-school experience and the children's education from the Soviet point of view and to place the events in the context of Soviet education and nationality policy. Even when scholars discuss education, there is limited use of the materials in Russian state archives.[13] The best work to date comes from Immaculada Colomina, who has used the Russian archives, but her goal was to highlight the Spaniards' experiences, not the Soviet project. Two other scholars have mined archives, but they tell us little about the Spaniards' education. A.V. Elpat'evksii's book on Spanish emigration has only one section on child refugees but little about education.[14] Daniel Kowalsky's excellent study of Soviet intervention in the Spanish Civil War deals broadly with war, diplomacy, and politics; its one chapter about the children focuses on only their first two years in the USSR as the civil war raged in Spain.[15] Although some scholars have suggested why the Soviet Union accepted 2,895 Spanish children, no one has yet explored all fourteen years of the expensive and privileged education and upkeep and how this transformed the children and youth into Hispano-Soviets.

Stalin's Niños excavates the educational process within a Soviet context in order to explicate Soviet intentions, policies, and practices. Its main contribution is understanding the Spanish boarding schools as part of a broader modern state practice of using education to transform children into patriotic citizens who are capable of becoming intellectual, political, cultural, and productive resources for the state. Moreover, the study asserts that we should not view these relatively isolated boarding schools as exceptions but rather place them in the context of Soviet nationality policy – particularly the model of "non-Russian" schools where national minorities retained native languages and customs while learning supranational Soviet behaviours and ways of thinking. Here they could use their national forms to learn socialist content. Therefore, I emphasize Soviet archival documents more than letters, memoirs, and oral histories that reveal memories of the experiences but which cannot tell us about Soviet intentions. As Karl Schlögel has so aptly noted, "history 'takes place' not simply in time, not merely as a sequence of events unfolding in turn, but in a specific space, a locality."[16] Understanding the transformation of the child refugees requires placing them in their boarding schools and in the context and space of a Soviet Union navigating extremes of repression and inclusion, increasing nationalism and international engagement, and war and peace. This approach allows an investigation of the Soviet nurturing and educating of Spanish children to become Hispano-Soviet youth who retained a connection to their native tongue and culture while acquiring and internalizing an internationalist world view and Soviet normative behaviours that could lead to their own self-governance.[17]

The Soviet homes for Spanish children were a "third space" somewhere between Spanish and Soviet milieus in which the Spanish children's new meanings, behaviours, and cultures were enunciated, practised, and negotiated.[18] A third space, somewhere between the dominant culture and the other, is a place for recognition of cultural diversity while also containing cultural difference. It is a place in which the dominant culture can articulate and try to control cultural norms while the "other" culture can try to exert its cultural forms either as a form of resistance or as an attempt to preserve a self-identification. These third spaces permitted a hybridity that allowed the Spanish children to cross boundaries of identification, and it equally frustrated many of their attempts to belong fully and exclusively to either culture. As was common in the 1920s, particularly for Gypsies and the people of Central Asia, the Soviet state also sought to fix populations to a defined location and to "modernize" their daily behaviours.[19] An investigation of this non-Soviet group of Spanish refugee children shows many of the same dynamics of a Soviet educational system that aimed to modernize and transform children.

This case study helps us situate Soviet education within the larger context of modern schooling, which disciplines and transforms children into agents of the state. Many countries forcefully assimilated indigenous populations and ignored and demeaned the cultural heritage of immigrant populations.[20] In the USSR, however, the party state's emphasis on promoting national cultural difference in Soviet non-Russian schools at a time of increasing russocentrism suggests a fundamentally different understanding of how to modernize populations viewed as backwards. Previous studies of the *niños de la guerra* (children of the war) have omitted connections between the Spaniards' education, a shift to modern state education practices, and changes in Soviet education – including "non-Russian" education and a return to a disciplined and teacher-centred classroom. By reforging these connections, *Stalin's Niños* shows us that "modern" was less about standardizing language and customs of minority groups and more about recognizing linguistic and cultural pluralism and using it to transmit new hegemonic ways of thinking and behaving.

Transformation of human capital has been part of a pan-European modernization process of which Russia was a part.[21] Modern education has sought to transform a national resource – humans – into a national asset. Schools have become more than places to learn to read and to write; they also teach hygiene, discipline, and order and prepare children for productivity. Schools act upon children and attempt to tame the wayward, to create patriotic citizens, to mobilize them for war and work, and to alter lifeways.[22] Soviet education also sought to transform and modernize children; the first Soviet decades saw numerous experiments as authorities vascillated on how and whom to transform.

The years between the great wars caused many countries to rethink their understanding of childhood and the role of families and the state in the collaborative effort of raising the next generation of productive citizens. Kate Ferris has argued that "the place of the family within European dictatorships is crucial to our understanding of how these societies functioned under the weight of the state's totalizing intentions."[23] However, dictatorships also have control over education and children's organization; therefore, schooling is an equally valuable lens for understanding how states want to refashion the new generation of citizens. It is schools – in both democracies and dictatorships – that develop the civilizing mission of a nation's youth.[24] If we consider families, schools, and faith traditions as formative in developing children and youth, then we should not ignore the Soviet boarding schools that served as surrogate families, educating and nurturing the young Spaniards and teaching them to have faith in Marxism-Leninism-Stalinism.

Boarding schools for foreigners are an ideal laboratory for study because here the state has around-the-clock surveillance and no interference from parents to undo the work of transformation. We now know how the Lenin School (1926–38) prepared young adults to return to their countries armed with a "proper" understanding of Marxism-Leninism, how Chinese communists at the International Children's Home failed to retain a close connection to their language and culture, and how Polish children – the offspring of an "enemy" diaspora nation – suffered abuse in Soviet orphanages and schools.[25] What we have not seen to date is a case study of a large group of foreign children who remained in the Soviet educational system for over a decade.

The Soviet boarding schools for Spaniards, however, shared some traits with boarding schools elsewhere. Similar to colonial and anti-indigenous movements, the Soviet educational system – unlike racial theory that created fixed, primordial categories and believed in nature over nurture – promised the "rescue" and "uplift" of "backward" peoples as part of an enlightened modernization process, whether the "backward" people wanted it or not.[26] In all of these systems, authorities invaded the intimate spaces of families and homes to foist perceived universal values and improvements upon the population.[27] Institutional authorities and the states they served became a new locus of authority for children, competing with families and faith institutions. Yet, the Spaniards in the USSR were not without their own agency. Adults in the schools sometimes tried to undermine Soviet teaching, and children enforced group discipline, ran away, stole, engaged with the black market, and acted out in school sometimes as means of survival or to challenge authority.[28]

It is also imperative to understand the Soviet context into which the niños were arriving. While the Soviet regime was murdering its own citizens in the Great Terror and deporting "unreliable elements" like Germans, Poles, Koreans, Chinese, Turks, and Bulgarians, it was also spending lavishly for fourteen years to protect and provide for Spaniards.[29] Much like modern educators in many countries in the twentieth century, Soviet educators viewed children – Soviets and refugee Spaniards – as resources to be moulded, sculpted, and reforged to serve the further development of the arts, sciences, industry, and defence of the country. Unlike Polish children, the Spaniards were from a "heroic," not an "enemy," diaspora. Spanish adults, including the PCE leadership that resided in Moscow, took a great interest in their education and material conditions, which was not the case for Chinese children, for example.[30]

National operations during the Great Terror targeted diaspora nationalities like Poles, Germans, and Chinese and particularly so-called bourgeoise nationalists and groups from bordering countries.[31] Spaniards were likely less persecuted because their home was far from the USSR. As children could be transformed more than the Spanish adults could, the latter were caught in the Terror and the purging by the Communist International (Comintern) in ways that the niños de la guerra were not. Dual loyalty for "enemy" nations condemned some groups to persecution; yet, the dual loyalty constructed in the *casas de niños* (boarding schools) preserved the preferred image of the Spanish as future fighters against fascism. However, the Great Terror established in the minds of the population that there were powerful forces among "others" who were anti-Soviet and had group loyalties to another nation, and we can see hints of that in some criticisms of the Spanish children during the Second World War evacuation. As the war approached, the attempts to prevent a fifth column intensified.

Moreover, caring for the "little heroes," for them to become both fighters against fascism and seeds of communism in the Spanish-speaking world, provided the opportunity for a good return on investment. Soviet officials had a deep-seated fear of wayward children, and by accommodating the niños well, they created opponents to Franco and a vanguard of communism in Latin America, while also avoiding the problems seen in post-war displaced-persons camps in Europe where children "live[d] in hordes and live[d] by maurauding ... to become new gypsies, undisciplined, untrained, ready for any political disorder and without any sense of communal responsibility."[32] This context helps us understand the relative privilege felt by the niños.[33]

Transforming non-Russian children was part of the Sovietization project and consistent with other modern educational systems. The education and upbringing of this foreign population shows the consistency of Soviet approaches to education and nationality policy. *Stalin's Niños* illustrates that unlike the international schools mentioned earlier, the boarding schools for Spanish students closely mirrored the so-called non-Russian schools in the Soviet Union in which the native tongue was the language of instruction and Russian was learned as a second language.[34] Russian was the lingua franca of the Soviet Union, and the "road to social mobility ran through Russian language acquisition."[35] Yet, instructors also taught the children to appreciate their native language and culture. It is on the cultural front that we see the greatest distinction with non-Russian schools because Spaniards had no titular republic or region in the USSR; thus, Russian language education took on greater importance as a mode of integration into a Soviet community. Whereas a Georgian, for example, could survive without acquiring Russian well, a Spaniard would have nowhere in the USSR in which to speak Spanish as a primary language and use it to open doors to Soviet social and economic advancement. Living in boarding schools set apart from Soviet society also made the use of Spanish language and cultural forms essential for the learning of socialist content. Thus, the casas replicated the intentions of "affirmative action" and "state-sponsored evolutionism," and the schools augmented the "form" of national culture with the "content" of a Soviet world view and Soviet disciplinary behaviours.[36]

The Spanish schools in many ways mirrored Soviet education. They followed a standard Soviet curriculum that provided a Marxist world view and anti-religious attitudes, which was novel for many children who had grown up in Catholic Spain where even the Basque Communist Party was pro-Catholic. Moreover, students learned collective activity and responsibility, an appreciation for labour and hard work, and the importance of hygiene and other forms of self-discipline. With the start of the Second World War, physical and military training – though not new in the schools – took on greater importance, as did Russian language proficiency.[37] Together, these and other traits marked a person as a modern Soviet who was no longer "backward" and was ready to fulfil one's responsibilities in adulthood. The whole child, mind and body, was to be nurtured and transformed into an asset for the state.

Children and youth had had a privileged place in Soviet society from its inception, but their role in society changed over time. They served both as a promise of transformation in the future and as sites of the transformative process in the present. The ubiquitous 1936 recitation of "Thank you, comrade Stalin, for our happy childhood" placed Stalin as the gift giver and children as the grateful and deserving recipient of his largesse.[38] There were hierarchies in the doling out of Stalin's gifts: urban over rural, party members over non-party residents, and heroes of labour and art over cogs in the machine. Children as a group were also near the top of the hierarchy, and just as there was a hierarchy among workers, there was also a hierarchy among children.[39] Those who worked to mould themselves into the Soviet ideal received prizes and vacations to the Artek Pioneer camp on the Black Sea. Children from suspect nationalities or parents were often ignored or abused. Just as there were hero labourers, however, there were also "little heroes," like the niños de la guerra who were the future fighters against fascism. Therefore, they received far more attention and material comforts than did typical Soviet children.

The Second World War radically changed the narrative from Stalin's gift of a "happy childhood" to a period of "sacrificing childhood," in which the state mobilized its youngest resources to support the war effort and defend socialism.[40] This "civilizing mission" was a dynamic process as war-time internal failures and external pressures led to changes in policies and approaches. Soviet autarky and russocentric statism coexisted with an engaged internationalism and a humanitarian approach to Spanish refugee children that far outmatched in time, effort, and expense the activity of European democracies that also accepted – though grudgingly – Spanish refugees. The well-appointed Spanish schools, as homes for the young defenders of Spanish democracy, received even more of Stalin's gifts, but the Second World War began a levelling process in which the young refugees started to suffer the same hardships as their Soviet counterparts, to work for the front, and to learn what it meant to be a Soviet citizen living in a crisis economy.

Researching the displacement of these young Spaniards and their experience of geographical, social, and cultural re-placement in the USSR provides scholars with a window into the Soviet project of forging the "new man and woman." A consideration of Soviet education, health care, and adult role models to cultivate the children's physical and mental development and their acquisition of "correct" character traits reveals aspects of the regime's wider strategy of social and cultural transformation. This is consistent with research that has shown displacement not merely as a condition of refugee life but also as a cultural phenomenon that allows for the construction of new identifications within the population.[41] Focusing on a non-Soviet population during a period of tremendous change increases our understanding of Soviet modernist transformation agendas. Relative consistency in education policy in times of turmoil suggests some enduring values. Rather than represent the 1930s as a period of either socialist humanist experimentation or ever-increasing violence and terror, it seems more helpful to engage in understanding the coexistence of what appear to be binaries or dichotomies.[42] Much as "socialism in one country" and a commitment to international engagement coexisted – albeit uneasily at times – the bifurcated Soviet upbringing that sought to maintain Spanish language and culture while simultaneously fostering Soviet political and social values led to unintended consequences of multiple identifications.

Stalin's Niños is not the first study to note the paradoxes in Stalin's USSR. Since the acknowledgment of a "Great Retreat," scholars have been trying to make sense of the seemingly non-Marxist policies in what purported to be the first Marxist state.[43] The policy of *korenizatsiia* (indigenization) was both a maker of nations and a breaker of nations.[44] It promoted national cultures and the people from these cultures; it both brought people together in their own territory and provided them with education, alphabets, and their own leaders; however, it also eventually led many to identify more with their nation than with the USSR.[45] Terry Martin posits a retreat in the 1930s from a sociological understanding of constructed nations to a primordial sense of fixed national characteristics and the needed promotion of national minorities at the expense of majorities. Francine Hirsch, however, describes a state-sponsored evolutionism that sought to modernize and raise out of backwardness all peoples, except "bourgeois nationalists," and to help them move through Marx's stages of development. Rather than it being a retreat from "affirmative action," Hirsch argues that the process of national amalgamations accelerated in the 1930s. Like David Brandenberger, who has demonstrated a shift in emphasis between internationalism and russocentrism in the late 1930s, Hirsch rejects the notion of a definitive retreat from Bolshevik commitments to national heterogeneity.[46] *Stalin's Niños* concludes that although the Spaniards were a highly privileged minority that a few Soviet citizens resented, they were not promoted above national minorities, but rather alongside them in order to one day merge with the ethnically heterogeneous Soviet citizenry, fulfilling their duties to their second homeland and their first.[47]

The amalgamation or hybridization, the blending of Spanish and Soviet cultures, resembles Francine Hirsch's notion of "double assimilation" in which national cultures and categories took shape at the same time as nationalities were assimilating into a supranational Soviet state and society.[48] One could be Soviet and from a national group at the same time. They were not mutually exclusive. Hirsch, however, studied the double assimilation of Soviet nationalities. The hybridization of a non-Soviet group of Spaniards suggests a relatively consistent educational outlook because the niños became Soviet while remaining part of their national unit. Soviet educational goals for the Spaniards also suggest one reason that many of them had difficulty adapting to Spain upon their return decades later: many had learned to internalize Soviet behaviours and a world view that was at odds with Franco's Spain.

Soviet national heterogeneity was alive and well in the Spanish homes, and *Stalin's Niños* illuminates the process and policies of constructing a supranational Soviet citizenry that also retained national traditions as the children began learning Russian and new behaviours and ways of thinking. Like double assimilation, *korenizatsiia* of the affirmative action empire, and education in non-Russian schools, the amalgamation and hybridization of the Hispano-Soviet children created at least three possibilities: to become fully Soviet, to prefer one's national affinities, or to adopt both and adapt to a national culture within a Soviet system and mindset. They learned Soviet content through their own national language. Depending on their particular circumstances in the USSR, some Spanish children readily adopted Soviet cultural and behavioural norms, and others rebelled against or struggled to conform to their new homeland. Many of the children benefited from the affirmative action empire and grew up to become award-winning Soviet artists, academics, and athletes; others returned to Spain in the mid-1940s, and yet others in large numbers from the 1950s onward, to a backward, paternalistic society that represented everything that their time in the USSR had trained them to loathe. A third set of the children – armed with a knowledge of the Spanish language, a communist outlook, and specialized skills and education that would have been difficult to attain in Spain – later aided Fidel Castro's revolution in Cuba. Privileging the Soviet or Spanish identifications or comfortably accommodating to both likely became a key factor in the decision to remain in the USSR or to return to Spain.

The Soviet policy of categorizing and marking the Spaniards seemed to have worked. Not only did it create élan amongst the Spaniards who often referred to classmates as "family" and their schools as "home," but Soviet citizens and institutions also perceived Spaniards as a group and often failed to differentiate individuals among them from the larger group. Even though regional differences were clear to the children, such divisions rarely appear in Soviet reports. Before 1941, Basque and Asturian children typically lived in separate homes in the USSR, but the early war years brought them together in large numbers for the first time.[49] Where they lived together, violence between the two groups was not uncommon; they fought with fists and attacked each other with forks and knives.[50] One Basque recalled: "We arrived in Russia more savage than civilized. After all, our families were all large and poor. We were totally uncultured, without any academic preparation."[51] The absence of such stories in archival documents suggests that although ethnic identification was to be secondary to a Soviet supranational identification, Soviet schooling was attempting to foster a unified Spanish identification alongside Soviet and international identifications that also valued regional cultural differences. For example, in one night of Spanish culture a Galician educator organized performances of Galician dances and the sewing of traditional costumes, and a dance troop of eight Basque boys performed in traditional white uniforms with red sashes and berets.[52] Thus, *hispanidad* (Spanishness) became a supranational equivalent of Soviet. One's cultural traditions could be Ukrainian, for example, while one's citizenship and behaviours were Soviet – national in form and Soviet in content. Similarly, identifying as Galician or Basque might have evoked certain cultural forms, whereas *hispanidad* could relate to a broader history and culture that enveloped the regional variations.

What exactly it meant to be Spanish in the Soviet Union is still unclear, especially given that many of the young Spaniards were Basque. Publicly, regional and national differences were often elided. When a Basque soccer team toured the USSR, journalists interchangeably used *Basque* and *Spanish*. When a group of Spaniards arrived in late June 1937, an article entitled "*Basque* Children Arrived in Moscow" reported Soviet Pioneers shouting "Long live the *Spanish* people" and singing "Song of *Asturias*."[53] In another article specifically about Basque children, journalists reported that "hundreds of *Spaniards*" cried "Long live Russia."[54] *Stalin's Niños* shows us, however, that modern educational practices for this non-Soviet nationality followed the Soviet mantra of "national in form, socialist in content" because Spanish language, culture, and traditions were used to transmit Soviet values and transform Spanish children into resources for the USSR, Spain, and beyond.

Chapter Summaries

The chapters of *Stalin's Niños* illuminate the lived experience of the Spanish refugee children and how they were educated and raised by the Soviets. The first two chapters examine their displacement from Spain and placement in the USSR to understand the outpouring of fond memories found in first-hand accounts. Chapter 1 examines letters, memoirs, oral histories, press coverage, and archival documents to uncover the lives of the niños in war-time Spain, their journey to the USSR, and the warm receptions in their new and much different homeland. Chapter 2 explains the structure and staffing of the boarding schools and argues that the close attention to daily needs and the removal of poor adult role models from the schools allowed many Soviet values to replace traditional Spanish educational and child-rearing practices, like corporal punishment.

Chapters 3 and 4 insert readers into the schools to examine the techniques used in education (*obuchenie*) and upbringing (*vospitanie*) to Sovietize the Spanish children and acculturate them in a manner that would allow them to access Soviet society through a common culture and language. Education in the boarding schools sought to construct numerate, literate, and well-rounded students who would have patriotism for their two homelands, Spain and the Soviet Union. The curriculum mirrored that of other Soviet students, particularly those in non-Russian schools. The refugee children studied Russian as a second language and used Spanish to learn all other subjects from Soviet textbooks that had been translated into Castilian. As in non-Russian Soviet schools, the Spaniards were able to learn and express their national language, culture, and customs because the Soviet leadership believed that national expressions were merely forms without content. Vospitanie work in study circles (*kruzhki*), outings, entertainment, and labour and military training reinforced the patriotic education of the classroom and added the disciplining of bodies and minds. Hygiene, obedience, respect, self-discipline, comradely behaviour, self-sacrifice, labour skills, and a communist world view all developed from after-class activities, which were carefully overseen by the Communist Youth League (Komsomol) and other organizations.

Chapters 5 and 6 detail daily life during a period that ended childhood for many and proved as traumatic as the separation from parents in 1937. Chapter 5 explores the horrific Second World War evacuation of the Spanish boarding schools away from the front lines, the bleak conditions in the interior, and the way in which this period changed pedagogical approaches with the greater emphasis on self-discipline and labour. Chapter 6 asserts that Soviet authorities continued subsidies to the Spaniards as they transitioned into adulthood and came into prolonged contact with their Soviet counterparts in labour training and factory work. These subsidies created animosity among some of the Soviet population and led Spaniards to understand their relatively privileged position in the USSR. The ambivalent and sometimes contradictory approach of maintaining Spanish national forms of culture initially limited the niños' socialization into Soviet norms of conduct and thought. Many of the Hispano-Soviets struggled to become Soviet and remained, to some degree, dependent on Soviet and PCE authorities into early adulthood. A conclusion briefly narrates the Spaniards' lives after the boarding schools closed in 1951, juxtaposing the many successful careers and lives in the Soviet Union with the difficulties of reintegration into Spanish society for some of those who returned home starting in large numbers in the mid-1950s.

1 "Like Reaching Paradise after Being in Hell": The Turbulent Transition from Spain to the USSR

Eleven-year-old Juan Rodríguez, son of a policeman from Oviedo, recalled that arriving in Leningrad in 1937 was "like reaching paradise after being in hell." In doing so, he juxtaposed his impoverished homeland – wracked by civil war, hunger, and conservative institutions – with his arrival in the peaceful Soviet Union that had dynamism and a relative bounty of opportunities and resources. "The Russians looked after us with the greatest devotion, spoiled us endlessly," he remembered. "We, who were little more than savages really, lived the life of the *grandes señores*."[1] The children had little preparation for their hasty evacuation to the USSR, which was so foreign that the young Spaniards "could not paint a picture of their future life."[2] Fantastic images filled the children's heads of a snow-covered country with no trees, where kids went to school on skis. After an arduous journey the children arrived in the USSR to the cheers of a population well primed by media to embrace the "little heroes" from Spain "with great enthusiasm"; they were "received with great affection from all the Russian comrades."[3] However, although many of the niños have expressed fond memories of their early days, unbeknownst to them the Soviet authorities struggled with how best to accommodate the new arrivals.

The children could not know that, as they arrived in 1937–8, they were entering both a paradise and a hell. Their arrival marked a year of contrast: political show trials and executions of the Great Terror coincided with celebrations of aviators and arctic explorers, Aleksandr Pushkin's jubilee, and the Paris International Exhibition. The Soviet Union led the campaign against fascist enemies in Europe while it manufactured enemies at home. Marxist internationalism persisted at the same time that russocentrism became more prominent. The regime starved and abused the prison labourers who were building the new Moscow-Volga Canal while it took in 2,895 children from Spain and provided for their every need.

Despite the traumatic and tragic separation from their country and families, the children quickly learned that the Soviet Union would meet their needs much better than they could have expected. They came primarily from the Basque region and Asturias – regions beset by class division, poverty, limited educational opportunities, and workers' uprisings – which stood in stark contrast to their adopted homeland of the Soviet Union in the late 1930s. Their first years in the USSR laid the foundations for both successes and failures. Accommodating the children meant privileged care and greater opportunities than those offered in Spain; yet, that same care in boarding schools failed to adequately prepare the older students for transition into independent and acculturated (*kul'turnyi*) Soviet adults.

Living in Hell: Life in Republican Spain

Life in Spain in the 1930s was bleak. From 1936 to 1939 the Nationalist interventionists and their German and Italian allies violently pushed their way through Republican Spain and had few hesitations about killing civilians – men, women, and children. Republican loyalists also had been brutalizing clerics and large landowners and destroying property. Daily life became insufferable. Hunger spread widely, particularly in the cities. "To this day," one person remembered, "I cannot eat lentils without recalling those months when that was all we had to eat, day after day, with a bit of rice. Whenever my wife cooks them, they seem to give me indigestion."[4] Memories of the hunger years, rather than his wife's cooking, unnerved him. In a country and region beset by poverty, food was understandably a key focus for urban children whose parents did not live off the land. Bountiful receptions in Leningrad made their former hunger even more memorable by comparison.

This generation of Spaniards also lived through extraordinary violence. Children witnessed friends and family killing and being killed. Air raids led to lives underground when Italians from the sea and Germans from the air sent families scrambling for shelter.[5] In March 1937 General Emilio Mola began his northern offensive against Republican forces. At the end of the month German and Italian airplanes bombed the Basque town of Durango, and during the following week Francisco Franco's forces blockaded the north coast. On 26 April Nazi planes intentionally targeted the market town of Guernica, a non-military target at the heart of the Basque national imagination, which was later made famous by Pablo Picasso's painting of its destruction. It was under these conditions that parents had to make the gruelling decision to send their children away or to die together. One child reportedly brought German and Italian shrapnel with him to the USSR as a reminder of the choice his parents had made.[6] The levels of violence on both sides of the civil war were excessive and continued long after Franco's 1939 victory.[7]

A research team headed by Marie José Devillard has provided us with the best statistical understanding of the niños evacuated to the Soviet Union.[8]

Table 1.1 Place of origin of Spanish children evacuated to the USSR

Origin	Total children	Origin	Total children
Andalucía	20	Galicia	8
Aragón	6	Madrid	114
Asturias	896	Navarra	30
Cantabria	86	País Vasco	1,315
Castilla–La Mancha	3	Rioja	11
Cataluña	47	C. Valenciana	43
Ceuta y Melilla	6	Others	30
Extremadura	30	Unknown	72

Source: Devillard, *Los niños*, 233. This table accounts for only those children for whom birthdates were known.

Overwhelmingly, the 2,895 evacuees came from industrial provinces in northern Spain. Asturias (896 children) and País Vasco (1,315 children) accounted for over 76 per cent of the total evacuated children. The next largest province was Madrid (114). The children were also concentrated in particular locations within the regions. For example, in País Vasco (the Basque Country) over 80 per cent of the refugees were from the province of Vizcaya (1,055 children) and over half (700) were born in its capital city of Bilbao. Many of these children had already moved from family homes to *colonias escolares* (school colonies) where educators sought to meet their social, physical, and academic needs.[9]

All evacuating children were supposed to be between the ages of five and twelve, but some were as young as three. Oral testimonies suggest that there was much obfuscation about age as parents tried to evacuate their children from war-torn Spain.[10] Although only about a dozen children seem to have been younger than five, Devillard has concluded that 270 boys and 168 girls were thirteen or fourteen years old. Most of the children (2,103) evacuated with at least one sibling, leaving fewer than eight hundred who were without immediate family on the journey. The majority travelled with two or three siblings, but there were two families of six children and one family of seven children.[11] Although we do not have statistical data about other family relations, we know that many children travelled with cousins, and often times entire schools evacuated together.[12] Thus, the number of children travelling with no relative was much lower than eight hundred. Owing to this fact and the regional density, there were likely even fewer children travelling completely without companionship. By gender we find a more male group (58 per cent) accompanied by an overwhelmingly female staff.[13]

We would need to have much more information about the children's families to make any conclusive statements about social origins. "Characterizations" in the Russian archives describe most children from working-class origins as sons and daughters of miners, dock workers, and metalworkers.[14] Yet, we also know that a small percentage of the children in the Spanish homes were from elite families, including those of Spanish pilots, military figures, and political leaders like Dolores Ibárruri (herself from a Basque mining family), and came primarily on the first and last ships to the Soviet Union. The working-class group far outnumbered the elites.

Although we do not know individual biographies for the children, we can say that the majority, although not all from Asturias or the Basque Country, came from these two northern regions, where workers' living standards had decreased because of lower wages, higher costs of living, and increased immigration from around Spain. Most of the first children evacuated to the USSR "were from the very poorest sections in Bilbao – the industrial belt, laced with rows of old decaying six-story stone apartments, surrounded by the noxious steel mills linking the filthy miles of the city's harbor."[15] They had little money for their daily needs. Hunger was the norm even if full rations could be found. Workers' political fragmentation – even within the left – and decreased standards of living vis-à-vis land and business owners led to violent strikes and street fighting that certainly became a part of many children's lives.[16] For children who lived daily with poverty, hunger, and violence, one can only imagine the shock that was in store for them when they finally reached the Soviet Union where they initially stayed in hotels, palaces, and resorts and ate as much as their stomachs could hold. Yet, they first had to endure further trauma as Franco's forces advanced with Nazi air attacks and Italian bombardments from the sea.

Troubled Evacuation While Escaping to "Paradise"

During their four-hundred-mile walk from Málaga to Valencia, the five Molinas children, ages six to thirteen, endured attack from land and air. Having already lost one of her children to the war, their mother decided to send her remaining children to the Soviet Union, although France and Belgium were also possibilities. "Many [families] cried. My mom cried," one of her children told a Soviet reporter. "Me – no. I knew that in Russia it would be good."[17] It is difficult to understand how this child knew it would be good, but the newspaper account of the story of Remedios, Alfredo, Carmen, Manuel, and Francisco, while extreme in some cases, shares much with the stories of other refugee children.[18] Most participants expected a short-term evacuation of three or four months; some children thought it could be an exciting getaway, an adventure.[19] For others it was a frightening leap into the unknown. There is little typical about evacuation stories except the assurance of change.

The periods before and during evacuation were often harrowing. Ángel Rodríguez was ten years old when his mother insisted that her children leave Asturias and go to the Soviet Union.[20] Once families had made the decision and completed the paperwork, all that remained was the agonizing wait. Ángel's basement became his safe place while waiting to leave from Gijón: "Windows in the basement were shut with sandbags to protect us against the guns. We had to run to that basement five or six times a day, covering our ears not to hear the whistle of bombs that were dropping near our home."[21] His mother carried a gun so that she had some protection on her travels. Ángel was relieved when he finally boarded the French ship. He reported five decades later that he was not overly anxious, because he did not know the concept of homeland (*patria*), and the children had been assured that they would return as soon as the war was over. Little did he know that the war would drag on and that he would not return for decades.

Other children recalled being agitated from the start. Adolfo Cenitagoya remembered the tears as bombs and shells fell and cries filled the air and his fourteen-year-old ears. The children boarded an old French ship with an international crew and hoped for the best as a German Junker dropped bombs.[22] This result of "non-intervention" of European democracies allowed for German, Italian, and Spanish Nationalist attacks on civilians and gave no relief to the children or adults onboard the refugee ships.[23]

Between March 1937 and December 1938 four expeditions took the Spanish children to the Soviet Union in what was part of an international effort to provide humanitarian assistance. The first small group of seventy-two children – including the Molinas family – left Valencia on 21 March 1937. The Republican Ministry of Public Instruction directed the ship *Cabo de Palos* to Yalta, where the children recuperated at the Artek resort, the premier Pioneer camp on the Black Sea.[24] Following a summer on the beaches the children moved to Moscow and entered the first of the homes for Spanish children on Bol'shaia Pirogovskaia Street, which is today the embassy of Vietnam. This was the only expedition not made up primarily of children from the northern coast of Spain.

The next three evacuations came from northern Spain as it began to succumb to the combined brutality of Nationalist forces and the German Luftwaffe. The Basque government's Department of Social Assistance and Culture (Departamento de Asistencia Social y de Cultura) along with the Communist Party of Euskadi (Partido Comunista de Euskadi) and the Comintern-affiliated International Red Aid (Socorro Rojo Internacional) organized these northern evacuations.[25] Evacuation presented real dangers, as the republic's enemies did not intend to let Spanish children leave the country. On 13 June 1937, just days before the fall of Bilbao, the Basque government responded to the offensive by loading the ship *Habana* with nearly 4,500 children. Approximately three thousand children either disembarked in Bordeaux, France, or continued to Southampton, England. On 22 June mostly Basque children arrived in Leningrad after having boarded the *Sontay* in France. The next expedition left Gijón on 24 September on the French cargo ship *Deriguerina*. The Council for Public Instruction of the Provincial Council of Asturias and León organized this evacuation of 1,100 children from Asturias, Santander, and the Basque Country. The hungry children arrived in Leningrad aboard the Soviet ships *Kooperatsiia* and *Feliks Dzerzhinsky* on 4 October after transfers in Saint Nazaire, France, and London, England.[26] The final official expedition, in October 1938, crossed the Pyrenees in buses and then evacuated further by train to Le Havre, France, where the children boarded the *Mariia Ul'ianova* and the *Feliks Dzerzhinsky*; the latter did not arrive until the end of November.[27]

Evacuation was difficult for the loved ones left behind in war-ravaged Spain. Mothers sometimes suffered from the absence of and separation from their children and the judgment of others who did not understand their decisions: "Many times I have heard reasoning regarding the mothers who sent us to different countries to save us from the war. I have heard reproaches: 'What a horror! How could they abandon their children like this?' And I must add that I believe in the love of our mothers."[28] The perceived short duration of evacuation caused further confusion for parents who had "sent all us children thinking that now we were on vacation for three months, and what happened was that we could not return until many years later."[29] Some children tried to flee during the evacuation, like the Mezquita siblings (ages five to eleven) who, even though they were told it would only be a three-month evacuation, hid on the *Habana*'s lifeboats, hoping to return to Spain rather than carry on to their destination.[30] The sense of separation might have been tempered for roughly three-quarters of the children who evacuated with at least one sibling. Others, like Carlos Roldán's brother António, who was hospitalized with measles and therefore separated from his brother, escaped (though briefly) from an institution so as not to be parted from a sibling.[31] This is but one example of the children trying to regain control over their lives.[32]

Fear dominated many children's memories of their evacuation from Spain. A child on the second expedition recalled: "I remember the day we had to leave they were constantly bombarding the port and we could not go. We left the next day escorted by a Soviet submarine."[33] For the children who traversed the "German waters" on their way to Leningrad, their fear of Nazi Germany also coloured their letters home, which described battleships, planes, torpedos, submarines, and bombs.[34] The voyages were arduous, and several narrators remembered the dark of the cargo hold where they bedded down on mats, surrounded by the sounds of crying children. Retching was frequent as people tried to overcome seasickness. The ocean was "as bad as the Germans," one evacuee recalled. Unfortunately for Ana del Bosque Arin, who had just seen the film *The Mask of Fu Manchu*, the crew of the coal ship *Sontay* was mostly Chinese. Like others, Ana remembered the discomfort of the rolling waters, uncomfortable mats, and the filth where she lived in the cargo hold; at thirteen years old, she felt trapped below decks because the Chinese mariners frightened her so much that she would not walk the corridors. One refugee claimed: "The treatment on the Chinese ship was horrible, we were all in the hold, everyone vomited. All the time they gave us rice to eat and the rats that were in the ship were like cats. Moreover, the whole way we could not change clothes or anything." Another recalled being "dizzy all the time" and asking to go home. Many simply could not eat in such conditions. Spaniards often recalled "everyone sleeping on mats in the ship's hold," "throwing up on ourselves," going "without eating," and "children crying."[35]

Unlike typical Soviet knee-jerk "storming" and "campaigning," preparations for the children's arrival in the USSR had been more than a year in coming. Planning for the physical care of children started at the highest levels, and most Soviet citizens – infected with "espanophilia" – followed the plight of Spanish children in print and film from the first days of the Spanish Civil War.[36] The combined efforts of bureaucrats and the media laid the groundwork for receiving the refugee children, who were lavished with attention and became heroic symbols for Soviet children.[37] Even before the initial plans for housing refugees had been made, the Central Committee of the Soviet Communist Party and the International Organization for Aid to Revolutionary Fighters (MOPR) had been in contact with the Spanish Republic. This liaison ranged from simple letters of greeting and support to invitations for Spanish delegations to tour the Soviet industrial heartland so that they could then return to Spain as propagandists.[38] Throughout 1936, daily columns in Soviet newspapers kept the public informed about the progress of the war. In addition, periodic campaigns to raise money and awareness personalized the war. During September, for example, the pages of *Pravda* reported numerous stories about women's meetings and fundraising for the women and children of Spain, including articles about individuals, families, and groups giving money for the cause.[39] As one scholar has noted, "the reports of the fighting in Soviet newspapers show how the war had begun to seep into the very pores of society."[40] "We Spanish children," wrote José Fernández in his memoir, "were famous at the time like [Valery] Chkalov, the aviator, or [Lyubov] Orlova, the actress."[41]

The Central Committee of the Soviet Union had been granting special and separate aid to Spanish children for months before the evacuations began, but a letter written on 22 September 1936 by Comintern official Dmitrii Manuilskii, requesting that Stalin accept refugee children, might have set evacuation planning in motion.[42] Although the first flotilla of niños was still months away, MOPR opened a home for foreign children in the autumn of 1936.[43] With an international home like this as precedent, it took little time to act on Marshall

1.1 To the Pioneers of Heroic Spain from the Pioneers of the City of Lenin. España, Ministerio de Cultura y Deporte. Centro Documental de la Memoria Histórica, P.S. Fotografías, carpeta 36, folio 2922.

Kliment Voroshilov's request to Stalin to open a home for eighty to one hundred Spanish children. Voroshilov's letter of 20 December 1936 specified that one of Moscow's best orphanages should be used and that priority should be given to children of dead Spanish fighters.[44] This was not to be mere warehousing of refugees; this was to be a recognition of sacrifice in the fight against fascism and a meaningful humanitarian gesture. Not surprisingly given Voroshilov's military status and membership in the Politburo, the latter approved a decree on 2 January 1937 that placed the Red Army Intelligence Service in charge of the first set of boarding-school-style homes for Spanish children.[45] In October the Comintern, seeing the ongoing calamity in Spain, issued a call to "organize as soon as possible the evacuation of the civilian population of Asturias (children, women, old people) because in Asturias there is a shortage of both food and housing ... We must appeal to the humanitarian feelings of the population of all countries."[46] The Soviets had already started accommodating Spanish children, and in November 1937 the People's Commissariat of Enlightenment

(Narkompros), which was responsible for Soviet schools and orphanages, took over responsibility for the niños. By the end of 1940 it had opened twenty-two homes for Spanish children and youth in the Moscow and Leningrad regions, Evpatoriia, Odessa, Kiev, Kherson, and Kharkov.

Staff for the new homes, drawn largely from Soviet schools and orphanages and including the Spanish adults who arrived with the children, first had to deal with separation anxiety. Parting from parents was excruciating for most of the children, and their misery became infectious. One older child remembered the weeping cascading from one young child to the next. It escalated, and the Russian caregivers, also crying, had to leave the room.[47] Unlike the willing departure of the Molinas children, one boy recalled "screaming and crying all the time because I did not want to leave anything. My mother would never forgive herself for sending me to the Soviet Union." Another stated: "Like many, I came here deceived. I did not want to come."[48] The evacuation had forced children to leave behind everything they knew. "We missed everything," one child recalled. "We missed our homeland, we missed our parents, we missed our religion, we missed a Spanish education, we missed everything because we were very little."[49]

As traumatic as the loss and the fear of evacuation and transport were for some children, other niños felt relieved to have escaped the violence, poverty, and hunger that had accompanied war in Spain. The fear of war and the arduous journeys across rough seas patrolled by German submarines made landfall in a peaceful city a pleasant change for many of the children who lived "like princes and princesses, being educated in the best manner possible, like being in Paradise."[50]

Soviet newspapers conveyed the joy of abundance and hope that tempered the sense of fear and loss felt by many of the young children. Eleven-year-old Charito Bruno, daughter of a Republican air force pilot, was the first Spanish child to speak to the Soviet press. Her story became a template for reporting on this first wave of refugees by highlighting the absence of a happy childhood in Spain. Charito's mother sent her and her brother from bomb-ravaged Madrid to Alicante. It was here that she joined the children's communist organization, the Young Pioneers. Charito's story brought fascist violence and brutality into Soviet homes. She recalled witnessing shootings and explosions and watching as Republicans killed fascists after the latter had gunned down her people. Germans and Italians shelled Alicante from offshore as bombs fell from above, which made her last night in the city "frightful." War had altered the routine and everyday existence of this young child, but it had also given her purpose and focus. She now dreamt of one day becoming a communist and flying like her father – an aspiration that would have been impossible for a woman in patriarchal Spain. She now preferred the happy life of Soviet children: "Here children are pleased and merry, but in Spain there is no kind of merriment possible for children because of the fascists."[51] Soviet protection and concern equalled a happy childhood where children could dream of becoming something. "I am so surrounded by love," she said, "that I feel like I am in a second homeland."[52]

Charito's story suggested that the Soviet Union was a land of opportunity where light could overcome darkness. In this one story we can see the process of re-placing the children, discursively, into a world of hope and opportunity, and their modelling of gratitude towards the Soviet Union as the Great Terror shattered many Soviet families.

First Encounters in the Soviet Media

Films and print stories prepared the Soviet public for the arrival of the Spanish children. Historian Daniel Kowalsky has shown how Soviet authorities set in motion a campaign to construct Spanish children as both victims of fascism and "little heroes."[53] In his analysis of the twelve-minute film *Spanish Children in the USSR* (1937), Kowalsky noted that the "apocalyptic images of a darkened and terrorized Spanish Republic soon give way to daybreak in sunny and tranquil Moscow." A fifteen-second shot of crowds cheering the children's arrival "is sufficient to paint a sharp contrast between the sun-drenched, joyful arrival in Russia and the panicked departure from the shrinking Republican zone."[54] Later in the same year Elena Kononenko published *Malen'kie ispantsy* (Little Spaniards) – the chief long-form propaganda piece about the first refugee children – in which she used similar imagery of a life of darkness and fear that is turned sunny and happy in the Soviet Union.[55] Although film shorts likely reached a wider audience, their brevity could not tell a child-centred story and enable viewers to "know" the subject. Written stories became the main vehicle for greater humanization of the children, and an elaboration on their experiences sought to impart lessons as much as to distract from current problems in the USSR, like the Great Terror. If tomorrow brought war, the Spanish children could serve as an example of sacrifice and fortitude.[56]

Journalists were the first to report on the evacuating Spanish children and painted a verbal portrait, occasionally with photographs, that often told individual stories of the journey from darkness to light. The first laconic report in *Pravda* noted the arrival of fifty-three boys and nineteen girls in Suuk-Su on the sun-drenched coast of Crimea.[57] This brief story did little more than narrate the initial steps of reception: shower, receive new uniforms, play in the flower garden, and settle into comfortable quarters. Readers found a list of teachers and medical personnel who came with the children; they learned that many of the children were Pioneers from Málaga, Madrid, and Valencia, and read that they brought notebooks, literature, and school supplies with them. The author identified the children as the offspring of workers, peasants, fighters, commanders, and pilots in the Republican army. Thus, the reader received a collective sense of the seventy-two children but no personal stories to increase one's concern and compassion.

Izvestiia's first report could not have been more different in length and substance.⁵⁸ Not only was the article twice as long at sixty lines, but the reporter also humanized the children and wrote of them as more than just a collective of war-weary children. The children were given a voice, albeit briefly, as they disembarked with cries of "Saliut! Viva Rusia!" while waving the Spanish revolutionary flag. They were marked by language and symbol as "other," yet they were not entirely alien because they shared a revolutionary spirit and an understanding of Russia (read: the USSR) as a special entity, the first socialist state. They were both "us" and "them." *Izvestiia* was developing the image of an internationally minded Hispano-Soviet hybrid that would become central to the children's self-understanding in the years to come and part of their dual patriotism for two countries. *Izvestiia* also narrowed the demographic breadth to children of workers and peasants instead of the more accurate, privileged offspring of commanders and pilots. Eschewing their fathers' military backgrounds also helped cast the children as innocent victims of fascist aggression and encouraged readers to sympathize with the children. The mission and ten-day journey were secret, the reporter noted, because the fascists had threatened to sink any ships carrying children to the Soviet Union. Thus, the children were relaxing and recovering in the motherland of socialism and meeting their Soviet counterparts. The Soviet Union also had rescued them from almost certain death.

Soviet newspapers had been filled for a year with stories about Spain's civil war. Daily briefs from the various front lines were usually front-page news and accompanied by various stories of Trotskyist spies arrested in Europe, of German and Italian collaboration with Franco, and of communication from Spanish leaders with the Soviet Union, other countries, and international bodies about the plight of the people and about the democratically elected government in Spain. The August–September 1936 campaign to raise funds for Spanish women and children dominated the press for several days. With the arrival of the refugee children, the Soviet press began showing the much more direct humanitarianism of the Soviet Union's defence of the future of the republic – saving and taking care of its children. This advanced preparation in the press is likely one reason why the Spaniards did not have to endure the neglect, violence, and abuse meted out to Polish children.⁵⁹

Continuing coverage in *Pravda* and *Izvestiia* set the tone for the film *Spanish Children in the USSR* and for Elena Kononenko as she established a revised narrative in her book *Little Spaniards* in November 1937.⁶⁰ The reporting in June and October 1937 added two key features that were essential in Kononenko's book: more personalized storytelling and photographs. Later reporters often told readers the children's names and something about the hardships of life in Spain. Occasionally photographs were included, often of Spanish children wearing fresh new outfits on their backs and smiles on their now-clean faces and raising their arm in the *puño* (the fist salute). Readers learned about the horrors of living through aerial bombardment, the malnutrition and illness that special resorts and clinics sought to combat, and the children's fierce desire to learn from their Soviet comrades so that they could return to Spain to fight fascism. This was the courage and happiness that was supposed to be found in the USSR.

When the first group of refugee children finally reached Yalta at 11:30 a.m. on 30 March 1937, it was sunny "as in southern Spain. The children shrieked from happiness and surprise," according to Kononenko.[61] They were warmly and immediately welcomed into their new family and a land full of sunshine, trees, and a happy childhood. A "throng of people" gathered at the pier. They were smiling, cheering, throwing white and pink flowers into the air, and playing music. A child introduced as Saragossa, waving his hand, cried out in two languages: "Viva Rusia. Da zdravstvuet Sovetskaia Rossiia!" He was answered with "Da zdravstvuiut deti geroicheskoi Ispanii!" Remedios and her siblings began to disembark, and a female worker swooped up little Alfredo and held him to her heart as tears spurted (*bryznut*) from her eyes. Rosario and Consuelo descended, and the latter had already stopped crying and was laughing. Tatar Pioneers gave her a big bouquet of flowers. The Spanish sailors bid them farewell. The kids kissed and thanked the sailors for their good care, and the captain started crying. Emiliia ran to him and hugged him tightly. The tough girl who had carried communist newspapers to school in Madrid broke out in tears of happiness "that strangers greeted the Spanish children just like their own [*rodnye*] ... She left from the steamer as from the last bit of Spanish land."[62] They had arrived in a country of sunshine, friendship, and concern for others where tears flowed freely, but out of joy and love rather than fear, darkness, and sadness.

Whether from the press, films, or books, no one could have escaped hearing about the niños, but by the end of 1939, with Franco's victory and the start of the Second World War, the children had disappeared from public view as Soviet press and film coverage of the children had all but ceased. So too did their letters home. Two years of reporting on the Spaniards to a Soviet audience helped to reiterate the values and ideals of Soviet life. Even to foreigners, the reports suggested, the Soviet Union lovingly cared for children and ensured they were fed, clothed, and housed. As Kononenko pointed out, most of the Spanish children did not dwell on their suffering and the absence of family, which was an important lesson for Soviet readers during the Great Terror. Instead, they persevered and improved themselves. The Soviet Union welcomed future fighters against fascism and extended care to children who would one day join the battle for their home country and for communism. Moreover, the stories prepared the Soviet public to receive and welcome these children, a welcome that would be tested as some behaved poorly and others competed for scarce war-time resources.

Spaniards Remember Their First Days in the Soviet Union

There is no doubt that Kononenko's official Soviet story about the arrival of the first niños was propagandistic, but the children's letters home and the memories they related decades later suggest that there was some truth in the propaganda. The children often fondly remembered the warm reception in the Soviet Union. José and Pilar Fernández wrote to their father in Bilbao that music and flags among the excited crowd greeted them in Leningrad before they received a shower and clothes and travelled to the south of Russia.[63] The large crowds singing (either the "Internationale" or the Spanish Republican anthem "Himno de Riego"), dancing, waving flags, and saluting led many refugees to feel that they were welcomed.[64] One letter noted that in the two days in Leningrad before onward transit the author had already seen palaces and cathedrals, enjoyed the affectionate welcome of the Soviet people, and been to dances and the opera to see the best Soviet artists.[65] Adolfo Cenitagoya reported that everything was "perfectly organized" and that Soviets welcomed them with "open hearts."[66] Juliana, who arrived in October 1938, expressed the totality of the accommodations: "On arrival we had chocolate cake and many gifts. Then they took us to a room full of toys. There we stripped and bathed, then came some doctors and they gave us a checkup."[67] Food, leisure, and health care all were immediate concerns and previously unavailable luxuries. The juxtaposition of a life in war and an economy in crisis with a new residence of ebullient welcomes and abundant material provisioning likely has led to the remarkably fond memories found in oral histories and memoirs.

Students were equally impressed with the places in which they were living. One child wrote about "a brilliant glimmering floor here ... wardrobes full of jewellery, perfumes of all types ... walls full of paintings."[68] Ángeles Pérez, an auxiliary worker who accompanied the children, commented that she lived in a "precious house" in Leningrad for the first two days.[69] Girls described the homes, formerly the property of Russian nobles, as large, grand buildings with rooms that were stately and spacious, with marble floors, exquisite decorations, and numerous musical instruments. The boys welcomed the soccer fields on the grounds. This was a "Soviet paradise" where one could dance on the terraces and play in the nearby forests and rivers; good health was now possible because of abundant soap, good hygienic conditions, and a dentist to care for one's teeth.[70] Another Spaniard recalled fondly the beautiful architecture, extensive garden, a fish pond, and the large auditorium in Home No. 7 in Moscow.[71] Milagros Latorre was enamoured with Home No. 5 outside Moscow, nestled in the forest where the children could swim in the nearby river.[72]

Letters suggest that Soviets – both communists and other elites – often intervened personally to make the refugees welcome. One of the older boys, fourteen-year-old Daniel Monzó Carbonell – who would later work in the aviation industry – wrote to his father and siblings in Alicante that Pioneers waving

"Like Reaching Paradise after Being in Hell" 29

1.2 Soviet Pioneers greeting the "little heroes" from Spain. España, Ministerio de Cultura y Deporte, Centro Documental de la Memoria Histórica, P.S. Fotografías, carpeta 36, folio 2928.

flags greeted him at a "building that looks like a palace" with gardens and trees all around, a loving Russian official, and "everything we want."[73] Another young Spaniard recalled Marshal Aleksandr Egorov's visit to his boarding school. Egorov inspected the food, the toilets, and even felt the quality of the children's blankets. A few days after his visit he sent new "beautiful, soft, and warm camel hair blankets" to replace the others. José Fernández and the other children were crushed when Egorov was arrested and executed during the Great Terror.[74] Carlos Roldán noted more than six decades later that each time he went to Leningrad, all he could remember was the music and sun greeting him as he walked down the gangplank.[75] Another Spaniard noted, "We lived like aristocrats, like marquises, we were treated like queens."[76] Although these positive letters in 1937–8 likely were scripted partially, we will see later that complaints too were passed on to parents.[77]

Kononenko's official story tells us of the white tablecloths, cocoa, and hot pirozhki that awaited the Spanish arrivals, but the children's testimonies place even greater importance on the abundance of the food.[78] After having made an arduous journey from a land where hunger was common, the children had an obsession with food, which should not surprise us. The topic of food filled Isidro San Baudelio's letter to his brother. After his arrival in Leningrad Isidro started to fatten up on bread and butter, cheese, *café con leche* (coffee with milk), and rice pudding.[79] He had so much to eat that he wanted to send a packet of food back to his parents. Enrique Undiano and José and Pilar Fernández reported that they "lived in luxury" with "good food that was different every day" and "everything [they] could want." Enrique wrote to his mother and sister six days after reaching Leningrad. The twelve-year-old seemed fascinated by the Soviet submarines and warships that he encountered in port. Most of the letter, however, detailed his daily regime, which revolved around food. The four meals per day with unlimited bread and butter were clearly the highlight for young Enrique. Fruit, cheese, and chocolate (both to eat and to drink) topped his list of favourites. Three Carazo Pereda children – Juan, Emilia, and Estanislao – wrote that they were "sick of cheese and butter" because it was so abundant, something unimaginable at home in Spain. Divina García from Bilbao claimed that they ate "like kings and [slept] like princesses," and José María Laparra, who later died at the Leningrad front and posthumously received the Order of the Red Star, crowed, "They stuff us until we do not want anymore ... They give us meat and chicken and later pastries and all the bread we could want ... Here we eat white bread." When juxtaposed with the paucity and poor quality of food in transit, luxuries like meat and white bread must have been astounding for the poorer children in the group, hence the description of royal treatment. From their first days in the Soviet Union the children felt the largesse of their new homeland and were amazed at its contrast with war-torn Spain.[80]

Kononenko's *Little Spaniards* tells us of the abundance of new volleyballs, bicycles, swings, toys, dolls, teddy bears, cars, and building blocks and also of the beaches, fishing activities, flowers, nightingale songs, and the familiar cypress and laurel trees. "But," she added, "the young Spaniards especially liked to go to the children's technical station."[81] Eating and playing were fine and part of a normal childhood, but a Soviet childhood had to be practical. Here children learned about railroads, radio stations, needlework, and art. This recounting of the arrival story shows children who were grateful for the abundance of Stalinist care and impressed by the food, the toys, and the beautiful surroundings. Yet, what did the "little heroes" like most? Kononenko asserted that the children preferred practical learning and work that would prepare them to contribute to society in future years; Spanish children, however, remembered the toys and fun more than the practical learning. Isidro San Baudelio was happy just to swim at the beach of his sanatorium with its "free air."[82] Enrique Undiano noted with pleasure the abundance of entertainment available to the children, particularly the "billiards, swings, balls, tennis courts, bicycles, and cars with big pedals."[83] Fourteen-year-old Araceli Sánchez Urquijo was amazed by the toys but more so by the white nights in Leningrad.[84]

New opportunities and experiences could be therapeutic, edifying, and entertaining. Teachers taught children how to draw flowers.[85] These lessons, Kononenko told her readers, showed that Spanish and Soviet children were not the same. The Spaniards depicted death and war, "what they not long ago saw in their homeland ... Our [Soviet] children drew trees, flowers, animals, passenger trains, the metro, and the Arctic."[86] Kononenko implied that a Soviet child could see and depict beauty and human possibility and achievement because they represented life in the Soviet Union. When a Spanish girl who had drawn burning homes was shown how to draw a flower, this represented progress: "Their childhood, stolen by the fascists, is returning to them."[87] Kononenko's retelling reiterated the Soviet understanding of children as malleable, as people transformable by nurturing.

Kononenko's presentation of the circumstances might have been melodramatic, but the children certainly appreciated the abundant opportunities now that they were living in a new country not yet embroiled in war. One boy seemed fascinated by the many novelties in addition to the abundant food. Electric buses and the women he saw driving trains and repairing roads starkly contrasted with the patriarchy and lack of infrastructure and development to which he had grown accustomed in Spain. The suburban Moscow camp, which he described as a "wonderland" (*jauja*), was a launching pad for his hopes and dreams.[88] He looked forward to field trips to Lenin's mausoleum and to museum exhibits about the tsars and Republican Spain. He noted, probably mistakenly, that in a month he would begin training as an aviator. Whether he was correct or not, his brief letter showed that he saw opportunities in the Soviet Union, where even women could drive trains. Another student appreciated the three pianos and even a microscope for botanical investigations. Excursions, especially to the beach during vacations where students could "recuperate" and replace the vitamins and minerals lost during the winter, were also popular.[89] Students like Jesús Oyarzábal enjoyed swimming, although they got sunburns, and playing soccer during vacations.[90] In short, playing games and luxuriating in many new experiences like billiards, tennis, bicycles, go-karts, and volleyball punctuated their early Soviet experiences.[91] The young Spaniards were gaining something akin to a "normal" Soviet childhood, in which children were freer from worry than were their Spanish counterparts. In chapter 4 we will examine the after-school and out-of-school opportunities that were a conscious part of Soviet child-rearing strategies and remained part of the Spaniards' lives in the Soviet institutions until their closing in 1951.

Not all recollections were positive, and in this way they were distinct from the Soviet public representations of the niños' early days in the USSR. Soviet writers essentially created undifferentiated and wholly positive stories about the Spaniards' arrival in the USSR. The children, however, related tales of fear and loss, especially a loss of family, traditions, and belongings. Although most children remembered the first days in the USSR much more positively than they did the evacuation and the journey, some reported ill treatment on arrival. The children were filthy and lousy after the long journey, so showers, a change of clothes, delousing, and medical inspections were the first priorities. Decades later, one woman recalled that the treatment was "very caring and attentive" and that the shoes were too big and a coat reached to her ankles.[92]

At this point, cultural differences sometimes clashed. Before the Spaniards had even stepped on Soviet soil, one official called them "frighteningly undisciplined" when compared to Soviet children.[93] António Martínez remembered that a row of sorts started when the girls and the boys, although only a few years old, were told to shower together, which was scandalous to those raised in Catholic Spain. Others reported that being washed by naked women illustrated a difference in the modesty of the two cultures.[94] On a different occasion, Martínez recalled the stomping of feet to protest against the classical music played to the children in Leningrad. The niños only stopped their outbursts when the band played the only "Spanish" songs it knew, the popular Mexican tunes "La Cucaracha" and "Cielito Lindo."[95] Children also complained that Soviet officials took their material goods – sometimes the children's only tangible connection to home. Although many children arrived in tatters and welcomed the crisp uniforms they received on arrival, others wanted to keep their clothing. One woman reflected that her clothing "was made of [...] smocking, which was very fashionable then and I looked so good in it, and suddenly, they give me the same as everyone else, and I never saw the other dress again ... where can it be? ... but oh well."[96] On the one hand, she expressed a desire to keep her finery and individuality, but, on the other hand, she seemed resigned to her fate and the loss of connection to home. This was all part of a disciplinary routine that typified Soviet education and upbringing.

For other children, clothes had an even more personal meaning. One former refugee recalled her arrival at three years of age: "Mom made us a couple of little black dresses ... when my father died ... [W]e took very few things [to the USSR] but what bothered me most was that mom bought us raincoats because we had no money for coats, and they took them away from us ... they made us tear up the only Bible we had."[97] The dresses represented a connection with her father, and the raincoats symbolized the family's financial sacrifice. The disposal of the Bible was an immediate recognition that the girl's religious traditions and identity were no longer going to be part of her public life. The norm was to take all the Spaniards' possessions and burn them or throw them into the sea, presumably as a prophylactic measure.[98]

Some adult Spaniards also questioned their reception and new life in the USSR. An auxiliary worker wrote to her mother that the food was beyond description: "they eat such strange things!" She was deeply disappointed in the Russian salad, and caviar so disgusted her that she could not even swallow it. She also complained that the weather in the south where she resided with the children was too hot, and she worried about the frigid cold that would be coming in the winter. However, she still hoped to go soon to nearby Odessa to speak with the Spanish sailors who, because of the war in Spain, were not able to return. Like most of the Spaniards who were not living in Soviet urban centres before the end of the Second World War, she felt isolated from the world and begged for news from home. Soviet authorities promised that she would learn Russian in two or three months, but she found it quite difficult. Given that she did not know Russian and there were few around her who knew Spanish, she spoke French, which became the language of translation. Her semi-disillusionment (she still expressed a desire to stay in Russia) probably derived from her current location at some distance from Odessa. Furthermore, her life certainly was not a "wonderland," because the lack of water required that everyone wash "like cats," and the potable water tasted terrible.[99]

There clearly was a dialogue between those with positive and negative memories. One woman stated it succinctly: "Some people will tell you that we [lived] like kings, that the [Soviet] Home for [Spanish] Children gave us this ... Have you been told this? ... I'll tell you what, I was never in the Home for Children as a queen."[100] So much time had passed between the events and the recorded memories that we cannot be certain about the intervening experiences that might have coloured the narrators' recollections. To cite just one example:

> As soon as we came out of the ship, we were taken to the bathrooms, to clean us up, take a shower, and because I came from a well-off family, of the high society, then, I carried some clothes that I got the last day, that I had in a suitcase ... I get there [Leningrad] and they took everything away from me. My sister was sent to the shower, those of us who were younger, we were separated right away. I saw my sister coming out of the shower, she used to have long hair, little braids, and now she had her hair cut off. They took away all her clothes. She was wearing, well, something we would never wear.[101]

Many of these recollections are hard to accept. In the case of this last woman, she was three or four years old when she arrived in Leningrad. Granted, traumatic events might take hold in memory in ways that prosaic events might not, but to remember an event in such detail more than six decades after the fact likely betrays elements of constructed memory. As this last respondent noted, notions of class could certainly have coloured one's views. This girl from Spanish "high society" could not bear the tasteless, undifferentiated uniforms, whereas the more numerous children of miners and steelworkers likely were grateful for shoes and a new outfit. Without extensive knowledge of the narrators' biographies (e.g., political affiliations, levels of education, employment) in oral history projects, it is difficult to interpret these responses fully.[102]

Soviet Authorities' Concerns for Child Welfare

Although Soviets used the tale of the Spanish refugees in propaganda during the Spanish Civil War, when looking beyond 1939 we need to broaden our understanding of Soviet intentions, otherwise we cannot explain the anguished conversations among Soviet officials, out of the public eye, about how to provide for the young Spaniards. The archival records that were not meant for public consumption do not connect the need for adequate food, health care, and education with any propaganda goal. Indeed, the first fully fledged inspection and review of sanatoria, where many of the sick Spanish children resided for their first months in the USSR, showed that there was tremendous concern for their well-being, and fury at the lack of success in meeting objectives.[103] The children's health was a priority for both the PCE and the Soviet government so that the niños could return to build socialism in Spain. Starving children would have undermined the children's propaganda value, but a lack of humanitarian concern would also thwart the value of these future fighters for socialism.

In August 1937, after approximately half of the children had arrived in the USSR, various agencies met to discuss conditions in the sanatoria in Crimea, Odessa, and Berdiansk. The secret police (NKVD), Narkompros, the health ministry (Narkomzdrav), the agency in charge of resorts (Soiuzkurort), and the official tasked with receiving the children were all represented. Two problems – the identities and the health of the children – plagued Soviet officials. Disorganization began when the children came ashore in Leningrad. Troianovskii from the NKVD noted that one ship arrived in Leningrad at 2:00 a.m. and that to disembark at night would have been too much of a shock for the children. Troianovskii had measles at the time – which makes one wonder why he boarded the ship – and therefore health officials quarantined the children who had been near him. Much like the story of the Roldán brothers, the report recounted that some of the older children ran away with the little ones when medical personnel started vaccinating the Spaniards. Many of the children also arrived with no documents, and the representative in charge of reception suggested that the comprehensive list of children might have remained in France where the children had changed ships. Many relatives had been separated in transport despite Soviet intentions. Twenty young Spaniards remained missing at the time of the report. The worst cases occurred when the children arrived in Sevastopol after a long train ride from Moscow. The reception in Sevastopol was "disgraceful." The sick children needed transportation from the train station, but photograph-hungry onlookers – an unintended consequence of the media coverage – delayed them. A "huge scandal" broke out at the station, and the reception leader from Moscow seized vehicles to transport the sick children to their final destination. These are details that one cannot find in the press, circumscribed letters, or the memoirs and oral histories of decades later.[104]

A Narkomzdrav official named Barkman provided the most detailed of the reports on the seven locations under examination. By the time of the August 1937 report, 1,053 of the 1,498 niños in the USSR after the second voyage were in sanatoria.[105] What is not clear is whether those numbers included the non-Spanish wards who were also at the sanatoria. Nevertheless, Narkomzdrav reported that its chief goals were to halt the declining health and to quarantine infectious cases. Children with rheumatic fever, for example, received forty days of treatment before re-evaluations. An unnamed NKVD camp, which was set to close soon after the report appeared, received praise for being the best camp to isolate and track its population; however, Barkman noted that this was largely because the NKVD facility had a stable population, unlike the other institutions, which had children arriving and departing.

The malnourished children arrived with numerous medical conditions, some of which were communicable, and the climate worsened some maladies like tuberculosis. Twenty-four of the 1,053 children had been isolated: fourteen in hospitals, ten in sanatoria. Barkman claimed that there was too little oversight of the many sick children, and there were too few specialists, especially otolaryngologists. Another disruption occurred when, despite the children having received full disinfection before their departure from Leningrad, medical personnel again shaved and disinfected them upon their arrival in Crimea. This included girls who had not cut their hair for years. A woman named Lebedkina took the children's things, including reminders of their parents like letters and cards, which of course begat weeping. As the children were under "severe stress," some procedures like taking blood for analysis, checking the temperature (when the children were not in quarantine), and listening to the heart were omitted. Health maintenance also suffered because standard food allotments were inadequate for recuperating children, and some children were so ill that they could not eat their entire ration. Many children also missed their full ration because, according to Barkman's estimates, the food designated for 100 people was used to feed 120 to 130 people, including additional adult personnel. On the bright side, however, whereas some foodstuffs were scarce, the children ate "colossal amounts" of vegetables and potatoes because they were used to them.[106]

The trauma of separation from family and friends certainly was not easy. The vast cultural changes, medical examinations, standardization of dress, and other factors did not ease the transition for many children. Few children, however, argued with the care they initially received. As one woman born in 1934 recalled:

> We were fine in Leningrad, although I cried a lot, because I was separated from my sister, and because I was crying all the time. I don't remember who told me: "Relax, go to the fence and when you see a little blue bus, it means that your mother is coming." Well, I spent a year and a half in Pushkin, a town close to Leningrad,

> I spent a year and a half looking out for a blue bus, yelling: "Mom is coming, mom is coming ..." and mom didn't come. I even had a nervous break. And here I am now, old ... and I had all the diseases you could get. I had everything, it was hell. But we were very well fed. We were looked after very well.[107]

In the face of all the psychological and physical problems she suffered, the former Soviet niña judged her childhood positively because of the treatment she had received in the Spanish homes. Although Soviet officials lamented the chaos and disruptions, it seems that most of the recipients, having lived through much worse in Spain, appreciated Soviet humanitarian largesse and understood their maladies as a consequence of something other than fine nurturing.

The Soviet Union was not paradise, but it was also not the hell of civil-war Spain. Whether a Soviet Spaniard remembered the first years in the USSR with glee or consternation, the archival record shows that the Soviet regime tried, and sometimes failed, to create a new happy childhood for the children. Although there were problems in the institutions charged with their care, these failures to create paradise paled in comparison to the hell of the Second World War years during which the niños de la guerra were twice evacuated, suffered extremes of cold and hunger, and transitioned out of the homes and into labour, the military, or further education. Franco's treatment of leftist families also was far worse than the children's lives in the USSR. All these horrific events made the early years seem rosier. The variety of sources that we have about the Spanish refugee children in their first months in the USSR allows historians to uncover differentiated experiences and perceptions. The experiences of privation that the narrators had after returning to Spain in the mid-1950s, or soon after Franco's death, often colour their oral testimonies. Those who returned during Franco's era may have perceptions refracted by his repressive regime. The Spaniards who remained in the USSR recall their childhood through the lens of the economic collapse of the 1980s and 1990s.

The Soviet press in the 1930s created an undifferentiated image of Soviet largesse in accommodating the young refugees; yet, archival reports show numerous shortcomings. We know that Soviet censorship prevented journalists from criticizing the state's efforts. In contrast, the culture of criticism in the bureaucracy led to reports that focused on problems as often as on successes. All three sets of sources – journalism, archival reports, and letters and oral histories – show the lengths to which Soviet officials went to feed, house, and provide health care. This laid the foundation for institutional care that privileged Spaniards as a group and provided resources in greater abundance than those given to Soviet counterparts.[108] As we will see, this institutionalized care was critical to a healthy childhood, but it also prevented sufficient independence for the young Spaniards to transition seamlessly into Soviet adults.

The USSR was not the only country to take in Spanish child refugees. As one scholar has noted, "France was not only the first, but she was also the most generous," in accepting the tens of thousands of refugee families. However, refugees in France were torn apart as the Catholic Church separated boys and girls, and most adopting families only accepted one sibling.[109] Moreover, because Franco and the Catholic Church largely succeeded in branding the displaced as "reds," the warm reception of Basque children was limited primarily to the first wave of refugees.[110] With British business and diplomacy being openly hostile to the Spanish Republican government, war refugees in Britain fell into the hands of charitable organizations and labour unions. When the Home Office finally agreed, on 30 April 1937, to allow child refugees into Britain, it did so on the condition that private funds, not government money, provided for their education and care. The Basque Children's Committee had to raise funds equivalent to ten pounds per child per week and promise that private citizens would house the children. The initial number of ninety camps for refugee children was halved a year later, and only five remained open in 1939. As in other countries, the press soon ran stories about the terrible lack of discipline among the older boys.[111]

From spring 1937 until the outbreak of the Second World War, about 3,200 children from northern Spain lived in Belgium with adoptive parents, in orphanages, or in refugee colonies. Socialist and communist organizations greeted the first arrivals, and then almost two months later the Catholic Church in Belgium arranged adoptions and opened new colonies. The Church often placed older boys in Catholic institutes, convents, pensions, rectories, and boarding schools, frequently separating siblings and friends. Unlike other countries, Belgium paid adopting parents a family allowance, a subsidy to care for the refugee children.[112]

Of all the countries accepting Spanish refugee children, Mexico was the only one to join the USSR in accommodating a large number of children at state expense beyond 1939. About five hundred Spanish "niños de Morelia" arrived in Mexico, where the Escuela España-México opened for them a Soviet model of high-quality, well-resourced co-education as preparation for their return to liberated Spain. An all-Mexican staff cared for the children after school administrators immediately rejected the Spanish teachers. Hispanophobia was common among the Mexican staff after the 1910 revolution that had glorified indigenous Mexicans and vilified the Spanish conquest. These popular attitudes became more hardened after the arrival of shiploads of Spanish adults in 1939. Press reports noted, as in the USSR, that the special school cost much more than the typical state schools did. To make matters worse, the "Honorable Spanish Colony" in Mexico City, a group of wealthy, mostly pro-Franco Spaniards who had set up clubs and businesses before 1910, viewed the poor, leftist children with disdain. After the socialist, reform-minded president Lázaro Cárdenas ended his term in 1940, the school changed a great deal, and the dilapidated, centuries-old buildings and rapid turnover of personnel led to the closure of this socialist educational experiment in 1943.[113]

By September 1937, just months after the arrival of the initial refugees in the USSR, the Soviet government had already prepared special boarding schools in time for the new academic year. Schooling was part of a normal Soviet childhood, but schools were also disciplining institutions and sites of socialization. The boarding schools for the Spaniards were no different; they became sites for the Sovietizing of Hispano-Soviets. They also were sites of the humanitarian care of a population that needed to be educated, cared for, and prepared for adult lives of socialist contributions. The Spanish experience in the USSR differed dramatically from the experience of exile in other countries because the USSR provided modern educational institutions that sought to surround the children with good role models, to provide a broad education, and to teach skills and behaviours that would allow them to transition into Soviet society and return to Spain to conquer Francoism.

2 "We, the Spanish, Were like an Island": Boarding Schools and Personnel as Loci and Models of Care and Soviet Values

[W]e had magnificent teachers, educators, pioneer guides, translators, guards, cleaning and kitchen staff, a magnificent director, assistant director, chief of teaching, instructor of gymnastics and sports, doctors, nurses ... For us nothing was spared, the Soviets treated us with caring and selflessness, working whole days in the boarding school without spare time, even though they also had their families, their homes and their daily problems. Always smiling, attentive, caring ... without ever forgetting we were Spanish, instilling in us love for our country and our relatives, taking care of our customs, art and literature, language, in short, everything that was most useful for our education.
   Isabel Argentina Álvarez Morán, *Memorias de una niña de la guerra*, 72

Isabel Álvarez's reflection on the care and attention of boarding-school staff points to the importance of the structure and function of these homes in the education and upbringing of the young Spaniards. When Jaime Camino said, "We, the Spanish, were like an island," he used the metaphor of the island to represent the isolated nature of the homes that allowed the Spaniards to forget sometimes that they lived in a distant land as foreigners.[1] Until the end of the Spanish Civil War the children could feel like they were living in two places at once. The Soviet commitment to rallying European anti-fascist solidarity kept the war in the news. The civil war "was a symbol for the more general war that threatened," and the international "campaign for solidarity" was not a fad but rather a symbol of the USSR's link with Europe and "proof that the Soviet Union did not stand alone."[2] Caring for youngsters – with assistance from the PCE and Comintern – was part of the Soviet obligation to the Spanish struggle against fascism, and, as Álvarez noted above, the Soviets went to extraordinary lengths.

During their times in the homes, the children lived among Spaniards and were able to speak Spanish regularly and share in some hopes and dreams that existed beyond Soviet borders. The Spanish children were not completely isolated from their Soviet counterparts, however. They often met at Pioneer events, at sports competitions, in hospitals, on playgrounds, and even during a rare visit to a Soviet apartment.[3] During the war-time evacuation, when educational space was limited, many Spaniards studied with Soviet children. In fact, some became "bosom buddies" (*zakadychnye druz'ia*), entered into romantic relationships, and eventually married.[4] Once the children had left the islands of happiness for work or higher education, they integrated, for better or worse, into the greater Soviet society. They had to confront Soviet culture fully without the protective barriers provided by their special institutions. Until that time, they lived a privileged and protected life.

Scholars have not yet situated the niños' arrival in 1937 amidst the great flux in Soviet policies. Soviet education was moving away from experimentation with the child-centred learning that was the fashion of the 1920s and was beginning to insist on discipline and teacher-centred instruction.[5] Much like the centralization of authority that tightened under Stalin in the 1930s, the schools began to teach and practise greater authority and discipline, which was hardened even further after the outbreak of the Second World War.[6] *Sovetskaia pedagogika* published its first issue in 1937 and launched discussions among educators about the "ideological perversion" and "pseudo-science" of child-centred schools, or paedology, which had dominated Soviet education since the 1920s.[7] This shift coincided with the reification of Anton Makarenko's teaching and the regime's continued concern about homeless and wayward children (although they were no longer reported in the press). Furthermore, the 1936–8 Great Terror, the 1939 purge in the Comintern, and Stalin's March 1939 speech on the importance of improving political knowledge among cadres showed an increasing focus on reliability, loyalty, and adherence to the party line.[8]

Even in times of great domestic and international turmoil, and while usually lacking sufficient resources, Soviet authorities tried to create spaces in which the children could adapt to their surroundings, maintain some of their Spanish heritage, and learn Soviet values and the Marxist-Leninist-Stalinist world view. The liminal third space of boarding schools created a sense of difference by maintaining Spanish language and culture, yet it also fostered a sense of commonality with Soviet peers because of an otherwise standardized Soviet curriculum.[9] In line with shifts in Soviet education and policy, Spanish schools emphasized discipline, patriotism, and the mastering of Soviet behaviours. Placed in the context of the new disciplinary policies in schools and society mentioned earlier, we can now understand the close attention to the education of the Spaniards and to the personnel who needed to act as positive role models for becoming Soviet.

Although the Soviet model of education was highly centralized with a national curriculum and rules for staff and students, each Spanish boarding school varied according the personality of the director, its location, and the students and staff within its walls.[10] As the Spaniards and the special homes of which they were a part often appeared to be isolated islands of foreign children, the personnel in daily contact with the children played a prominent role in their adaptation to life in the Soviet Union and in their overall development as Hispano-Soviets. Their displacement to the USSR and the distancing from family and friends created anxiety and stress, but they also created opportunities for the children to construct new identifications and to create new bonds. The "double exile" from Spain and then from Moscow during the Second World War deepened friendships as the children came to depend on each other and became inseparable.[11] K. Levterova, a worker in one of the homes, noted that to some degree the children formed a collective simply because of the shared experience of displacement. However, they did not know each other well until they were "welded" together through walks with school staff.[12] The boarding schools became family, school, and religion for the refugees.

The importance of the Spanish homes cannot be over-emphasized. Nearly all of the refugee children spent at least three years in the homes – youths aged fourteen often moved into labour in 1941. All but these oldest children spent more time in the Soviet homes for Spaniards than they had spent in Spain. Therefore, these Spanish homes, these secluded islands, were likely even more formative than regular Soviet schools because apolitical or anti-Soviet parents or grandparents were not waiting at home to undo what was learned in school. The absence of parents turned teachers and educators into surrogate family members, and the relatively isolated nature of the homes made the selection of party-minded personnel even more important. Without undue outside influences, these year-round boarding schools provided a type of laboratory for refashioning the Spanish children into Soviets, and decades later the Spanish refugees continued to refer to "my home" and "those from my home."[13] The reforging required proper facilities and personnel who could serve as teachers and role models. This chapter will discuss the formation and staffing of the homes, while investigating how and why in 1939–40 the Soviet authorities began to remove some adults from contact with the children.

Boarding Schools as Disciplinary Institutions

Araceli Sánchez Urquijo remembered her years in the homes for Spanish children as "the happiest" of her life.[14] Although her opinion was not shared universally, oral testimonies frequently comment on how privileged the Spaniards felt to have their daily needs of food, shelter, clothing, and nurturing met by the homes and their staff and to be studying in school, rather than fearing political violence in fractious Spain. The Second World War and life in evacuation were bleak, but even at this low point most Spanish children, simply by having an institution to protect them, avoided the calamitous life that befell so many Soviet children who starved, lost one or both parents, and often wandered the countryside homeless and alone.[15] From inception, the homes for Spanish children sought to meet all the daily physical and intellectual needs of the children; they sought to provide shelter, food, clothing, education, health care, and the guidance necessary for them to become adult members of society.

In November 1937 Narkompros received full responsibility for the children's homes, and by February 1939 there were 2,189 Spanish children in eleven homes in the Russian Soviet Federative Socialist Republic (RSFSR) and 646 children in five Ukrainian Republic homes, concentrated in the Moscow and Leningrad regions, Evpatoriia, Odessa, Kiev, Kherson, and Kharkov.[16] These varied greatly in size and location. Some homes were in the centre of Moscow or Leningrad, whereas others – often with primarily younger Spaniards – were in wooded suburbs, like Pushkin and Obninskoe, outside Leningrad and Moscow respectively. The more rural homes typically had schools attached, whereas the urban homes often sent children (especially the older ones) to separate classrooms within a nearby Soviet school. In 1940 a new dimension was added with two homes for Spanish youth (teenagers who generally had completed the seventh grade, or who were fourteen, and worked during the day and studied at night).[17] Three of the twenty-two homes were specifically for ill children.

Soviet children's homes in general, and the Spanish ones in particular, included administrators (e.g., directors, assistant directors, and accountants), teachers, non-classroom educators (*vospitateli*), medical personnel, and auxiliary staff (e.g., cooks and maintenance workers). Soviet administrators supervised the overall functioning of the homes and communicated with superiors at all levels of government and party and the various divisions of Narkompros. They oversaw not only the education of the children but also the provisioning of food, clothes, bedding, heating fuel, and more. Medical personnel oversaw the children's health and diet and the sanitary condition of the sleeping quarters, classrooms, kitchen and cafeterias, food-storage areas, and grounds.

One former student recalled that the Spanish homes "mobilized the best educators, teachers and professionals. They were men and women who taught us Spanish. Who ran the centres, who often behaved like parents. The constant concern of our educators was to not lose the love for our country, language and customs."[18] Although Spanish educators were concerned with maintaining the children's connection to Spain, some of the personnel – as was common in Soviet institutions – were less than ideal mentors and role models.[19] Retaining Spanish culture and language also interfered with the students' ability to learn the Russian language, which stunted their acculturation and made for a difficult transition to their adult lives outside the homes. For this reason many of the Soviet personnel and administrators grew increasingly concerned with the relative weight of Spanish to Russian. From their inception these bilingual and bicultural boarding schools suffered from competing interests and aims and inconsistent modelling of proper behaviour. Although most of the educators had not had higher education, "they taught [the children] to love Spain" through discussions of history and culture.[20]

Senior Administrators

The director of the children's home sat atop the pyramid of authority and was responsible for coordinating the various parts of the operation, implementing directives from above, and providing reports to his or her superiors within Narkompros. Directors held a great deal of authority in most of the homes and, in addition to carrying out the important administrative duties that largely would have gone unseen by the children, served as the central paternal or maternal figure. One woman recalled that the Spanish teachers and educators called their director "papa wolf" because he desperately protected everything in the home for the use of the children. Even though he was "very rigid" with the children, the respondent believed it was for her own good.[21] Good directors were often described as "phenomenal, a good communist, a person of integrity," and "energetic."[22] "Thanks to [our director]," Manuel Arce recalled, "we survived in those terrible [war] years of hunger, cold, diseases."[23]

Not all directors fulfilled their duties well. Some administrators stole food and other items designated for the children.[24] During the war and evacuation in particular, some directors were criticized for a variety of failures. One woman from the Obninskoe home remembered her director as a "shameless director, you could see he had no guts, he had no character to insist." Another woman from the Pravda home complained that her director "was very cruel, punished the children so much, and we worked a lot, ... and the headmaster knew how to take products from the government but he would make us starve anyway."[25]

Directors also set the tone and direction of the homes. Some were quite lax or disorganized, while others preferred more structure. Students like Valerio understood the differences: "The director [of Home No. 9 in Leningrad] was very soft, did not have any kind of authority. Everything changed when a new director came, Comrade Marlovni, who came to be director from a reformatory of Soviet children where [they] applied a lot of discipline. Thereafter, we had every hour occupied, the schedule was very tight and it was set very well."[26]

Discipline and structure feature prominently in recollections about directors, but respondents judged them quite differently. Some, following the Soviet line, viewed discipline and order as necessary and correct. Others believed that there was too much structure. However, it is important to understand that "discipline" meant organization, structure, and proper behaviour. We should not confuse "discipline" with punishment or violence. Proper Soviet discipline was "conscious discipline," not the blind obedience created through fear that was associated with "bourgeois" education (as in Spain). Soviet conscious discipline was to be developed from neither fear nor self-aggrandizement but from

Communist ideals and deeply held convictions.[27] Katerina Clark has shown that Soviet literature also sought to demonstrate the transition from spontaneity to conscious discipline; this was precisely the task of the boarding-school teacher in reforging the Spanish children into Soviets.[28] Discipline, literature, education: all were part of the larger scheme of Soviet socialization of children.

Anton Makarenko was an ever-present figure in the homes' administration, and Comrade Marlovni was one of his many disciples, as was Arce's director, Kiselev. Makarenko was widely publicized and admired in the 1930s – especially after his death in 1939 – for his system of raising wayward children and rehabilitating them into useful Soviet citizens. His books and articles were mandatory reading for educators. Once described as having a place in the "golden reserve of Soviet pedagogues," Makarenko set forth a theory and practice of child rearing that received official sanction.[29] His best-known work, which was widely read in the Soviet Union and the Soviet Spanish homes, was *Pedagogical Poem*, also known as *Road to Life* in English. Published in 1934–7, it recounts some of the stories from his time spent in establishing and administering the Gorky colony for children. By reading his stories of wayward youth – some were orphaned by the Russian Civil War, and others became thieves and hooligans – parents and teachers were able to understand how children could transform into productive Soviet citizens. Makarenko did not hide his failures and made clear to his readers that much of his prior training had been useless; he had learned more from his day-to-day experiences with the children in the colonies. The preference for practical learning over theoretical training became an important part of Soviet discourse at this time.

Some of the central themes in *Pedagogical Poem* were instructive for the people in charge of the Spanish homes. Makarenko believed that children learned best from an organized environment in which clear boundaries existed for their behaviour. Although he condemned violence against students, coercion was not only acceptable but also expected. He believed that students and staff needed to work collectively in order to create a sense of self- and mutual respect. As with Makarenko's teaching, Soviet authorities had banned corporal punishment, and instead children were ostracized, which symbolically or physically served to remind them and their peers of normative behaviours. This worked on some children; for example, one girl willingly accepted public shaming after she had abused her position on the children's council (which gave her access to the kitchen) and had stolen potatoes.[30] Rewards included special excursions and admittance into normative groups, like the Pioneers with their uniforms and red neckties as symbols of their inclusion. Grades, awards, and teacher evaluations created normative thresholds that allowed the categorization and ranking of students. As Michel Foucault has noted, states govern not only with coercion and violence but also with subtler means: "to govern ... is to structure the possible field of action of others."[31] The intended result was to construct a child who could learn to self-govern. Modern education in general is a disciplinary institution that "compares, differentiates, hierarchizes, homogenizes, excludes," and thereby normalizes.[32] Through observation and surveillance, and punishments and rewards, teachers, administrators, and peers help to set normative behaviours. The Soviet regime was no different.

Medical Staff

Just before the arrival of the Spanish refugees, Soviet authorities had also increased attention to children's hygiene.[33] On 31 May 1935 decrees brought attention to sanitation and hygiene in schools and other children's institutions while also focusing on control of the content of children's literature and film.[34] These new rules signalled greater attention to both physical and mental hygiene. Contagion from ideas was as dangerous as contagion from viruses and bacteria. One decree called for regularly scheduled and thorough cleaning of children, linens, and the sites they inhabited. From laundering clothes and bed linens to washing floors and windows with bleach to fumigating and isolating newly arrived children, controlling contagion was a top priority. In boarding schools – with children living and learning in close confines – tuberculosis, typhus, and other maladies could spread rapidly. Children's mental or ideological hygiene was also important. Soviet authorities removed from cinemas and libraries any adventure stories that glorified criminality and replaced them with heroic tales of men, women, and children who sacrificed themselves for their comrades and the motherland. The journal *Sovetskaia pedagogika* drew the most succinct connection between the disciplined mind and body and the need for proper role modelling: a teacher's "undisciplined" and "slovenly" thought was a "destructive infection."[35]

Medical personnel supervised physical hygiene and well-being, whereas teachers and educators supervised mental and behavioural development.[36] Medical issues – including food, sanitation, quarantining, and treatment – were primary concerns in the Spanish homes. Many of the Spanish children arrived under-nourished and infected with a host of diseases. Given the conditions of life in war-time Spain, this should not be surprising. In the USSR, reports from doctors and nurses paid close attention to weight gain, height increases, and spread of infection. In 1939, for example, there were seventy-nine medical personnel in the RSFSR Spanish homes for 2,250 children, or 28.5 children per caregiver, which was not too much greater than the 22.0 students per teacher.[37] It is safe to assume that, like teachers, these medical personnel were distributed unevenly among the homes. The homes with a sanatorium regime for the sickest children would be expected to have a higher concentration of medical personnel.

Nearly all the children from the first two evacuations found themselves in sanatoria at some point. For most, these were merely places to rest, breathe fresh air, get some exercise, and put on weight. However, a report on 1 August 1937 showed that physicians institutionalized many new arrivals to prevent their health from declining or to prevent them from infecting others. Twenty-four of 1,053 children under examination (2.3 per cent) recovered in hospitals or in isolation wards with serious health problems.[38] Although good intentions persisted, quality medical care did not always follow.

As with directors, not all medical personnel lived up to the Soviet ideal. One of the most striking examples concerned a physician who seemed to have been incompetent in the extreme. "Dr. Rufino [Castaños],"[39] though finally removed for a "criminally negligent attitude to medical work," spent nine years practising in the USSR. He was remembered by one man as "very nice," "old," and with almost no knowledge of Russian.[40] He had served as a doctor during the Spanish Civil War, and he went to Home No. 5 in 1938, but without any evidence of his qualifications. He followed the school into evacuation and then went to the home in Evpatoriia in 1943 when Home No. 5 closed. The director in Evpatoriia dismissed him because Castaños showed little knowledge of epidemiology or diagnosis. Castaños moved to Moscow but found no accommodations, so he moved into Home No. 3 because he still did not know how to speak Russian after eight years. Once in Home No. 3, Castaños began to interfere in the work of its physician in charge, Dr Ponkrat'eva. When Ponkrat'eva had to leave for medical reasons, Castaños stepped in. He failed to diagnose cases of measles and scarlet fever and allowed infected students to re-enter the school population and even to visit family elsewhere in the USSR during holidays, thus spreading the epidemics.[41] However, when he did intervene, as he did in evacuation when he forbade children to eat rice on which gasoline had accidentally spilled, the cook and children ignored him and ate it anyway because food was scarce.[42]

Teachers and Educators

Whereas medical staff supervised physical development, classroom teachers, both Soviet and Spanish, oversaw the children's academic growth. Living conditions, like work conditions, varied dramatically from one home to another. Many homes had living space for the staff in the home or nearby; others did not. Alejandra Soler – a teacher of Spanish language and literature, history, and geography in Home No. 12 – lived in the Hotel Metropol. Although the accommodations were good, and she could see friends, she had a long commute to work each day. Other adults reported a type of shift work that required standing guard until 2:30 a.m. or arriving at 5:00 a.m. so that the children had adequate supervision.[43]

The Soviet and Spanish teachers provided learning opportunities for the children that most, especially the girls, could never have attained in conservative, patriarchal Spain, and many children remembered their inspirational teachers fondly.

> We had an excellent [Russian] teacher ... she told us [about] all of Walter Scott's literature books, all the classics, and the Russians and Turgenev and, well, all of them, and Tolstoy ... [W]e went to the orchard to work, we walked next to her, to her left, her right, behind her ... because she would tell us about that literature on the way there and that's why I think she played a very important role in our group, because all of us, almost everyone, finished 10th year [the final year in Soviet schools] and had careers after. No one went to the factory because we were very interested in studying ... she was a history teacher but would introduce all that literature within history.[44]

This unnamed history teacher passed along her love of learning, and she modelled the Soviet ideal of a love of books. Though not a literature teacher, she conveyed an infectious enthusiasm for reading.

Like their Soviet counterparts, teachers in the Spanish schools were responsible for more than teaching subject matter like mathematics, physics, history, and art. Like the teacher who led her cohort to the orchards, good teachers followed Makarenko's advice and were involved in the daily life of their charges. In and out of the classroom, teachers were to teach patriotism, the current political line, and all other ad hoc measures. They often had responsibility, with educators and Komsomol leaders, for organizing field trips, evening lecture series, and other learning events outside of regular class hours.

Spanish teachers sometimes had additional roles in the children's lives. Twelve-year-old José Fernández from the coal region of Ablaña, Asturias, had moved into a Spanish military orphanage after his father died in February 1937, and eight months later he entered Home No. 7 in Moscow. Fernández understood the mission of teachers and the influence of Spanish teachers. They "came from Spain and logically wanted to see in us the perpetuators of their effort and with the same degree of ideological passion as they had ... [They said,] 'You must study hard. You are our hope, our greatest treasure.'"[45] Fernández perceived adult Spaniards as role models who continued to remind the children of their homeland and their obligations to it. The presence of Spanish adults were critical symbols of Spanish heroism and valour who helped to connect children's Soviet learning with their future in Spain.[46] In some ways, the behaviour of Spanish adults towards the poor behaviour of their younger co-nationals mirrored the self-policing seen in displaced-persons (DP) camps in Europe after the Second World War, in which those in positions of authority articulated "behaviour deemed 'appropriate' to the nation." PCE leaders functioned in a manner similar to that of the "patriotic leadership [in DP camps] that claimed refugees for the nation."[47] They helped to define what it meant to be a Spaniard in the USSR.

Classroom teachers were evaluated not only on their credentials and knowledge of subject matter but also on their ability to be a positive influence on the lives of the Spanish children. When the youth misbehaved, it was common for reports to blame their actions on the influence of the Spanish adults around them.[48] Some teachers also were physically abusive. "The director," another man remembered, "found out that [a male teacher] had bitten a boy, he called for a meeting of all the educators and teachers, Spanish and Russian along with the translator ... And so he said that the first one to even touch a child would be sacked and no one ever touched a child again."[49] With so much close contact with the children, it was imperative to employ the correct personnel in order to achieve the homes' objectives of raising educated, cultured, and communist children.[50]

Limits on advancement among Spanish adults suggest the importance of cultural differences in education and discipline. Soviet authorities were concerned with transmitting Soviet norms of behaviour while also raising the children with Spanish language and culture to prepare them for their return to Spain and building socialism there. Álvaro Peláez, a former postal official and second PCE secretary in Toledo who became a military commissar and then worked for Narkompros in the USSR, tried to place his candidate, Luis Balaguer, in charge of one of the homes for Spanish youth. The problems within the homes would not be fixed, Peláez said, until a "Spaniard, and not a Soviet person, a member of the party," was in charge. Balaguer was a communist who had been working with Spanish youth in Moscow and Samarkand, but he was not a Soviet citizen. The current director of the home, Chembrovskii, was Soviet but not a pedagogue. The row continued with Peláez being chastised for "organiz[ing] an intrigue," until the home was closed five months later with Chembrovskii still acting as director.[51] This incident illustrates how important Narkompros felt it was for a Soviet citizen to be in charge. Directors were vetted communists, and even PCE members seemed less politically reliable than their Soviet counterparts. Chembrovskii did not have teaching credentials, but he did have ideological credentials vetted during years of work in the Soviet Union. Spanish officials, however, seemed to believe that a Spaniard in charge could improve a boarding school's performance because of better communication with the niños. This incident shows the tension in the homes between modelling Soviet values and maintaining Spanish identifications.

Arguably the most important, least trained, and overburdened of the personnel were the educators. They were responsible for children during every waking and sleeping hour outside of class. Normally they worked all year with a specific group of about twenty children. They had to get to know "their" children and the children's problems and potentials. The educator was usually the first person consulted when a child had a problem because the close contact meant that the educator should have known the child best.

Educators, with their wide mandate within the homes, needed more positive traits than did any other position in the school. It was educators who oversaw completion of homework, monitored respect and comradeship towards adults and other children, maintained group and individual discipline, and ensured that students cleaned their living spaces and bodies. Bernardo del Río remembers Luis Balaguer, who had lost a leg during the civil war and was only thirty years old when he evacuated with the youth to Sarmakand, as an inspiration and the man who likely saved their lives because he was always intervening to secure them more food.[52] Some educators apparently possessed "infinite patience" with the "pirates [who] were accustomed to spend all [their] time on the streets" and who in Spain were "only going home to sleep."[53]

Oral testimonies are generally silent on auxiliaries – a broad and ill-defined group who maintained the home and provided various services like cooking, cleaning, and maintaining the facilities – but their service was no less vital. There are a few examples of auxiliaries who did more harm than good, but the archives' relative silence about them while the homes continued to function during periods of crisis and relative normality speaks volumes about the number of Spanish and Soviet men and women who – whether or not proper resources existed – cooked, cleaned, maintained the buildings and grounds, and carried out numerous other tasks that were essential to a happy and healthy childhood.

The First School Years: Modelling Proper Soviet Values and Behaviour

"Many of us were little hooligans. With our Spanish temperament imagine what might have happened if there was no discipline."[54] This recollection from one of the Spanish children who was raised in the Soviet Union underscores a key issue for boarding-school administrators: how to merge Spanish culture with Soviet values. Although Spanish authorities wanted the special homes primarily to maintain and advance Spanish language and culture, Soviet authorities by the start of the Second World War had increased their attention on Soviet behaviours and norms. Spanish Communist Party leader Dolores Ibárruri was quoted as saying: "We Spaniards considered ourselves always united, and our politics were Spanish and oriented toward maintaining the children so that they might not forget their language and accustom themselves to think of their country, to which they would return and where their lives would continue. To this end, every help was given us by the Soviet authorities, including bringing Spanish teachers, organizing schools for the children – everything we needed."[55] Similarly, General Hidalgo de Cisneros, whose daughter Luli lived in Home No. 1, called the living conditions there "luxurious," and his wife, Constancia de la Mora, insisted that Spanish-language instruction persisted to prepare the children for "when they can return to the homeland."[56] These Spanish leaders, and much of the Spanish scholarship on the subject, did not understand the context of Soviet education for non-Russians.

"Non-Russian" schools in the multilingual Soviet Union were *supposed* to educate children in their native language and national culture. Spanish boarding schools in the USSR followed this model.[57] Only in rare cases, as with Chinese students at the international children's home, was training in students' native language all but ignored.[58] Although the USSR administered a national curriculum, learning one's native language and culture – as in the non-Russian schools – distinguished the curriculum of the better-provisioned Spanish homes from that of their regular Soviet counterparts. Therefore, it seems shortsighted to focus only on the Spanish and not on the Soviet intentions.

A Soviet director of one of the Spanish homes understood, better than Ibárruri did, the bilingual education and how it applied to Spaniards. "From these pupils, entrusted to us by the heroic Spanish people, we must forge not only strong and fearless fighters for the liberation of their compatriots, but faithful sons of their Fatherland, and loyal followers of the great teachers of humanity – Marx, Engels and Lenin ... A love and devotion to the Communist Party of Spain and the VKP (b) [Soviet Communist Party], and to Spain and the USSR – these must be the first priorities in our endeavor to raise [the Spaniards] as our own children."[59] The director understood that the children could be transformed – or "forged" – into new and better people through, among other things, patriotism and political knowledge. Spanish language, culture, geography, and history remained in the homes, but the Soviet world view and behaviours were taught also.

As we will see in the next chapter, some teachers changed the history curriculum, for example, to highlight the moments in Spanish history that taught lessons of patriotism and perseverance, but the curriculum overwhelmingly used standardized Soviet lessons. These values – along with discipline, comradely behaviour, and hard work – were the focus of vospitanie in the homes for Spanish children. Thus, the homes' personnel sought to forge Hispano-Soviet children much as the non-Russian Soviet schools placed national particularities under the larger umbrella of universal Soviet values.

The Spanish homes were sites of the "production of cultural *differentiation* as signs of authority."[60] The homes taught Soviet culture and values and often juxtaposed them with the "natural" behaviour with which the "little hooligans" had arrived and which had to be overcome. These were spaces for cultural and behavioural education. When the narrator who opened this section recalled "our Spanish temperament" and feared "what might have happened if there was no discipline," he showed the authority that came from differentiation.[61] Decades later he still recalled fellow Spaniards as undisciplined and implied that Spanish behaviour was destructive. Having learned discipline in the Soviet schools, however, he was redeemed and transformed. His response sounds much like school tales in children's literature in which by the end of the school year "the slingshots are forgotten, will is disciplined, and the bad grades are corrected."[62]

From the beginning, Soviet officials clearly understood that, although Spain's Republican government wanted to preserve the children's heritage, Soviet training was to be the mainstay in the classroom. In fact, the first set of rules governing the Spanish homes did not refer to the maintenance of Spanish culture.[63] In 1938, as the Spaniards prepared for their first full year of school in the USSR, a set of regulations governing the boarding schools detailed the Soviet priorities in providing for the refugees and suggested what a successful program would achieve. A preamble of sorts dominated the first page of the regulations and set out the four main tasks of the new institutions: (1) "to raise [*vospitat'*] energetic communist builders of society, selflessly devoted to the socialist fatherland of workers from around the world – the Soviet Union, the fighters against fascism, the fighters for a free, independent Spain"; (2) to protect the health of children, providing them with attentive care and the cultural conditions necessary for physical health and the creation of a familial feeling in the home; (3) to provide education fully through the middle-school level (grade seven, typically age fourteen); and (4) to raise the children's love of the socialist attitude to work, help them choose a profession that would allow them to leave the homes for work or higher education, and equip them with job-skills training in order for them to master the profession.[64]

Whereas the PCE had insisted that Spanish culture be *the* priority in the homes, the four goals show that Soviet *kul'turnost'* (culturedness or acculturation) was more important than Spanish culture. Kul'turnost' included traits like behaviour, hygiene, broad education, and political consciousness and had become a central part of the remoulding of Soviet citizens in the late 1930s.[65] The second and third tasks are more politically and culturally neutral in the desire to educate the children and keep them healthy. The first and fourth tasks, however, focus primarily on Soviet goals. The first task sought to create an internationalist mentality that prioritized the honouring and protection of the Soviet Union; the fight against fascism and for an independent Spain were dependent parts of support for the Soviet Union, the socialist fatherland and leader in the fight against fascism. The regulation suggests that to fight against fascism and for Spain one had to understand the Soviet system and its place in the vanguard of uniting forces against fascist regimes. Although it might be important to embrace Spanish language and culture in order to fight for an "independent Spain," the first task signalled an ideological and attitudinal disposition. Home administrators were given the fourth task in forming a Soviet mentality and set of behaviours that often fought against the stereotypes of Spanish tendencies towards laziness, sloppy work, violence, and a lack of hygiene and decorum. Although the boarding schools changed over the next dozen years, these four pillars remained.

An obligation to work hard was central to the revolutionary culture of the USSR, as labour edicts against parasitism attest.[66] The 1939 internal regulations for the Spanish homes developed the fourth task and noted that labour was a "matter of honor, a matter of glory, a matter of valor and heroism."[67] Each person had a duty to work for the greater benefit of society. There was no room for "parasites" in the Soviet Union, and the Spanish homes, like the schools for Soviet children, sought to instil in their charges a love of labour and a sense of duty and obligation. The regulations made it explicit: "All training and educational work in the home is completely subordinated to the tasks of communist upbringing and education of the younger generation in the USSR."[68] Both *vospitanie* (upbringing) and *obuchenie* (education) were by definition to be first and foremost political and Soviet, despite the beliefs of PCE members to the contrary. Classroom education was important in creating a literate, numerate, and politically informed student; vospitanie in and out of class helped to inculcate kul'turnost', or the behaviours and attitudes that marked one as a new Soviet man or woman and led to one's success in life.

With Franco's 1939 victory, as other countries returned evacuated children to Spain, the Soviet and Spanish communist parties thought it better to continue to raise the children in the USSR and to create an educated, skilled, and ideologically sound group that could one day liberate and enlighten Spain. The young Spaniards would need skills to contribute to the Soviet Union until the day they could return to Spain and use those same skills to rebuild their country.[69] They would also need good role models to help them learn how to be good communists.

From the first days in the Soviet Union, and even more so after Franco's 1939 victory and the stranding of the children for an indeterminate time, the children became surrounded increasingly by and inculcated with Soviet values. Certainly, Spanish language and culture were taught in the schools, but they existed beneath a much more influential Soviet system of education and upbringing. Fourteen-year-old Emiliano Aza Ocaña of Bilbao wrote to his family in January 1938 from Odessa: "Father, this is the first nation to rise up and defeat the cruel tyrant, and the beast of fascism will be defeated by Red Spain ... and in the whole world will reign equality and all the workers will work and eat and around the world will reign peace and joy. Father in the Soviet Union all are equal as carpenters and mechanics and engineers and railworkers. They all eat the same and work the same."[70] If the adolescent Emiliano could parrot, if not internalize, the Soviet internationalist world view so soon after his arrival, then we must assume that the even more impressionable preschoolers could, also, and that this world view would become clearer after more years of education.

The rapidity of learning displayed in this and similar letters suggests that counter-narratives were rare or at least minimally effective given the saturation of Soviet teaching in boarding schools. Cisneros, Mora, and Ibárruri were correct: Spanish teachers remained in the homes, and Spanish language and culture lessons continued, but Soviet instructors and values trumped the Spanish as a priority for Narkompros. The retention of national culture followed from Stalin's statements in 1913 on national rights and his later April 1948 statement: "Every nation, whether large or small, has its own specific qualities and its own peculiarities, which are unique to it and which other nations do not have. These peculiarities form a contribution that each nation makes to the common treasury of world culture, adding to it and enriching it."[71] However, for the Soviets, an island of Spanish children who were almost without exception isolated from parents and grandparents became an ideal site to propagate Soviet teaching. The story of Pavlik Morozov, among others, shows the authorities' fear of the children's being taught one thing in school and then going home to parents who were not ideologically correct in their thoughts and actions.[72] Young Pavlik overcame his home circumstances and denounced his parents; boarding schools allowed the Soviets to avoid undo negative influences as long as the adult staff could be trusted.[73]

Without good discipline of mind, body, behaviours, and attitudes, however, no gains could be made. Soviet understandings of child development placed "nurture" over "nature."[74] Therefore, the establishment of a good social milieu for the children was imperative for them to grow up as proper adults. Adult role modelling thus became a priority because role models were part of a disciplinary system in which children were both observed and observers. Although the following section will address adults, the children's peers increasingly became part of the disciplinary network.

When Soviet authorities began to house the newly arrived Spanish children and arrange for their schooling, discipline was becoming one of the most pressing issues in the USSR.[75] Their Spanish temperament indeed may have made many of them little hooligans, at least in the eyes of Soviet administrators and teachers who were now focused on asserting adult authority and enforcing disciplined behaviour among their charges. We need to read archival reports with this in mind, but later Spanish oral histories and memoirs also recount numerous instances of misbehaviour, which lends support to Soviet perceptions. Before his transfer to Home No. 2 in Krasnovidovo, António Martínez from Oviedo remembered staying in the relatively luxurious Hotel October in Leningrad, where he and his pals skated on the waxed floors, vandalized the buildings, broke things, and shouted down the orchestra that had come to play.[76] Viewing similar behaviour, the director of a Spanish children's home noted the need to overcome the "lordly bourgeois inclinations" of the refugee children.[77] "We had everything," one former niña remembered, "but some of us we were a little too much [in need] of responsibility or, as it was said there, of discipline." Yet, "nobody laid a hand on us, nobody scolded us raising a voice or offending [us] ... everything boiled down to making us understand that we were wrong in being disobedient."[78] It is noteworthy that, like Makarenko, the respondent equated responsibility and discipline and stressed that Soviet educators sought not by punishment but by gentler means, such as persuasion and the provision of positive role models, to cultivate responsible, disciplined young people. Reports and Spaniards' memories decades later recall these unruly behaviours as Spanish characteristics, but Soviet children could be hooligans, too.[79] Understanding the pedagogical changes, and especially a renewed emphasis on discipline in the USSR as the Spaniards left Spain, helps us to understand the spaces in which they were reforged.

In the Spanish homes, students and staff served as role models to emulate and were to chastise the improper behaviour of their peers. Peers made jokes about children who lacked effective study habits, and they published caricatures and poems in wall newspapers condemning bad behaviour.[80] Beginning in 1940, Soviet journals discussed Makarenko's methods, and archival reports provide evidence of teaching workshops in the Spanish schools about his writings and methods.[81] Sometimes new staff had to be introduced to them. Incorrigible boys in Home No. 12 in Leningrad required two new educators from the Makarenko school. One former student remembers that, when order broke down in evacuation, "Shulman, an official of the Commissariat of Public Education, was sent to our home. Shulman was a specialist in education for difficult children, author of a doctoral thesis on the pedagogical methods of Anton Makarenko."[82] The children and Spanish educators remembered at least four directors as Makarenko's disciples.[83] Many niños linked the quality of directors to their training with Makarenko, who had insisted it was imperative that staff members be involved in the daily life of the children, including eating meals together and working or playing after school hours.[84] Manuel Arce's evaluation of his director Kiselev as "kind, fair, hardworking" and an "extraordinary man" stemmed largely from the director's doing manual labour, like hauling firewood, with the children rather than sitting at a desk.[85]

Various organizations also provided leadership and organizational roles for the students. The Young Pioneers and the Communist Youth League (Komsomol) served the same purpose in the Spanish schools as they did in regular Soviet schools. Both organizations served to transmit Soviet values and ideology to the students and provided opportunities for them to be squad leaders, liaisons with the staff, meeting planners, classroom monitors, and more. In this way the administration created opportunities for them to learn leadership and responsibility, which Makarenko saw as a primary function of such institutions. The children's council (*detskii sovet*) liaised with the adults in the school and helped make decisions. The children's council and the leaders of the Pioneer and Komsomol groups policed their fellow students, pointing out shortcomings in learning, hygiene, political knowledge, Soviet morality, and more. By creating a fear of rejection by the peer group because of deviations, the councils set norms in the schools and guided proper behaviour.[86] As the journal *Detskii dom* noted, councils worked with teachers and directors in cases of rule violations so that children could take some responsibility for how the home operated and their peers behaved.[87] There is substantial evidence that in the post-war period in particular the children's councils, typically composed of the best Pioneers in the school, were leading the organization of hygiene and discipline and improving schoolwork, often with Komsomol assistance.[88] In theory these organizations were supposed to police the school, but adult intervention was the norm. Participation in the organizations and various forms of self-policing provided purpose to the refugee children and taught them Soviet values of personal and collective responsibility.

Communist Party organizations were ever present in the Spanish homes, just as they were in Soviet schools. In 1936 at the Tenth Komsomol Congress the organization shifted from training and guidance in the workplace to a greater emphasis on working with children in schools. Thus, the year before the Spanish refugees began to arrive in the USSR, the Communist Party had tasked the Komsomol with a greater presence in Soviet schools to ensure discipline, organization, party-mindedness, and attention to studies. In the same year, children's cinema received its own studio, Soiuzdetfilm, signalling the regime's increasing focus on controlling the messages children received.[89] The Pioneers, Komsomol, and members of the children's councils were also supposed to be examples of good Soviet behaviour for the children and the adults.[90] However, membership in these organizations was never as high as desired. According to a boy named Hugo, Komsomol membership was much like religion in Spain: if one did not join, then that person was marginalized. Although Komsomol membership remained low, a boy named Andrés recalled that Spaniards were forced to join, which shows the problem of relying on memory.[91] In addition to Komsomol leadership, the Spanish schools also had oversight from the Spanish Unified Socialist Youth (OSM in Russian, JSU in Spanish). Although not mentioned as often in archival reports because school officials were reporting to Narkompros and thus highlighting Soviet organizations, the JSU served to raise the political knowledge of the young Spaniards and to serve as role models and a connection to trusted Spanish mentors and Spanish culture.[92]

Groups for the adults were common too. The methodological council sought to improve training for teachers and educators. At times there were also various councils and conferences to raise the general political knowledge or cultural level of the employees so that they could be good role models. Spanish teachers struggling with language instruction attended workshops and additional training on language pedagogy, Marxist philosophy, Soviet pedagogy, and Soviet psychology.[93] This suggests that teaching was about much more than subject matter; it also emphasized the acquisition of Soviet and communist values by students and teachers. A host of journals from this period, like *Sovetskaia pedagogika, Narodnoe obrazovanie,* and *Detskii dom,* served to inform the adults in Soviet and Spanish schools about the most recent decisions of party and state and how to implement them. There were both theoretical articles and what we today would call "best-practice" articles that discussed examples, for instance, of how to teach Soviet patriotism in history classes or evening meetings. The director and/or one of the assistant directors in each home supervised all of these pedagogical activities for the students and staff.

Sometimes the attempts to instil discipline in the Spanish homes begat violence, and the staff crossed the line in their treatment of the children.[94] However, a female educator, who was barely twenty years old in 1937, recalled that the administration vigorously condemned violence as a form of punishment. The Soviet administrators "were saying that [slapping] was counter-educational .... that it is necessary to speak to the child, it is necessary to convince him that he has to do the things well but not to punish him, that not at all."[95] When adult violence occurred in the Spanish schools, Soviet officials sought to stamp it out. Several Spanish educators "tried to beat the children, saying that they were incorrigible, that they were bandits, criminals, etc." The only way to redress this problem, the report noted, was to teach the Spanish adults, who in this case had just arrived in the Soviet Union, that "there are no bad children, but there are bad educators."[96] The Spanish adults, and not just the children, had to be trained anew. The condemnation of adult violence differentiated proper Soviet behaviour from poor educational methods learned in Spain.

As scholar María Encarna Nicolás Marín notes, "discipline characterized all daily activities."[97] Learning was not limited to children; adults were also constantly learning new skills, ideas, and behaviours. This was even more important in the Spanish boarding schools because the Spanish adults had not already internalized Soviet norms of behaviour and thought, as had their Soviet counterparts. Moreover, many in the adult staff, especially among the younger Spanish educators, were poorly educated. Adult personnel were required to take classes on *The History of the Communist Party of the Soviet Union (Bolsheviks),* known as the *Short Course,* to remedy the situation.[98] Some personnel studied the constitution, literature, and art, took excursions to historical places and collective farms, and studied the Russian and Spanish languages.[99]

Some children justified their bad behaviour by referring to the failings of their adult caregivers. "[T]here were several uprisings of the children because of the poor management by the directors," recalled one adult respondent in an interview. "In our home, in Leningrad, there were many abuses and we children, we were always the losers. We were seven to ten years old. We lacked food and everything ... And they beat us a lot ... Sure, we behaved badly because we were hungry."[100] This recollection, likely from the early war years, though not a fond memory, shows that the respondent and his peers had by adulthood internalized cultural differentiation. The director, neither the state nor the children, was to blame; the children's poor behaviour was a function of poor adult leadership.

Remarkably, other niños de la guerra respected their abusers. One of the youngest children, born in 1933, recalled later of his director: "Let's be honest, he used to hit us, yes, but I remember him as an extraordinary person ... although yes, he did make me lose a tooth and all that ... [W]hen one of those Spanish naughty boys [pelagatos] would start to threaten or something, he would give a few slaps for sure!"[101] This understanding of the need at times for physical discipline recalls the story of Zadorov in Makarenko's *Pedagogical Poem*. When the wayward boy Zadorov acted disrespectfully, and Makarenko, who disapproved of violence towards children, slapped him, Zadorov apologized and reflected on the appropriateness of the punishment. This scene marked the transition point for Makarenko from teaching in a relatively unstructured, child-centred environment to a system in which the children, through adult and peer role models, received clear boundaries and discipline.[102] Both Zadorov and the niño expressed that ultimately the violent means justified the ends in creating Soviet discipline within children. The boarding schools helped to define the boundaries of Spanish and Soviet cultural differences.

The Expulsion of Bad Influences

Soviet pedagogy considered that the disciplining of children by violence in most cases failed to instil self-discipline. Instead, the journal for Soviet children's homes, *Detskii dom*, stated clearly in its first issue that teachers and educators needed to be good role models, be organized, tidy, and precise, and have good self-discipline and the ability to produce disciplined behaviour among their students.[103] The values expected of adults mirrored the student rules that required tidiness, accurate schoolwork, and cultured speech. To teach academic subjects and proper Soviet behaviour, influential adults had to embody the behaviours themselves. Just as the Bolsheviks viewed the religious grandmother as a threat during the militant atheism campaigns of the early Soviet years, so did the Soviets consider that teachers and educators without a sense of their Soviet duties threatened to undo the training of Soviet children.[104] Unfortunately, the ill-trained staff of the boarding schools often could not function effectively as positive Soviet role models. The sacking of adults who could not positively reinforce Soviet teachings created a transparency of discipline by showing the authority of the institution and by purging and putting on display models of the unacceptable from which the children and other employees could learn.

Beginning in 1939 a host of Russian and Spanish workers left or were dismissed from the Spanish children's homes, likely as a result of Stalin's March speech about the importance of cadre development. Nearly 129 Spanish teachers and educators had arrived with the children in 1937–8, and one hundred remained in the homes after reductions in 1940, a 22.5 per cent decline. Of the twenty-nine Spaniards "reduced" during 1940, fourteen of them were without jobs but still lived in the homes, which was considered to be "harmful to the educational work with the children" because they had no positive social role.[105] Most of the Soviets who left were auxiliaries, like cooks and cleaners. Some, however, had had direct and extensive contact with the children and therefore could threaten the harmonious and unified message that the Soviets wanted to project in classrooms and in extra-curricular activities. In the first half of 1940 alone, a separate report enumerated thirty-three Spaniards and eighteen Soviet personnel who were fired, mostly for low levels of "political development" and "low general education." A subset of the Spaniards also had "unhealthy political attitudes" and suffered from "errors" in their work.[106] For some of the adults who left the homes we have evidence of the causes.

Many of the Russian staff members who left the homes had done nothing wrong; they were moving on to other activities. For example, the Ursat'evs were moving to Crimea, nurses Likhacheva and Voloshikina resigned to continue their studies, nurse Lipushnik and educator Antonova left for family reasons, and other workers in Home No. 1 departed because of general staff reductions. However, administrators sacked some of the Soviet workers for their personal or work-related behaviour. Several were truant, Mal'kov pilfered produce, Miatisova stole from Spanish comrades, Filatov came to work drunk, Shevel'kova failed to return to work after leave, and nursemaid Kalinina stole children's goods. Still others were sacked for "poor work."[107] It is striking that none of these dismissals was for political reasons or gross misconduct. Rather, they occurred because of disregard for labour and personal discipline, which the administrators could not tolerate in adults who were supposed to act as positive role models. It does not appear that any of these dismissals led to criminal proceedings.

Details on the firing of Spanish workers at this time show a different set of issues, which were more frequently construed as political in nature and were not merely lapses in labour discipline. In December 1939 one Soviet investigator urged that Juan Bote, a science and mathematics teacher from Alcuesca who had arrived with the children, should not "remain in the children's home because he was not providing a communist upbringing or devoting time to the principles of communist education. He prefers to discuss his travels and avoid work with the collective of other communists." The author of the document feared that Bote also could foment unrest among a "part of the Spanish collective which is less prepared and understands political questions poorly."[108] Thus, Bote not only refused to serve as a model of Soviet communist values but also behaved as an individualist rather than working with others. Both his political values and his personal behaviour challenged the Soviet norms taught to the young Spanish charges and positioned him as a negative role model that could lead others astray.[109]

In other cases, directors removed "politically illiterate" Spanish women because they refused to improve. In addition to being politically illiterate, Teresa Rodríguez from Oviedo, twenty-seven years of age, was described as having "weak professional preparation." The recommendation also emphasized her deafness and asked that she be moved to manufacturing work. Another "politically illiterate" woman, twenty-four-year-old Dolores García from Córdoba, had little regard for her work and little interest in the children. Moreover, her work was "undisciplined," which led to a recommendation that she be reassigned to a manufacturing job in Kolomna where her husband lived. The twenty-four year-old Asturian América González from Candas was deemed "illiterate" and "completely uninterested in receiving a minimal education." She further flouted Soviet norms because she neither studied nor showed interest in "questions of political development," and she was "uninterested in the children."[110] The fact that Soviet administrators moved these Spanish adults to factory work rather than arresting them suggests that they were seen not as political enemies but as direct threats to the proper upbringing of children. They failed to instill Soviet vospitanie and kul'turnost' in the children.

There is a degree of consistency in these cases. Adults in positions of nurturing the next generation of Spanish communists had to be willing to transmit the values of a good Soviet communist: education, political awareness, and proper behaviour. The process of eliding public and private and of ascribing political meaning to private acts like drunkenness was typical in the establishment of Bolshevik normative behaviours.[111] Educational preparation among all these dismissed employees was deemed weak, and some had combined their intellectual lethargy with political and personal behaviours that did not provide an authoritative model of correct Soviet behaviour for the children.[112] None of this should be surprising given that most of the Spanish educators were poorly educated young women who, at home in Spain, had had no professional childcare experience and had demonstrated little or no political commitment (only a meagre few were PCE members).

Some charges were far more explosive than those of simple illiteracy or lack of political knowledge or engagement. Twenty-four-year-old Lina Chao was judged unfit to work with children because she "admitted to sexual contact with individual pupils." As if that were not enough, she was also uninterested in politics. A March 1940 report by the chief of the Division of Children's Homes of Special Purpose, Dubrovskii, sheds more light on this case. His short characterization noted that this PCE member, who had been a milliner before becoming an educator in Children's Home No. 1, worked as both a cleaning woman and an educator (although she lacked any training for this latter role), "displayed a dishonest attitude to work," and had also been caught in "anti-Soviet conversations."[113] It is unclear whether these charges preceded or followed the charge of sexual misconduct with students, but it suggests that the first recommendation to remove her went unheeded and that the authorities were trying to build a stronger case against her. She remained in Home No. 1 even after being sacked; in April 1941 another official complained that she avoided work and had cynically stated, "I don't want to work, I'll soon be leaving."[114] Someone wanted her sacked, and the combination of allegations of improper behaviour and political hostility likely sealed her fate.

In some cases it was not what persons did or did not do, but rather who they were, that marked them as suspicious. A Soviet investigator claimed that the age of Elías Bajo (born 1895) made it likely that he was attached too deeply to his roots and traditions. The report deemed him conscientious in his educational work but noted that he bore the "influence of a bourgeois scholastic school," perhaps owing to his theological training. In Spain, Bajo had belonged to a party of "republican-federalists," but the Soviet official could not discern what his political attitudes were in the USSR. To be sure, the Spanish political left was so fractured that being a socialist or even a communist in no way guaranteed support for the Soviet Union or even that one was an atheist or an internationalist. Bajo apparently neither refused to attend public events nor eschewed political speeches of a "deeper character." However, in his daily life he was supposedly often "insincere" and at times "two-faced."[115] This was far from a ringing endorsement but apparently not quite enough to have him sacked. Nevertheless, a new investigation in January 1939 noted that he had an "unhealthy attitude" and that officials in the children's home were suspicious of his "relations with older girls" and his "dubious political physiognomy."[116] Here we see the Soviet fear of "masking" that was so prominent during the Great Terror, which was in full force as the Spaniards arrived in the USSR.[117] The teacher showed no outward evidence of political unreliability or hostility, but his biography – his age, his training and experience, his uncertain political affiliations – prompted concerns. He might be a conscientious and loyal Soviet pedagogue on the one hand or a lecherous, anti-Soviet personality on the other. His Janus-like character, behaviour, and political leanings were all suspect or "dubious," and he could not be left in a classroom of impressionable Spanish children if they were to be reforged into Hispano-Soviets. In this instance, as with Lina Chao, investigators introduced allegations of sexual misconduct to strengthen the case for dismissal.

Although the 1938 *Regulations Concerning the Children's Homes for Spanish Children* demanded that all Soviet employees of the homes should be Komsomol members approved by their regional committees, the records of employees show that in fact most were not Komsomol members.[118] However, this rule reflects the authorities' desire to have only positive communist role models for the children. It was natural that the boarding schools would sack Soviet citizens less frequently for political reasons. Soviet staff had already been vetted and could therefore be trusted to raise the Spanish children as Soviets. With the politically suspect Spanish adults being increasingly culled from the homes, children interacted more often with good role models of Soviet behaviour.[119] In this way Soviet authorities differentiated for the children between proper Soviet culture and the old ways of Spain.

The Spanish children came to recognize the cultural differences between Soviet and Spanish adults and children. As one former student remembered, "the Spanish [teachers] were more liberal, less disciplined, more happy-go-lucky [*más viva la pepa*] in every way."[120] Another former student noted, "It was difficult to work with the Spaniards, because we were more mobile, more playful than the Russians, we had more energy and we were very insolent, so that the teachers had to endure us."[121] Soviet staff shared these views: "Spanish children are generally temperamental, and most of the children's characters were dominated by features of a choleric temperament."[122] They were undisciplined and did and said what they wanted. Although the archival record clearly shows that Spanish adults frequently frustrated or antagonized the homes' Soviet administrators, one has to wonder if the differences were as dramatic as some children remembered. Much of the learning in the homes focused on Soviet behaviour and values, including hard work, a love of education and books, and personal discipline. That the children decades later labelled Spanish teachers and children as the antithesis of Soviet values like self-discipline suggests an internalization of those Soviet values as "good." Those not personifying proper Soviet values earned the label "bad." Thus, the boarding schools had successfully characterized cultural differences.

The existing studies of the refugee children have not contextualized or understood fully the motives and methods of the Soviet authorities in structuring the homes and their staff. We need to see the homes' staff turnover in 1939–40 in the light of the attacks on paedology and the child-centred classrooms of the 1920s and a return to classroom discipline and the adoption of Makarenko's methods. Equally important was Stalin's discussion of cadres at the Eighteenth Party Congress in March 1939 in which he called for raising the political knowledge of cadres throughout the Soviet system. Many Spaniards seem to have fallen short in both political knowledge and the administration of proper discipline. Some of the Spanish workers who were removed from the homes also may have been victims of the purge of the Comintern and other foreign communists at this time. How, for example, do we understand the motivation to remove the Argentine Jewish math teacher Abraham Volma? Was the charge of trying to kiss one of the Spanish girls his real offence?[123] Or was Volma caught up in the Comintern purge or an anti-Semitic persecution? It is likely, given the propensity to simply move the offenders from the boarding schools to factory work rather than to the Gulag, that the "purged" Spanish workers had failed in their duties as role models. They had not learned to "speak Bolshevik" by 1939.[124]

Had this been an attack on Spaniards in general, the special schools for Spanish children, which still maintained a sizeable contingent of Spanish teachers and staff, would not have remained – at great expense – until 1951. Furthermore, what would have been the logic in creating the Centro Español, a Spanish centre in Moscow, to maintain Spanish culture and traditions for the now adult Spaniards in the decades beyond 1951?

From the moment of Stalin's speech on cadres, attention turned to ensuring that the staff, both Soviet and Spanish, within the Spanish homes had sufficient and proper political training. Political illiteracy on the part of teachers threatened the working class, the state, and the internationalist education of the Spanish children.[125] Behavioural problems and uneven political education necessitated a review of the adult staff because only good role models could educate and raise children to become good Soviets and internationalists with the discipline required by recent educational changes. Critical reading and discussion of core texts was proposed as the best solution for adult learners who had failed thus far to acquire the proper political outlook.[126] Only through these role models could schools forge displaced Spanish children into self-disciplined, comradely, and educated contributors to the Soviet Union and Spain as required in the 1938 regulations. The niños had to learn what "socialist in content" meant in the USSR, but they also celebrated their language and culture and thereby remained "national in form." Therefore, Spanish role models were still imperative.

Katerina Clark has argued that it was in the 1930s that the Soviet Union attempted to fashion Moscow as the cosmopolitan centre of a transnational secular enlightenment.[127] The case of Spanish children in the Soviet Union supports the notion of a regime that was still committed to internationalism at precisely the same time that Stalinism highlighted Russians as first among equals in the multinational USSR. The children were raised to love two countries and to care for the development, freedom, and equality of all peoples. Fascism and capitalism, they learned, were the two greatest threats to global freedom and equality. The homes' staffing, education, and health care were designed to ensure that healthy minds and bodies were prepared to advance global socialism. However, these early attempts to construct a safe and ideologically sound living and learning environment with good role models for the refugee children also had to be implemented with careful attention to how and what the children learned in their classrooms.

3 *Obuchenie*: Classroom Instruction, Patriotism, and the Instilling of Soviet Values

[L]et me finish with a "Long live the father of the world proletariat, comrade STALIN!" And another Viva to our beloved homelands Spain and the USSR, imperishable bulwarks that exterminate fascism in all its manifestations.
State Archive of the Russian Federation, f. 2306, op. 7, d. 5993, l. 3

As *Pravda* noted in 1942, "educators must subordinate the whole of their teaching to the tasks of patriotic upbringing of the pupils."[1] Ibárruri, in a speech at the Kharkov children's home, said, "You ought to study hard and learn from the Soviets so that tomorrow you may be useful to a democratic Spain."[2] Learning from and emulating the Soviets thus became a duty to one's family and native land. Classroom lessons and the values they projected, particularly patriotism for the USSR and Spain – the two homelands – helped to construct the Hispano-Soviet identifications in the young Spanish refugees. The epigraph to this chapter is the conclusion of a letter from teacher Elías Bajo to Narkompros that illustrates the pervasiveness of the dual patriotism expected in the boarding schools. Bajo's letter is a plea to allow his children to join him in the USSR. As we saw in the last chapter, Soviet investigators had questioned Bajo's reliability as a role model. Yet, as a supplicant, he had learned how to deploy Bolshevik language. The letter states that he wants his children to be safe from the "clutches of fascism," and he also notes that his three young children could soon become "conscious comrades who will fight with faith and enthusiasm for the common cause." They will become part of the two "imperishable bulwarks" that under the guidance of Stalin will defeat fascism.[3]

This chapter argues that classroom instruction did more than create literate and numerate students. Soviet education had a transformative purpose. Like modern education generally, it sought to create notions of patriotism and citizenship, highlighting for students the values important in society. As in other Soviet non-Russian schools, the Spanish boarding schools sought to blend respect for particularist native language and culture with universalist Soviet values of internationalism, patriotism, and civic duty. The outcome was to be new Hispano-Soviet students who had learned to value the best aspects of their two homelands. This is reminiscent of what Terry Martin has described as an "affirmative action empire," one in which the Soviet regime promoted local languages, cultures, and leaders as a bulwark against denunciations of being Great Russian chauvinists.[4] One method of strengthening non-Russian cadres was through education. Martin and the scholarship on non-Russian education help us see that the Soviet Spanish schools were operating within Soviet parameters, despite the intended influence of the PCE. The boarding schools promoted Spanish language and culture and prepared the children to become future leaders of socialist Spain. Rather than being a bulwark against charges of Great Russian chauvinism, however, affirmative action among the Spanish children sought to strengthen international communism and burnish the USSR's international humanitarian credentials. Spanish children were promoted as a minority population that deserved its language and heritage and an education that could help create Spanish cadres. Francine Hirsch argues that the Soviet desire to modernize "backward" peoples lasted much longer than Martin contends. The Spaniards' upbringing through 1951 is evidence of this. The chief difference is that, rather than becoming Spanish cadres within the USSR as other national minorities did, the Spanish children developed into cadres for the USSR, a liberated Spain, and the communist movements throughout Latin America. Although Spanish children were still living in the USSR during russocentrism – a Soviet shift in the mid- to late 1930s to popularize Marxist ideas using traditional Russian imagery – the niños were able to maintain much of their Spanish culture while being Sovietized to share new educational and attitudinal values and Soviet international concerns.

Scholar Guy Neave has argued that in several European countries during the Second World War "education was an instrument of social mobility, a vehicle both for the struggle of hearts and minds and means of stating and restating the goals for which both sides contended."[5] In addition to teaching reading, writing, and arithmetic, many countries – and not only the dictatorships that emerged in the inter-war period – viewed state education as a vehicle for teaching nationalism, patriotism, and civic duty.[6] In some countries a cult of violence emerged. In Japan, children learned that defence of their country and the emperor's life included sacrificing their own lives.[7] In Nazi Germany, violence was even more prevalent as young boys learned to brawl in Hitler Youth camps, and boys and girls learned the lessons of racial hierarchy and violence in the schools that all but ceased to offer a traditional education.[8] These were no longer innocent and protected children. Even when children's experience seemed to take similar forms on the surface, such as camping in the Boy Scouts of America and in the Hitler Youth, the lessons learned from these times away from parents took on national forms that supported individualism on the one hand and collective action on the other.[9] Democracies, too, mobilized children and taught nationalism.[10]

Soviet education mirrored those modern practices, viewing children as resources to be mobilized. From 1939 to the end of the Spanish Civil War to the start of the Russo-Finnish War, to the Second World War, and into the post-war period, heroism and patriotism became central in Soviet discourse; for children, this meant showing greater attention to and love of labour and political matters.[11] Patriotism was to be the focus of every class and every teacher.[12] Even librarians were to "inculcate in our children a boundless love for the motherland and the most intense hatred of the Fascists."[13] Patriotism was *admiration for the heroic struggle* of the Soviet people at the front and the rear, a sense of *solidarity with oppressed peoples, pride in the country* in the vanguard of the war of liberation from Fascism, the *certainty of victory*, the nearness of the hour of reckoning and the *readiness and desire to devote all one's powers to the service of this struggle*."[14] The emphasis on admiration, solidarity with oppressed people, pride, certainty, readiness, and desire shows the continuum of Soviet thinking from recognition of the problem to mutual ascription to active participation. Stated another way, the teaching of patriotism was meant to move children from feeling and emotion to action. In the Spanish boarding schools, Spanish patriotism grafted onto this russocentric patriotism. The refugees learned to love their two homelands. As Julio Mateu stated, "Two homelands I carry with me, both in the heart."[15] They had to defend the homeland of communism in order to extinguish fascism in their Spanish homeland.

Education from Spain to the Soviet Union

Spain's Second Republic (1931–9) had reformed education, but it was starting from a devastatingly low level. Spain had no ministry of education until 1900, and at the turn of the century illiteracy remained at 60–70 per cent (compared to about 30 per cent across the border in France), and at about 90 per cent for girls alone. Approximately thirty thousand municipalities had no school at all, and many others had only a primary school. Before the Second Republic the state had given the Catholic Church – known to Soviet pedagogues as the "bulwark of reaction and fascism" – virtually free rein to education.[16] At nearly every turn the Catholic Church ignored illiteracy, limited female education, and contributed to the general cultural backwardness in Spain.[17] An "obstinately conservative oligarchy" insignificantly funded education; spending amounted to 25 per cent of per capita levels in France and Italy and to only 10 per cent of that in the United States.[18] Despite conservatives' attempts to keep Spain in the nineteenth century, during its half decade in power and its attack on Catholic hegemony the Second Republic built over 9,300 schools and increased female enrolment in secondary school from 14.6 per cent in 1930–1 to 31.6 per cent in 1935–6, only to see Franco's regime constrict learning after 1939.[19] The children who evacuated to the Soviet Union began mandatory, co-educational, secular learning in at least the first seven grades; this provided opportunities that most could not have realized in Spain.

The curriculum at the Spanish children's homes in the USSR varied little from that of the typical non-Russian Soviet classroom, except for the initial prioritization of Spanish language and culture instead of a Soviet language and culture. Soviet textbooks, translated into Castilian Spanish, were the norm, and teachers for the most part followed the standard syllabi approved by Narkompros. The Spanish Republic had sent books to Narkompros via the All-Union Society for Cultural Relations with Foreign Countries (VOKS) in 1936, and later in 1937 as the children began to arrive.[20] The republic continued to send books in 1938, but it does not seem that Narkompros distributed them to all the schools.[21]

Teachers in all courses, except Russian, initially used Castilian Spanish. In many cases the classroom teacher was a native Russian speaker who worked through a translator or a Spanish teacher or educator. Memoirs also suggest that Spanish-speaking teachers and faculty from Moscow State University were moved to the boarding schools.[22] Although there had been intensive Spanish classes for Soviet teachers just before the children arrived, their abilities to communicate were extremely limited. In the early years Soviet teachers assisted the several Spanish lead teachers, most likely as a check on the ideological content and pedagogical methods of courses. From the beginning, Soviet authorities wanted to ensure the delivery of a Soviet education accessorized by Spanish content. The longer the homes stayed open, the fewer Spanish teachers remained. One way we can interpret this is that there was a growing desire after Franco's victory to prepare the Spanish children to become long-term Soviet residents. Although this eventually meant Soviet citizenship for many, both the Communist Party of the Soviet Union (CPSU) and PCE prepared for the day that these Spanish children, now patriots of two countries and armed with a "proper" view of Soviet Marxism and a command of the Spanish language, would be able to return to Spain to modernize it and bring it into the fold of communist nations.

Patriotism in Soviet education predated the Nazi invasion, and the revival of pre-revolutionary Russian heroes was already a hallmark of pre-war russocentrism. From the first issue of *Sovetskaia pedagogika* in 1937 as the first niños made their way to the USSR, one of its central goals was to show how and why patriotism belonged in schools.[23] Teaching patriotism became central to all coursework and training in Soviet schools, children's homes, and *internaty* (boarding schools for gifted, troubled, or disabled Soviet children). Wherever there were children learning, messages about love of country and people bombarded them. Pedagogical journals emphasized that instilling patriotism in young children was the task of each school worker and that it should not be limited to just one or two subjects.[24] Narkompros head V.P. Potemkin noted as much when he said, "Education in such conscious patriotism is the primary duty of the Soviet teacher. In this sphere, all our school subjects give the educator inexhaustibly rich material."[25] Even though science had hero scientists – like Michurin, Lysenko, and Pavlov – and the great feats of the 1930s in aviation and polar exploration, the teaching of heroism and patriotism was most prominent in the social sciences and humanities. History lessons highlighted popular uprisings against foreign invaders and the inevitable downfall of oppressive empires. Literature courses preferred national classics, patriotism, and writings about the Great Patriotic War. While all these ideals were fine in theory, classrooms and extracurricular activities had to promote them.[26]

History, Geography, and Patriotism

Education in the Spanish homes, as in the Soviet schools, consisted of core courses like history, geography, politics and the constitution, Spanish and Russian languages and literature, mathematics, and the sciences. Some disciplines were more important in developing the students' Soviet mindset. Courses dealing with politics and the Stalin Constitution for older students were the most obvious and direct in teaching a specific world view. Study of the constitution, moreover, served as a platform for other disciplines. As a leading educational journal noted, "the history teacher, the geography teacher, and the literature teacher will find in the Constitution the most gratifying material for the enrichment both of their discipline and the improvement of their teaching."[27] However, history had long been a privileged discipline in the Soviet Union as the party and teachers reinterpreted the past to make it fit the Marxist-Leninist-Stalinist ideas of the day. By also directing students' attention to past Russian heroes, history lessons could develop both a Soviet world view and patriotism. By the late 1930s, "heroes and heroism would come to stand at the center of a series of Soviet propaganda drives that were designed to promote a newly populist vision of the USSR's 'usable past.'"[28] The centrality of heroism and patriotism in the Spanish schools suggests both a consistency in Soviet non-Russian education and the realization that the Spaniards were becoming long-term residents of the USSR.

Students took part in an increasing number of activities and classroom lessons that began their transformation into Hispano-Soviets. The history curriculum was rather straightforward: a focus on the "glorious historical past of the Russian people."[29] Pre-revolutionary peasant uprisings led by Ivan Bolotnikov, Stenka Razin, and Emilian Pugachev showed how the masses could revolt against injustice and oppression. Similarly, the Decembrists and the October

Revolution showed a seemingly natural Russian propensity to fight against exploitation and abuse of power. Third graders could study military leadership in the more distant past from Aleksandr Nevsky, Kuzma Minin, and Prince Dmitry Pozharsky and, in the following school year, learn about Peter the Great's war with Sweden and the 1812 war against Napoleon. Political education then linked the past to modern-day heroes like polar explorer Ivan Papanin, Red Army soldiers during the Battle of Lake Khasan, and pilots Valery Chkalov, Mikhail Gromov, and Valentina Grizodubova. International history focused on important events like the French Revolution, the Paris Commune, and the founding of the First International (the International Workingmen's Association) and thus further develop an internationalist mindset.[30]

In Home No. 1, teacher N.G. Maksimova's history classes for grades four to seven serve as an example of instruction to develop dual patriotism – Soviet and Spanish – and the certainty of the folk's defeat of fascism.[31] In the fourth grade, after completing the full syllabus for "History of the USSR," Maksimova and her students reviewed the lives of pre-revolutionary Russian heroes and the "historical exile" of comrade Joseph Stalin. In 1242 Nevsky outwitted the Teutonic Knights in the "Battle on the Ice."[32] Donskoi, in 1380, staged the first major defeat of the Mongol Golden Horde in the Battle of Kulikovo Field. Minin and Pozharsky led an uprising in 1612 to repel from Moscow the forces of Polish King Sigismund III and thereby helped install the first Romanov on the throne. Aleksandr Suvorov was one of Russia's greatest generals, leading the conquest of Poland during the partitions, fighting in the Russo-Turkish wars, and commanding Russian and Austrian forces against France. Suvorov's contemporary Mikhail Kutuzov also fought in the Russo-Turkish wars and, having outlived Suvorov, oversaw the expulsion of Napoleon from Russia. All the heroes appeared in the Russian and Soviet canon as defenders of the motherland against outside invaders from the Mongols and the Teutonic Knights in the thirteenth century through Napoleon's invasion in 1812 and the wars with the Ottoman Turks.

Maksimova's focus on the Russian and Soviet homeland must have confused a number of the students, so she improvised and modified curricula on ancient history and the Middle Ages to generalize about the power of peasant armies and the long history of brutal German invasions across Europe. In these ways she sought to balance her russocentric curriculum with what she called "moments of nationalization of the curriculum," using examples from Spanish history to make the general Soviet syllabus more meaningful to the Spaniards. For example, in Roman history Maksimova discussed the fight of the Iberian people during Hannibal's siege of Saguntum (219 BCE) and for independence from Rome during the uprisings of Viriatus (147–139 BCE) and Quintus Sertorius (80–72 BCE). These examples, she said, were meant to strengthen the children's hearts to be future fighters for the new Spain. Maksimova linked Spanish valour in the deep past to the present conflict against the Nazis and the children's future in fighting against Franco. Although not a student in this school, Isabel Álvarez recalled that the heroism of the Leningrad siege that she had to endure "could be compared with Sagunto and Numancia," so this connection certainly made sense to some children.[33] That Spain was not united during the period taught by Maksimova does not seem to have entered her teaching. The apparent lapse in discussing a fragmented Spain likely helped to form a common *hispanidad* with minimized regional differences. In this way she echoed the hopes of Ibárruri and other PCE leaders who had consistently informed the children that their great task was to learn from the Soviet Union and prepare themselves for a return to unite Spain and to liberate it from fascism while building a new progressive, socialist state. The fight against fascism, and oppression generally, they believed, inextricably bound the Spaniards and the Soviets together. Maksimova's lessons bridged the Second World War and Spain's history, the broader fight against oppression, and the fights against fascism in Spain's civil war and the Second World War. Soviet anti-fascism and socialist internationalism thus became timeless struggles against repressive regimes.[34]

Maksimova's teaching of Russian history, situated within larger struggles, was so exemplary that on the school's fifth anniversary she won a cash prize. Her suggestions for teaching history indicate what she and perhaps the regime valued most about the instruction of this subject. By selecting her for an award, the regime was signalling that her teaching was an exemplary model for others to follow. She felt that students needed to perceive their people as legendary heroes. They needed to understand that the goal of fighting fascism meant more than mere survival; people fought together to liberate countries from oppressors. She illustrated the barbarity of the Nazis by showing the damage inflicted by German soldiers on the estate of the writer Lev Tolstoy and the brutality visited on Ukraine in 1918 and during the Second World War occupation. Her intent was to help the students understand the battle and strengthen "their love for their second motherland and its leader, Stalin."[35]

The idea of patriotism for two homelands is consistent throughout the period under study, and it highlights the notion that schooling was transforming the children into individuals with two languages, two "families," two homelands, yet one world view. Soviet minority populations had a native tongue and culture but also learned Russian language and culture, all the while learning to ascribe to a Soviet world view. They were to value both their native homelands and the USSR.

The PCE also did its part to merge Spain's history with the Soviet narrative of peaceful people fighting against aggression. A monthly periodical entitled *Ahora* (Now), published in Moscow by Spanish communists, taught lessons from the Spanish past. The seventeenth-century wars of Catalonia against French and German invaders, and Napoleon's aggression nearly two centuries later, were but two examples.[36] Regular repetition of these lessons from the

Russian and Spanish past was meant to foster dual identifications among the children and to create affinities with their birthplace and their new homeland. History lectures like those of Maksimova, and publications by the PCE, were critical for the development of patriotism and a Soviet world view, but other disciplines also had much to offer.

Like history lectures, geography coursework also taught politics and patriotism, and study of the USSR's natural resources proved the autarkic possibilities of the country. War-time use of maps of physical geography contributed to the militarization of the curriculum, although map drawing and orienteering were lacking.[37] Geography, both physical and cultural, served to improve students' knowledge of the richness and cultural diversity of the USSR.[38] Teachers could include maps of pilot heroes' exploits, Arctic expeditions, nature, the USSR, and the world. Teaching about the Red Army and military also was a vehicle for teaching maps.[39] And, of course, the niños followed the Spanish Civil War on maps. Even before the arrival of the refugees, Soviet Pioneers had written to their Spanish counterparts telling them about their attention to the war in newsreels and newspapers and their use of maps to follow the action.[40] Komsomol members in some factories were studying Spanish history, geography, and economics. One group wrote to the Unified Socialist Youth: "We wait with impatience ... Each of us would like to fight alongside you in your ranks against traitors to your country and the supporting troops of German and Italian fascism."[41]

The goal of geography study in the Spanish homes was precisely the same as that in other Soviet schools, but with a Spanish inflection. Geography lessons taught "about the life of the Union Republics, the people of the USSR, to show the great Soviet Union, its wealth, strength, etc."[42] As early as the fourth grade, students learned the climactic zones and republics of the USSR, topography, main rivers, industrial and agricultural centres, natural resources, communication networks, and the peoples of the USSR. Geography lessons – and newspapers – also apparently included significant attention to Spain. A Soviet geography teacher noted how the study of maps and current events in Spain "created great interest among the [Soviet] children." Students used maps to follow events in Japan and the feats of Soviet aviators.[43] Visits to the Spanish schools by Ivan Papanin and Valery Chkalov likely reinforced the in-class lessons.[44] Bernardo del Río recalled that he saw maps of Spain with red pins marking the front lines in schools, clubs, and factories.[45] In 1940 the Ministry of Education published a new textbook for Spanish geography that was important "for the welfare of their country" and to develop a "great love for their heroic homeland ... And for this purpose the first and most necessary is to know Spain well."[46]

History and geography courses taught about both Spain and the USSR and sought to cultivate knowledge and a love and appreciation of both their homelands and their people; thus they opened the possibility for students to ascribe

3.1 Children in a Leningrad home, meeting hero aviator Valery Chkalov. España, Ministerio de Cultura y Deporte, Centro Documental de la Memoria, P.S. Incorporados, carpeta 17, folio 1.

to one or more cultures. The success of these endeavours likely depended largely on the quality of instruction, the availability of materials, and the linguistic abilities of teachers and students. At least before the Nazi invasion, some Spaniards recalled having no knowledge of current events or newspapers because they "were limited to living and nothing more."[47]

Language and Literature, Culture and Inculcation

Language and literature courses sought to train the young Spaniards in their native and adopted languages and introduce them to literature from around the world that conformed to the parameters of socialist values; at the same time, the literature courses increasingly focused on Russian classics and contemporary Soviet prose and drama that foregrounded the thinking about Russian and Soviet greatness. Party and education officials vigorously debated the place of Russian-language instruction in schools for non-Russian children. New regulations in 1938 mandated Russian-language instruction in all Soviet schools, but Stalin's support for native-language instruction remained unwavering.

In an attempt to produce a lingua franca for the military, Stalin believed that Russian should be taught as a second language and not become the language of instruction (except in Russian language and literature courses) in non-Russian schools.[48] The dominant language of instruction and the students' performance in both languages remained key concerns for the entire decade and a half of the Spanish homes' existence. Both languages were required to master Soviet values, to maintain a Spanish community, to prepare the students for work in the USSR, and to seize Spain from Franco.

Although Spanish-language training remained a priority throughout the boarding-school years, a lack of trained pedagogues and good instructional materials complicated instruction. The "Children of Spain," an introduction from a 1938 primary-school reader, began, "Never forget while you live the fascist criminals who have murdered so many of your little brothers and who want to kill and sink into misery your parents and siblings."[49] Learning Spanish was an existential necessity for the future of Spain and humanity. Yet, Home No. 2 in Mozhaisk reported that in the 1938–9 school year it lacked a qualified Russian and Spanish language teacher and that education continued "without interruption ... but in very difficult circumstances."[50] The eight Spanish teachers in Home No. 2 were so overworked that two became ill and the director had to ask for two more Spanish and Russian language teachers, none of which was forthcoming. In this home, as in most others before the war – per a resolution of the party and the government – Spanish was the language of instruction in history, mathematics, geography, and natural history. By the end of the war, however, it was common to teach only Spanish language, literature, and geography in Spanish.[51]

Most of the Spanish adults who accompanied the children from Spain had had no pedagogical training, and even fewer had studied languages. There were thirty-seven languages of instruction in Russia and forty-eight in the USSR, and not enough trained teachers, which led to failures in both Russian- and native-language training.[52] Spanish was not a priority language in the USSR, so there were few Soviets qualified to take on the task of teaching it. In July 1940, for example, a senior Narkompros official overseeing the Spanish homes directed the Institute of Foreign Languages to send six recently graduated French specialists to teach Spanish in the boarding schools that lacked Spanish specialists.[53] One must wonder how the Comintern purges affected the lack of Spanish teachers. The South American sector lost all its translators and Spanish-speaking teachers, and the students noticed the disappearance of international teachers like Comintern members Edmund Peluso from Italy and the Hungarian husband of educator Meri Suárez, both of whom were arrested.[54]

Before the war some Spanish boarding schools had significant Spanish-language libraries. Home No. 5, for example, housed about four hundred Spanish-language titles in its library, but this was far smaller than the Russian collection and insufficient for the 467 children in the home.⁵⁵ Perhaps the relatively high volume of Spanish books came with the thirteen Spanish teachers in the school. We do not have complete inventories of school libraries, but annual reports often provide highlights of the collections and the books that students enjoyed reading. In many cases Spanish literature is completely absent, and when an author like Cervantes appears, it is not clear if the text was in Spanish or translated into Russian or whether the children read it or had it read to them.

The almost complete silence on the issue of Spanish literature and other reading material suggests that the PCE and Comintern were not the primary audience for most reports. Yet even PCE investigators and Spanish personnel in the homes who wrote unsolicited letters to PCE leaders focused more on daily life and less on literature.⁵⁶ Thus, we should not take the absence of Spanish topics in many reports as an acknowledgment of the neglect of Spanish topics altogether. Rather, report authors were likely highlighting the themes and topics demanded by their superiors, which included Russian-language acquisition and preparation to enter Soviet society with the proper world view and personal behaviours.

First-hand accounts suggest that Spanish literature was less prevalent in the homes. Eyewitnesses note that, for example, the 1939 Vasilieva literature anthology written for them had excerpts by Gorky, Ostrovsky, and Ibárruri, but none by Chekhov or Dostoevskii, and Spanish literature included only the writings of relatively minor figures like poet Pía y Beltrán. Moreover, the "splendid library in Spanish and Basque" remained behind when Home No. 7 evacuated in 1941.⁵⁷ It was Spanish educators like Rubén Landa who tried best to keep alive the Spanish heritage. He introduced students to the beauty of masterpieces like the Castillian epic poem *El cantar de mío Cid*, and then he fled to Mexico in 1938. That same year, Isabel Álvarez entered her "romantic period" and read – on her own, it appears – Ramón de Campoamor, Lope de Vega, García Lorca, Nicaraguan Rubén Darío, and "other famous Spanish poets."⁵⁸ Some Spanish schools shared similar problems with non-Russian schools: good intentions battled with insufficiently trained staff and materials to teach the native language.

Literature served two major functions in Soviet education: it highlighted the creative talent of the nation and illustrated the feats of heroism that children should emulate. As in other disciplines, literature was used to promote patriotism and develop Bolshevik attitudes and behaviours: "True Soviet patriotism must strive to be the all-round culture-bearer of the motherland and the people, possessing firmness of character, Bolshevik toughness and persistence, courage and goal-directedness. All these qualities can and must be inculcated by literature."⁵⁹ Classical literature provided abundant examples of fine writing with heroism as the subject, and it often complemented history courses. Bogatyr' Il'ia Muromets fought against steppe invasions, and "he served the motherland and the interests of the people [*narod*]."⁶⁰ Students could read the narrative poem about him and the other *bogatyrs* (knight-like warriors) and examine Viktor Vasnetsov's painting on the subject. In this instance, as in many others, multi-disciplinary approaches – here history, literature, and visual arts – reinforced ideas like courage, patriotism, defending the state, masculinity, and more.

Medieval and imperial literature also provided numerous heroic narratives for the children. The late-twelfth-century fight against the Polovtsy steppe nomads in the "Lay of Igor's Campaign," and stories of legendary battles against Mongols and Germans from the early thirteenth century – such as "Story of the Invasion of Batu in Riazan," "Story of a Tatar Invasion," and "The Life of Alexander Nevsky" – all brought the long history of Russian literature and heroic fights against invaders into the Soviet and Spanish classrooms. Tolstoy's *War and Peace* and Mikhail Lermontov's poem "Borodino" about Napoleon's 1812 invasion illustrated the more recent Russian heroism against great odds.⁶¹ Soviet schools also taught Pushkin's poetry and the works of Gogol, Nikolai Nekrasov, Nikolai Chernyshevskii, Maksim Gorky, Vladimir Mayakovsky, and others.⁶² Reifying a classical Russian literary canon legitimized the Soviet state historically and politically and further provided a rich cultural legacy to draw upon for inspiration and pride. Moreover, canonical texts forged a "coherent identity for the new Soviet society by placing a reinterpreted Russian cultural narrative at its core."⁶³ Spaniards shared this canon, which provided a common cultural language with their Soviet peers and aided in their acculturation as Soviet adults.

In addition, Soviets and Spaniards studied more contemporary heroes, like Pavel Korchagin (the protagonist in the civil-war novel *How the Steel Was Tempered*), Oleg Koshevoi, and the heroes in Gorky's *Mother* and Sholokhov's *They Fought for Their Country*.⁶⁴ Teachers reported that the Spaniards enjoyed the most Polevoi's *Story of a Real Man*, Elena Koshevaia's *Tale of My Son*, Petr Chervinskii's *Blood for Blood*, Iakov Bash's *Professor Buiko*, Semen Rozenfel'd's *Doctor Sergeev*, Il'ia Ehrenburg's *Storm*, and Alexander Fadeev's *Young Guard*. These novels are primarily martial texts that address self-sacrifice in war time. Many of the books also became films. The Spaniards' other favourite authors included Tolstoy, Anton Chekhov, Ivan Turgenev, Gorky, Victor Hugo, Romain Rolland, Jack London, and the early critic of Nazism, Lion Feuchtwanger, thus displaying the international character of the socialist ethos.⁶⁵

When we examine the children's assigned reading, which was both entertaining and instructive, we find clear themes of heroism and sacrificial actions for the students to emulate. For example, Ehrenburg and Feuchtwanger were not only prominent Soviet and German writers, respectively, but also outspoken Jewish critics of Nazi Germany. Ehrenburg won the Stalin Prize in 1947 for *Storm*, a novel set in France and the Soviet Union that highlights the heroic efforts of the Red Army and touches on the Soviet defence of Spain during its civil war. War novels took precedent, as with Polevoi's story of the Second World War fighter pilot Aleksei Mares'ev who continued flying after losing both legs. Fadeev's 1946 Stalin Prize–winning account of the martyred partisans near the Ukrainian city of Krasnodon, and Koshevaia's biography of her son Oleg, who was the leader of the Krasnodon partisans, also became part of the martial genre for Spanish children.[66] These exciting stories reportedly helped to develop a love for reading, a central goal of Soviet education, and showed Soviet heroism, collective effort, determination, and sacrifice. It is important to note that the Spanish boarding schools had complete control over what students could read. The guided reading promoted and overseen by teachers and librarians narrowed the ideals to which the children could strive and thus provided new possibilities as they negotiated their new identifications through literature that taught normative values, morals, and behaviours.[67] With control over reading and extracurricular activities to reinforce books' themes, it became easier for educators to pass along the most salient collectivist messages to their students.

During their visits to the school library younger readers also read lighter literature from the international canon. By the end of the third grade, Spanish children enjoyed reading the books of Daniel Defoe, Mark Twain, Harriet Beacher Stowe, and Jules Verne along with Russian works like Valentin Kataev's *Son of the Regiment*, Sergei Girgor'ev's *Victory at Sea*, and Nikolai Chukovskii's *Submarine Chaser*. The older children read a variety of light and serious literature: Turgenev's *A Nest of Gentlefolk* and *Rudin*; Tolstoy's *War and Peace* and *Anna Karenina*; Gorky's *Mother*, *Stories*, and his autobiographical trilogy; Chekhov's stories and plays; Victor Hugo's *Les Misérables*, *Ninety-Three*, and *Hunchback of Notre-Dame*; Jack London's *The Sea Wolf*, *A Daughter of the Snows*, and *Hearts of Three*; Walter Scott's *Ivanhoe* and *Richard the Lionheart*; Thomas Mayne Reid's *The Scalp Hunters* and *The Headless Horseman*; James Fenimore Cooper's *The Pathfinder* and *The Last of the Mohicans*; and Alexandre Dumas's *Three Musketeers* and *The Count of Monte Cristo*.[68] Instructors carefully selected international literature so that the stories supported Soviet teachings. Some books were adventure stories, a genre that Soviet publishers had dramatically curtailed in the 1930s. Adventure stories were popular, but some educators feared they would distract students from "serious" literature. The authors noted here, however, became acceptable because they commented on heroism, initiative, valour, American racism, tyranny of elites, and comradery. The use of international literature also helped to highlight to the children that in countries around the world, even in fascist and capitalist states, there were people who understood oppression and believed that everyone should work together for equality. This was designed to help develop students' empathy and internationalist perspective. Nationality did not matter; each country had enemies and champions of the repressed.

Staff or Komsomol members who supervised or led book festivals, readers' conferences, and workshops aided the "correct" readings and understandings of the messages.[69] Of course, this does not mean that every reader came away only with the official understanding. It would be quite easy to read many of these stories simply for the adventure, while ignoring, misunderstanding, or trying to dismiss the political and ideological questions on display.[70] However, access to the text and reading groups to probe the text likely increased the number of students who emerged with the essential meaning that Soviet educators wanted to impart. Just as the literature itself expanded on ideal Soviet values, student reports about literature developed desirable character traits like initiative and public speaking.[71] Film adaptations of some of these novels and lectures by adult mentors before exams further reinforced many of the themes and values in literature.[72]

Spanish literature likely was less prominent in Soviet schools because it was less politically clear. There was no Spanish socialist-realist canon from which the homes could pick. The work of Federico García Lorca resonated well with Soviet values, but there were not many other masters to whom the homes could point as good socialist writers. Cervantes – like Shakespeare or Pushkin – could not be ignored, and the farce of romantic chivalry in *Don Quixote*, its meditation on deception, and its arguments against nationalism could be illustrative for Soviets also. Children could have read it as simply a great adventure tale and a masterwork of Spanish language and literature; therefore, discussions about it were crucial. Reading Golden Age literature showed the children that Spain too had literary masters about whom they could be proud. Literature and culture lessons became what we might call "heritage work," passing on valued traditions to the next generation.

For the Hispano-Soviets, obuchenie shifted from being more Spanish centred in 1937–40 to being more Soviet centred thereafter. Throughout the era the Spanish boarding schools insisted on educating children with a patriotism for two countries and a willingness to serve humanity. Heroes guided the way and provided inspiration and a target for aspiration. Although Soviet heroes were most prominent, Spanish examples helped keep alive dreams for the first homeland. Like the non-Russian schools, the Spanish boarding schools had to promote the students' native culture while at the same time fostering Soviet values, among which were patriotism and internationalism. Niños were emerging from backwardness and being trained as cadres.

War dislocates, disrupts, and causes educational institutions to adapt. Moreover, in belligerent countries, patriotic and nationalist education begins to prepare new warriors and workers. Soviet schooling mirrored modern schooling generally. Teachers and school officials were tasked with raising literate and numerate citizens with the skills and social dispositions that would make them valuable to the nation. In Japan the outbreak of war intensified pre-war trends towards nationalism and militarism in school. In Germany the teaching of racial hierarchy and hatred intensified during the war. In Italy state textbooks taught the fascist values to "believe, obey, and fight" and revered Mussolini as a hero and father figure.[73] As in other combatant nations, patriotism and nationalism took hold in new curricula in the United States and Australia, although in the latter direct political education was more muted. Increased attention to science, mathematics, and physical education typically increased in most belligerent nations.[74] In all these countries, educational systems realized that the exigencies of war necessitated greater attention to behaviours and citizenship training outside the regular curriculum.

Whereas classroom education in the Spanish schools taught numbers, letters, patriotism, and heroes, learning the discipline, labour skills, and fortitude of heroes and the traditions and aesthetics of a cultured person were best learned out of class in Soviet vospitanie.

4 *Vospitanie: Kul'turnost'* and *Kruzhki* as Techniques of Normative Behaviour Training

After studying they brought us breakfast at school, they gave us bread with butter, with sweets, in the middle of the morning ... so in the afternoon we did our homework and they gave us a bus ride to the pioneer's palace so that we could learn whatever we wanted; music, photography, dramatic art ... all the arts ... a palace, because that thing was a palace, drawing, whatever you wanted. (Female, born 1928)
                Devillard et al., *Los niños españoles en la URSS, 1937–1997*, 87

Throughout the Soviet period, *kul'turnost'* (culturedness or acculturation) became a key component of the Soviet process of human transformation. Although it was never a clearly articulated policy, a host of measures between 1934 and 1938 indicated what kul'turnost' entailed. Vadim Volkov has suggested three distinct phases in the articulation of kul'turnost': 1934–6, behaviour, hygiene, and consumerism; 1936–7, knowledge and education; 1937–8, consciousness and ideological commitment.[1] This periodization reveals a shift from the external and performative part of culturedness to the internal and reflective. In all three periods, however, there is a clear articulation of the need for self-control and self-discipline. Kul'turnost' thus served as a complement to the coercion and violence of the Great Terror of the same period. Coercion and violence physically disciplined the body and the body politic; kul'turnost' civilized people by actively engaging them in acquiring and mastering normative behaviours. The Spanish children had little agency in acquiring the material goods (e.g., white tablecloths, curtains, lampshades) that were physical markers of the cultured, acquisitive Soviet; these had to be provided by the boarding schools. All the other components of kul'turnost' (e.g., behaviour, hygiene, education, and political consciousness) were omnipresent parts of the remoulding of the Spaniards as Soviet residents. For the Spaniards, as well as for Soviet citizens, becoming Soviet was as much about behaving in a particular way as it was about thinking "correctly" and creating a common culture that would allow them to enter Soviet society in adulthood.

The homes served as a safe and nurturing transition point that began the process of teaching Spaniards to be Soviet, and the Spanish children viewed the homes as a place of protection: from the war, economic concerns, dislocation from Spain, and a world that was foreign to them.[2] The transition went beyond language training, though this was a chief concern of school officials, to teaching and modelling norms of hygiene, comradely relations, connection with labour and agriculture, a love of reading and nature, respect for the arts, and a socialist world view. Thus, as the epigraph to this chapter recollects, the upbringing – vospitanie – of children outside of the classroom was an important counterpart to lessons learned in academic studies. Whereas academic studies helped to develop patriotism, it was the out-of-classroom moments that nurtured the passions of students, developed their aesthetic sensibilities, and taught them how to behave as Soviets. As much as, if not more than, obuchenie, vospitanie acculturated the Spaniards to Soviet life.

For the first years of the Spanish boarding schools the goals of vospitanie varied little. The first set of rules and regulations in 1937–8 stressed the importance of a "familial feeling" in the homes, which were to foster a love of work and a selfless devotion to the Soviet Union, Spain, and all workers.[3] Thus, from the beginning, dual patriotism and an internationalist perspective were important. However, the 1939 regulations added, "All training and educational work in the home is completely subordinated to the tasks of communist upbringing and education of the younger generation in the USSR."[4] Both obuchenie and vospitanie were by definition to be primarily political and Soviet. With the war in Spain lost, it became imperative that work in and out of class transform a Spanish child into a Hispano-Soviet adult ready to contribute to Soviet society and rebuild a post-Franco Spain. The boarding schools thus carried on the intent – albeit with much younger students – of the Lenin School (1926–38) to Sovietize international students and return them to their place of birth.[5] The 1939 turn reflects both the reality of Franco's victory and the onset of war in Finland that necessitated greater attention to training youth to contribute to and protect the USSR and its internationalist agenda.

A 1940 letter to Ibárruri from a Spanish colleague urged her "to provide these children with special attention so that soon they can acquire not only a technical qualification and develop their cultural preparation but also be used as prepared political cadres according to Spain's future needs."[6] Spain would need engineers, teachers, doctors, and politicians. Soviet officials believed that the same cadres also needed to behave in particular ways. Out-of-class activities in vospitanie complemented coursework, instilled values, prepared bodies for labour and war, and began to teach practical skills for being in the workforce among Soviet citizens.

In the middle of the war, the new rules for all Soviet schools in 1943 focused almost exclusively on disciplining the mind and the body. With food and soap being in short supply and living conditions bleak, cultured speech and behaviours – particularly those that dealt with hygiene and health – were paramount. Service to the Soviet motherland came through obedience, diligence, and hard work. The rules created a familial environment by respecting parents, teachers, and school directors and by developing empathy for and helping the weak, sick, old, and young people.[7]

In 1947–8, annual goals continued to stress the inculcation of patriotism, cultured behaviour and speech, a familial environment, and labour discipline.[8] As we will see in the next chapter, the Second World War created dramatic changes in the boarding schools, but for over a decade the core elements of the 1937–8 regulations remained: create a family feeling, teach patriotism for two countries, and raise disciplined children. All these "Soviet" characteristics could, of course, develop children to contribute to Spain, Cuba, Mexico, and other countries, too. Indeed, António Martínez reflected decades later that the Soviets "were training and educating us but trying to preserve our idiosyncrasy, our nationality as Spaniards, because in the future we would be the liberators of Spain." He could not wait until Franco's demise; Martínez, who was educated in engineering and construction in the USSR, took his skills to Cuba instead.[9]

Owing to the relatively abundant material resources, the happy childhood promised in Stalin's USSR was more attainable in the Spanish homes. Extracurricular activities, though they varied among the institutions, allowed children to pursue their interests. There were darkrooms for photography, workshops for wood working and metalworking, rooms for making model airplanes, and studios for painting, music, and dance.[10] As a Spanish student noted with a bit of hyperbole in this chapter's epigraph, Soviets allowed the niños to learn whatever they wanted. They sought to create more well-rounded students, whereas the Spanish officials preferred more narrow vocational training. Some Spaniards recalled: "If we can complain about someone ... it is not the Russians, but many of the Spanish leaders of the PCE."[11] Other Spaniards recalled Ibárruri cajoling a girl with painted fingernails, saying "These are not the hands of the daughter of a proletarian." José Díaz reportedly said, "We prefer a peasant who says '*trujo*' before an intellectual who is not faithful to his people."[12]

Before and after the Second World War, opportunities abounded for the Spanish children in the USSR. Although the Spaniards often retell these stories as part of great Soviet humanitarian concern, out-of-school activities served a purpose, too. Whereas some vospitanie occurred in the classroom at the same time as obuchenie, out-of-class activities were most important for teaching proper Soviet behaviour. Soviet emphasis on nurture over nature viewed children as material for socialist transformation, and the Spanish boarding schools were ideal sites for reforging youngsters and preparing for their long stay in the USSR.

Soviet officials understood that boarding schools posed particular challenges and provided opportunities. Around-the-clock care for children required more supervision, staffing, and organization than for those in day schools; some pupils later remembered the extra security as protection against kidnapping, spies, and enemies.[13] More contact time with the children also created more possibilities for instructing them in Soviet attributes. In one of the first sets of goals for the special Spanish schools, the Commissariat of Education placed responsibility for all out-of-class activities like physical culture, defence work, art, and technical kruzhki in the hands of educators and Pioneers leaders. The intention was to develop activities according to the interests of the children, expose them to a wide variety of literature, inform them about political life in the USSR and capitalist countries, and instil in them a "feeling of Soviet patriotism and proletarian internationalism." These events included systematic anti-religious education and instruction in "organization and collectivism, courtesy" towards comrades, and correct use of school property. Komsomol and Pioneer organizations supervised all political education and mass cultural work.[14] Quite simply, out-of class-activities were to instil "discipline among workers and children" in the boarding schools and to raise "the political, cultural and industrial growth."[15]

Political education – an understanding of Marxism-Leninism and its international role – was one aspect of disciplining the Spaniards; yet they also had to learn to be comradely and hard working. As with classroom education, the upbringing for Spanish students varied little from that of their Soviet counterparts. Some after-school activities were merely fun and games; others were dull lectures. In many extracurricular activities, however, we see a combination of both fun and learning.[16] Many organizations – Narkompros, the PCE, the Komsomol, the Pioneers, and, of course, the boarding schools – intervened to instruct the new arrivals about the benefits of living in the first socialist state and their responsibilities as good socialists. As the chief pedagogical journal argued, boarding schools were to "substitute for the family, to become for [children] a real school of life."[17] As a substitute for the families left behind, the boarding school taught values and conduct aimed at socializing children into adult society. Behaviour, hygiene, discipline, consciousness, and ideological commitment were all important elements of extracurricular education in the Soviet Union, and, without parents or grandparents to undermine instruction, the boarding schools aimed to foster development more consistently. Spanish comrades began to emphasize the need for niños to "emulate" their Soviet counterparts, which for some meant shaving their heads like Red Army soldiers did.[18]

The return to adult authority and structured learning in the late 1930s was intended, first, to improve education. Proponents of the new approach declared that the child-centred schools had created crude children with no respect for authority.[19] Some Spanish students understood the initial permissiveness of their lack of discipline as a signal that Soviet educators were indulging them because of their perceived trauma.[20] Yet Soviet students were known to disrupt class by breaking out into arias from *Faust* and greeting teachers with,

"Hi ya, grandma" (*Zdrastvui, babushka*).[21] Operatic prowess aside, the reformers believed that discipline would lead to greater success in studies, reduce tardiness and absenteeism, and eliminate rudeness. Educational authorities embarked on several experiments, such as creating new rules for student behaviour, introducing a student identity card, and even providing single-sex education in urban schools.[22] The new pedagogy presupposed that the young person was malleable and therefore improvable.[23] Second, the new practices sought to regulate the child's social training in order to cultivate proper citizens. In the words of Soviet president Mikhail Kalinin, vospitanie was wider than obuchenie, and Communist vospitanie was the "development of political consciousness, a common culture, and a raising of the intellectual level of the masses."[24] The development of a "common culture" meant not only learning Russian language and literature but also acquiring normative behaviours. Social training would then provide the will-power and self-discipline necessary for children to engage in and contribute to Soviet society.[25] Developing a common culture would allow the Spaniards entrance into Soviet social networks.

There were numerous ways to teach proper Soviet behaviour and values. In-class lessons, especially in history and geography, surely played a large part in the new formation of Soviet identification, but life outside the classroom was just as important in establishing Soviet values and ideals. The dormitories were learning laboratories for discipline, and so too were playgrounds and future work sites. Leisure opportunities abounded for most of the children, and in these moments education occurred also. Thus, vospitanie and obuchenie reinforced each other; they were two parents that would bring forth the new Soviet child. Spanish boarding schools were also modern transformative institutions and brought normative Soviet behaviours to the niños.

Disciplining Time and Bodies

Many of the Spanish children arrived with little or no schooling, and the vast majority had not been in combined living and learning environments like boarding schools in Spain. Soviet perceptions of and prejudice against undisciplined Spaniards (both children and adults) created the need for routines and discipline. Discipline had become a prominent educational goal in the Soviet Union since the 1937 rejection of paedology and the reinstitution of teachers' authority in the classroom as a form of role modelling and behaviour training.[26] The Spaniards and their perceived backwardness arrived as pedagogical journals had begun to emphasize the need to transform children's behaviours. As we saw in chapter 2, role modelling by adults in the home was of paramount importance, but disciplined behaviour was taught in many other ways, too. Effective learning among children required making cultural work "more interesting," much like outdoor science classes were to enliven formalist teaching.[27]

While time out of class could involve fun and games, the best directors knew that extracurricular activities reinforced the academic, ideological, cultural, and behavioural work of the classroom.

Time discipline was one of the most basic, but most important, ways to reorient students' thoughts towards attention to detail and collective responsibility. Some of the early boarding schools housed two to four hundred students. In this setting, logistics were important. Although the daily schedule for the Spanish children varied a little, especially during the war, a typical pattern was to rise at 6:00 a.m. for ten minutes to exercise and twenty minutes to use the bathroom and clean the sleeping areas. After one hour for breakfast, lessons took place from 8:00 a.m. to 1:00 p.m. A ninety-minute lunch started at 1:30, followed by reading from 2:00 to 4:00 p.m. From 4:00 to 7:00 p.m. the children worked on homework, followed by two hours of extracurricular and "mass" work. On Mondays those two hours were devoted to politics, on Tuesdays to kruzhki, on Wednesdays to reports and lectures, on Thursdays to films, on Fridays to meetings, on Saturdays to dancing, and on Sundays to physical culture, theatre visits, and more film. This schedule, when enforced, cycled students throughout the grounds in regular order, ensured proper feeding and hygiene, and kept them busy and out of trouble. Unfortunately it allowed only seven and a half hours for sleep – far too little for most children and adolescents and far short of the mandated nine hours of sleep for eight- to eleven-year-old children.[28]

Just as keeping to schedules and routines was a central part of the daily life training for the Spaniards and the development of disciplined behaviours, crowded conditions necessitated extra attention to hygiene and to disciplining the body. Daily habits had been part of the Bolshevik project of creating a new kul'turnost' since the civil war,[29] so the Spanish schools provided lectures on hygiene, some with particular emphasis on girls' needs during menstruation.[30] The halting of epidemics started with the washing of bodies, clothing, bedding, and residential and communal areas. Education officials instructed boarding-school directors to make students change their undergarments once every six days, and linens every ten days. Beyond regular hand and face washing, the children used the *banya* once every six days and laundered everything at least once a month. Each boarding school had an isolation ward for infectious children and sent children to sanatoria or health resorts when their needs became more serious.[31] Bernardo del Río recalls that even pre-war visits to military barracks and their scenes of order and hygiene transformed the Spaniards' attitudes and behaviours.[32]

Locating learning on the body also established disciplined behaviour through sport and exercise. Directors understood that "calisthenics organizes and disciplines the children's collective for the whole day."[33] Daily movement and exercise also strengthened the body, prepared it for labour, and helped to keep sickness at bay. Refugees remembered "games of all kinds," gym class, skiing and skating, and sports examinations as part of the weekly rituals.[34] Some new activities, like skiing, did not come easily, but Delfin Val from León remembered how a Russian educator brought new skis and quickly taught the children to conquer their fears. This also led to interactions with Soviet children with whom they could practise Russian.[35] Summer vacation was a time to have fun with Soviet children. Jesús Oyarzábal wrote to his parents, "We played soccer with [Soviet children] and we beat them."[36] Soccer, of course, was a favourite activity, and Spaniards like Agustín Gómez, who captained the Obninskoe home's team and later the Torpedo Moscow team, stood out.[37] Other Spaniards wrote home to their parents, describing all the activities that were available: "We have here all kinds of games: billiards, hammocks, tennis, bicycles, and go-karts."[38] But as Spanish investigators noted, girls participated in sport at much lower rates than boys did, presumably as a result of gendered notions of sport from their upbringing in Spain.[39] The disciplined mind and body were central targets of attention in the Spanish homes and in Soviet schools generally as preparation for adult lives.

Outings and Entertainment

Understanding that children have a limited ability to focus for long periods, the boarding schools sought to train children through entertainment, too. All Soviet life was a laboratory for learning and self-improvement. The Spanish homes in major cities often used nearby cultural facilities as sites of leisure and education. Some of the outings, like visits to the zoo, were merely relaxing days out. Others brought the students into contact with high art, but not necessarily specific Soviet values. A third category of outing had clear political motives. Excursions to political museums and performances with specific ideological merit brought the students to spaces of agitation and learning that for some children might have been entertaining, too. The children's own performances were similarly instructive, as when children played for a Soviet audience in evacuation in Unterwalden, and the local secretary of the party, who enjoyed the jazz performance, informed them that performing in blackface was racist.[40]

These outings did not need to have direct propagandistic motives to serve well the Soviet desire to teach the Spanish children that all people were equal in the USSR. Most of the children, coming from humble backgrounds in Spain, would have seen folk dances, but they would not have gone to the ballet. The Soviet niños, however, not only watched ballet for free but also observed world-famous ballet troupes in Moscow and Leningrad.[41] Orchestral performances also were rare luxuries for most of these children in their home country, but now they could see world-class musicians performing the great masters. These were not performances for only the rich and famous to attend; the accessibility of the arts to all classes in the USSR was a stark difference from Spain where only the moneyed and propertied classes had access.[42] By taking children on cultural outings, Soviet and PCE officials emphasized the egalitarian nature of the Soviet experiment while encouraging an aesthetic appreciation for the arts as counterparts to academic knowledge and job-skills preparation. One Spaniard remembers the willingness to send even the marginally talented to study at a conservatory.[43]

Teachers led several excursions each year to theatres, museums, and concerts. Students went to the Tretiakov Gallery, the Museum of the Revolution, the Historical Museum, Novodevichii Cemetery, and the Moscow-Volga canal. Each student attended at least one excursion, and some attended as many as three trips.[44] For students interested in the arts, the Tretiakov Gallery allowed them to learn about the long history of Russian visual arts.[45] Sources do not give the itinerary to the Novodevichii Cemetery, the most famous burial site in Moscow, so we cannot know which of the historical, cultural, and political luminaries interred there were discussed by the children. The cemetery, and the contiguous sixteenth-century convent of the same name, provided opportunities for a variety of instruction as well as a fun day out of school amidst a magnificent aesthetic ensemble.

Other outings had clear didactic benefits. The Museum of the Revolution and the Historical Museum reinforced classroom lessons about Russian and Soviet history and the struggle of the working classes against their oppressors. The excursion to the Moscow-Volga Canal took the children into a natural setting to view the feat of engineering and the twenty-five-metre-high statue of Lenin – which was completed in the year they arrived, 1937 – and likely allowed for a discussion of collective and corrective labour by Gulag prisoners.[46] The students probably did not hear about the thousands of prisoners who had died on the work site or were executed when the canal opened for traffic. We cannot know if or how students internalized messages of collective effort and class-consciousness from these particular excursions, but memoirs state clearly that seeing Soviet life outside the boarding schools transformed behaviours and even allowed the children to find joy in harvesting crops with Soviets.[47] All of these excursions were to sites of learning, but for some students the chief benefit might well have been merely a much-needed respite from the routine and surroundings of the home.

Many excursions were part of the educational experience for all students, but some students earned their excursions. The Spaniards seem to have become fond of and adapted to the Soviet reward system: "Another prize for studying well, an excursion to Moscow ... the Mausoleum of Lenin, the Museum of Revolution to see the capital ... then, in [19]40, was when we were taken to Pushkin. In [19]41, when I finished the course, because of a prize, I was allowed to go to Artek, which was the prize dreamed of by all children."[48] Milagros Latorre loved her prize, also a trip to Artek, because despite four days of being quarantined for diphtheria she was able to swim every day at this "paradise"

4.1 Spanish Pioneers with the *puño* salute at Artek. España, Ministerio de Cultura y Deporte, Centro Documental de la Memoria Histórica, P.S. Fotografías, carpeta 36, folio 2931.

with its military discipline and beautiful surroundings.[49] Excursions served as an incentive to behave and perform well. On a visit to the Red October chocolate factory, for example, the children were told that if they refrained from touching the chocolate being made, they would each receive a packet of treats. "Some couldn't restrain themselves," and they received treats anyway.[50]

Although many children remembered outings as special times away from the boarding schools, sometimes opportunities came to the Spaniards. Ángel Gutiérrez, who arrived in the USSR in 1937 at five years of age and grew up to teach in Soviet theatres and drama institutes before returning to Spain in 1974, remembered how they "spoiled us ... treated us with true love. There I studied music with the director of the Bolshoi orchestra ... he came expressly to the boarding school to give me harmony classes."[51] We cannot know the motivation behind this tremendous opportunity – was it volunteerism, or was the director compelled to go? – but this is merely one example of the Soviet system and its citizens' reaching out to the Spanish children to nurture their interests and talents. Gutiérrez learned skills that did not apply to work in a field or factory; his supplemental education maximized his talents so that he could then contribute to the greater Soviet project, which he did by becoming a teacher.

Summers and holidays provided additional opportunities to move beyond the Spanish schools and to enjoy new experiences in their adopted homeland. Delfín Val was concerned that Christmas in the atheist Soviet Union would not be the same as in Spain, but the New Year's holiday celebration was still wondrous. In the game room of one home a huge spruce reached to the ceiling. A crystal stood at the top, and toys, ornaments, balls, and coloured bulbs covered its branches. Small fluffs of cotton gave the sensation of snow. Of course, Grandfather Frost and the Snow Maiden arrived in their beautiful costumes and distributed toys to all the children for the new year. The Spaniards also went to the House of Trade Unions and the Hall of Columns in the Kremlin where they performed folk dances and songs. The children's performance reinforced their connection with their first homeland much as non-Russian Soviet nationalities found that their Sovietization – with its insistence on local elites, national institutions, and performance of national cultures – fostered a deeper understanding of their nationality.[52] The children appreciated that they could celebrate in peace, which was impossible in Spain.[53] For Soviet authorities, the celebrations showed the regime's largesse while avoiding nativity scenes, processions, and other religious superstitions associated with the seasonal celebrations in Spain. Celebrations taught that obscurantism begat poverty, class division, and repressions, whereas progressive societies lived in abundance, happiness, and equality.

Spanish holidays, particularly the remembrance of the 18 July 1936 start of the Spanish Civil War, brought luminaries to the Spanish children. For the tenth anniversary of the children's flight from Spain, Santiago Carrillo – a

4.2 Celebrating their first New Year's holiday in the USSR. España, Ministerio de Cultura y Deporte, Centro Documental de la Memoria Histórica, P.S. Fotografías, carpeta 36, folio 2921.

member of the PCE Politburo and secretary of the Unified Socialist Youth – and other Spanish leaders visited the homes to celebrate with the children. If children had relatives in the USSR, they could visit and transform the holiday into family reunions.[54] In 1940 Communist Youth International sent a Spanish adult leader to each summer camp during the July holidays to teach the Spanish children about the working class before the civil war, the Spanish Communist Party at the outbreak of the war, and the participation of Spanish youth in the struggle for liberation. Girls sewed national costumes, and the artistic kruzhki performed scenes from Spanish classics like *Don Quixote* and *Fuenteovejuna*.[55] Children who liked physical labour could recreate Asturian peasant huts, episodes from the war, the defence of Madrid, or the crossing of the Ebro River. Many Spanish workers received leave from their factories in order to participate in the festivities.[56] These shared experiences helped to redefine national identifications. Remembrance and re-enactment of national culture reaffirmed the connection to Spain; yet the Soviet Union made it possible. Not surprisingly, in oral histories Spaniards often speak with gratitude about the USSR's role in maintaining their connection to Spain and Spanish culture.[57]

The children celebrated Soviet holidays quite differently than they did the Spanish holidays. The newly arrived niños had no idea how special it was to be seated near Lenin's tomb for the military parade on the twentieth anniversary of the Bolshevik Revolution.[58] The Komsomol planning for the thirtieth anniversary included speeches and reports on the revolution, Lenin, and Stalin, and numerous excursions punctuated the holidays with some fun and excitement. The sites visited included the Museum of the Revolution, the Lenin Museum, and the Tretiakov Gallery exhibit on Soviet art. At the "best theatres of Moscow" the niños saw films and performances that stressed Russian history, defence of the homeland, collective activity, and doing one's best work. The children wrote wall newspapers and assembled montages on industry, village life, education, and the friendship of peoples. Socialist competitions included challenges for the best clean-up work. There were meetings with veterans.[59] Soviet holiday celebrations reinforced normative behaviours of cleanliness, collective labour, and sacrifice for others.

Other holidays, like May Day, were equally political while still allowing entertainment. Elena Kononenko reported that the camaraderie on their first May Day in the USSR stunned the children. A diverse group of youngsters at the Artek Pioneer camp exchanged national songs and dances as they welcomed the new Spaniards to the Soviet Union. The Spaniards danced and sang around the bonfire and played with puppets and toys. They tried to teach a dance to their Soviet counterparts, and together they sang and read in many languages: Russian, Ukrainian, Tatar, Spanish, and Mongolian. Then the Soviet children performed a scene from *Chapaev*. Kononenko's readers learned that the most important lesson, as one would expect on May Day, was the Soviet notion of friendship of peoples.⁶⁰ Collective effort and equality marked their first celebration in their new home. The May holiday also blended fun with learning. Lectures on Moscow's history and new science combined with chess tournaments and boxing against Soviet children. Films, car trips for young children, mass games, excursions, dances, and even a grenade-throwing competition rounded out the day's fun.⁶¹ A child named Rosario stated: "It seems to me like a magical fairy tale ... Suddenly we will wake up and find ourselves in the basement again and above ... bombs?!"⁶²

Excursions and holidays sought to entertain children while also showing the stark difference between the superstition, class exploitation, and poverty of Spain and the rational, progressive, socialist equality of a prosperous USSR that loved and educated all children. Celebrating Spanish and Soviet holidays further reinforced the dual nature of these children's lives. Some celebrations reinforced ethnonational identifications whereas the universalist celebration of childhood with fun, games, toys, and excursions bridged those ethnonational boundaries and taught that children were children, regardless of their conditions of birth. They were valuable members of society who should be nurtured and honoured. These shared experiences also developed a common culture that should have allowed connections between the Spanish children and their Soviet peers when they left the homes for good.

Film and Drama for Fun and Instruction

Not surprisingly, movie nights were among the most popular forms of entertainment. Film was a chief conveyor of both entertainment and values, and most homes had film nights on Fridays, Saturdays, or Sundays. The Bolsheviks had learned early on that film was a wonderful complement to the power of the written word. With the unionization of filmmakers and the imposition of socialist realism in the 1930s, much of the avant-garde experimentation of artists like Dziga Vertov ceased, and political messages became imbedded in musical comedies and dramas. Studios in the 1930s – from Moscow to Berlin to Hollywood – specialized in musical comedies, and in none of the locations was politics absent from film.⁶³ The films shown to the Spanish children seem to have been carefully selected, which is not surprising given the 31 May 1935 decree to "exercise enhanced supervision of children's literature and films, and not to allow any literature and films which might have a pernicious influence on children."⁶⁴ The censorship regime made every film "official" and therefore approved as a vehicle of values. But many of them were also entertaining.

When choosing films, teachers were to look for realistic stories that avoided fantasy and anything sexual; theft, murder, and suicide were also avoided. The best films, whether used with lectures or in kruzhki, would augment the curriculum.⁶⁵ Although Spanish films found their way to the children's homes in the early years, a survey of archival records shows that they were nearly absent (or not mentioned) once the civil war had ended.[66] School personnel placed films into categories: "film material was used in lessons or as learning, or as an educational [*vospitatelnyi*] moment."[67] The former category included historical feature films and short films on science; the latter category used story lines that promoted the characteristics of proper Soviet behaviour. As film scholar Jamie Miller has noted, "the cinema industry became both part of the quest for legitimacy and part of the frontline of political and ideological defense ... Thus cinema was to play a fundamental role, not only in politically educating and moulding the new man, but also in showing ordinary people that their feats and sacrifices were in their own interests."[68] For Spanish children, films introduced them to the traits of the new Soviet, taught sacrificial rather than individualistic behaviour, and opened their eyes to Soviet and Russian history and culture. This helped to reinforce Soviet "legitimacy" and political and ideological training. Spanish and Soviet children viewed the same films, leading to a shared cultural vocabulary and set of normative behavioural ideals.

The students enjoyed *vospitatelnyi* films, not least among them the popular musical comedies *Circus* and *Radiant Path*. Light films often had music that was easy to sing and therefore were remembered. *Circus* teaches about the Soviet value of "friendship of peoples": the Soviet circus audience passes a bi-racial American boy from person to person, singing a lullaby in various Soviet languages and chasing away the Hitler look-alike von Kneischitz. *Circus* thus taught the Spaniards to equate the capitalist United States and Nazi Germany because of their shared racial discrimination. The Soviet Union, however, welcomed all people in a land of equality and collective responsibility. Most importantly for the Spaniards, *Circus* argued for the acceptance of national minorities and thus taught proper Soviet behaviour and the meaninglessness of ethnonational categories.

A series of films showed the children that Soviet citizens – and thus Spaniards, too – could transform into ideal citizens. *Radiant Path* glorified labour for the good of society. *A Girl with Character* showed perseverance against corruption and bureaucratic waste, from which the children could learn the Soviet virtues of criticism and self-criticism, an important part of the Stalinist political culture of problem solving.[69] *Red Necktie* showed the power of mentoring and peer ostracization as methods of behavioural transformation and improvement. In *Rural Teacher* Spaniards could witness sacrifice for others, engagement with the party, and then the work to end class exploitation in the countryside. *First Grader* showed the transformation of a selfish and capricious little girl into a disciplined and responsible student who eventually got along with her classmates and teachers. This 1948 film was ideal for Spanish students who themselves had been experiencing similar transformations towards Soviet kul'turnost'.

Historical films about the Russian revolution and subsequent civil war, great military leaders, and even some tsars became increasingly common in the

1930s, and the Spanish children watched them on a regular basis.[70] Historian Stephen Norris has noted about post-Soviet film that "historical films in particular subvert pre-existing narratives as often as they reinforce them."[71] Under the state censorship of the Stalin era, historical films portrayed the correct way to interpret the past.[72] State building and defence of one's homeland featured prominently in nearly all historical films. On celluloid as in history and literature classes, Russian and Soviet history became a story of defence against invaders and of sacrifice to create a state strong enough to defend its people.

Tsars and imperial military officers who forged a strong Russian state found their way into films shown in the boarding schools. Historical films in general, and *Peter the First* and *Ivan the Terrible* in particular, are evidence of Stalinist russocentric etatism; both films appropriated royal histories to show the defence of Russian lands against invaders and the conquest of new lands for the expansion of the Russian state.[73] *Aleksandr Nevsky* and *Suvorov* showed the cunning and heroism of imperial Russian military leaders who refused to give up, even when outmatched. *Giorgi Saakadze* also recounts a historical character, the controversial seventeenth-century Georgian warlord. The cinematic Saakadze became a symbol of Georgian patriotism and a fight against nobles. Stalin had recast Saakadze as progressive.[74] Flawed characters and their violent regimes (though minimized in the films) found a place in Soviet culture because they helped to create unity and strength in a vast and diverse land.

Revolution and civil war films such as *We Are from Kronstadt*, *Chapaev*, *Lenin in October*, and *Man with a Gun* were common viewings in the Spanish homes.[75] From these films, the children would have learned the Soviet interpretation of the 1917 revolutions and the Russian Civil War, and the role that heroes, both political and military, played in creating and defending the first socialist state. "In reading books about heroes," notes scholar Evgeny Dobrenko, "children also enter into the collective spirit."[76] The process of becoming, reforging, and transforming via heroic literature had a counterpart in Soviet heroic films, many of which had been adapted from literature. Entering the "collective spirit" through film and literature certainly provided Spaniards with a common cultural vocabulary that granted access to Soviet social relations.

Classroom films extended learning beyond books and brought to life the objects of study. Biographical films introduced Spaniards to ethnographer Miklukho Maklai and musical, literary, and scientific luminaries in films like *Glinka*, *Mussorgsky*, *Alisher Navoi*, *Pirogov*, *Michurin*, and *Pavlov*. It is unclear whether feature films like *The Great Force*, the story of a disciple of botanist Ivan Michurin who instead became an advocate of agrobiologist Trofim Lysenko's plant breeding, found their way into lesson plans. Listed as a popular film in the schools in 1950, *The Great Force* rails against kow-towing to Western science and could have lent support to the biographical films, science education, and increasing cold-war rhetoric.[77]

One Spanish-school director noted specifically that post-war and early cold-war films increased Soviet patriotism and national pride, and former students remembered illegal border crossing as a common theme in films.[78] Some films featured children as heroic fighters for the homeland. *Young Guard* shows students becoming deeply devoted patriots and underground partisans and saboteurs. These young fighters in Krasnodon became fearless, courageous, and disciplined. Similar to *First Grader*, *Young Guard* hails youth and the power of transformation. Other films like *Life in a Citadel*, *Marite*, *Third Strike*, and *Story of the Furious* venerated adult heroes of the Second World War – partisans, soldiers, sailors, and everyday citizens. In all these films the protagonist makes the correct choice to put the motherland above all else and thus serves as a model for Spanish children that sacrifice for the greater good is a socialist behaviour.

Cold-war foes and increasing xenophobia became themes in post-war films such as *Encounter at the Elbe*, *Court of Honor*, *The Oath*, *Secret Mission*, and *The Russian Question*. These films likely stirred Soviet patriotism in many of the refugees, but at the same time their messages about the dangers of the "other" likely made the transition back to Spain in the mid-1950s – when Spain drew closer to the United States – more difficult for some. The children had been taught to despise capitalism and collaboration with it.

Film viewing in the boarding schools served to transmit a variety of values to the Spaniards. Protagonists modelled the Soviet ideals of hard work, perseverance, commitment to the greater good, co-operation, vigilance, and party-mindedness. Some of the films also taught historical lessons that situated the Soviet Union within a narrative of state building and fights against invading oppressors. Although everyday people had a role in these fights, heroes and leaders showed the way, thus reinforcing the hierarchy of the Soviet party state. Films also made literature more accessible, particularly for students whose knowledge of Russian was still limited. The moving images in some ways could make up for the lack of understanding in the dialogue. Questions of reception, however, remain unclear. Few memoirs discuss films in the schools. One Spaniard recalled *If Tomorrow Brings War* as a favourite, but José Fernández, for example, says nothing about these specific films. He and his friends enjoyed especially *Three Musketeers* and musicals with Mario Lanza and Diana Durbin, but these he saw in evacuation in Saratov cinemas outside the supervision of the boarding schools.[79]

Excursions to Soviet theatres had a different objective than watching films did. School officials stated that taking Spaniards to see dramatic performances of "Soviet art and its ideological orientation" would develop their taste and culture while often reinforcing a Soviet world view.[80] Many of the films, like *Kremlin Chimes* and *The Russian Question*, were also plays. Some of the historical characters, such as Ivan the Terrible, appeared on both stage and film. Other historical stagings, like *Prince Igor*, followed the film model of bringing to life important characters in the history of Russian state building. However, the opera *Prince Igor* did more than retell the tale of the twelfth-century battle between Rus' prince Igor Sviatoslavych and the Polovtsian tribes. The libretto combined material from the medieval Kievan chronicles and the epic poem *Lay of Igor's Host*. One of the "Mighty Handful," Aleksandr Borodin, had composed the opera, but he died before completing it. His fellow "Handful" member, the great Nikolai Rimsky-Korsakov, completed *Prince Igor* with the assistance of Aleksandr Glazunov. The Spanish children, largely the children of miners and other workers, were privileged to watch and listen to the work of great Russian masters and learn about the defence of the Kievan state, all from two of the most important documents of medieval Russian history. We do not know which theatre the students attended for each performance, but we do know that they visited the best Moscow had to offer: the Bolshoi, Moscow Art Theatre, and Vakhtangov, among others.

Other classic performances included *Rusalka*, *Pygmalion*, *Evgenii Onegin*, *The Cherry Orchard*, and *Cyrano de Bergerac*. The performances about a water sprite, the power of education and nurture over nature, a Pushkin tale, and social change and the dissolution of nobility have a social or cultural lesson. However, some performances must have been chiefly for their artistic merits. Those like *Cyrano de Bergerac*, the story of a large-nosed French noble pining for his beloved Roxanne, hardly fits the historical or ideological norms of Soviet performances. Although theatrical performances could and did teach Soviet values and Russian history, the list of plays, operas, and ballets suggests that aesthetic training and appreciation were at least as important as didactic lessons. Appreciation of the arts was a key component in Soviet kul'turnost' that was absent from education in Spain. Moreover, aesthetic appreciation had little or no place in education in other authoritarian regimes like Nazi Germany or in capitalist democracies. This desire to create well-rounded people led some former niños to call the Soviet aesthetic training "generous."[81]

Mass Political Work

Disciplining time and the body and enlivening aesthetic appreciation through the arts was important; yet Kalinin stated that the "development of political consciousness" went hand in hand with creating a "common culture" and "raising the intellectual level of the masses."[82] Following Andrei Zhdanov's speech on culture and formalism, the 1947–8 school year brought greater attention to the political upbringing of Spaniards as a way to raise the knowledge, culture, morals, and the ideological level of students and adults. Educators needed to teach the importance of the Soviet system, the interests of the people, and the future of democratic Spain. Various methods were employed, including individual reports, class meetings, educator group meetings, "mass measures," and kruzhki.⁸³ Kruzhki also were part of the larger category of "mass political work," which likely was less enjoyable than creating model airplanes and participating in other fun and creative kruzhki. For example, for the older children, a *kruzhok* on Stalin's "Short Course" history of the Communist Party became an obligatory part of mass political work.⁸⁴

Since the niños arrived in 1937, political education outside of the classroom had taken a variety of forms and often sought to strengthen the children's understanding of international affairs and the USSR's place in transnational engagement. In the first three years political education in one school included following the decisions of the party and the government, international relations, and the defence of the USSR. Lectures on youth and children in capitalist countries and the international proletariat's struggle against world imperialism complemented radio and newspaper reports. Political education also took place away from school grounds with excursions to the House of the Red Army, the Lenin Museum, the Historical Museum, the Pioneer camp of the civil air fleet, and nearby children's camps. Spanish students even travelled as far as Samarkand for a two-day trip about friendship of peoples, which was part of a summer-long set of exchanges. In addition to the holidays discussed earlier, the children celebrated the anniversaries of the Red Army and Lenin's birth and death. In 1940 PCE leaders José Díaz and Dolores Ibárruri attended Lenin's birthday celebration, and Ibárruri and Andre Marti were at the opening of the summer camp. Ibárruri even accompanied the students to see a performance of the ballet *Schast'e*. She spoke to the children about Spain and the fourth anniversary of the start of the Spanish Civil War. Celebrating Spain's civil war featured Spanish songs, dances, and poetry, the students' radio report (which pleased Ibárruri), and displays in a "Spanish corner" of the school on daily life in Spain.⁸⁵ Both of the great heroes of the day, polar explorer Ivan Papanin and aviator Valery Chkalov, visited the homes, as did painter Petr Konchalovsky, the Spanish military leader El Campesino, and many others.⁸⁶ Effective political education thus meant much more than lectures. Interaction with people and visiting sites personalized learning and forced the children to learn with multiple senses.

Mass political work in school was also part of the weekly routine. Director Zvorovskaia noted that political education was the "foundation of the school."⁸⁷ Every Monday evening after dinner there were ninety minutes of study that included lectures and reports like Molotov's speech on the thirtieth anniversary of the Russian Revolution, the capitalist system of tsarist Russia, the second and third Five-Year Plans, the Second World War, peaceful construction in the post-war period, and the Anglo-American zone in Germany. Students provided most of the reports, and throughout the year there were thirty additional reports on Soviet topics and eighteen on Spanish themes. Anniversaries were common subjects for political education, including the anniversaries of the Asturian revolution and the death of Kirov, Constitution Day, and Stalin's birthday. Active student involvement found expression in making albums, publishing wall newspapers, and leading discussions.[88] Mass political work also included reading newspapers and journals and following international affairs and reports from Sovinformburo. In these, students learned about the life of Lenin, Bloody Sunday, the Red Army in the fight for the motherland, the Paris Commune, the role of women in the Great Patriotic War, the defence of Sevastopol in the Second World War, May Day, Francoist Spain, and the struggle of the Spanish republican youth against fascism.

In one school there were twenty-nine Komsomol members charged with aiding academic success, increasing discipline, overseeing mass political work, and assisting in publishing Russian and Spanish wall newspapers.[89] In all these events we see Spanish children as both passive recipients of knowledge and active producers. They were agents in their learning by participating in the creation of reports, newspapers, and more, typically with Komsomol supervision. Regular columns such as "Spain Lives!" served to help the student writers to process news about their homeland and transmit to the young readers the hope that they could one day return there to rebuild. Wall newspapers also served to discipline peers as authors called out their comrades for poor behaviour or academic performance, such as nineteen-year-old Jacinta Fernández from Turón who reportedly studied poorly and left the home without permission for a "not entirely beautiful friendship with a Russian boy."[90] Thus, the Spanish youth and their cultural products became part of the surveillance and disciplinary network of the schools.

Heroes came to life in newspapers, on the radio, on the screen, and in periodicals and books. Although the niños followed the same set of heroes as their Soviet counterparts did, the Spaniards had particular Spanish heroes as well. Leaders of the PCE stood atop the pantheon of Spanish heroes for the children, although some viewed them as members of "a kind of mafia" and a "privileged caste" who took care of themselves, their families, and their friends.[91] Greetings for the heroes on their birthdays and on major holidays – and, in the case of José Díaz, on memorials at their death – were regular occurrences throughout the homes. Upon the death of Díaz, the leader of the PCE, the children produced lectures, newspaper articles, and more about his life. Arguably the chief icon for the Spanish children, Dolores Ibárruri served as a maternal example alongside the "second father," Stalin.[92] December hosted the birthdays of both Stalin and Ibárruri. Therefore, the final month of the year was festive but also highly politicized. Mass political and cultural work helped to teach Soviet values and provide a common Soviet cultural vocabulary, thus preparing students to understand Soviet life, but they did not provide many life and labour skills that would allow the refugees to contribute effectively to Soviet society and productivity.

Kruzhki led by teachers, educators, or Komsomol and Pioneer leaders served an important purpose in Soviet upbringing by connecting study and play, providing future vocational skills, and instructing students on how to become Soviet. Spanish-culture kruzhki also kept alive a memory and hope of home, which was important because the stated goal was to prepare the young charges to be the liberators and builders of a new Spain.⁹³ The greater gender equality in the Soviet Union amazed the Spaniards, yet many kruzhki were gendered. For example, the needlework, sewing, and dressmaking kruzhki typically were the most well attended in the various schools, but they were strictly for girls. It was in these kruzhki that girls mended students' clothing, made garments for front-line troops, and learned the basic skills for their future professions. The male domain included metalworking and wood working. Here too, when facilities allowed, boys would make products like furniture for their boarding school while learning skills for work after their education had concluded.⁹⁴ Many of the children expressed their thanks and gratitude for the opportunities provided in the kruzhki. Writing to her grandfather and aunt, a girl named Mercedes expressed her "endless thanks to the Great Soviet people" for the opportunities, including her work in the sewing, music, and drawing circles.⁹⁵

The creative circles typically were not segregated. Before and after the Second World War, when resources were plentiful and the Spaniards lived in close proximity to cultural institutions and instruction, the children participated in brass orchestras, dance and theatre groups, choirs, film and radio clubs, photography and painting studios, and much more. School officials attempted to maintain the children's culture by providing books from the Golden Age of Spanish literature and by taking them to dances, operas, and concerts.⁹⁶ Students performed for the army, and some were fortunate to have prominent Spanish artists in their schools, like sculptor Alberto Sánchez, who taught drawing.⁹⁷ The Belorussian actor and director Aleksandr Shaps and artists of the State Philharmonic often visited to perform, instruct, or both.⁹⁸ The House of the Red Army also provided free concerts and films for the children.⁹⁹ In other circles, instruction came from Spanish or Soviet adults or even former students. The artistic production could be highly politicized, including, for example, students painting portraits of Ibárruri and producing radio programs of news, information, criticism, and updates on life in the boarding schools.¹⁰⁰

It is in the creative circles that we find the greatest balance of Spanish and Soviet culture, with Spanish traditional cultural forms and performances steeped in Soviet values. Dance, music, and drama circles in particular were sites of Spanish culture. Reports typically do not note repertoires for the creative kruzhki, but the sources we have are informative. Enrique Zafra, a Spanish adult who worked in one of the schools, noted that the small orchestras often played Spanish-themed music, and niños's letters to parents, discussing castanets and tambourines in some homes, suggest as much.¹⁰¹ The orchestra of Home No. 2 performed Soviet and Spanish hymns, five marches, five waltzes, eight Western dances, two ballroom dances, a fairy tale, a funeral march, two songs about Stalin, a French revolutionary song, a Spanish revolutionary song, "Young Guard," "Tian-Shian," "Suliko," a song from *Faust*, "Valencia," "Spain ... Spain," "Rodina," and "Ty vzoydi, soltse krasnoe."[102] This eclectic and extensive performance schedule introduced students to folk and symphonic music (Russian, Soviet, and Spanish) and revolutionary songs from Russia, Spain, and France.

Songs like "Ty vzoydi, soltse krasnoe" were ideal types in that they taught the Spaniards about forms of Russian folk music, praised youth and nature (the Volga River), and introduced the great peasant rebel Stenka Razin. In this one song the Spaniards learned music, geography, a love of nature, and part of the history of class struggle in Russia. The song "Tian Shan" transported students to the mountains of Central Asia. "Valencia" evoked romantic images of orange groves and open skies, calling listeners back to that paradise. The repertoire thus situated the young performers in both of their homelands. Romantic and lyrical poetry and music were less common in the Stalin era; however, "Valencia" is an overtly romantic paso doble from the Spanish lyric or drama style. Similarly, "Suliko" introduced the children to the soulful and heart-wrenching Georgian love poem of Akaki Tseretelli, which had become a staple on Soviet radio with Sulkhan Tsintsadze's composition. The young musicians thus had a trip around the Soviet Union and its diverse cultures and began to cross borders and blend the cultural traditions of their two homelands.

Performances in the drama circles centred on the works of the Golden Age, which, along with the works of more recent leftist authors, formed the core of Spanish literature in the Soviet boarding schools.[103] The work of Cervantes, Lope de Vega, and Pedro Calderón de la Barca occupied shelves next to the writings of Antonio Machado, Federico García Lorca, Juan Ramón Jiménez, and Rafael Alberti. When books were available, the Spanish children read the best poets and playwrights of the Golden Age, the Generation of '98, and the Generation of '27. Even though many of these later, Silver Age writers sympathized with leftist politics and in some cases were Marxist, Soviets typically would not have celebrated their aesthetics. Much of their work was lyrical and/or modernist, styles that the Soviet Union of Writers had denounced and banned in the Soviet Union since the adoption of socialist realism in the early 1930s. This suggests that in the boarding schools, drama circles and literature were meant not merely to reinforce the socialist realist aesthetic but also to maintain Spain's cultural traditions amongst the refugees. Adult Spanish communists had a prominent role in leading many of the drama circles, and therefore Spanish art forms took precedent.[104] There also was an attempt to educate the Spanish adults on how Marxist criticism understood Golden Age literature so that they could couch the Spanish masterworks within the Soviet political idiom.[105]

The ideal kruzhok was both educational and fun. For example, the journal *Detskii dom* suggested a young-naturalist kruzhok for orphanages because children were naturally attracted to the outdoors, and with proper guidance they could learn to see and understand nature. The youngest children would create nature calendars that tracked the first butterflies and blooms. Eleven- and twelve-year-olds would do the same and prepare the soil for planting. The thirteen- and fourteen-year-olds would be ready for more scientific study and then practise how to maximize yields and their manual labour. All of these activities would site students in the fresh air and reinforce biology lessons.[106] In reality, these were not always successful, owing to poor or lack of leadership by adults.[107] Some kruzhki were not fun, such as those in which children helped to clean the building and grounds and worked in the kitchen.[108] Students thus learned the union of labour, learning, and working for others.

When resources allowed, vospitanie helped to develop patriotism, a work ethic, and an aesthetic sensibility that Spaniards shared with their Soviet peers and which could have bridged cultural differences. The cost and logistics of kruzhki and outings show that raising the Spanish children for fourteen years was an ardent attempt to create well-rounded, educated, cultured, bilingual students equipped for future service to the USSR, Spain, and global communism. The boarding schools endorsed a wide range of opportunities to develop a Soviet aesthetic and an appreciation for Spanish art and culture so that the refugees could maintain contact with their native culture and acculturate to life in the USSR, thus becoming Hispano-Soviets.

Displacement created opportunities for children to construct new identifications and to create new bonds with Soviets and Spaniards.[109] The staff and students of their home became their new family, such that in adulthood the Spaniards viewed marriages among children of the same home as "quasi-incestuous."[110] Shared experiences helped form group identifications as niños de la guerra, Piarists (*los escalopios*) who went on to higher education, or "migote" brigades who harvested wheat with peasants and cooked *galushki* (*migote*, in Spanish).[111] Even for those Spaniards who left the USSR rather early, like Milagros Latorre who was among twenty-one adolescents to leave for Mexico in 1948, the Spanish Civil War and the Second World War evacuations and suffering created a common set of experiences.[112]

An understanding of the classroom and extracurricular training of the Spanish children provides insights into the Soviet transformation project. Except with a few minor variations, Spanish refugee children were educated and trained like their Soviet counterparts. They took the same classes, played the same instruments, watched the same films, and visited similar sites. We see variance primarily in the preservation of their culture, much as would occur in non-Russian schools in the Soviet Union. Scholars like Brigid O'Keeffe, Matthew Pauly, and Ali Igmen have shown how the Soviet attempts to modernize members of a particular population through education and culture Sovietized them and created or hardened their understandings of themselves as a particularistic population.[113] This same approach with a non-Soviet Spanish population suggests a high degree of consistency in Soviet child-rearing. Preparation of a healthy body and a trained mind necessitated a focus not only on coursework but also on behaviours, complementary entertainment, and the establishment of a world view that included a recognition of mutual interdependence and created a common culture that would link the Spaniards to their Soviet counterparts.

5 Becoming Soviet in Traumatic Times: Life in War, 1939–1944

> We drank milk directly from the goat to the mouth ... there was no electric light or water ... the food was always the same: a porridge of wheat or pearl barley or some other grain; they also gave us some soup that didn't taste of anything and a piece of black bread.
>
> Milagros Latorre Piquer, "De niña española a mujer en la URSS," 81

After settling into new homes and schools during 1937–8, the Spanish children experienced several disruptions. Significant staff turnover plagued the years 1939–40, and the evacuation of the children deep into the Soviet heartland in 1941–4 disrupted their lives in such profound ways that they recall it vividly as a key turning point in their lives.[1] The chaos and violence of the Second World War tested the Soviet designs and abilities to provide for all the material needs of the Spaniards. Everything the children had started to take for granted since their arrival – food, electricity, water, safety – again became scarce and objects of longing. Like Milagros Latorre's recollection in this chapter's epigraph, other niños also remembered drinking milk straight from the teats of a Jewish tailor's goat and eating breakfast of only terrible black bread and sunflower oil.[2]

The events of 1939 had a dramatic effect on the Spanish children in the Soviet Union, influencing where and how they lived and shifting Soviet priorities for their education and upbringing. On 1 April 1939, five months before the Second World War broke out on the continent, the Spanish Civil War ended, as did the children's hopes for a prompt return to Spain. Those who had found refuge in France, Great Britain, Belgium, and other countries began filtering back into Franco's Spain,[3] but, fearing Franco's retribution after their life in the socialist motherland, the PCE refused to allow children to return from the USSR.

Two years after Franco's victory, the horrors of war landed on Soviet soil. With the Nazi invasion of the Soviet Union on 22 June 1941, Soviet and Spanish officials began to worry about the welfare of the children in the western USSR.

In 1941–2 the homes were consolidated, and their children evacuated deep into the Russian heartland and Central Asia. In war time the Spaniards "began a new stage in [their] lives."[4] The sudden and poorly coordinated movements led to the separation of siblings, to lost children, and to hostile reception in their new residences; in one example, Volga Germans awaiting deportation as a suspected enemy nationality assaulted the children who were to move into the Germans' homes.[5] Accidents were frequent, such as when fourteen-year-old Marcelino Sáinz Castillo was crushed and killed in an automobile accident in the Volga Geman town of Galka.[6] In another case, when a train started moving without warning, it amputated the legs of two girls who had disembarked to urinate.[7] Between 1939 and 1944, the darkest period for the Spaniards and most Soviet citizens, thirty-six children died in the Spanish boarding schools from disease, hunger, and accidents.[8]

Many of the Spanish refugees remembered war as a time of chaos and disorder without the usual protections afforded by the boarding schools.[9] Milagros Latorre, who drank from a goat, remembered the Second World War evacuation as one of hardship: "Life here was going to be most inhospitable. We would have to work hard to make the place and make it more or less habitable."[10] This view of war-time evacuation is not unlike the experience of approximately sixteen million Soviet citizens displaced by the Nazi invasion, likely the largest evacuation in history.[11] What Latorre captures, however, is the active role that the Spanish children played in their own survival. The cause of evacuation was out of their control, but their survival depended on their own abilities to gather food, water, and heating fuel to survive the harsh winters and an economy in disarray. This was a time for growing up and gaining resilience at a time when there were fewer adults around for comfort and "to give you a caress."[12]

Untethered from their comfortable and protected surroundings, the refugee children began to live for the first time more like their Soviet counterparts did. They experienced privation, had to fend for themselves in the struggle for survival, and adapted to rapidly changing educational and behavioural expectations, now designed to prepare them for long lives in the USSR. Soviet and PCE organizations still tried to protect the niños, but the children were also forced to begin transitioning into independent adults, which meant taking more personal responsibility. As shortages increased, front lines approached, and the children prepared for longer lives in the USSR, their education and upbringing shifted towards increased labour and military training, more Russian-language acquisition, and even greater attention to disciplined minds and bodies.

The story of Isabel Álvarez, while not typical, shows a range of hardships endured by many of the young Spaniards at this time. Álvarez, though a good student, rejected PCE suggestions that she continue schooling beyond year seven. After initially wanting to work in a textile factory, she took up nursing in Leningrad. She suffered through the siege before making the dangerous evacuation across Lake Ladoga in late March 1942. She endured a long journey from station to station, cold and hungry, before she began to trek through the Caucasus Mountains with Nazis all around. As she had no shoes, she wrapped a jacket around her feet and eventually climbed up and down the mountains, ending up with rocks embedded in her bare feet, suffering from altitude sickness, and fearing the sexual advances of the Soviet troops who sometimes came to her aid. The precise nature of her horrific story differs from that of her compatriots, but it shares the cold, hunger, separation, isolation, lack of adult supervision, and more that became common. Life was "full of risks and difficulties to survive in that sad reality."[13]

This chapter seeks to illuminate the war-time daily life in the homes for Spanish children and the shifting educational priorities towards Russian-language instruction and additional labour and military training. The war was a pivotal moment for dividing the fates of the younger children from those of the older ones, who moved into factories or to the front lines. Some Spaniards transitioned into becoming adults, though, as we will see in the next chapter, they were not truly independent, while others remained in the familial and paternal environment of the Spanish homes with fewer mentors and resources. In 1944, children and youth returned to Moscow *oblast* (province) where the PCE could continue to watch over them and where the Spaniards could be reunited with their compatriots and resume a life of relative privilege.

War-time displacement is always traumatic, and for Soviet citizens it jeopardized resources like housing and the rations that were tied to one's residence and workplace. "In the absence of state funding and in the face of soaring prices," writes historian Rebeccay Manley, "the survival of evacuees was contingent on their ability to insert themselves into the state-run system of supply. As displaced persons, this was a particularly difficult task. One needed connections, acquaintances and friends."[14] Prior to 1941 the Spaniards had been far better provisioned than their Soviet counterparts had been. With war-time evacuation came a rapid decline in standards of living and a greater scarcity of all material goods, which led to increased reports of theft and pilfering, trading on the black market, hooliganism, petty crime, and running away. However, the Spaniards still had numerous institutions supporting them and therefore, despite their privation, lived a relatively privileged, though often horrific, life during war. The dislocation of war and the movement of adult role models to the front and to factories meant decreased supervision and made daily life tenuous, which likely caused an increase in troublesome behaviours and a need for greater attention to discipline.[15]

The Chaos of Evacuation

War-time evacuations rarely go smoothly, and the Spaniards suffered in many of the same ways as their Soviet counterparts did. The intent was to evacuate Spanish children and youth to avoid the pains of war again. It was unsuccessful. The children based in Leningrad suffered from terrible hunger and cold. Juan Ricardo recalled, "We visited many buildings, we saw a horrible panorama, many [people] were almost half dead in their beds or dead already from hunger and cold." He evacuated on 19 March 1942: "We boarded open trucks and passed through the lake [Ladoga] until we reached the mainland. We were then assembled in a freight wagon that was alone at the platform. It was a terrible cold. The train was very slow, very slow and I remember that we were only Spanish, I think we were about a hundred and ninety."[16] During the evacuation, children encountered numerous hardships. An interviewee named Carlos recalled an "afternoon [when] it rained a lot [and] we stopped to rest next to a river and a few [of us] went to collect water for the others ... In the river, from afar we saw soldiers who, by their uniform, we were sure were not Soviets, and we went to warn the others and we fled as best we could in different directions. A group went straight to the river but they could not cross because it was very mighty and they were caught. They were hunted by the Germans and taken to Spain."[17]

Even in the absence of capture and forced repatriation, seventeen-year-old Marina recalled that "evacuation to the interior was generally a disaster."[18] She waited for three days to cross the Volga River because the tiny boats could shuttle only a few people at a time to the other side. Others crossed the Volga at Stalingrad "under a rain of bombs."[19] Once they had resettled, the chaos did not change for some of the Spaniards. A Fernando recalled his time working in Stalingrad to rebuild a destroyed rail line. He wore mittens because of the cold, but his hands stuck to the rail, and "the mittens peeled off my skin and my hands were bare."[20]

Disorder in evacuation led to dramatic changes for the Spaniards.[21] Two months before the Nazi invasion there were 2,253 Spanish children in the RSFSR, but nine months later, in January 1942, significant shifts occurred in their lives. Homes No. 3 and No. 4 in Odessa merged and fled to Saratov. The home in Kiev combined with one in Lepinsk and moved to Stalingradskaia oblast. Home No. 8 split; 64 children in the younger classes went to Bui in Iaroslavskaia oblast, and the seventh through ninth grades moved to Mostovskii raion in Krasnodarskii krai. Home No. 6, formerly in Evpatoriia, moved to the village of Orlovskoe in Saratovskaia oblast, and then the children transferred to homes No. 1, No. 5, and Kirov No. 3. All these moves, and others, left eleven children's homes in the RSFSR.[22] By September 1941, 698 children had arrived from the Ukrainian SSR, and 5 from living with their parents. The RSFSR system integrated all 703 children, for a total of 2,956. These disruptions upset the routines and learning environments as children moved into new institutional cultures where directors sought to create living and learning environments, albeit with significantly reduced staff and resources. The transferred students had to adapt quickly.

With less supervision during the chaos of evacuation, children went missing, too.[23] In one bizarre story Juan Ricardo recalled a girl who became separated from her group during evacuation and ended up in Georgia. A group of Spaniards who evacuated to Tbilisi in 1943 met her. She could understand Spanish, but she could no longer speak it. In the years since she had evacuated she had learned Georgian and gained only a rudimentary knowledge of Russian. The newly arrived Spaniards tutored her in Spanish until her adopted Georgian father found out, put a stop to it, and prevented her from seeing the Spaniards again.[24] Some children left hospitals and could not find their relatives; others were urged to write to their mothers who were worried about them; and still others received inquiries from relatives abroad who were seeking to be reunited with their siblings.[25] Similar evacuation stories caused worry among parents and siblings who wrote through the International Committee of the Red Cross, the Soviet Red Cross and Red Crescent, the Ministry of Foreign Affairs, and other agencies, trying to locate their relatives.

The children knew that they had organizations outside the Soviet government and party, like the Comintern, to which they could petition. José Fernández recalls a "moment of cheerful anarchy" with new freedoms and cigarettes as supervision waned. A new specialist on troubled children named Shulman, who had written his doctoral thesis on Makarenko, arrived to reimpose order. He forbade movement on the school grounds without a pass – punishable by confinement in the potato cellar – and put some of the older boys in charge as guards. But his experiment failed as the children protested, and director Vorontsov assumed control.[26] The children did not respond favourably to changes in leadership. They reportedly said, "Now it will be bad, it is necessary to write to the Comintern."[27] The children's council tried to explain that the changes were all for the good of the party, Spain, and the Soviet Union, and to prepare the children for labour. However, having lived in privilege by comparison to Soviet orphans and school children, the Spanish children must have found it jarring to shift from living in hotels and palaces with abundant food to living in ramshackle and crowded shelters and often having unsatiated bellies. Naturally, this caused tensions as school officials could no longer provide abundant food, warmth, and entertainment in evacuation.

Daily Life during War-Time Evacuation

The lack of advanced central planning and the shortage of information in the periphery led to terrible journeys and to difficult living conditions in the homes during the first months of evacuation. It also did not help that many of the children were left in the care of Spanish educators who were not much older than the children. The niños recalled that the adult Spaniards "did not speak Russian, they did not know what the Soviet institutions were or how different the Soviet mentality was."[28] With few allies on the ground in the new locations and little knowledge of Soviet bureaucracy, school staff often lurched from one crisis to the next. The Spanish experience resembled the experiences of their Soviet counterparts. As John Dunstan has noted, "the war had not only affected young people's attitudes ... it had also damaged the efficiency of schools by removing teachers and administrators and leaving them with replacements inadequate in both numbers and experience."[29]

The evacuation years were often quite brutal as displacement, hunger, and cold were present more often than textbooks. Teacher Alejandra Soler recalled the winter on the steppe greeting them with a "white curtain" of snow that was much worse than in Moscow.[30] José Fernández remembered a snow that fell not "in gentle flakes, but dry, hard, hurtful, brought from the steppe by a wind that shook everything."[31] Paired with a paucity of soap and the inability to effectively wash children, their clothes, and linens, it was no wonder that sicknesses periodically swept through the schools. Manuel Arce recalls rolling clothes under heavy weights to squash lice and then plunging the clothes in water and hanging them on a line in minus forty-two- degree weather.[32] A woman named Sofía remembered a terrible epidemic, yet "in the creek where we were bathing the water was cold and we were barefoot, naked, dirty, starving."[33] During the war students ate only once or twice a day, rather than four times a day as before the war.[34] Home No. 2, having already evacuated once from Mozhaisk, had its building seized on 24 October 1941. This forced the students to move in with Home No. 12, now in Birsk in the Bashkir Autonomous Soviet Socialist Republic (ASSR). Children had to study in corridors and sleeping quarters because there were not enough rooms, tables, and chairs for two sets of students. Sanitation and hygiene in the buildings was "very bad, mainly thanks to (a) great overcrowding, (b) the small quantity of water, (c) an insufficient quantity of natural and artificial light."[35] Cases of typhoid fever and paratyphoid emerged, and one child died of tuberculosis.

Although by 1942 most Spanish boarding schools had found stable accommodations, all was far from perfect. Inspections in 1942 showed ongoing problems in the evacuated boarding schools. Food supplies in Home No. 3 from the oblast were insufficient and did not meet the norms established by Sovnarkom (Sovet Narodnykh Komissarov, the Council of People's Commissars) and the party, and the supply of fuel in the Volga German region was "catastrophic," making heating and cleaning impossible. The home had transferred from Odessa and arrived in Saratov with 367 children, one hundred staff, and their families. They had been living in train cars in Saratov for ten days without hot food or drink. Children and adults had developed "massive stomach illnesses, angina, bronchitis, etc." Fifty of the children were still ill in May 1942 when the Saratov oblast's executive committee tried to move the Spaniards to another location.[36]

In the evacuated Spanish boarding schools the learning spaces were often abysmal, and necessities were difficult to attain. Even in Kirov, where Narkompros had relocated during the war, resources were scarce, and municipal officials had to be cajoled into providing adequate facilities to the evacuated children.[37] Classes took place in hallways, dining rooms, and bedrooms in the repurposed buildings, now transformed into makeshift schools.[38] Studying became difficult because of frozen ink, few books, and a lack of teachers, who often had mobilized for the war effort.[39] Home No. 2, for example, consisted of twelve staff members: eight Spaniards (only one of whom had documented pedagogical training) and four Russians from the nearby middle school. Three of the Spaniards left in the following year. The school lacked physics textbooks, and it "had not one art book." Home No. 3 needed "workbooks for both Russian and Spanish language," and, in the city of Miass, Home No. 8 had "only one workbook for every ten people," and one Spanish adult – a cook.[40] At sixty degrees below zero, the children's hands froze, too.[41]

The niños now had to contribute to their own survival.[42] The hardships of the war were nearly universal in the Soviet Union, and they were also felt by the Spanish children. The conditions of the Volga German removal made their plight precarious. "The poor [German] people could not take anything they had and left everything," a respondent named Verónica recalled. "We were warned on the way there that we should not eat anything that was in the homes of the Germans, who had poisoned everything and that we could die. And we believed it, we were very hungry. In the village there was everything, animals and food, we ate nothing, out of fear, but we were hungry. In the end we ate and it turned out that everything we were told was all a lie."[43] In another Volga German village, the NKVD was trying to prevent the theft of grain and other products left behind. The older Spaniards in the group managed to steal food so they did not starve, but "we were [there] almost six months and the misery was so terrible that many of us began to get sick and die. At least five or six children of our group died."[44] José Fernández remembers quite differently the encounters with Volga Germans. He and his group sang Spanish and German songs with the people they were supplanting, even forming a type of camaraderie with them because they all worked the fields together for their common survival.[45]

Stealing food from the state or people was a common strategy of survival, particularly as food availability declined in 1942, but the Spanish children also had to work hard.[46] Manuel Arce did chores for his home's doctor and accountant in return for potatoes, but most of his recollection of evacuation in the home consists of various strategies to steal food.[47] Home No. 4 had its own resources: ten hectares, two cows, eight piglets, five horses, and gardens to supplement state supplies.[48] Spanish children also collected firewood, sewed clothes, tended gardens, brought in the harvest in nearby collective farms, and hauled water.[49] In Leningrad under siege, Spaniards made gloves, cleared snow from railroad tracks, and burned their furniture for heat.[50] Similarly, in the Volga German village of Basel, Spanish children burned furniture and roofs to warm themselves as they tore down huts piece by piece. "Our life had become so basic," recalled one former student, "that we did everything ourselves," which included growing their own food.[51] In Home No. 1, also in the Volga German region, the cold weather and the need for the children to haul water from the river led to frostbitten, blackened extremities.[52] Home No. 7 could heat only sleeping quarters, so they doubled as study rooms.[53] The children and staff of Home No. 8 had to build their own kitchen and cafeteria after arriving in Krasnodarskii krai in March 1942.

The children's health – which was closely related to food availability, quality, and variety – was a key concern for most home directors and Spanish and Soviet inspectors. The amount of willing assistance by local organizations varied widely.[54] Many of the Spaniards had arrived in poor health in 1937. Although some improved dramatically through treatment in sanatoria near the Black Sea, several became worse during the war. The war-time evacuation caused additional problems because food, medicine, and medical personnel and equipment often were in short supply. Soviet humanitarianism towards the children continued, but the evacuation placed pressures on local residents already concerned about scarce resources.

Numerous municipalities from Saratov to Kirov to Samarkand tried to avoid taking in the Spaniards, fearing correctly that local institutions would have to provide shelter, clothing, and food during the war.[55] Accommodating hundreds of children and their caregivers in a new location not infrequently led to resentment and even hostility because some Soviets perceived that, despite dangerous living conditions, in many ways the Spaniards were privileged over Soviet children and youth.[56] Spaniards often received scarce goods and stipends that were unavailable to Soviet orphans or children and youth in similar positions. Soviet orphanages were particularly under-resourced, and their wards suffered from a widely held stigma of unruly and unredeemable hooligans.[57] Home No. 6 appears to have been one of the most troubled locations in the network of Spanish facilities. A letter written directly to Stalin from someone named Perchik at that institution is also instructive about the way in which some Soviet citizens perceived the Spaniards. After acknowledging that Stalin had things that were more important – like the war – to occupy him, Perchik listed several problems with the children in the home. They were servile before foreigners, they ate better and received 50 per cent more food than Soviet children did, they had "open sympathy for Franco," and they behaved like "occupiers." The general tenor of the letter is that the niños were spoiled hooligans who had a much better life than their Soviet counterparts did.[58]

However, E.V. Koniakhina, chief of the RSFSR Administration of Orphanages, immediately sent a retort to the Central Committee's Department of Schools in which she stated that Perchik's letter was "without grounds and incorrect." The children were doing a great deal of the upkeep in the home, helping collective farm workers with sewing and harvesting, cutting wood and hauling water for the kitchen, and repairing furniture, shoes, and clothes in their workshops. Some had made underwear and gloves for the Red Army, many had volunteered to fight, and 150 had participated in the defence of Leningrad and other fronts. She continued by noting that many youth over sixteen years of age had requested citizenship, and many had already earned it. As for Home No. 6 in particular, the director was taken into the army, and his deputy evacuated the home from Evpatoriia to Krasnodar krai and then to Saratov oblast. Koniakhina finished by noting the carousel of directors who followed. At no point, however, did she directly rebut Perchik's claims that ungrateful Spaniards were too pampered.[59]

Almost exactly a year after the Nazi invasion and the eventual evacuation of the homes, the party and government officials began to meet to discuss the well-being of young children and the needs of a country on a full war footing.[60] In 1942 alone, ten children had died of tuberculosis in the Spanish homes, which led Sukhov, deputy chair of Sovnarkom RSFSR, and Vladimir Potemkin, commissar of Enlightenment RSFSR, to write to Rosalia Zemliachka of Sovnarkom SSSR (USSR) that, "in light of [health concerns], the need is ripe for an immediate transfer of the children to other healthy climactic conditions."[61] However, even in the proper locations, the health care could not live up to expectations without proper hygiene, sanitation, and medical care. The paucity of everyday items was critical in the attempts to meet the children's health needs, and recollections suggest that boarding schools consistently lacked even cups, plates, and silverware.[62] Therefore, the central committees of the party and Komsomol called for various agencies to provide soap, clothes, kitchen items, and medicine and to isolate students with infectious tuberculosis.[63] Whether the institutions fully complied (or could) is unclear.

As late as January 1944, conditions remained horrible for many. Even as patronage (*shefstvo*) by factories, collective farms, and other institutions brought in food and material goods, several homes struggled to find adequate resources for survival.[64] Some of the most vulnerable children housed in the sanatorium in Alekseevskoe, Saratovskaia oblast, still had to sleep two to a bed, while another 160 of them slept on beds they had made from planks. Bedding and underwear were filthy, and there was no warm winter clothing. "The children's home is called a sanatorium," reported the director Sharanova, "but that is only a name because living conditions are worse than a normal home." There was no water, sewerage, or heating, and no electricity in the treatment areas. Food and soap were also in short supply.[65] In February 1944, Home No. 12

ran out of bread and drank nettle soup after many fell ill from eating rotting wheat.[66] Milagros Latorre remembered meat in her soup only once during evacuation; the meat appeared after the camel that they used to fetch water from the Volga had died because, as Manuel Arce recalled, it was blind and could not find food for itself.[67] Although the conditions were still far from ideal, directors could report improved nutrition and weight gains even as all types of shortages still plagued most schools.[68]

Living conditions had come to the attention of various authorities. Georgi Dimitrov, head of the Comintern, had been receiving reports, likely from Spanish cadres, about the "unfortunate" material conditions in the evacuated homes. As early as January 1942, he charged Potemkin with looking after the Spaniards in the Narkompros system and suggested that Álvaro Peláez be brought into the system with a mandate to accommodate Spanish comrades.[69] Dimitrov's letter led to Narkompros inspector Morgunova's being sent on a tour of the homes in Saratov oblast, and Peláez taking a place in Narkompros. Spanish adults and members of the communist parties of Spain and the Soviet Union in the homes played a significant role in the war-time care of the children and youth. Even though reports and memoirs detail horrific conditions, the refugee children at least had numerous organizations looking out for their welfare. In an unsigned letter from April 1942 to secretaries of the Komsomol Central Committee, the author asked that the Executive Committee of the Communist Youth International (IKKIM) put communists and Komsomol members in all homes to help with political work among the Spanish staff. This suggests that communist oversight had been limited in some homes. Moreover, the letter requested placing a plenipotentiary of the PCE's central committee in oblast centres where Spanish children were concentrated. However, one student reported seeing neither Vicente Talón nor Tomás Huete, the PCE members responsible for Saratov province, even when he was in hospital for three months after losing both legs.[70]

Soviet Communist Party members and Komsomol activists, in an effort to increase supervision and improve role modelling and socialization, would have to answer for the political training of both the Spanish children and the workers in the homes.[71] From the archival record it appears that inspections and reports increased, and conditions began to improve, but memoirs suggest that these claims could not be generalized, because some Spaniards recall being "feral because of the circumstances we had to live in, without any authority or firm paternal hand."[72] Moreover, not all Komsomol leaders were ideal role models. One of the more striking cases was that of twenty-year-old José Amiama from San Sebastián, secretary of the Komsomol committee who – along with Isabel Zapatero, Paco Basurto, José Malea, Amor Ferro, and Anita Argüelles – "lurked in dark corners" at night and then insulted the staff who "substitute[d] for his father and mother."[73]

The Spaniards were doing a great deal to aid their survival (and the survival of others), and because Spanish and Soviet agencies were helping them, the children likely had access to scarce goods that their Soviet counterparts could not obtain. The very presence of the Spaniards in these new locations far from the front lines also put them in direct competition for food and other goods with Soviet residents. The Great Terror and Comintern purge had created the expectation of enemies among foreign populations. This may have influenced some charges against Spaniards, but resentment towards perceived privilege was not directed to the Spaniards alone. Average citizens felt aggrieved about the privileges of party officials and others who had access to scarce goods. Soviet citizens feared evacuation and the unknown assistance that may or may not be offered depending on their place in the hierarchy: "Everyone is afraid of the possibility of getting laid off somewhere far away in an unknown city – finding themselves without living space or a salary while food prices are rising sharply."[74] People in advantaged categories throughout the Soviet Union gained access to greater variety and quantity of food during the war. Foreigners – after party and government officials, military officers, and intellectuals – were one such group.[75]

Studying While Trying to Survive

The turmoil of war and evacuation changed not only standards of living but also Soviet priorities for education and upbringing in the Spanish homes. As Ann Livschiz has noted, the Second World War brought several dramatic changes to Soviet educational policy, like increased discipline and labour and military training.[76] The only significant differences for the Spaniards were the absence of single-sex education that came to some cities in the USSR and a sharp decline in Spanish-language instruction.

War-time shortages necessitated a reduction in Spanish-language instruction; however, other curricular changes sought to meet new needs for war-time mobilization. During the war, instructors placed greater emphasis on core subjects like Russian language, mathematics, and literature while promoting military and physical education for the new needs of the country's defence and industry.[77] Mathematics problems, as in Germany, began to use military examples (e.g., plotting flights of projectiles), and biology renewed a focus on hygiene and health.[78] Military training included hand-to-hand combat for boys and nursing and communications operations for girls. Summer camps taught "marches, construction of anti-aircraft shelters, and other paramilitary activities."[79] In rural schools agricultural work came to the forefront, whereas in urban schools labour training occurred principally in workshops.

According to Spanish children and staff, the niños arriving in the USSR in 1937 had refused to clean floors, toilets, and even potatoes; they also had failed to care for communal goods like furniture and toys. By necessity, they soon learned to tidy the grounds, dig anti-tank ditches, and cut wood.[80] Teaching political, cultural, and social values in schools was part of the typical Soviet educational system, but with the start of the Russo-Finnish War in 1939 labour and military training became more important as a vehicle to train the body, develop discipline and friendship, and learn how to be bold, resourceful, and successful.[81] War-time conditions forced the boarding schools to shift from providing for the children's material needs to helping them become self-sufficient, hard-working, selfless Soviets. A teacher named Yagokina is reported as saying, "Each potato you dig is a howitzer against the enemy," and the children were proud to show their calluses to Ibárruri.[82]

In 1940 – a ground-breaking moment for the youth labour movement – Arkady Gaidar published *Timur and His Team*, which was quickly made into a film and served as inspiration for youth participation in labour. The Timur story captured the imagination of Soviet youth and became a central text and film for labour and moral education for the rest of the Soviet period. Timur and his team of village children secretly did good deeds in their community, stood up to local hooligans, and aided the families of Red Army soldiers. Loyalty, community, and service to others aided the development of a child's social persona (*lichnost'*). Serving the community was not done to mark one's individuality or to display publicly one's efforts. The secrecy of the Timurovtsy, or children emulating Timur, was an integral part of the spontaneous movement that developed from the story. Children were sacrificing their own interests for the greater good, not for self-aggrandizement. Thus, initiative was encouraged, but individuality was not.[83]

Spanish children seem to have responded to the Timur movement with the same enthusiasm as their Soviet counterparts. Many Soviet and Spanish children wanted to join the fight against fascism; however, for most of them, their age precluded front-line fighting. The Timurovtsy provided much needed service away from the front by recycling materials, bringing in harvests, collecting medicinal herbs, helping soldiers' families, and tending the graves of the dead.[84] In Home No. 2 in 1942, for example, thirty-four Spaniards formed a Timur brigade on arrival in Bashkiria and began to cut firewood, bring in the local harvest, and more. Other children recalled doing many of the same activities to secure additional food and thus avoid starvation.[85] The fictional Timur represented the pinnacle of socialist child-rearing: he had internalized the values of the Soviet Union so well that he could use his own initiative – without further guidance from adults or the state – to serve society.

In January 1941, following the enthusiastic reception of *Timur and His Team*, a conference of writers and critics met to discuss literature's role in developing military readiness and a strong work ethic in children.[86] Part of the training program at the children's home included labour to create self-discipline and self-sufficiency. Labour obligations were neither typical nor widespread in the

Spanish homes in the first years, but the war years made such labour a key strategy of survival. Educators often viewed labour as a panacea; it could teach "discipline, collectivism, initiative, persistence, respect towards working people and disdain for idlers, and development of willpower and character."[87] Labour showed children how to work together, provided discipline and a sense of social responsibility, and in many cases connected them with nature.[88] Soviet schools had been directing students to perform tasks that aided society, but farm labour was not merely a way to achieve class-consciousness during the war. Child farm labour was an attempt to alleviate food shortages.[89] Taking the cue from *Timur and His Team*, Spaniards located in a village along the Volga River formed into groups to sanitize the complex against sickness and disease, to guard harvests, and to prevent the encroachment of flood waters.[90] Like Timur, the Spanish children hauled water and firewood, gathered scrap metal and medicinal plants, sewed items for front-line soldiers, and tended gardens and livestock.

Protecting the children also meant training them to protect themselves and their schools, but ideal and practice often were at odds. In 1941, before the Nazi invasion of the USSR, children in some boarding schools already had completed military training in a kruzhok. Their preparation included studying the lives of the military heroes and marshals of the Soviet Union Semen Budennyi, Semen Timoshenko, and Kliment Voroshilov and the civil war heroes Mikhail Frunze, Vasilii Chapaev, and Grigorii Kotovskii. The children listened to reports in Spanish about Stalin as the leader of the Red Army, and they followed the war in Finland. They went to a nearby army camp, lived there like the soldiers, and later divided into two teams – one trying to protect the home and the other trying to invade. The Spanish children devoted a significant portion of their time to the new war-time needs. They heard lectures, and some students completed courses in preparation for air or chemical warfare. Older students took 110 hours of military-preparedness courses, and sixth and seventh graders studied civil defence. A group of sixteen female Komsomol members voluntarily formed a group to study modern weaponry. In total, 231 students earned awards for military and civil-defence preparation.[91] Fearing paratroopers, teenagers armed with knives and one rifle per ten students scoured the forests near Moscow for Nazis.[92] Although authorities improved civil-defence training, the shortages of a crisis economy limited their ability to achieve all their goals.[93] Firefighting equipment was barely adequate in most locations, and training in artificial resuscitation and the treatment of chemical injuries was completely absent.

Military and labour training also found their way into children's daily routines. The fifth anniversary of the Spaniards' arrival in the USSR was a "sports holiday," allowing the children to "demonstrate their preparation for labour and defence."[94] Fun had a function. Students took part in team sports like volleyball, soccer, and gymnastics to condition their bodies in a collectivist manner for labour and defence. When not learning to protect themselves

5.1 Niños familiarizing themselves with rifles and a compass. España, Ministerio de Cultura y Deporte, Centro Documental de la Memoria Histórica, P.S. Fotografías, carpeta 36, folio 2926.

and their bodies, they wrote individual and group letters to front-line soldiers, made and sent gifts to the front, and even staged an exhibition about the Great Patriotic War. Thirty-three of the older children left school in February 1942 to attend factory training schools to aid the war effort. Younger students, led by Komsomol members, raised funds for the war effort and the home. As malnutrition took hold, the students tended the fields in a nearby village and thereby learned the value of labour and saved themselves and villagers from hunger. Despite all the cold and hardships, the "period of the Great Patriotic War significantly raised the discipline and organization of the Spanish children." The staff and students met their "responsibility before the Motherland and the glorious Red Army," which included building rail lines near Stalingrad and between Saratov and Astrakhan.[95] Yet José Fernández remembered that his "childhood had been lost" as his home descended into anarchy.[96] The war forced the children to become more responsible for themselves and others, and no two situations were the same.

Some Spanish youth also worked for the survival of the USSR by joining the war effort.[97] One Spaniard recalled that the desire to fight was important to his understanding of his place both within the Soviet Union and as a Spaniard: "Remembering the Spanish War, we dreamed of being heroes. We wanted to participate more actively in the defence of the Soviet Union in the struggle against fascism. And we believed that the best we could do and where we could contribute was by staying in Leningrad. When the bombers came, we would go up to the roof to remove or bury the incendiary bombs, which were the ones that caused the most damage ... It was a Dantesque spectacle!"[98] When Bernardo del Río, Francisco Navarro, Vicente Delgado, José Zaragoza, and Adolfo Cenitagoya arrived at a recruiting station to volunteer for the Red Army, many of the Soviets cheered, "Spanish brothers!"[99] From the time the niños had disembarked in the Soviet Union, authorities had hailed them as "little heroes." In their education in the boarding schools they were taught Soviet patriotism – as was standard practice in Soviet schools – and encouraged to work and study hard so that they could one day defeat fascism and liberate Spain. Their life experiences in the Spanish Civil War led many to understand that the Soviet fight against fascism was also a fight for a free Spain.

Spanish-language instruction was another casualty of war. Since there was little history of teaching Spanish in the USSR, there were no textbooks or workbooks available. With fewer qualified instructors because of war-time mobilization, Narkompros could not readily develop new course materials. In June 1943, three teachers were freed from teaching duties in order to restructure the Spanish language and literature curriculum. In addition, an August 1944 conference of all Russian and Spanish teachers convened to review teaching methods and goals.[100] Nothing came from these efforts, and the lack of workbooks remained a problem for at least another five years.[101] Therefore, oral and aural Spanish developed more than reading and writing because "out of class [the students] only speak Spanish," and, starting in sixth grade, most subjects were taught in Russian.[102] Without good instruction in the classroom, the acquisition of grammar, syntax, and vocabulary lagged far behind those of the older Spaniards who had arrived after the end of the civil war and therefore had spent more of their time in Spain.

A report from the last war-time school year noted a variety of reasons for the students' limited abilities: they lacked a Soviet work ethic, and the absence of grammar books and literature in Spanish led to small vocabularies and many punctuation and orthography errors.[103] One student recalled that the absence even of Spanish dictionaries forced him to use a Russian-Italian dictionary to translate a *Komsomolskaia pravda* article about the war-time death of Dolores Ibárruri's son.[104] Of course, students learned to read; their textbooks, after all, were in Spanish. However, textbooks and copies of the PCE newspaper *Mundo Obrero* (Workers World) and the occasional poetry reading of Antonio Machado's works were not quality substitutes for a more significant grounding in Spanish-language literature. Claims about poor work ethic among students, however, runs counter to other war-time reports that stressed improved attention to studies because of the war. Schools varied, and so did students. We cannot expect a single report or memory to represent the multiplicity of experiences.

Decreasing attention to Spanish literature by 1941 likely derived from multiple causes. There was simply a lack of Spanish texts in the USSR. With the outbreak of the Second World War and the darkening of relations with Franco, the importation of texts from Spain ceased, and libraries were not evacuated with the children, therefore leaving homes with little Spanish literature. One school report noted that in 1946 "books for reading in Spanish are completely absent."[105] The only contact with Spanish literature in the school was teacher Alfonso Lagos's occasional readings from the journal *International Literature*. Another school staged two successful evenings of Spanish poetry – one dedicated to Republican poet Antonio Machado and another devoted to the memory of José Díaz – but the report noted that to organize more was difficult because of the lack of Spanish literature available. Use of the library and reading rooms in this home was high, yet the plan to have weekly oral readings of Spanish literature was cancelled because teachers "could not get the appropriate materials" in this the most well-appointed of the Spanish boarding schools.[106] This suggests two things: Spanish literature was hard to find, and many of the students apparently could not read Spanish well enough on their own because of the war-time deficiencies.[107]

In class, Spaniards rarely read much literature in Spanish. However, in evacuation they apparently missed much of the Russian canon, too. One report noted that students who were returning from evacuation and then reintegrating into Soviet Spanish schools were behind in both mathematics and literature because they had been studying a "program for non-Russian schools." As a result, they had not covered required topics like polymath Mikhail Lomonosov, poet and statesman Gavrila Derzhavin, Gogol's *Dead Souls*, Goncharov's *Oblomov*, Turgenev's *Fathers and Sons*, Saltykov-Shchedrin's *Golovlevs*, and Tolstoy's *War and Peace*, all of which were obligatory in the Spanish homes.[108] This report suggests that although in many ways the Spanish boarding schools operated like non-Russian schools in allowing native-language instruction, the literature coursework was more Russian than non-Russian. Moreover, despite all the horrors of war-time evacuation, Spanish schools seems to have been better provisioned than the non-Russian schools in which some Spaniards had to study. Although shortcomings abounded, it appears that the boarding schools maintained their desire to celebrate the literary heritage of two countries.

In addition to the greater availability of Russian literature, the heightened emphasis on Russian-language mastery in the Spanish homes coincided with more Spaniards entering the workforce in 1940–1. As we will see in the next chapter, with the outbreak of war, the older children, especially those with lower aptitudes or desire for advanced study, entered labour training and then factory work to aid the war effort. However, officials in training schools and factories complained about the Spaniards' limited Russian-language abilities, and job skills, which made it difficult for them to follow directions and operate equipment safely.[109] Poor language instruction and learning was not limited to non-Russian speakers.[110] Owing to the poor Russian-language skills of many national minorities, which led them to fail entrance exams, Russian as a second language garnered more attention. Narkompros's attacks on formalism pointed to teaching Russian grammar by "catechism" in Soviet schools, which led to low levels of cultured speech and dramatic grammatical and stylistic mistakes, even among Russian speakers.[111] Other problems in non-Russian schools included pronunciation difficulties and a lack of specialists for teaching Russian to non-Russian speakers.

The shortage of good language instruction during the war left Spaniards struggling with the Russian sounds for Б/В, Л/Ль, и/й/ы. In addition to drilling these articulations, teachers assigned two-way translations, had students listen to the radio and watch films, and added six to nine more vocabulary words to each lesson so that students would have 1,700-word vocabularies by the time they left the schools. Russian literature courses had been less effective because students struggled with the Russian-language textbooks.[112] Some students remembered struggling in class and being baffled by the Russian case endings: "Russian comes from the mother's milk ... but we had already been weaned on another."[113] Although Russian was "difficult and complex," diligent students who struggled early in their new homeland soon acquired Russian well enough that in evacuation they were sometimes appalled by the inability of other Soviet nationalities to communicate in Russian, which highlights the Spanish boarding schools as being relatively more successful than other non-Russian schools.[114] Soon after the war the Spanish students who were on track for higher education, such as those who remained in the homes for ninth and tenth grades, often had additional Russian-language courses after the regular school day. Students who still needed remedial work could go to a "Russian corner" where teachers and/or Komsomol members posted lists of difficult vocabulary and grammar rules.[115] After the war-time failures, schooling in the homes began to pay much closer attention to the improvement of second-language acquisition in preparation for the Spaniards' entrance into Soviet daily life at the workplace or in higher education.

The annual report from Home No. 1 in the 1941–2 school year shows the pervasiveness of the turn towards Russian and Soviet themes at the war's onset in the Soviet Union, even though José Fernández has insisted that a policy of Russification "never existed," because his fellow students were simultaneously reminded of their Spanishness.[116] This year of departures, when the Spanish schools evacuated further from the front lines, brought additional political education to the students. After laudatory phrases about Stalin and the party, the report notes that the "day-to-day work in the school" consisted of instructing the children about the merits of Leninism-Stalinism: "fortitude, courage, stoutness, without fear of the fight, preparedness to give one's life for the great work of Lenin-Stalin." The lessons were to encourage "love for studies, work, [and] careful, economical consumption of state resources."[117] One needed to be a disciplined student and labourer, but during the war one also had to conserve resources for the front. Although not mentioned directly in this passage, the underlying current of all these traits is discipline. In fact, a school administrator noted that the war created a "turnabout in the children's psyche." The trauma did not depress or frighten them; apparently it merely steeled the children for greater effort. They "strengthened their love for our [Soviet] homeland and willed to change their relation to studies, labour, discipline and many other responsibilities." In order to improve their "studies, discipline, labour, defence and physical culture work, overcoming the existing difficulties arising from war," the Spaniards studied Stalin's writings and engaged in socialist competitions with other homes.

Clearly, we cannot accept the report as a factual representation of all Spaniards' behaviours and thinking, but oral histories and memoirs corroborate that patriotic feelings increased during the war years. We know that some of the boys rushed to enlist and that those who were too young were turned away at the recruiting station or hindered by Spanish adults. However, some Spanish adults thought it was a great honour for Spaniards to fight for the USSR and felt more Russian after the Nazi invasion.[118] Military training, increased Russian-language competency at the expense of Spanish, and labour skills all began to train the Spaniards for the adult lives ahead of them in the USSR.

Discipline, *Vospitanie*, and Role Models

Decreasing supervision and the need to begin to prepare students for entry into Soviet society necessitated even greater role modelling and attention to vospitanie and especially discipline. Discipline appeared to deteriorate during the war as many adults moved to the fronts or factories, leaving fewer role models and less supervision. A September 1942 report from Home No. 10, in which nearly half the children had lower behavioural evaluations than before the war, provides the most thorough glimpse into changes in daily life.[119] Immediately after evacuation the behaviour was described as "disgraceful," with the remaining Spanish adults pampering the children, smoking pipes, and playing dominoes rather than helping the children with homework. Instead of denouncing Spanish adults for corporal punishment of the children, the director (deploying a common stereotype) reportedly said, "Spaniards, you see, are hot-tempered," and he did nothing else. Thus, survival strategies like stealing watches and money and selling textbooks continued.[120] Students also remembered well the collapse of discipline when boys in particular "believed themselves the owners of the world [who could] do what they wanted, taking advantage of the goodness of the personnel who could not put a finger on them."[121] At the start of the school year a new regime directed the children's council and Pioneers to bring better supervision and order, and personnel had a "weekly battle with the words 'I don't want to'" and "we are not slaves."[122] Rooms needed cleaning, and the children were "protesting, being rude."

New behavioural norms were instituted to discipline students' time and bodies and reduce the chaos. "It was agreed" in May 1942 that the children's council and Pioneer staff would salute the director in a show of respect and that each morning one child would give the command "Attention!" and exchange salutes before reporting students' readiness. Uniforms and shoes were to be cleaned and stored properly, no one was to leave the grounds without permission, and all were to take part in obligatory labour. Students were forbidden to bring unnecessary things to class like toys, chewing gum, and slingshots. All students were to stand when the teacher entered the room, refrain from talking during class, complete homework without mistakes, sit only in their assigned place in the classroom, raise their hands instead of crying out, and bring books and writing instruments.[123] We must assume that, before these new rules were set, chaos reigned, with children hurling missiles in class, playing with toys, ignoring the dwindling ranks of teachers and staff, and wandering about without the knowledge of school officials.

During and after the war *Sovetskaia pedagogika* published numerous articles that reminded teachers and school administrators about the importance of character training. Schools were to be sites for inculcating self-control, decisiveness, persistence, constancy (*postoianstvo*), initiative, tactfulness, attention to one's health, and a love of labour and one's people.[124] Honesty and truthfulness were also "characteristic features of the new man – communist."[125] With less supervision and more need for order, the new rules for students in 1943 developed these themes by mandating that students arrive on time, leave and speak only when given permission, raise their hands in class, and remove their caps when meeting teachers or administrators on the street. Respect for teachers, elders, and parents and the insistence that the students "obey without question the orders of the school director and teachers" illustrate the growing importance of discipline and hierarchy in schools during the war.[126] Truthfulness was central to the success of students and the entire collective; therefore, the new student rules stressed the importance of doing one's own homework.[127]

School rules also emphasized cultured behaviour, including prohibiting students from gambling, smoking, and speaking coarsely.[128] As textiles and footwear were prioritized for front-line troops, care for clothes, shoes, and school materials was also important. In addition, good communists in training were required to be attentive and helpful to others. Hardening (*zakalivanie*) was another element of character development to transform children into war-time defenders and workers. "A courageous person is not born," wrote one commentator; "courage is learned."[129] The urge to action came through physical education and military training, both of which gained greater emphasis during the war. With less supervision of children at school and home, authorities feared that chaos would reign again as had happened in the wake of the Russian Civil War, collectivization, and famine.[130]

Although some reports suggest great self-sacrifice during the war, the number of cases of war-time theft and flight from the boarding schools suggest that some students felt that their survival depended on their individual action and that with fewer adult mentors they could get away with it. Theft was a result of scarce material goods and personnel. Milagros Latorre remembered: "There is nothing to sharpen ingenuity like need." She made a scrap-metal spoon and stole butter.[131] Manuel Arce's memoir, however, has the most dramatic cases of ingenuity for survival, including catching hens with fishhooks, skinning cats and pretending they were rabbits, easing down a bakery's chimney to steal flour and oil, and selling the plaster eggs that were made to stimulate laying as real eggs at market.[132] Fourteen-year-old Francisco Serrano from Gijón was identified as the ringleader of four children who ran away to Ufa after stealing from their residence.[133] Twelve-year-old Juan José Caballero and eleven-year-old Fausto Naves fled to Home No. 3 in the village of Iazykova. Four others fled their worksites in 1945 for the Spanish home in Evpatoriia. At age eighteen in 1944, future dance teacher Gerardo Viana ran away from the aviation technicum in Ufa, stayed at the apartment of his former Russian teacher, and there stole shoes, underwear, and galoshes.[134] Fifteen-year-old María Aya Sierra stole a coat, a dress, and other things, fled from Home No. 2, and then escaped again from the police.[135] Spaniards also remembered being part of a "Russian-Spanish gang of roustabout loaders" who stole food from trains and warehouses in order to eat or sell it at market for cash.[136] Others gladly accepted stolen and forged ration cards from well-known Soviet miscreants.[137] Not only do cases like these counter reports that suggest greater discipline in war time, but also they show privation even in the relatively better provisioned Spanish homes.

Incomplete acculturation among these Spaniards led to a series of anti-social, if not anti-Soviet, behaviours. The Spaniards' belief that they were only in the Soviet Union "temporarily and in a very short time ought to go back to their homeland" led to tardiness, absenteeism, indiscipline, and impertinence. "It's all the same to us," one young woman reportedly replied when confronted about her behaviour; "nothing will be done [about it]." This "suitcase mood" of evacuees refusing work because they believed their evacuation was temporary seems to have been relatively common among Soviet citizens, too.[138] When we remember that by 1940 not only theft but also workplace absenteeism and tardiness were punishable crimes, it is remarkable that more Spaniards were not arrested. This is likely another example of the preferential treatment towards Spaniards; Soviet authorities likely did not want to rile the PCE unnecessarily, nor did they want to admit that the Soviet project was not successful in transforming these young Spaniards into conscious Soviets.[139]

Soviets believed that role modelling was essential in creating an ideal learning environment, and the many changes of adult personnel during evacuation affected the children's fate. For example, one report shows that fourteen Spanish teachers who were no longer "fit for purpose" left the homes. The director of Home No. 6 was arrested, and the directors of Homes No. 2 and No. 12 went to serve in the Red Army.[140] This followed the soft purge of staff in 1939–40 discussed in chapter 2. Whereas in 1940 there were 103 educators for 2,258 children and youth, there were twenty-six fewer educators for only seven fewer students the following year. This means an addition of more than seven children per adult in one year (21.92 to 29.23), leading to less adult supervision in extraordinarily difficult times in evacuation.[141] Other staff just got lost. A Spanish educator and a translator unknowingly ended up in Mozdokskii raion in Ossetia without any idea that the school had evacuated from Kiev to Leninsk in Stalingradskaia oblast.[142]

As a part of role modelling, Spanish communists provided lectures in the homes. For example, the plan for 1945 listed a dozen Spanish lecturers (and never a Russian speaker) providing political lectures such as "Life of a Student in Spain," "Spaniards' Struggle for Independence," "The Workers' Movement in Spain," and "Relations between Spain and Latin America." Lectures also educated the children about their culture as in "Theatrical Art of Spain," "Spanish Monuments and Ideas about Architecture in Spain," "Folk Music and Song," "Spanish Artists, and Spanish Language: Its Dissemination and Significance."[143] José Fernández recalled that the news bulletins and study circles about current events "served to seal our solidarity and keep alive the consciousness of Spaniards."[144] Bernardo del Río has suggested that artistic performances and sports were avenues for practising their collectivism.[145] Both the political and the cultural topics seem designed to bridge the children's associations with the USSR, Spain, and the wider Spanish-speaking world.

As it became increasingly clear that the Spanish children were not going back to Spain soon, it became imperative that they learned how to live as Soviets and integrate into society. Discipline and living amongst and as Soviets became important, especially for those Spaniards transitioning into adulthood. In the school year of 1944–5 significant concerns continued. In Home No. 2 there were no teachers for physical education or military studies, a shortage of books (including for Spanish history, language, and literature), electricity for only half the day, poor Russian-language acquisition, and a poor understanding of Soviet attitudes towards work.[146] Many of the Spanish teachers did not have teaching qualifications, and they treated Soviet property "like vermin." The solutions to these and many other problems were simple: teach "patriotism, love for the Soviet Union, the Communist Party, and its leader comrade Stalin, for free Spain and to hate the enemy of humanity – fascism."[147] Political work and lectures were imperative for the Soviet development of staff and students. However, the actions of some adults continued to undermine instruction in ideal behaviours and attitudes. War time necessitated new rules for the homes, but it was hoped that a change of location would make vospitanie easier.

Re-evacuation and Continued Supervision

From the first days in 1937 the children dispersed throughout the Ukrainian and Russian republics from Leningrad to Yalta. The war-time evacuation spread them even further, from Tbilisi to Saratov to Samarkand. In these circumstances the PCE found it difficult to maintain regular contact with the children. The turn of the war at Stalingrad in the winter of 1942–3 opened the possibility of the return from exile of millions of Soviet citizens and of the Spaniards, too. In 1944 Spanish children and youth returned to Moscow oblast where the PCE could continue to watch over them and where they could be reunited with their compatriots. Whereas the 1941–2 evacuation seems to have developed with little forethought, the PCE, already in 1943, had urged the Soviet state to return Spaniards to the Moscow region. In this way, the PCE leadership could supervise the development and education of all the Spanish children and youth. However, full repatriation to the centre ran into several problems, though not as many as had plagued the initial evacuations eastward.

In 1943 PCE leader Dolores Ibárruri wrote to the State Defence Committee member and deputy chief of Sovnarkom Georgii Malenkov, stating that the homes in war-time evacuation were inadequate for normal educational development and the maintenance of hygiene, health, and food supplies. She therefore submitted a request to relocate all the residents of the Spanish children's homes to the Moscow region, "if it is possible."[148] On 5 April 1944 Ibárruri sent a letter to Malenkov, telling him of a lack of direction and control in the homes, which had led to "moral problems" in the evacuated institutions far from Moscow. The decision to advocate for the children's return to Moscow, she noted, came after she had received correspondence from the Spanish adults in the homes.[149] In an undated letter of the same year, Leonor Estévez, speaking on behalf of the Spanish adults in Home No. 1, wrote to Ibárruri, asking her to request that Malenkov hasten their return to Moscow from the Saratov region because of the health of the children, "catastrophic" economic conditions, the political and moral atmosphere among the population, hygiene, and a lack of cultural work.[150] It might be Estévez's letter that prompted Ibárruri's second appeal to Malenkov.

The Spanish communists clearly wanted to maintain a strong community among the niños, and concentrating them, for the first time, in one region would allow the PCE to provide political and cultural education and thus reduce the "moral problems" caused by the lack of supervision and good role models in the periphery. In her 1943 letter Ibárruri focused on education, health, and welfare; a year later she suggested that the lack of supervision had led to un-Soviet behaviour. She adopted Soviet rhetoric and returned to some of the central themes of the 1938 regulations discussed in chapter 1. In these two letters to Malenkov, Ibárruri stressed the need for greater material aid and supervision in order to improve daily life and behaviours; she brought local concerns to the attention of the highest levels of power and set in motion the young Spaniards' centralization in Moscow. She had learned to speak Bolshevik and act as an intermediary.

Given the general breakdown of discipline during the war, Soviet authorities likely also saw the benefit of bringing the Spanish children, youth, and adults under closer supervision. There was a sense that in Moscow they could be educated better in communist values. Adults could be monitored and removed if necessary. Teenagers could be placed in factories that had capable Komsomol oversight and taught Soviet values like love of labour and working with and for a collective. Children could move into boarding schools within easy reach of Moscow's educational and leisure opportunities and thus see the best the USSR had to offer. The newly relocated children's homes could be outfitted with workshops and visited by dignitaries, both Spanish and Soviet, to prepare the niños for life beyond the schools and as contributors to Soviet society. Authorities also likely hoped that concentrating the Spaniards in Moscow might help reduce resentment towards their relatively privileged position vis-à-vis Soviet children.

The re-evacuation process began on 24 April 1944 with Sovnarkom USSR resolution no. 466, "On Improving the Conditions of Work of the Children's Homes of Spanish Children Located in the USSR."[151] Potemkin's petition to RSFSR Sovnarkom chief Aleksei Kosygin earlier in the year made clear that Soviet authorities were following Ibárruri's request. They noted that war-time evacuations in far-flung locations made inspections and supervision much more difficult, and the Soviet government wanted to improve conditions and supervision in the homes after a nearly three-year evacuation, during which the children's daily lives had declined dramatically. The typically vague directives of the resolution obligated several agencies to provide food, transportation, accommodations, and even livestock for the homes that were relocating to the Moscow suburbs. An addendum to the resolution detailed the 1,000 to 1,600 pairs of shoes, shirts, trousers, and more that were promised for the children, but it said nothing about size, colours, or even how many of each were to be sent to each home.

The return to the Moscow region was problematic, but not as much as the initial evacuations eastward had been. Two months after Sovnarkom's 1944 re-evacuation resolution, Narkompros issued order no. 413, "On the

Table 5.1 Relocation of homes for Spanish children in 1944

Name and address of relocation	Students	Re-evacuation from
No. 1 Bolshevo station, Mytishchenskii raion, hospital 2960 VTSPS	281	Privolzhskoe village, Saratov oblast
No. 2 Town of Solnechnogorsk, hospital 2957 VTsSPS	156	Birsk, Bashkir ASSR
No. 3 Tarasovska station, Mytishchenskii raion, hospital 2686 Narkomzdrav SSSR	145	Iazykova village, Blagovarskii raion, Bashkir ASSR
No. 4* Krasnovidovo, Mozhaiskii region, former Spanish Home No. 2	222	Home No. 6, village of Orlovskoe, Markovskii region, Saratov oblast
No. 7 Village of Zheliabino, Istrinskii region, Children's Home "Kommunisticheskaia zhizn"	80	Village of Tundrikha, Zalesovskii region, Altaiskii krai
No. 8 [Istrinskii region]**	92	City of Miass, Cheliabinsk oblast
No. 10 settlement of Cherkizovo, Mytishchenskii raion, building of Tarasovskii detgorodok	142	Molotovsk, Kirov oblast

*GARF, f. 5451, op. 28, d. 40, l. 15 (1944) lists Home No. 4 as a sanatorium in Meleuz, Bashkir ASSR, with 118 students. The higher number of students listed in the table must have come from merging the students from Homes Nos. 4 and 6.
**No location is given, but below the original table it says Istrinskii region, which is in northwest Moscow oblast.
Source: GARF, f. A-2306, op. 70, d. 6084, l. 3.

Re-evacuation of Children's Homes for Spanish Children," which pinpointed the location of the new homes. Narkompros soon began to report on the re-evacuation process, and it quickly drew attention to the poor and even dangerous living conditions in the new Moscow-region children's homes. Most of the preparations proceeded as ordered, but Home No. 10 had to delay its return to the centre because the Moscow oblast Department of People's Education (MosOblONO) had yet to find a place to relocate the Soviet children who were currently housed in properties set aside for the Spanish home.[152] By late June 1944 the department in charge of the Spanish children's homes had taken possession of properties in Bolshevo, Golovkovo, and Tarasovka and received confirmation that two trains were ready for June and July transfers from the evacuated regions.

In July the head of Narkompros RSFSR's Administration for Children's Homes, I. Naumov, reported on the final re-evacuation details for the seven Spanish children's homes remaining in the RSFSR and on the intransigence of some Soviet organizations to accommodate them. Homes Nos. 1, 2, 3, 8, and 10 arrived at their new destinations near Moscow in time for the new school year. Homes Nos. 6 and 7, though also scheduled for an August return, remained unsettled.¹⁵³ Home No. 7 was in transit at the time of the 19 September report. The special sanatorium for Spanish children in Evpatoriia had deteriorated greatly during the war, and, despite requests, the military construction agency had still not completed capital repairs, because of a lack of labour and building materials. The new location of Home No. 6 in Krasnovidovo needed massive capital repairs, but Moscow State University, which possessed the buildings, had thus far refused to make repairs or furnish the building properly. Moscow City Department of People's Education (MosGorONO) had borrowed the furniture left behind at the Spanish home on Bol'shaia Pirogovskaia and provided it to City Orphanage No. 58. As a result of the Spaniards' privileged status, those Soviet orphans were being told that they had to return the furniture to the Spanish children, something that MosGorONO initially refused to do.

These examples tell us a great deal about the accommodation of the Spanish children. Higher-level organizations, both Soviet and Spanish, seemed well intentioned to meet the children's material needs, but lower-level units often did not have the means or inclination to fulfil mandates. Resources in the war-ravaged country were in short supply, and ministerial infighting was the norm. Although there was some resentment towards the Spaniards, most of the recalcitrance likely derived from competition for scarce resources during war and reconstruction and because authorities had prepared the population to perceive evacuees as potential enemies and spies.¹⁵⁴

As with the 1937–8 arrivals and the 1941 evacuations, Soviet institutions could not respond quickly or sufficiently enough to the vague and last-minute demands for action. The re-evacuation was "poorly organized," and as a result, two groups of children had to sleep "under the open sky or at the rail station" for nine to twelve days, while others waited to move into a building that "threatened to fall down." The children in Home No. 2 remained in the cold for an entire month, with boys sleeping in the cafeteria and girls with adults. Children in Home No. 1 slept two per bed. Not only was bed sharing a poor reflection on the means of the state and Stalin's care for his new children, but the sharing of beds and cups, such as in one boarding school where 176 children shared forty plates and drinking glasses, also increased the spread of diseases.¹⁵⁵ This type of "uncultured" living had been under attack since the first days of the revolution as peasants tried to learn new urban ways of living and working.¹⁵⁶ Many of the health problems that plagued the USSR after the Second World War were products, at least in part, of overcrowding, which joined lack of sanitation and personal hygiene as key factors inhibiting the control of epidemics.¹⁵⁷ Tuberculosis, which had been a constant problem since the arrival of the Spaniards and afflicted 85 per cent of the children, accompanied typhus and other infections of proximity on lists of ongoing maladies in the Spanish homes.¹⁵⁸

Near-constant change in the early days back in the Moscow region did not help in creating a stable living and learning atmosphere. Home No. 2, for example, increased enrolment by almost one-third over the previous year and now had two Russian children studying in its school. The additional children must have been younger because Home No. 2 now taught grades four to seven instead of starting in the fifth grade. This enrolment increase necessitated more personnel, but drawing, military studies, and physical culture had no teachers. Books, especially for Spanish history, were in short supply, lights flickered for only half the day in the cold building, and the school continued to operate in two sessions.[159]

By the end of the Second World War a host of systemic failures, including a lack of materials and personnel, had prevented the achievement of the goals set forth in 1938 to provide job-skills training, foster a positive (socialist) attitude to labour, create future builders of communism, or even instil individual self-discipline, the foundation of kul'turnost'. Students did not study after class, because there were few books, and there were also few toys with which to play. The paucity of teachers further limited motivation to study. After-class supervision was minimal, and the children went, without adults, to the market or the rail station, where they often caused trouble. The students had a "great aversion to studying Spanish" because none of the Soviet teachers knew Spanish, and most of the Spanish speakers had no pedagogical training, which led to the children "often being taught by [Spanish] postal workers, pharmacists, pilots, and others."[160] Narkompros was to have rewritten the Spanish-language curriculum in 1939, but "in the course of 6 years Narkompros RSFSR could not find the time to rework the program." Its evacuation to Kirov and loss of staff to the war likely caused some of the problems. "The success of the children is low," the inspector noted, "labour education is not being put into effect, labour workshops haven't been created, [and] discipline among the children is weak."[161] Many instructors had gone to the front, leaving boarding schools without vocational training.[162] One inspector drew a common connection between labour supervision and discipline: "During the current [1945] school year," he reported, "weak discipline in the classroom was the main severe deficiency."[163] The director of the boarding school lamented that the children still had not adopted the Soviet attitude to work. Not surprisingly, in the third quarter of 1945, 37 of the 146 students in one boarding school failed their courses, and in another school 73 of 176 students failed.[164] As important, the inspector found that training for life outside the homes, in the form of self-discipline and skill, was insufficient. The war had created conditions that severely hindered Soviet attempts to acculturate the growing Spaniards for the next stage of their lives.

Spanish educators, it seems, also adapted at uneven rates. Officials characterized many of them as lacking a desire for independent reading and as misusing Soviet property.[165] The importance of proper role models manifested as early as 1939, and Spanish adults continued to come under scrutiny well into the war years.¹⁶⁶ A report on the 1944–5 school year showed that Esther Álvarez from Laviana, who had no teaching certificate, taught mathematics and botany to students in the fifth grade and Spanish geography to those in the fifth to seventh grades. Her performance in mathematics left much to be desired, but the director forgave some of her shortcomings because of the "colossal difficulty of teaching children in different grades." However, she was also faulted for not making teaching plans, not showing any desire to improve her training, and not working with the collective. Thus, the failures were both personal motivation and a lack of resources (i.e., personnel) that left Álvares spread too thin. In 1946 she moved to Mexico.¹⁶⁷

Some Spaniards received better evaluations than did their Soviet counterparts. Mercedes París from Oviedo, a member of the Unified Socialist Party of Catalonia and a feminist activist, excelled in teaching fourth grade even though the children had come from different schools and therefore had uneven preparation. The future Spanish instructor at the Institute of Foreign Relations, Carmen Roure from Lerída, also received a glowing evaluation. The home director valued both teachers much more than some of the Soviet teachers who were said to lack discipline, were unprepared, and did not do enough with students outside of class.¹⁶⁸ Much as with the 1939–40 sackings, these evaluations suggest that officials defined success and failure less by nationality and more by one's ability to act as a Soviet should. A lack of Soviet virtues (e.g., discipline, order, and concern for students) united the failures of Spanish and Soviet staff. Dedicated and prepared teachers, regardless of national origin, received the highest praise. The presence of superior role models and supervision created a stark contrast with those adults who were deemed deficient.

Staffing was only one concern; Soviet institutions were keenly aware of the nexus between resources and the health and success of the children. Illness and material and educational deficiencies led the All-Union Central Council of Trade Unions (VTsSPS) to create an eight-point program for Narkompros RSFSR in 1945 to improve the health, learning, and behaviour of the children with the hope that they would become better Hispano-Soviet workers. The program included (1) moving Home No. 10 to a safe location, (2) quickly transferring the children who remained in Saratov and Bashkiriia to Moscow oblast and setting up a sanatorium in Evpatoriia, (3) fully outfitting homes and organizing labour workshops, (4) organizing additional resources for the children, (5) strengthening educational work among the Spaniards to develop a love of labour, organization, tidiness, discipline, and politeness, (6) working with personnel on their pedagogical training to help the children improve and succeed in school, (7) preparing the children better for independent lives after they left the homes, and (8) preventing directors from releasing talented older students into "independent lives" until the completion of a full middle-school education through grade seven.¹⁶⁹

The program sought to remedy several problems. The first two points focus on health and safety, important parts of Soviet concern for child welfare. The third and fourth points emphasize material provisioning and labour training. The fifth point stresses the importance of several behaviours that, with proper upbringing, would lead to kul'turnost'. Soviet authorities judged Spanish children as not appreciating the importance and value of labour for themselves or the collective, of lacking discipline and organization, and of displaying personal habits that failed to live up to Soviet norms of hygiene and comradely behaviour towards others. Children had to master these traits for a successful transition to a Soviet adulthood in which they would contribute to the common good through their labour. The sixth, seventh, and eighth points focus on home staff and their mentoring and preparation of children for life beyond the children's homes. The eighth point is most interesting because it signals a shift at the end of the war. Rather than encouraging students who had completed seventh grade to enter the workforce, as they had done during the war, this final point in the program encouraged the *retention* of the best students for additional education in the homes with an eye towards higher education and a profession.[170] Immediate assistance for the war effort was now secondary to developing skilled cadres for the USSR and Spain.

Here, as in the 1938 regulations for the boarding schools, we see an emphasis on meeting the children's material and educational needs while also preparing them for work and independent lives beyond the homes. The reiteration of these key points in 1945 indicates both the war-time failure to achieve the 1938 goals and the continued attention to the importance of safe and healthy material conditions to strengthen the body and mind. Proper education, attitudes, and behaviours were all essential to becoming Soviet. No longer was it expected that students could leave the boarding schools and go straight to the factories. The war had shown the need for the schools to focus more intently on developing their skills for labour and life. Independence, which necessitated discipline, tidiness, politeness, and love of labour, now became something learned through the homes' careful planning and supervision. Only when the war-time devastation was overcome could the necessary resources be mustered.

As a type of post-war normalcy returned to the boarding schools now located in the Moscow suburbs, material assistance increased dramatically and new priorities emerged. Dynamism marked the post-war years as the Soviet Union tried to recover from devastating destruction and losses. Post-war education clearly shifted in this period from viewing the students as refugees to rearing them fully as Soviet children, albeit with Spanish accents. Whereas between 1937 and 1939 Spanish language and culture had been high priorities, the war and the early post-war years promoted cultured behaviours, patriotism, Russian-language acquisition, and military and labour training. For example, following are the six main tasks for the 1947–8 school year in Home No. 1:

1 "to ensure a high-quality knowledge [among] students and their ideological-political orientation"
2 to strengthen "Soviet patriotism ... both in the schools and the homes"
3 to create a "united, friendly family" out of the new and old students
4 to strengthen "labour discipline" and "cultured behaviour"
5 to further the students' Russian-language skills and "cultured speech"
6 to coordinate the work of teachers and caregivers in the rearing of "literate, cultured, healthy" students[171]

The focus turned to modelling behaviours and raising the children as Russian-speaking Soviets. Although Spanish instruction continued, there is no mention of maintaining the students' Spanish heritage. In fact, the subtext of these points is an attempt to homogenize a heterogeneous group, and the dominant theme is to make them cultured.

The first two and last two tasks stress the Soviet demands for quality obuchenie in the Spanish homes. Graduates would leave the school understanding Marxism-Leninism, the Stalin Constitution, and a Soviet world view. The post-war period continued the inculcation of Soviet patriotism, especially as Western democracies began to move closer to embracing Franco. Consistent with the curriculum in Soviet non-Russian schools, the fifth task emphasized the importance of Russian as a lingua franca and the language of mobility. Highlighting "cultured speech" and "cultured behaviour" illustrates the concerns for kul'turnost' among Soviet citizens. The final task recognizes that to transform a child, curricular and extracurricular activities must work in tandem and reinforce one another. The ongoing and coordinated approach to teaching academic subjects and transforming ways of thought and behaviour occurred best in a controlled environment with close teacher and caregiver supervision of the children.

As students grew older and moved into the workforce during and after the Second World War, some homes closed, and the younger students were increasingly transferred to Home No. 1. This posed new challenges for the administrators charged with the health, education, and discipline of the Spaniards.[172] The new students in the third task were likely the Basque children – whom Soviets and Spaniards (and even some Basques) perceived as less disciplined and cultured – and children who had come from families that had less structure and discipline. One Spaniard, betraying his social position as the son of a Basque Republican pilot noted, "The sons of miners and workers came from the north, foul-mouthed, badly behaved, destroying the toilets, making extra work for our teachers."[173] Discipline, cultured behaviour, and a friendly family were becoming increasingly difficult to perpetuate as regional and class distinctions collided. Prior divergent experiences in Spain likely also posed a challenge to the creation of homogenized "family" units in the boarding schools. Participants have recalled, however, that their fellow students seemed to enjoy the performances of Basque, Galician, and Asturian cultures in the homes: "our children's group became rich with the representation of other regions of Spain."[174] Spaniards also struggled to merge their past selves with their present. The students simultaneously negotiated identifications as Spaniards and Soviets, which, along with other roles like gender, created varied experiences, understandings, and self-constructions as "earlier beliefs also continued to interact dynamically with the individual agency to shape subjectivity."[175] The rhetoric of "little heroes" in the propaganda published before their arrival could not completely replace some popular notions of hot-blooded and backward Spaniards.

Soviet party-state elites maintained their concern for the welfare of their young charges from their arrival in 1937 throughout the war and beyond. Massive amounts of resources were used to evacuate and accommodate them, but the children's survival in the early war years came from their own labour as much as anything else. The Comintern and PCE remained engaged reminding their Soviet counterparts about the material and political needs of the Spaniards. Without a doubt, the PCE had the greatest influence in the return of nearly all the Spaniards to the Moscow region where PCE members could nurture their compatriots and raise them with respect for their native language and customs. The Comintern and the Soviets shared many of the PCE's assumptions and hopes of raising the Spaniards with the ideological purity and cultural knowledge that would one day allow them to return to Spain and change its political course. The Soviets, however, also had a competing agenda: for as long as the Spaniards remained in the USSR, they had to become useful members of society. This meant becoming Hispano-Soviet, learning Russian well enough to survive independently, and embracing Soviet norms of behaviour and attitude towards labour and state property. The war years thus served as a major transition moment. Alejandra Soler recalled that in one way the war was positive because it forced the adults to learn Russian "whether we wanted to or not," which allowed them to lead a "more independent life" and become "more incorporated into Soviet society."[176]

Spanish children had to endure privation that was common for Soviet citizens but from which the Spaniards had been protected prior to 1941; they also began to learn more about life in the USSR. War-time obuchenie and vospitanie shifted the niños' non-Russian education towards more Russian-language instruction and labour and military training, combined with reinvigorated attention to disciplined minds and bodies, as preparation for a longer residency in and contributions to the USSR. As in other combatant nations, the children were being mobilized and were sacrificing their childhoods for the greater good.

The war years also led to the first significant number of Spanish adolescents leaving the homes and thus differentiated the experiences between younger and older Spaniards. Many of the niños de la guerra were no longer children, and hundreds had left the Spanish homes since June 1941. Some went to fight the Nazi invasion; others went to labour in fields and factories. The war years, therefore, divided the experiences of the niños in yet another way. Some adolescents transitioned to adulthood while others remained in the familial environment of the Spanish homes. The transition to adulthood was anything but smooth as Soviet largesse continued and counterproductively stunted the ability of many Spaniards to acculturate quickly and become fully independent in Soviet society. The symbolic fear or resentment of the "other" manifested both when the boarding schools evacuated during the Second World War into communities that could not accommodate them and when the now young adults moved into the workforce and lived primarily within Soviet society. These experiences, unintentionally, helped to further the refugees' identification as Spaniards. As we will see in the next chapter, the All-Union Central Council of Trade Unions (VTsSPS) had seen the effects of poorly trained Spaniards in war-time factories, and it also understood that in peacetime these students were to become the vanguard of the Hispano-Soviet intelligentsia and serve as important links with the Spanish-speaking world in the coming cold war. However, strong group identification among Spanish youth also posed problems when they were trying to integrate into Soviet society.

6 No Longer Children: Transitioning to Adulthood during War and Reconstruction

After leaving the Children's Home we mixed for the first time with the Russians, we slept, we lived and we shared everything with them.
      Immaculada Colomina Limonero, *Dos patrias, tres mil destinos*, 120

Recalling her time as a student in the Soviet Union, a woman named Juliana recognized one of the chief limitations of the special Spanish boarding schools: there had been little assimilation or preparation for adulthood. Both the in-class and the out-of-class training sought to create numerate and literate children with aesthetic sensibilities, a Soviet world view, a love of two countries, and a set of Soviet dispositions and behaviours. However, many of the oldest children who remained only two years in the homes before moving to labour training or employment did not learn Soviet norms and had only sporadic contact with Soviet life outside the homes. These teenagers, who, as in Soviet schools and orphanages, typically moved out of the institutions between the ages of fourteen and sixteen, were unprepared for independent lives. Isabel Álvarez recalled that she knew little of "life and less of domestic affairs, because I always lived in groups without greater concerns, and that change was too rough."[1] Complaints by the Spanish youth who now lived outside the homes and about their indiscipline and unwillingness to work were part of a larger Soviet discourse on the need to "harden" children and teach them to commit to the greater good. Throughout the 1930s "Soviet children were noticeably becoming spoiled," which was one factor in constructing the Labour Reserve system in 1940.[2]

 This chapter explores how Soviet institutions during and after the Second World War sought to transform the aging youth in the boarding schools from wards of the state into independent Soviets, all without the loss of their Spanish heritage. There was much continuity during the fourteen years (1937–51) of the Spanish boarding schools, but the Second World War forced officials to work specifically towards training Spaniards to behave like Soviets. Much as the end of the Spanish Civil War and the start of both the Second World War and the Russo-Finnish War in 1939 led to changes of personnel and education within the schools, the period also brought further changes to the older Spanish teenagers living and working outside the homes. Testimonies show that the Spaniards understood this period of transition as a time of disorder, lacking the control and protection they had come to expect in the boarding schools. For the first time in the Soviet Union, as they moved to vocational schools, factory labour, or the short-lived homes for Spanish youth, some experienced personal economic hardship and, as younger Spaniards also did, resorted to crime as a survival strategy.[3]

As adolescent Spaniards moved into war-time labour, Soviet and PCE leaders alike realized that the insularity of the dutifully cared-for children had created a culture of privilege that had not prepared the Spaniards for independent adult lives in which they had to provide for themselves and the collective; there was also a continuation of privileged care and subsidies in institutions like the new youth homes and the factories. During the Second World War, when their labour in fields, forests, and gardens was essential to their survival, the Spanish children began to learn and understand that professionalism, responsibility, and hard work would lead to benefits within the Soviet labour system. However, when they left the homes, they often had few skills that were transferable to employment.[4] The central committees of the Soviet Communist Party and the Komsomol realized that the relative isolation in the boarding schools had led to "youth [who] know little about our Soviet life [and] are little interested in social life in the enterprises."[5] Boarding schools and labour enterprises had to become the models and trainers of Spanish youth as they moved towards adulthood. Soviet institutions continued their preferential treatment of the older Spaniards, with stipends and free clothing, during a period of war-time crisis and shortages, and some Soviet citizens expressed their hostility or resentment. However, the institutions eventually crafted a system of material support and vospitanie for Spanish youth in factories and trade schools that mirrored the accommodation of the boarding schools.

Adolescence is a time of transition between childhood and adulthood in which one learns the skills necessary to join society and the workplace and to live independently from families, schools, and other institutions. Narkompros's model charter for children's homes in 1921 envisioned state homes that provided standard education, clubs and circles to keep students busy and entertained, and a series of workshops and gardens for labour training, "self-service," and "self-government" in which the children had chores and limited administrative responsibilities. The goal was not to warehouse these wayward children but rather to teach hard work, collective responsibility, and respect for manual labour as preparation for adulthood and life beyond the children's homes.⁶ Although Soviet children's homes often failed to live up to these aspirations, the Spanish children's homes and youth homes took up the challenge nearly two decades later. The Soviet accommodation of Spanish children now continued into adolescence, protecting them from the worst economic privation, with the unintended consequences of delaying their full acculturation into Soviet society.

Founding of Spanish Youth Homes

The two years prior to the German invasion of the Soviet Union brought two key changes. As we saw in chapter 2, a Russification process began in the homes that led to the sacking of many Spanish personnel in 1939 and 1940. Also in 1940, two homes for Spanish youth – one in Leningrad and one in Moscow – opened for the refugees who had completed the seventh year of school and had little interest in or aptitude for further academic schooling. Teenagers posed a particular problem for Soviet and Spanish authorities: they were becoming too old or unwilling to study full time, yet they also lacked practical skills to join the workforce and had acquired little Russian language in the one or two years in the boarding schools. The two short-lived Homes of Spanish Youth (1940–2), separated geographically and by mission from the children's homes, served as transition institutions for continuing some formal education, like language study, while also providing job training for at least half of the day. The young Spaniards were not truly independent and continued as wards of the state while receiving clothing, food, medical care, and cash stipends. The continuance of oversight and material subsidies prolonged the path to independence and led to some resentment from Soviet citizens who were living through the privations of war and reconstruction without additional assistance.

The increasing age of some students and the need for labour during war provided the impetus for this transition from children's homes to youth homes, but it was also part of a larger discussion about failures in Soviet education. During the Eighteenth Party Congress in March 1939, Molotov advocated for more practical work in Soviet schools because children were becoming soft and unable to work with their hands. The decline of labour education and the move away from valorization of workers in the mid-1930s had led to more students becoming interested in higher education and fewer imagining their future as factory workers. One interview project has shown that a minority of Soviet students wanted to enter factory labour or agriculture; half of the students preferred the arts or professions, especially engineering and nursing.⁷ With war on the horizon, the need for additional factory labour became acute, and some of the young Spaniards were willing to work to defeat fascism. Many other

Spanish children – like José Luis Vidal and Antonio Díez – went to factory work because they were unlikely candidates for further education. Other Spaniards, like Milagros Latorre, left the boarding schools under the assumption that workers would eat better than students would. However, she found at her tank factory in Saratov that the black bread – not the better white bread often found in the Spanish schools – was more water than bread, and most of the time there was nothing to eat.[8]

Failures during the Russo-Finnish War clarified the need for children to learn practical skills as well as to improve their basic education. Military training, order, and discipline affected both military and civilian life in adulthood. Therefore, in January 1940 the Komsomol Central Committee held a meeting on vospitanie work to ensure that students in all Soviet schools learned skills that were useful to society instead of "living off everything ready-made" and growing up "like hothouse plants," completely dependent on others.[9] In October 1940 the Supreme Soviet passed an edict on creating the Labour Reserves system to provide vocational education and a steady supply of new young workers.[10] Placing the August 1940 opening of the Spanish youth homes in the context of these other events shows that the youth homes were a particularist approach to a larger concern about Soviet adolescents' preparation for adulthood and the problems of Soviet child-rearing generally in a time of war. Much as the children's preparation in the Spanish homes mirrored that in the non-Russian schools, the Spanish youth now had institutions to mirror broader Soviet practices.

From the beginning, these hastily implemented Spanish youth homes suffered from several problems. Eight months after their founding, an April 1941 report showed 218 Spaniards in the Leningrad youth home. Of them, 138 worked and studied in the home, and seventy-six were in a trade school. Another ninety-nine had full employment. This Komsomol report touted that several Spaniards were making up to eight hundred rubles per month, which was a good wage for entry-level work. The cashier in the youth home was supposed to hold half of their wages, but in the first month this did not happen and many Spaniards spent their wages on wine and cheap cigarettes. Not surprisingly, another report suggested that residents in the homes for Spanish youth were frivolous and undisciplined. Perhaps because of the greater freedom, Isabel Álvarez Morán remembered that before the Nazi invasion "our life in the youth home was happy and promising."[11] In the Moscow youth home everyone studied, but only three of the girls worked. The report charged that the youth homes were not preparing Spanish youth for independent life, which was their mandate. Moreover, it stated: the adolescents have become "used to life with everything prepared"; the "Spanish children and grown-ups study very little Spanish history, their folk and national heroes, they are insufficiently acquainted with the facts of the struggle of the Spanish communist party and its leaders José Díaz and Dolores Ibárruri for the interest of Spanish workers, and also [only] a few of them are acquainted with the condition of workers and their children in Francoist Spain."[12] Furthermore, wasteful consumerism on alcohol and tobacco and low-levels of female employment showed a lack of socialization to Soviet ideals.

This summary points to several key concerns in the rearing of the Spanish refugees and shows the tension caused by the shift in emphasis in 1939 from the primacy of maintaining Spanish culture to that of preparing for Soviet society. On the one hand, the Komsomol report suggested, Spanish culture and history had been neglected. Yet, on the other hand, the Komsomol also complained that the young Spaniards had failed to acculturate as Soviets by becoming independent and prepared to enter the Soviet workforce, because in the children's homes "the students are poorly prepared for independent life."[13] In essence, the youth were not being forged into Hispano-Soviets conscious of the struggles in their country and trained linguistically and dispositionally to defeat Franco and spread socialism. Moreover, institutionalized students had become "used to life with everything prepared" for them, and they had not learned to take initiative or responsibility or learned the skills that would allow them to contribute to the collective. These concerns that youth entered factories at fourteen years old with virtually no skills were common throughout Soviet children's homes generally.[14]

Conscious of the importance of role models in positions of authority in children's institutions, Spanish communist leaders expressed clearly their displeasure with some Soviets and Spaniards' being considered to lead the new youth homes. Federico Pita, a "well-known leader" of the Unified Socialist Youth who repeatedly stressed the importance of Spaniards emulating their Soviet peers, argued that director Saveliev of children's Home No. 7 was a terrible choice to lead the proposed Leningrad youth home because he completely lacked the "political capacity ... for educating our [Spanish] youth."[15] For three years he had failed to take charge of the "petty bourgeois" Spaniards in Home No. 7, which consisted of "anarchists, republicans, and socialists." His lack of political work was a direct cause of the spoiled attitudes of the children. José María Meseguer Ramos from Zaragoza – a teacher, a PCE member since 1936, and the regional secretary of the Spanish Federation of Education Workers in Aragón during the civil war – was a better option, but he had a "dry and unfeeling character" and he "absolutely does not know the character of Spanish children."[16] Pita further noted that his economic management was lacking, and cited Meseguer's saving on bread – serving black instead of white – as a major drawback. Pita cited three problems with director Molotnikov of the Leningrad Youth Home: he provided poor food and medicine to the children, he insufficiently led political work among children and adults, and he was hostile to all the Spanish staff.[17] In short, Pita was asking for a new list of candidates. His critiques were not nationalist; Pita was Spanish, and he complained about both Soviets and Spaniards. What united all three candidates, according to Pita, was that in some way each of them failed to connect with the Spanish youth and/or staff in order to discipline, mentor, and provide for them. The children needed someone they could emulate as Makarenko had advocated.

In reports and letters from Spanish leaders we can see the root of some of the problems in the Soviet institutions' preparations of Spanish youth for independence. In what Soviet orphanage or boarding school was white bread – as Pita demanded of Meseguer – anything but a luxury, especially during the war? Moveover, the PCE advocated a three-week vacation between the time the Spanish youth left the boarding schools and the time they entered the youth homes: "They need rest because the transformation that has taken place in their life ... has been very abrupt."[18] Soviet citizens moved directly from schools to jobs or job training, without long vacations. Even though Pita had the best of intentions, his suggestions would have built an even greater sense of entitlement among the young Spaniards and led to their sense that they were "better than Russian children."[19]

Many of these problems with discipline and socialization in general predated the opening of the youth homes. In August 1940 Pita reported that many of the youth in Home No. 7 were from "petty bourgeois" families and aloof from Russian children; he likely was referring to Spaniards who had arrived in 1939 with the start of the Second World War in Europe. Unlike the 1937 arrivals, they had not yet been socialized into proper Soviet behaviour and attitudes.[20] His observation stressed two key points that resonated with Soviet authorities: role models and "political work" among children as important parts of the solution in correcting behaviours and creating kul'turnost'. In both cases, supervision played a key role in the upbringing and forming (or reforming) of youth. A plan at the end of 1940 sought to "strengthen their love for the Soviet Union and for the affairs of the Spanish people" and to "overcome religious, anarchistic and other vestiges." Unfortunately for the recipients of this program, the plan consisted of a series of twenty-two lectures on such topics as the working-class struggle, false "friends" (anarchists) of the Spanish labourers, how life began on earth, and more.[21] Thus, the solution to changing behaviour among the Spaniards was political education through lectures, something anticipated in the 1938 regulations and quite common in all Soviet school settings.

Staffing within youth homes was also problematic. One report noted that "agents of Franco" – a convenient discursive weapon – in the Leningrad youth home had tried to prevent four of the Spaniards from applying for Soviet citizenship, which had become more common since Franco's victory. Only the intervention of the Leningrad party and Komsomol managed to "isolate the enemies" and put the young Spaniards on the "correct path."[22] The number of Spanish adults finding refuge in the Soviet Union had increased since 1939, which necessitated greater vigilance in the Soviet institutions for young Spaniards against "hostile" elements who interfered with their daily life and education and led them to hooliganism and away from proper Soviet behaviours. This echoed concerns during the soft purge of personnel in children's homes discussed in chapter 2.

The quality of instruction, work, discipline, and working conditions became frequent topics of conversation between Comintern and PCE Spaniards. After inspectors in January and April 1941 noted problems in the homes, PCE leader Dolores Ibárruri received reports, the outcome of which may have set the stage for closure of the Leningrad youth home a few months later. One report complained that Spanish youth who had arrived in April 1939 had entered factories and institutes around the RSFSR where the Komsomol and other communists were trying to help them, but they had virtually no grasp of the Russian language. These new arrivals, at the end of the Spanish Civil War, had had little preparation, socialization, or hope for a successful transition into Soviet life. The children with only a few years in Soviet schooling often had poor Russian-language skills, they had never had to live on their own, and they had had limited contact with Soviet citizens beyond those who worked in the homes. One of them, eighteen-year-old Manuel Recarey, in a letter to José Díaz, admitted that the students' Russian skills were so low that the machine-construction school had to place the Spaniards in a special class.[23] They also needed political training, training for professions, and material aid.[24] Bernardo del Río recalled struggling because all the training was in Russian in his electromechanical technicum; Milagros Latorre's brother Rafa was sent to a factory because his Russian was too poor for him to study in a technical school.[25] VTsSPS realized that many concerns among Spaniards also arose from material conditions; therefore, it arranged to meet all the needs for food, clothes, and shoes and to provide a stipend, but such efforts "created in youth a parasitical attitude ... and weakened the stimulus to shockwork at the enterprises and for successful studies."[26] Seeking to solve one problem only reinforced another and seemed to reduce incentives, at least in the minds of some supervisors.

In a long report to Segis Álvarez (also of the Unified Socialist Youth) Pita noted numerous problems as the Spaniards entered trade schools. Some boys refused to cut their hair, at one enterprise only one of fifteen Spaniards showed up, and one Spanish male had to be confined to a punishment cell for several days. The conditions in which they worked were also terrible, but emulating their Soviet counterparts, Pita asserted, led the Spaniards to gain greater interest in work, study, and discipline. Some of the improvement also came from the Spanish youth policing themselves. For example, when the boy returned from the punishment cell and again failed to report to work, his comrades took him from his bed at night and made him sleep in the bathroom. They dressed him later and threw him into the street, which was enough for him to reform his behaviour. The cultural level of some of the adolescents also concerned Pita: they did not read, were filthy, and drank too much. Most striking of all, perhaps, was an "abnormal" girl named Chelo who had befriended some Germans "of a fascist ideology" and brought them to the house. Pita turned the matter over to the NKVD, and he emphasized that one of the Spanish Unified Socialist Youth (JSU) leaders needed to be present in the homes at all times.[27] The policy of meeting the material needs and supervising the political growth of the Spanish youth who were now in enterprises continued even as the young Spaniards and the adults seeking their transformation argued for greater independence.

An April 1941 letter from Pita and teacher Vincente Talón to Ibárruri called for even more assistance from the PCE to the youth home in Leningrad. Recent budget cuts had had devastating effects on food provisions, and some of the Spaniards were working twelve to fourteen hours a day, with most working at least eight hours. This left little time for study even for those who were so inclined; only half of the Spaniards were attending classes. The authors asked Ibárruri for more materials for political and cultural education, which were desperately needed. The kruzhki on current events and the history of the Bolshevik Party were utter disasters, and the youth were not well engaged in the social life of the home or their places of work. Despite these complaints, the general message in the letter was that there had been a gradual improvement in nearly all phases of the youth homes' work.[28] Thus, we see a continuation of the tensions that had started with the 1938 boarding school regulations, which had sought both to meet students' material and educational needs and prepare them for independent lives. The need to protect the Spanish refugees complicated the desire to make them engaged citizens (or at least residents) in the USSR. The Russo-Finnish War had precipitated a shift to greater labour education, but resource deficits continued to provide challenges for Soviet and Spanish institutions and their ability to train young workers. Moreover, many of these older youth had arrived only in 1939, or were amongst the oldest who had arrived in 1937–8, and had had relatively little time to learn to be Soviet; thus, age is one of the most important factors when differentiating memoirs and oral histories.

Evacuating Youth Homes

In the first days of the war the youth homes – much like the boarding schools – evacuated and eventually consolidated. The new home in Samarkand housed 145 youth until its closure in 1942. The evacuation was badly botched; what should have been an eight-day journey took thirty-eight days. On 27 October 1941 a two-car train left for Yaroslavl, then Bui, Galich, Kirov, Sverdlovsk, Omsk, Novosibirsk, and Barnaul with 145 students and 12 Spaniards who had no connection to the home. The director, Chembrovskii, evacuated by himself because none of the other personnel at the home wanted to leave. He called ahead to Kirov where Narkompros had evacuated, but no one came to meet the train, and the evacuees had no money or food. The krai government and party in Barnaul decided that the train should go further because there was no place for a school in their town. The train next travelled to Tashkent via Alma-Ata. However, the Spaniards were not taken in, in Tashkent, either.[29] Similar to the evacuation of the children's homes, the paucity of advanced planning led to chaos and suffering.

On 1 December 1941 the train finally arrived in Samarkand after thirty-eight days. Food had been scarce on the journey, and youth and staff had to grab soup or kasha at one of the many stops. At one point, there was no food for a forty-hour period. Even though officials in Samarkand knew the youth were coming, nothing was done by the city or oblast educational officials for their arrival. The evacuees had to stay in the train cars until they finally moved into the old Jewish school, where there was no water, no electricity, and no one to assist them. They took their meals in a factory cafeteria, but the food was so bad that the students rioted. Director Chembrovskii reportedly appealed to everyone, including the Uzbek Sovnarkom, but nothing came of his protestations.[30]

For nearly three months, Narkompros, the Komsomol, and the Communist Party (presumably with some input from the PCE and leaders of the Spanish youth like Pita) deliberated what to do with Spanish youth in evacuation. Ironically, given the discussion of 1941 about the problem of isolating Spaniards from their Soviet counterparts, in April 1942 the Central Committee of the Soviet Communist Party suggested creating a special trade school just for Spanish youth in Tashkent, which would have prolonged their isolation from Soviet society. This plan was scrapped a month later.[31] A May 1942 proposal suggested stipends for Spanish youth to augment their wages: 250 rubles for Spaniards in technicums and 150 rubles to those working in various enterprises.[32] Without family on whom they could rely, like Soviet citizens could, the Spaniards needed these stipends for their survival. As we will see, this perpetuated their financial dependency on the party state, and they remained a privileged minority and often acted as such, which created resentment among some of their Soviet comrades.

In June 1942 the central committees of the Soviet Communist Party and Komsomol met again to discuss the fate of the remaining Spanish youth home in Samarkand. This was part of a general complaint about the unfavourable climate for all Spaniards evacuated to Uzbekistan, Kyrgyzstan, and Tajikistan and the need to move them elsewhere. A specific complaint concluded that the Spaniards' isolation in the special institutions like the youth home continued to separate them from Soviet society and hindered acculturation.[33] A draft proposal underscored the separation between Spaniards and Soviet daily life by focusing on problems with Russian-language acquisition. The central committees proposed that intensive Russian-language instruction start in sixth grade so that on completion of seventh grade the Spaniards would be prepared to go directly into trade schools with sufficient linguistic proficiency. Narkompros eventually made Russian the primary language in sixth and seventh grades, although in most schools Spanish remained in the language, literature, history, and geography courses.[34] Moreover, the committees called for a full review of all Russian-language instructors and for a better contingent of language teachers in the Spanish homes. The war revealed that language deficiencies were a major impediment to Sovietizing the Spanish youth. Much like it was for their non-Russian Soviet counterparts, Russian was becoming the lingua franca and a passport to mobility.

The central committees concluded that for the time being, despite the perceived disconnect between Soviet life and the youth who had lived in Spanish homes for the last five years, Soviet party officials should relocate all 140 students who had completed seventh grade from the boarding schools to trade schools. Furthermore, the committees discussed closing the one remaining Home for Spanish Youth in Samarkand. These youth would then join the 140 Spaniards in a trade school. However, there was also a recognition that the children's homes, and particularly the Pioneer and Komsomol members in them, needed to take more responsibility in preparing the Spaniards for their transition out of institutional care and into an independent life in Soviet society. Critiques, whether from Spanish or Soviet sources, spread blame around. The youth needed to conduct themselves better, yet inspectors also realized that the paucity of resources and role models raised additional barriers to Sovietization.

In June 1944, as Soviet troops pushed westward, 1,227 Spanish youth resided in seventeen separate cities, as far as 1,700 miles apart from Moscow to Samarkand. Tbilisi (307), Saratov (271), and Ufa (226) accommodated the most youth, followed by Tashkent (100) and Samarkand (91). In cities like these, Spaniards had comrades. In cities like Batumi, Gruz, Makharadze, and Stavropol with only one or two Spaniards, life must have been lonely.[35] Indeed, one woman recalled life in post-war Kirov where she did little more than read; she only saw a Spaniard when she was passing through Moscow on vacation or visiting her sister in Evpatoriia.[36] For many of these youth, there would have been no oversight from the PCE, which was hundreds or thousands of miles away.

Eighteen months later, the geographic distribution of Spanish youth was completely different. Whereas 1,227 youth lived outside the Spanish-boarding-school system in mid-1944, 1,660 Spaniards had left the homes by the end of 1945, and the latter figure does not count the 88 youth who were in the army or prison or who were neither working nor studying in 1944. Only 6.5 per cent of Spanish youth resided in Moscow in mid-1944; yet, a year and a half later, 89.5 per cent of youth (1,486 of 1,660) lived in either Moscow or the Moscow region. Samarkand, formerly home to 91 Spanish youth, now had only 9. Tbilisi's 307 Spanish youth had been reduced to 50, Saratov's contingent had declined from 271 to 3, and all of Ufa's 226 Spanish youth resided elsewhere.[37] Thus, we see a dramatic reversal of the war-time evacuation soon after the end of hostilities. Similar to the return of Spanish children from evacuation, the concentration of Spanish youth in Moscow was now higher than at any time, including at their arrival in 1937, thanks to Ibárruri's intervention with Malenkov.

Spanish Youth and Their Transition to Labour

War demands had mobilized many of the Spanish youth for labour, but the greatest shift in labour and location came at war's end as the niños were coming of age. Although one could portray this as forced labour for the Spaniards, and indeed some commentators have made just that argument,[38] it is quite clear from the evidence that many of the children had no desire or aptitude for further academic education and thus followed the same path as that of Soviet children of the same age. Even before the war there had been regular reviews or "characterizations" of children who had reached the seventh grade and who were fourteen to sixteen years of age. In the evaluations the boarding-school staff commented on the child's academic aptitude, discipline, physical and psychological health, and political views. A final statement generally stated the child's hopes after leaving the homes, whether it be for higher education or labour.[39] Some Spaniards recall that they refused the higher education suggested by the PCE and chose labour instead.[40] However, there is evidence that some students had hopes and dreams beyond what their academic record suggested was probable.

From a small sample of sixteen teenage Spaniards in Home No. 6, we can begin to unpack the values that were most important to Soviet investigators. Significantly, the characterizations show a clear understanding that children are malleable and transformable, that nurture trumps nature. Four of the youth in the sample were from anarchist families, which was a dangerous lineage in the USSR in 1941. María Fernández from Oviedo – who later served as a machine technician in Cuba – was described as "exceptionally capable" with a good attitude and good grades. Celestina Marinero from Bilbao "began to feel the horrors of capitalist domination" from an early age and actively pursued change. She was "exceptionally disciplined," became a leader in the Pioneer unit and in the children's council of the home, and was a talented organizer and agitator. Her academic work was excellent, for which she won awards. She was politically conscious, honest, and self-critical. She condemned her father's anarchist viewpoints and became a true "daughter of the Spanish freedom-loving people. An ardent supporter of communism."[41] These two children of anarchists, though only in the Soviet Union for less than four years, had managed to internalize Soviet concerns for discipline, self-criticism, academic fortitude, and political consciousness. Marinero, in fact, became a member of the PCE and the Soviet Communist Party.[42]

Although a lack of academic success sometimes led to more critical evaluations of the Spaniards, frequently it was the behaviours and attitudes that drew condemnation. For example, Luciano Bartolomé from Baracaldo, the son of a machinist who belonged to an anarchist party, initially was a diligent member of the Pioneers and had a talent for mathematics and literature. However, he soon went astray. He was described as "selfish and stubborn" and as one who had fallen in with a group of "disorganizers" in the home; they had pulled him away from his Pioneer duties. He was "secretive" but also "persuasive," with an "anti-Soviet" mood.[43] Although this is a rather damning portrait of the boy, he was not primordially bad because of his father's politics. He had been a conscious Pioneer until other students had led him astray. Here we can see Soviet notions of the malleability of children and the importance of role modelling. The boy learned to overcome his parent's political errors, only to be led down the path of anti-Soviet behaviours and attitudes.

In a final example we can see more clearly how a child transformed. Pedro Marinero, younger brother of Celestina, had arrived from Bilbao with "anarchic qualities," but through "systematic and purposeful influence" it was possible to instil in him "the elements of discipline, organization, and diligence necessary for learning" in the children's home. He was an excellent student and had begun to show interest in political issues. Pedro was still in the process of becoming an ideal Soviet youth. He had achieved discipline, organization, and diligence, yet he did not willingly accept the advice of adults and only admitted mistakes when there was "conclusive evidence."[44] Although these character flaws might seem minor, they were important in Soviet education. The Soviet regime feared too much initiative in children and youth and required the guiding hand of adults to keep students from going astray.[45] Pedro's inability to admit mistakes is another way to say that he was not self-critical. From the 1930s on, *samokritika* (self-criticism) was an essential trait for self-improvement. One had to learn not only how to accept the critiques of others but also to recognize shortcomings in oneself and to make the appropriate changes on the path to transforming into the new Soviet person.[46]

In these interviews of fifteen- to eighteen-year-old Spaniards we can also learn something about their hopes and dreams. Nearly all the students in this sample had applied for Soviet citizenship and were requesting placement in a trade school (mostly in automechanics), an energy technical college, or in aircraft construction. Moscow and Leningrad were the only destinations they had considered. Except for Luciano Bartolomé, who died in Tbilisi in February 1944, all went on to technical or higher education.[47] In this sample there is only one case in which the interviewers clearly altered a student's wishes. Ángel Soto Rodríguez from León, according to his characterization, expressed a desire to "study only in Leningrad," but not in a specific field of study. However, the reporters stated unequivocally, "We recommend he continue his studies in an agricultural technical school, in the field of rabbit breeding or poultry farming."[48] Although eighteen-year-old Ángel was interested in international political affairs, an important trait for a good Soviet, he was not a successful student and sometimes had an "unhealthy mood," which often is code for asocial behaviour or incomplete acceptance of Soviet communism. In this case, though, the "unhealthy mood" does not necessarily carry political connotations. The report makes it clear that his mood was likely a result of his physical disability, a missing right foot, and his feelings of inadequacy, not his political disposition. He had had a rough life, too. His mother had died when he was two, and his father had died at the front in Spain. Ángel was an active member in the Komsomol, the children's council, and the sanitary commission in the home, so he was politically active. The highly specific recommendation for animal husbandry likely stemmed from his poor academic record and the fact that, as a child in Spain, he had served as a village shepherd. Raising rabbits and chickens would not require as much walking for this child with one foot. Moreover, although disability was used as a visual symbol in the Soviet Union's welfare state, the most disabled typically were isolated and invisible in Soviet society. Yet, work was promoted as a transformational endeavour and a right – and then an obligation – for all citizens who could work in some capacity.[49] Manuel Arce, who had lost both legs when he was hit by an oncoming tram as he clung to the side of his overcrowded tram, eventually received prosthetics and went on to become a neuroradiologist.[50]

Of course, we cannot know if during the interviews the home personnel suggested a particular path for all children or whether desires were freely stated. Some respondents have noted that, even when they were given the chance to study after the boarding schools, the PCE in particular steered students to science, construction, and engineering instead of stated preferences for something deemed less useful to a future Spain, like choreography.[51] They "disposed of our lives and destinies at will," recalled one former student, and decided who worked, who studied, and who received privileges.[52] Many chose night school or correspondence classes so that they could continue some education while also working full time.[53] Spaniards characterized their classmates who went on to higher education as "privileged" and "connected."[54] However, much of the divergence between higher education and other work was simply a matter of age. With the end of the war and with demobilization, there was a decreasing labour shortage. Spaniards in the USSR were more likely to go to university if, for example, they had been under fourteen years old during the war. A student's aptitude and behaviour mattered, too.[55] Engineer and recipient of the Order of Lenin Virgilio Llanos has noted that Spaniards had greater access to higher education than did their Soviet counterparts, which also likely kept Spaniards out of poverty. According to Manuel Arce, scholarships were twice as generous for Spaniards, and they only had to pass an entrance exam; the rank of their score did not matter for admissions.[56] Another former student noted numerous benefits – not least among them, meeting his Russian wife – from his training at a railroad technicum and the Higher School of Transport Engineers in Moscow; yet, he added that the post-war years were difficult for many Spaniards in the capital because they had no family to help them.[57]

Given the poor academic performance of many of the children, however, it seems highly unlikely that many would have wished for more formal schooling. We must remember that most of the Spanish child refugees came from working-class families in Asturias and the Basque lands. University education, or even advanced general education, had not been family priorities or even dreams – and certainly not attainable – for most in Spain.[58] Therefore, the combination of their family backgrounds and the lack of success in the Soviet school system and in acquiring Russian likely caused most of the least successful students to realize, much like their Soviet counterparts, that a trade was their best path as they completed middle school.

Daily Life of the "Independent" Spanish Youth

Did the regime still have an obligation to the older youth who were supposed to be independent like their Soviet counterparts? Providing age-appropriate cultural and daily-life services continued for the Spaniards now living outside the purview of Narkompros's boarding schools. The enterprises where they worked and trained were supposed to take on some of the responsibility. Thus, the central trade union, VTsSPS, became key in accommodating the Spaniards.

As with the Spanish children, the relocation of working Spanish youth to Moscow at the end of the Second World War led to more supervision, albeit with limited resources. When VTsSPS inspected the facilities for Spanish teenagers in 1945, it found much that could be commended and much that caused dismay. It reported on the availability of material goods, the condition of sleeping quarters, the quality and quantity of food, and the work performance.[59] As the homes for Spanish youth closed, the factories and training schools were told to ensure adequate supplies of beds, bookshelves, nightstands, tables, chairs, lamps, clocks, teapots, and more in their dormitories. Clothes and linens were to transfer with the youth.[60] Of course, plans and realities are often quite different during the chaos of war and the devastation left in its wake. Lacking a family network and sufficient pay, Spanish youth relied on the Soviet state for nearly all their needs. This led to resentment from some Soviet citizens; yet, when aid did not materialize, the Spaniards acted to close the gap. For example, the youth in war-time Tashkent reported that they had failed to receive ration cards for bread and soap, leading one Spaniard to go without bread for an entire month and many others to buy soap at "speculative prices" at the market. The Soviet ideal of cleanliness could only be met through un-Soviet behaviour – speculation. When one adolescent was in hospital without adequate food, it was his Spanish comrades who visited every day and brought food even though they were not earning a salary in their apprenticeships.[61]

During the war the provisioning of the Spaniards had faltered, as had some public support for them. Increased anti-fascist rhetoric during the war had apparently led some Soviet citizens to conflate the Spanish refugees with Franco. Spanish youth were tired of working twelve-hour days, especially when Soviet citizens were calling them fascists, anti-Soviet supporters of Franco and Hitler, and bourgeois.[62] This is understandable because ethnonational groups in the USSR – like Volga Germans, Crimean Tatars, and Chechens – were now targeted as potentially disloyal groups. This signalled that "foreign" national groups could be enemies en masse. Furthermore, antagonism likely resulted from the competition for scarce resources. The limited aid that Spaniards received from the state came at the cost of even less aid to Soviet citizens.

Concentrating the Spaniards in Moscow made allocation of resources and supervision easier and removed them from peripheral regions where their foreignness might be more noticeable. When the war ended in May 1945, the accounting of the Spaniards began. As many of the Spanish refugee children had reached their fourteenth birthday since 1937, only 1,037 children remained in the children's homes of the 2,895 who had lived there before the war. Narkompros admitted that during the war it had lost track of children and that 239 young Spaniards still had not been found. Of the 2,895 Spaniards, 148 were currently studying in institutions of higher learning (VUZ), 282 in technicums, and 376 in trade (RU) and factory training schools (FZO), and 653 were working in industry. Seventy of the former boarding-school students had served in the Red Army, and the same number had died in the Leningrad blockade.[63] Fourteen of the Spaniards were in German camps, forty-four had died in the last six years, and fifteen remained in Soviet prisons for desertion, speculation, and theft.[64] Owing to the diversity of experiences, work with the Spaniards since the war had taken on a "more complicated character."[65]

In July 1945 the VTsSPS secret resolution "On Measures for Aiding Spanish Youth and Children" tried to address many of the material conditions that had often led to complaints. The resolution compelled numerous factories to provide specialist training, to repair and outfit dormitories, and even to organize the cleaning of underwear. Furthermore, factories were to pay for entertainment in the form of concerts, films, and clubs. The sports club Kryl'ia Sovetov had a role, too; the resolution demanded that it form a sports team from among the Spaniards and provide all the necessary equipment.[66] Again, we see a dual concern for both material conditions and training, here doubling as entertainment. It was at this point that a mass recentralization of Spanish youth occurred. Even Molotov acted, demanding that 195 additional Spanish youth relocate to Moscow.[67] Only when many more children and youth had been returned to Moscow oblast did VTsSPS and representatives of the PCE start mass political and cultural work among them. Reports noted behavioural improvements approximating the ideal Soviet attitudes set forth in 1938 for labour and kul'turnost'. In the attempt to create independent lives for Spanish youth, however, both Spanish and Soviet organizations mirrored the boarding schools' systems of accommodation, supervising and meeting their material needs and delaying the development of fully independent lives. Five months later, VTsSPS requested that Narkompros teach carpentry, sewing, and metalworking so that students in the children's homes could attain skills early and thus be prepared for factory work. Moreover, if there were more supervisors, particularly in the aviation factories with their high concentrations of Spaniards, workers' behaviour and performance might improve.[68] The proposals signal a realization that the Spanish refugees, who did not have the support of extended family networks like their Soviet counterparts did, needed a bridge between childhood in boarding schools and adulthood in factories. Children's homes needed to begin teaching workplace skills, and workplaces needed to continue vospitanie.

All the institutions, whether they be factories or schools, provided Spaniards with additional clothing allowances. This speaks to the low wages but also to the state's interest in maintaining the Spaniards' standard of living beyond the children's homes. The exact nature of the clothing gifts varied by institution, but the norm was for each of the Spaniards to have at least two sets of clothing and shoes at any time. As these new workers were teenagers, the chance of growing out of the offerings was quite high. Moreover, when one did receive new shoes and clothes, they were not necessarily the correct size.[69] Many youth also had to have special clothing for their work. Some enterprises provided suits, padded jackets, and multiple types of footwear (e.g., boots, *valenki*, sandals).[70] A report from November 1945 stated that 1,141 young Spaniards were working in factories, workshops, and educational institutions in Moscow and the Moscow region. For the year, they received 6,200 orders of clothes, shoes, and underwear. The 364 Spanish youth in trade schools and factory training schools received full uniforms. Even the youth who left for

Mexico earlier in the year received a full allotment of clothing and two thousand rubles in cash.[71] Thus, an emphasis on material conditions remained during this transitional stage of youth, and the provisioning of those leaving for Mexico suggests that the regime was concerned even for those few Spaniards leaving the USSR who would no longer contribute to Soviet society but who would become part of a larger international network of Hispano-Soviets and tell of their experience in the USSR.[72]

Conditions for the former students who were now in industry or in further training or education varied dramatically. Some of the institutions served as perfect examples of what VTsSPS inspectors had hoped they would find. In enterprises such as the Kapranov shoe factory and Proletarskii Trud metal works, the Spanish youth were living in comfortable dormitories (usually, but not always, separate from their Soviet counterparts), receiving three tasty and filling meals each day, generally performing their jobs well, maintaining order and discipline, and engaging in after-work activities such as chess, string bands, and newspaper writing.[73] Many of these Spanish workers were even singled out as superior workers who exceeded their assigned production quotas. In some cases, the Spanish contingent fulfilled over twice their production quota. Two Spanish youth in Tbilisi fulfilled planned targets by ten and fifteen times the requirement, respectively.[74] One Spaniard remembered, "There was a brigade of our Spanish girls that for all the Soviet Union had the name ... Stakhanov ... they put the red flag on [their] machine." Others recalled with pride receiving the Veteran of Labour award and seeing photographs of Spanish workers in Moscow's Park Kul'tury.[75] Clearly, these Spaniards had transitioned well to life beyond the homes. As is common in bureaucratic reports of the era, however, a litany of problems shortly followed the praise.[76]

Systemic barriers created problems for transitioning Spanish youth to independence. For example, some of the Spaniards had no specialization and had received little in the way of job-skills training in the boarding schools and therefore received low salaries. In these cases, either they could not afford three meals a day or their entire salary went for food with nothing left for other expenses.[77] The variety of experiences was completely dependent on one's circumstances. Soviet workers with nearby relatives relied on extended family networks to cling to survival in times of shortage, and the boarding schools in the post-war period heaped even more resources and opportunities on the Spaniards. For the young Spaniards at work or in higher education, VTsSPS supplied stipends. Spaniards studying in places like Moscow State University, where eleven Spaniards resided in 1945, received monthly stipends of 200 to 250 rubles, for a total outlay of 30,320 rubles for these university students.[78] Spanish youth in industry received a 300 ruble stipend for each of the first six months of employment, for a total of 82,000 rubles in stipends. The average annual stipend for these students and workers amounted to 2,451 rubles. When one factors in 252,000 rubles for clothing allocations, the annual state expense from VTsSPS for Spanish youth, not counting those still in children's homes, was 4,113,300 rubles for their material needs, or nearly twice the outlay of state benefits for single mothers with many children (2.1 million rubles).[79]

The language of reports shows both disappointment and frustration at the ingratitude of some Spaniards. A factory had "created beautiful living conditions, notably a newly repaired, well-equipped, warm dormitory," where Spaniards had three good meals a day, but "many of the Spaniards didn't value this ... [They] often skipped work in large groups, hung around the market, got into fights, got drunk, chased girls." They stole from the factory and threw explosives near the dormitories: "[Soviet] workers are afraid to go past the Spaniards' dormitory." The report's author noted a recurring cause: coming out of the Spanish homes, Spanish youth were "completely unprepared for independent life and labour."[80] However, one Spaniard recalled his illiterate Soviet counterparts blaming him and other Spaniards for their own mistakes.[81]

Unacceptable and, in some cases, dangerous behaviour was bad enough, but many Soviets also objected to the vast sums being spent on refugees who failed to follow community norms. Already in 1942 one Rachinskaia from the Uzbek Narkompros was so incensed that the Spaniards leaving the boarding schools were receiving stipends that she began to complain up the chain of command, and she was successful for a time. In her region, only the Spaniards continuing into higher education would receive stipends; those who were working were supposed to fend for themselves on their salaries and ration cards, just like Soviet workers did.[82] A Soviet employee in Home No. 6 wrote to Stalin, asking for his assistance in addressing the animosity between Soviets and Spaniards. He detailed the privileged life of the spoiled Spaniards who received far better clothing and food than the Soviets did, how the Spaniards flouted the law and regulations, and how many of the free and subsidized goods found their way back onto the market.[83] Evidently, some people with proximity to the Spaniards, either as teachers or administrators or simply living near the boarding schools, perceived the material provisioning of the Spaniards as a poor use of resources during the dire war-time and post-war economic crises. Moreover, with limited supervision, some Spaniards were living beyond the law. These private letters repeated many of the issues raised in official reports and noted in Spanish oral histories.

We can never know how widespread this type of reported behaviour was among the Spaniards, but because the former refugees themselves also recall that they behaved poorly and felt privileged, we can be certain that the reports are accurate to some degree. For example, Araceli Sánchez Urquijo from the small town of Sestao near Bilbao had moved to the Moscow Home for Spanish Youth in 1940 and recalled later that many of her friends went to work in factories when the war came. They were hungry, and studying was hard, but the "Spanish children were privileged. For example, we had the first-class ration card," which allowed for more food.[84] Isabel Álvarez recalled that during the siege of Leningrad her youth home was especially privileged to have high-vitamin pineapple extract, a bread ration, and a stove to heat the soup and bread. When a child died, however, the child's bread ration had to go to the gravedigger.[85] Manuel Arce claimed that "just because we were Spanish we were privileged." He had "better ration cards than the Russians ... [they] always gave us the best they had."[86]

The term *los enchufados* (the connected) was common among Spaniards; they understood the system of hierarchy, prizes, and incentives and sought to improve themselves and their work in order to obtain benefits.[87] They learned that work qualifications – and especially party membership – granted one access to better salaries, social benefits, special recreation, and commodities like high-quality meat and fruit, books, and high-demand tickets.[88] Therefore, some youth used their free time to study and to raise their work qualifications while also engaging in social and political activities.[89] On the other extreme, former refugees remembered gangs of Spaniards in Ufa volunteering to carry groceries for shoppers at the central market, only to then steal the food.[90] Hungry staff members in the schools also were not above stealing the food meant to feed the children.[91] One woman remembers stealing a kilogram of ice cream every day from her factory because "nobody puts their hands on us [Spaniards]." Selling her handiwork, in this case sewing, at markets or to private clients was a way to augment her income.[92] This set of experiences illustrates both the importance of luck – like living in a good home – and individual agency to get ahead, either through hard work or theft. These examples also suggest that whereas some Spaniards internalized normative Soviet behaviours, others ignored them because of need or disposition.

Even within the ranks of the 1937–8 Spanish refugee children there were vast differences in their perceptions of Soviet assistance in the post-war era. Some Spaniards claimed that they received double the typical Soviet stipend while others remembered that life was worse in the early 1950s than during the war because stipends were too low: "These years [the early 1950s] were something terrible ... much much hunger ... a terrible hunger."[93] This differed tremendously from the lives of Spanish children in the Bolshevo boarding school outside Moscow. One girl who studied there noted that after the "Stalin reforms" of 1948, ration cards disappeared, harvests were abundant, bread was available, and "everything ... it was all very good."[94] She lived in a home that was well equipped with parallel bars, boxing equipment, skis and skates, and all the material needs for thirteen different sports clubs – for boxing, hockey, gymnastics, track and field, chess, and shooting, for example.[95] One's position within the network of Soviet institutional care determined one's living standards.

Financial subsidies, clothing allotments, and other material aid went some way in alleviating the need for theft or the desire to shirk work duties, but, as in the children's homes, supervised upbringing and nurturing, or vospitanie, was another crucial element for improving behaviour and kul'turnost' as the USSR moved from the "indulgent" model of the 1920s to the "disciplinary" model of the Stalin years.[96] There remained a tension between keeping the Spaniards under Soviet wing and allowing them more freedom. On the one hand, some argued that, after finishing their studies at the children's homes, the Spaniards should lead independent lives just like any Soviet adolescent, but, on the other hand, the VTsSPS investigations, as we have seen, revealed persistent criminality among some Spaniards.[97] Under these circumstances VTsSPS ordered that vospitanie had to continue among the Spaniards and directed Komsomol and party members to help Spanish youth learn to behave like Soviets. This process of provisioning, propagandizing, and transforming the poor behaviour of young workers was consistent with the approach to Soviet youth.[98]

Since most Spanish children and youth had transferred to Moscow at the end of the war, VTsSPS was able to increase its supervision of mass work among them. Spanish clubs, houses of culture, and lectures and reports on political and general topics served as the chief vehicles for strengthening discipline and transforming the Spaniards into young men and women who behaved as Soviets. This mass political work would have been familiar to the Spaniards because it had been a point of emphasis during their time in the children's homes. Representatives of the PCE often gathered activists from among the Spaniards, discussed important issues of the day, and fostered a sense of community through entertainment and common experiences. In January 1945, as more youth began to join the Spanish children in Moscow, the Kremlin Hall of Columns hosted a New Year's celebration for the Spaniards after their four-year absence, and later the Spaniards organized a dance of their own. On another occasion, a PCE representative gave a talk about the fourteenth anniversary of the Spanish Republic to the older Spaniards.[99] "Because the greater part of the Spanish youth are concentrated in Moscow and Moscow oblast," noted the head of mass culture work in VTsSPS, "raising the educational [*vospitatel'noi*] work among [Spanish youth] has significantly improved."[100] VTsSPS had recognized the difficulty of educating Spaniards who had been dispersed across the USSR during the war, and their possibilities were now concentrated in Moscow. We cannot know how effective the increased cultural and educational opportunities were; however, this seems to support research that has shown how "participation in collective cultural activities could serve positively to stimulate national feeling among exile communities."[101]

The Aviakhim or Chkalov Club established by Luis Balaguer, Jesús Sáiz, and Enrique Zafra on Leningrad Prospekt in Moscow was the most tangible expression of continued vospitanie and paternalism beyond the homes.¹⁰² Initially the club of Factory No. 30 in Moscow, it transitioned in mid-1945 – with an initial 100,000 ruble outlay from the Fund for Aid to the Women and Children of Spain – into a club for Spaniards instead of Soviets. PCE members administered the club.¹⁰³ The Chkalov Club contained a library and a variety of rooms for dance, theatre, films, and chess. These spaces accommodated 1,500 people and allowed for artistic exhibitions, literary discussions, and commemorations of scientists, painters, writers, and more. Music and dance performances included both classical and regional favourites from the Basque Country, Asturias, Catalonia, Andalucia, and others.¹⁰⁴ The Chkalov Club introduced further cultural work to the Spaniards. There were free performances of Spanish classics by writers such as Cervantes, Lope de Vega, and Pedro Calderón and by composer Ruperto Chapí. Visitors watched recent Spanish films that were not available in the rest of the USSR and which contained themes beyond those allowed by socialist realism.¹⁰⁵ Archival reports suggest that the club and the good working conditions led Spaniards in Factory No. 30 to average 246 per cent of their production quota; yet, desertion and truancy remained a problem even there.¹⁰⁶ The club continued to celebrate regional particularism as part of a united Spanish culture, much like the Soviet Union did for its non-Russian regions.

When the Chkalov Club opened, it functioned much like the extracurricular opportunities in the Spanish boarding schools. There were political lectures, interest groups for music and dance, and a place to socialize. Now that most Spaniards were not living and working in Spanish-centred institutions, one crucial difference was that the Chkalov Club became a place in which workers who had less daily contact with their native customs could speak Spanish and preserve their traditions, culture, and folklore.¹⁰⁷ Fifty-five kruzhki were operating in various enterprises to teach party history and the history of Spain, and the Chkalov Club also offered lectures, reports, and political news, especially about Spain. The drama collective at the club performed Spanish masterworks like Lope de Vega's *The Stupid Lady* (*La Dama Boba*) and Cervantes's *The Puppet Show of Wonders* (*El retablo de las maravillas*).¹⁰⁸ These Golden Age masterpieces are highly entertaining and showed the best of what Spanish culture offered to the stage. Although the club typically served Spaniards, Soviet friends, guests, and those who simply wanted to learn about Spanish culture also attended.¹⁰⁹ Soviet artists and directors praised the performances and complimented the club's choir and dance group, too.¹¹⁰

The position of Soviet workers' clubs like Chkalov was critical, because here the workers had time for relaxation and entertainment in the form of music, films, and more. Clubs contained newspapers and journals, provided lectures, and in other ways brought workers into contact with party or Komsomol actives. Houses of culture and trade union clubs were ubiquitous in Soviet cities. They were points of vospitanie and further training in Soviet values that mirrored much of the activity of the Spanish boarding schools in trying to inculcate culture, proper behaviour, and a communist world view. For non-Russians, the clubs also promoted national cultures.[111] Therefore, we should not look on the inquiry into the Spaniards' welfare as something extraordinary. Certainly, they were singled out as a group within the larger ranks of workers and trainees, but political work among them was similar to that for other Soviet workers.

The "independent life" was not to be so independent after all. Acculturation most often took place in *groups* of Spaniards, not unlike what was happening in the boarding schools, and under the supervision of Soviet and Spanish communist organizations. Material subsidies and party-centred activities promoting the Soviet way of life and Spanish culture continued into the early years beyond the boarding-school system. However, this supervision was only possible once the majority of Spaniards had been concentrated in Moscow. The war years provided the experience needed for officials to understand and implement methods of training Spanish children to become Hispano-Soviet youth, and the methods for training youth to become Soviet adults looked remarkably like the 1938 boarding-school regulation that still had not achieved its aims seven years later. Dependency, though to a lesser degree, continued even as life in the workplace and Soviet organizations continued to stress the importance of becoming independent Soviets. The insular nature of many of the Soviet institutions for Spanish children and youth reinforced their sense of collectivity, fostered a tribal structure, and led them to view each other as family. Their performances for the "other," their Soviet counterparts, drew a sharp line between Spanish culture and the culture of their new homeland. They had been exoticized. The ambivalence – likely because of the PCE's presence in Moscow – between raising the refugee children as Spaniards and raising them as Soviets led to a cultural complexity that likely prompted them to a self-understanding as Spanish *and* Soviet, Hispano-Soviets.

The re-placement of Spaniards in the Moscow region in 1944–5 follows some of the same logic as post-war filtration generally. Historian Nick Baron has shown that war-time dislocation made surveillance and material provisioning difficult among a mobile population. The dislocated were now "to be fixed in place, both spatially and in the matrix of social regulation."[112] Although Spaniards did not have to endure the rigorous filtration to which Soviet returnees were subjected, the rationale of control and order over the location and bodies was much the same. We should remember that upon their arrival in the USSR in 1937–8 Spanish children endured the physical filtration (e.g., delousing, medical exams) common to filtration generally, and their existence within the boarding schools re-placed them into a liminal third space with near-constant supervision that mitigated their ability to infect (either physically or ideologically) the Soviet population. Displaced people, be they refugees or new arrivals to a place, signified disorder to the socio-political body; therefore, hygiene and sanitation became linked with the integration of new residents.[113] Not until they reached adolescence in the Second World War did large numbers of these refugee children interact with Soviet citizens on a daily basis and for extended periods. However, with the children having little opportunity to learn Soviet ways and not having extended families nearby to lend support, Soviet institutions during the war and post-war period had to continue providing stipends, material support, and vospitanie to Spanish youth so that their transition to adulthood would also continue their transformation into Hispano-Soviets with a love of two countries, correct political understandings, Soviet behavioural traits, and a bilingualism that would allow them to contribute to the USSR, Spain, and Spanish-speaking countries.

Conclusion: Life after Stalin

The first time I came [back] to Spain was in 1972, I immediately understood that
I could not adapt in Spain because I had an education.
I have two homelands, two places of mine.

Carmen González Martínez,
"El retorno a España de los 'niños de la guerra civil,'" 86, 90

The recollections of these two women, Elena and Francisca, represent two extreme perceptions of the Spanish experiences in the Soviet boarding schools. One the one hand, Soviet education and upbringing had succeeded to such a degree that a return to Spain, the Western European homeland, was a step backward. The second recollection, on the other hand, illustrates the effectiveness of following a non-Russian school model that allowed some of the former refugees to balance their Soviet and Spanish selves, blending the cultures and becoming Hispano-Soviets.

The Soviet experiment in educating and raising nearly three thousand Spanish children from 1937 to 1951 provided an education that divided them from their peers in Spain, yet it also developed a love for two homelands. Soviet schools for Spaniards were unlike the highly heterogeneous Lenin School or the International Children's Home in Ivanovo that raised youth and children from myriad countries. Although there were regional differences among the Spanish children, the Soviet schools promoted a unified *hispanidad* while also recognizing and in some cases promoting regional cultural differences. Therefore, we are best served by understanding the casas de niños as Soviet non-Russian schools that embraced the transformative agenda of modern educational practices but did so within a Soviet context in which minority populations were to be raised with a respect for their particularist cultures and languages. In line with prevailing Soviet nationality policy, the Spaniards accessed the socialist content through their national forms. The Soviet Union planned almost from the start to transform these young state resources into useful residents of the USSR or other countries and used the mantra of "national in form, socialist in content" to do so. As they were "little heroes" and not of an enemy nationality, they benefited from being in a privileged position in the hierarchy of resources.

Whether in dictatorships or democracies, educational practices in the early twentieth century had begun to recognize children as a resource for the nation, which necessitated greater attention to hygiene, discipline, and patriotism, in addition to reading, writing, and arithmetic. Unlike in conservative Spain, Stalin's niños – both boys and girls – had ample opportunities to gain a high-quality, secular education as they trained their bodies and developed a Marxist, internationalist world view both in and out of the classroom. With the coming of war and their coming of age, the teaching of labour and military skills and Russian language became more important while the Spaniards began their transition into adulthood as long-term residents of the USSR outside the daily supervision of school authorities. However, the Soviet Union never abandoned its promise to raise the children – at least in part – as Spanish, even when textbooks and teachers were in short supply. Maintaining *hispanidad* mirrored the Soviet policy towards national minorities and facilitated the development of a new cohort of Spanish speakers armed with Marxism-Leninism-Stalinism to save their country and other Spanish-speaking countries from fascism and capitalism.

In many ways Soviet institutions treated Spanish children and youth much like their Soviet counterparts, particularly those in non-Russian schools where local language, literature, and culture stood alongside Russian. Spaniards learned their history, language, geography, and culture at the same time as they began Russian-language training and acquired Soviet ideology and values. Many Soviet and Spanish youth worked hard during the war, spurred on by patriotism, a belief in the need to supply the war effort, and the desire to survive. Decades later, some Spaniards still recalled that the spirit of patriotism that had been instilled from their first days in the USSR created a work mentality that was far superior to Spanish work habits.[1] Others responded to the state's failed promises of support and compensation during the war and behaved in a most un-Soviet manner through theft and flight from work and school.

Previous research has rarely investigated Soviet attempts to reforge the young Spaniards, has not differentiated the changes wrought by the Second World War, or placed this grand experiment in a Soviet context. Yet we now know that Soviet officials modified their methods as circumstances changed or policies failed. However, the goal of constructing Hispano-Soviet cadres remained. The 1938 school regulations and Stalin's 1939 speech on cadre development laid the foundation for Soviet thought about transforming the Spanish children and extending humanitarian welfare. The niños entered the USSR as Makarenko's ideas about the importance of teacher-centred schools, discipline, and role modelling replaced child-centred, permissive paedology. With fascism on the march across Europe, teaching patriotism, internationalism, and physical fitness became increasingly important. The boarding schools were to be sites that strengthened health, sharpened minds, and taught socialist values. At the 1939 start of the war and Franco's victory, it became essential to remove from the boarding schools some Spanish adults who were poor role models and to enhance the teaching of Russian as a foreign language in order to improve the Sovietization of the children and thus allow them entry into Soviet society.

By 1940 many of the Spaniards were approaching working age (fourteen), so transitional institutions like the Homes for Spanish Youth opened in Leningrad and Moscow. In 1940 the Komsomol Central Committee required the teaching of skills that were useful to society, and the Supreme Soviet created the Labour Reserves. The shift of Spanish teenagers to trade schools, factories, or the new youth homes must be seen in this context. Preparation to enter Soviet society and contribute to labour and the war effort created a new emphasis on labour and military training to "harden" Soviet youth and mobilize them to work for others. Spaniards also needed additional language training, so the youth homes divided the day between school and work to prepare the adolescents for what now appeared to be a longer-term residency in the USSR. Yet, even with these initiatives, some young Spaniards still struggled to integrate into Soviet life, largely because Soviet and PCE officials continued to see them as wards of the state rather than as independent citizens. One could argue that the Soviet obsession with nurturing children into ideal types never allowed many of the niños to struggle and find their own way to integrate.

The war years thus served as a major transition moment in which Soviet values and institutions began to take precedence over Spanish. Russian-language instruction became a priority, and both Soviet and Spanish organizations fought to return the Spaniards to Moscow where they could be better supervised and prepared for their adult lives and integration into Soviet society and labour. The war demanded greater discipline and collectivist effort for the front and for survival. The pressures of war and the failure of the youth homes caused yet another shift; older Spanish youth entered into factory work while still receiving specialized attention and stipends. As the crisis of war subsided and Spaniards returned to Moscow, the Spanish Chkalov Club began to provide the vospitanie and Spanish cultural training that often were absent in the factories in evacuation. Young Spaniards began to enter higher education with larger subsidies and at higher percentages than their Soviet counterparts.

From their arrival in 1937, with accommodation in hotels and palaces, and through the dark days of the war, Spanish children had lived privileged lives vis-à-vis their Soviet counterparts. Soviet intentions went well beyond warehousing a refugee population. Even after the children had largely disappeared from the press in 1939, Soviet and Spanish leaders, though not always in complete agreement about the method, sought to meet human needs and transform the refugees into Hispano-Soviets who could serve the Soviet Union immediately and Spain and Latin America in the future. António Martínez, who as an engineer helped develop Fidel Castro's Cuba, has insisted that "no amount of money could buy the friendship, generosity, and kindness with which they treated us, the [Soviet] people, the common people."[2] Soviet institutions for children, youth, and adults attempted to transform the Spanish refugees through a dual process of obuchenie and vospitanie, to maintain Spanish culture, and to teach and model Soviet normative values and behaviours as was the goal in Soviet non-Russian schools. The little heroes also benefited from Soviet humanitarianism and internationalism that endured despite the ascendancy of mass violence and a turn to russocentrism during the late 1930s and 1940s.

Adult Lives in the USSR: Stories of Success and Socialization

Much as the Spaniards' lives in Soviet-Spanish institutions varied by circumstance, so too did their adult professional lives. Continuing education was the norm for most youth after the boarding schools. Training schools accepted 392 boys and 215 girls; another 182 boys and 228 girls attended technical schools. At 24 per cent, the largest category of students went into higher education: 375 boys and 317 girls.[3] Many of the technical schools had highly gendered populations of Spaniards. Seventy-two girls and only one boy went into nursing; forty-seven girls and only four boys studied textiles; machine agriculture took in ten boys and three girls; nine girls studied in railroad technicums alongside twenty-two boys; road building saw a disparity of thirty-nine boys and nineteen girls; and five times more boys than girls entered energy fields.[4]

After leaving the boarding schools the Spaniards took three main paths: into science and technology; translating and teaching; and industrial production. Several of the former niños, like Bernardo del Río, Florentina Díaz, and José García, studied for doctorates in economics, history, philosophy, biology, agronomy, mathematics, and pedagogy. Others, like María Pérez, Ramiro Rincón, and Esther Vicente, studied at institutes for medicine, agriculture, hydro-electricity, chemistry, foreign languages, aviation, instrumentation, transport, and many more, achieving skills and qualifications that would allow them to build communism in Spain, where they could not have received such training.[5] The Spaniards participated in grand Soviet experiments like the Virgin Lands campaign and hydro-electric dam construction, became members of the communist parties of Spain and the USSR, attained Soviet citizenship, and entered the Soviet elite with all the privileges that came with it. Several dozen of the Hispano-Soviets, like Joaquín Avelairas, Carmen Alcorta, Ventura Muñoz, Ángel Navalón, and María Pérez, went to Cuba to assist Fidel Castro in his revolution; they were a rare combination of highly educated and trained specialists and fluent in Marxism and Spanish.[6] Many earned Soviet medals, including at least two Orders of Lenin. Award-winning sculptors, ballerinas, and choreographers emerged from their ranks, as did soccer stars like Agustín Gómez, Jesús Varela, and Ruperto Sagasti.[7] The Spaniards could not have imagined such futures had they remained in Spain with its less educated and mobile society.

Of course, not all life courses were successful; other Spaniards did not fare well. Some, including Dolores Ibárruri's son Rubén Ruiz Ibárruri died in the Second World War while fighting in the Red Army, as did José Argüelles Fernández, Paulino Arrizabalaga Arana, the brothers Julián and Mariano Balaguero Ruiz, and many others.[8] A smaller number joined a total of 150–90 Spanish adults who were confined to the Gulag.[9]

For various reasons, many Spanish men and women elected to remain in the Soviet Union for the rest of their lives. Some Spanish women refused to leave without their Soviet husbands, who were forbidden to emigrate. Children, other family, and professions also led many to remain in the USSR. Having arrived as young children two decades earlier, they had spent most of their lives in the USSR and in essence had become Soviet. For those men and women who remained in the Soviet Union until the late 1970s, we have more data. In 1978 the Centro Español in Moscow gathered data on the remaining Spanish niños. Although they are not comprehensive, the data are illustrative. For example, we know that in 1978 at least 947 of the former niños remaining in the USSR were married. Of the 331 women, 260 had married Soviet men. The 616 Spanish men had an even greater imbalance, with 546 married to Soviet women. In all, 85.1 per cent had married Soviet citizens. Twenty-one Spanish men and sixty women were single in 1978.[10] There were many more single Soviet men and women than there were eligible Spanish partners; this explains the imbalance in intermarriage and suggests some success in acculturating the Spaniards to Soviet ways of life. Moreover, the appearance of a greater percentage of Spanish-Spanish couples returning to Spain may be attributed to the difficulty of intermarried couples to do so; the USSR forbade Soviet men to join their Spanish wives in Spain, but Soviet women could accompany their Spanish husbands.

Returning to *la Patria*: An Uneasy Reintegration

The transition to life in Spain was arduous for many. As we have seen in previous chapters, it is difficult to generalize a vast array of experiences. One's transition into Spanish life varied greatly based on gender, the date of return, the number of years (and what percentage of one's life) spent in the USSR, and more. For example, a woman returning to Spain during the Franco years could be taken aback by a society that was still fervently patriarchal and had fewer professional opportunities. The state also often viewed returning men in particular as a political threat and treated them as such.[11] However, a person who had been fourteen years old on arrival in the USSR in 1938 and one of the few who returned to Spain during the Second World War would have had a much different experience than a three-year-old who arrived in 1937 and returned after the collapse of the USSR in 1991. Therefore, we need to be careful about making general conclusions on the niños de la guerra from any one person's oral or written testimony many decades after events.

A few children, some of whom had been captured by German troops, had been returned to Spain in the 1940s, but the largest repatriation had to wait until 1956–7. A small number of niños had left for Latin American countries just after the war. In 1945–6 three expeditions reunited Milagros Latorre, Esther Álvarez, siblings Gonzalo and María Cruz Arjona, Josefina Valverde, Luis Rivas, Antonio Molina, Enrique Vázquez, Javier and Manuel Tourne, and others with their families in Mexico. In December 1946 another group went to Venezuela. In 1947 Mariano Frades, sisters Carmen and María Machado, and sisters Meri and Margarita Suárez joined family in Chile.[12] The PCE condemned as traitors those who left the USSR in the 1940s, but in 1946 the Kremlin had already begun secret negotiations with Spain about repatriation.[13] By the mid-1950s, refugees could return to Spain in large numbers.

Stalin's death in March 1953, political change in the Kremlin, and Spain's changing economic and diplomatic position in the 1950s made Moscow more amenable to finalizing negotiations.[14] Spain increased trade with Eastern Bloc countries and thereby indirectly with the USSR. In December 1955, amidst growing cold-war divisions as Spain's relations with the United States improved, the Soviet Union supported Spain's admission to the United Nations. All the while, various Red Cross organizations had been fielding requests from parents and their now-grown children for reunification. Nearly two and a half years after negotiations had allowed the ship *Semiramis* to return Blue Division prisoners, and some of the niños de la guerra had "camouflaged" amongst them, the large-scale return of refugees began.[15]

From September 1956 to May 1959 seven official flotillas left the Soviet Union for Spain, carrying 1,204 (630 men and 574 women) of the child refugees – between twenty-five and thirty-two years old – who had lived for two decades in the USSR. After just a few months, 69 men and 25 women returned to the USSR, mostly because of problems reintegrating into Spanish society.[16] A further 56 men and 68 women had emigrated to third countries by 1956–7.[17] In 1959 alone, an estimated 635 Spaniards fled Spain to "the second homeland" of the USSR.[18] Emigration to Spain continued after 1956–7, but it slowed tremendously in the next decades. One scholar suggests that from 1957 to 1967, only 17 Spaniards returned to Spain, with incremental increases to 43 in 1970 and 46 in 1977.[19] Fleeing economic hardship and rising national sentiments, a final wave of returns began after the Soviet collapse in 1991 when 44 to 53 people returned in each of the first three years.[20] However, it remains unclear how many of all these people were the original child refugees of 1937–8.

Most scholarship has viewed the approximately 1,900 Spaniards – both the former child refugees as well as adult political exiles, soldiers, and pilots who returned between 1956 and 1959 – as mere objects of the USSR, the Franco regime, or international agencies like the Red Cross, but more recently scholars have investigated returnees' efforts, too. Despite two decades of Franco's brutality against leftist families, there were attempts to ease the transition for returnees.[21] Franco's government issued secret directives to accommodate returnees; local officials and trade unions often intervened on behalf of the new arrivals; and returnees formed their own organizations like *L'Association en Espagne des Espagnols rapatriés d'URSS*.[22] Many people viewed as propaganda the attempts by government organizations to show the largesse of the Spanish state, but agencies also provided benefits for some. Recently historian Glennys Young has intervened to show that although returnees were constrained by Franco's dictatorship in what they could say and do, they were agents in their own lives and advocated for jobs, housing, and other services. As Young notes, their activity caused no dramatic change in policy, but some returnees achieved small victories at the same time that Spanish police surveilled, questioned, arrested, humiliated, and placed them in concentration camps and prisons.[23] Some of the Hispano-Soviets also found themselves at the centre of an international protest in 1960 against the arrest of two hundred to two hundred and fifty of the returnees in Spain.[24]

Life in Spain was dramatically different from that in the USSR. Franco's Spain lagged behind the Soviet Union in education and in equality of opportunity for men and women. At the time the highly educated refugees returned from the USSR, only 67 per cent of school-age children in Spain were even registered for school, teacher purchasing power was only 20 per cent of what it had been two decades earlier, and women comprised only 15 per cent of university students.[25] One man reflected on the ignorance he found on returning to Spain: "Look at my brothers, they are as capable as me, and because they have been educated in Spain, they have been made into donkeys."[26] Women who had been raised in the Soviet Union to believe that girls should have the same opportunities as boys returned to a Spain still under the thumb of Catholic patriarchy and Francoism.[27] These former refugees had benefited from Soviet largesse and realized, as they saw it, that life had been better in the USSR. Maintaining their Spanish language and culture was not enough for them to feel comfortable in Spain because everything else they had learned in the USSR was antithetical to their new lives in their old homeland. They had modernized, yet Spain had not. Some even reported that their position as former refugees and outsiders in Spain led to their being nicknamed "Bosnians."[28]

One report suggested that 1,192 of the Spaniards had received a Soviet higher education, 417 had attained expertise, and 1,114 were skilled workers, which separated them from other Spaniards.[29] In short, 2,723 of the 2,895 refugees – especially the women – received education and training that they likely would not have attained had they stayed in Spain. Women who had received high-quality education and careers in the USSR returned to a highly patriarchal and thus limiting Spain. Not only did this constrict employment opportunity, but it also caused rifts in families that were not accustomed to modern womanhood. These architects, agronomists, and engineers were "something that in Spain in the 1950s was unprecedented and caused a confused feeling between admiration, distrust, and a certain discomfort among men."[30] The Spanish state also refused or delayed recognition of many returnees' degrees and professional qualifications, thus creating conditions for unemployment or under-employment in an economy already struggling to employ its citizens. Returnees had better education and job skills than had their counterparts in Spain, and semi-skilled workers found jobs more easily than did highly educated and skilled workers, for whom there were fewer positions in the struggling economy.[31] For example, two brothers who were very skilled marble carvers in the USSR reported finding in Spain "no work except as labourers putting shelves on windows."[32] There were, of course, exceptions, such as Manuel Arce who, despite having lost both legs, had become a highly skilled radiologist in the USSR and in 1975 took a chest X-ray of a dying Franco– the latter certainly not knowing that Arce was a niño de la guerra who had returned to Spain illegally.[33] Unemployment and under-employment further hindered reintegration into Spanish daily life.

Problems in daily life concerned many of the returnees. The lack of sufficient employment and housing created a stark contrast to the relatively prosperous lifestyle most of the Spaniards had led in the USSR. Returnees imported Soviet goods – televisions, radios, record players, motorcycles, and even a Zil car – that were rare in Spain and even in the USSR in the mid-1950s.[34] A significant number of returnees reported problems with communication because they had developed a patois that one scholar has termed "Rusiñol."[35] The Soviet "character and customs" they had acquired separated them from their Spanish family and friends.[36] Having been absent from Spain for two decades, they found that everything they experienced was different from their childhood memories and from their experiences in the Soviet Union. Roads, bridges, transportation, and other infrastructure were far less developed in Spain. Family and friends were sometimes distant and seemed like strangers after such a long absence.[37] Franco's regime and many Spaniards viewed the returnees from the communist motherland as real or potential enemies, and surveillance caused additional problems.[38] Police and other state agencies, as well as the United States Central Intelligence Agency, interviewed the returnees.[39] Various government agencies had to validate Soviet diplomas, work certificates, and other official documents. Franco's government also issued new identity cards to returnees that were distinct from those of their Spanish compatriots. This marked them as "other" and facilitated discrimination. Although family ties had pulled many Spaniards to return to Spain, family also pulled some back to the USSR. Many of the Spanish women wanted to rejoin their Soviet husbands who had had to remain in the USSR. Just as they had suffered a separation from family in 1937–8, in repatriation the Spaniards endured another separation, from their Soviet family and friends, when they rejoined their Spanish loved ones. Family problems, poverty, and the inability to adapt to life in Spain eventually led about seven hundred returnees to petition to go back to the USSR.[40]

Many of the refugees had longed to return to Spain but were not prepared because of the hybrid identifications they had developed in the USSR. The conscious attempts in the Soviet boarding schools to keep Spain alive in the youngsters gave them the linguistic skills they needed to return to their native land, but they had also received a romantic notion of an "imagined Spain," the fragility of Francoism, and the inevitable victory of communism.[41] When Spaniards returned to Spain in large numbers in the mid-1950s, they often experienced resentment and suspicion from their fellow Spaniards much as post-war returnees did in Armenia, Upper Silesia, Ukraine, and other locations.[42] Their time in another place taught a normative set of behaviours and values that stalled their full reintegration into the community they had left in the 1930s. They had inhabited a third space, a type of limbo that was neither one nor the other.[43] Moreover, their learned Soviet values of atheism, equality, and international friendship and peace ran counter to the Spanish values they experienced upon their return. Soviet modernity with its disciplined minds and bodies, co-operative and collectivist ethos, curious blend of patriotism and internationalism, and more advanced economy and educational system made jarring a return to Spain with its Catholic conservatism and stagnant, autarkic economy.

Stalin's Niños helps us to understand the USSR as a modern state, not one outside the history of twentieth-century Western models of development. As in many other countries with different economic and political systems, education in the Soviet Union was a disciplinary institution; this was not merely a matter of ideology. Children were to be raised as young patriots and future contributors to society, and this required them to be literate and numerate, with healthy bodies, and with minds trained to a normative standard. Children were a state resource to be mobilized for the greater good. The Spanish boardings schools were slightly different in that the children were to be patriots of two countries, but this was not antithetical to Soviet education broadly. Soviet education sought to create an internationalist ethos among children that was not bound to nationality. The supranational ideal of class trumped nationalism. Thus, the Spanish schools took the form of Soviet non-Russian schools in which local cultures, traditions, and languages were used to teach and express the more important supranational Soviet values. "National in form" was a means to the ends of "socialism in content."

There are remarkable similarities between the education and upbringing of Russian and non-Russian Soviet children and those of the Spanish refugees. This suggests that Soviet nationality and education policies in the late 1930s and 1940s were relatively consistent and what we today might call best practices. All children needed to become modern, literate, numerate, patriotic, and disciplined. Children also needed to learn Russian; however, Russian was not supposed to be the language of instruction in non-Russian schools. As numerous scholars of nationality policy have shown, Soviet promotion of national difference – but not bourgeois nationalism – remained a constant throughout the Stalin period. This meant expending resources to protect and promote languages and cultures and to groom local elites. The case of the Spanish refugee children is similar. Attention to their needs far surpassed their small number as Soviet authorities lavished attention and resources to prepare a national group both to become Soviet and to spread socialism and modernity to their ethnonational territory in Spain and to their linguistic compatriots outside the USSR. Their language was preserved, and many Spaniards were groomed to become political, cultural, and scientific leaders.

Their difficulties in reintegrating after the Spaniards returned to Spain is similar to the outburst of national discontent in the USSR in the late 1980s, but in the inverse. Yuri Slezkine has suggested that Soviet "leaders found it harder and harder to explain what their 'socialist content' stood for and, when Gorbachev finally discarded the worn-out marxist verbiage, the only language that remained was the well honed and long practiced language of nationalism."[44] Owing to the need for greater attention to teaching Russian language to the Spaniards who had no Soviet language on which they could rely for social integration, one does not see much evidence of a divisive Spanish nationalism. Moreover, Soviet accommodation strategies led most Spaniards to thank the USSR for their survival.

Leaving the USSR brought them in contact with a regime that did not even pretend to promote equality and remained fixated on unity through the Catholic Church. For the Spaniards, it seems that their "socialist content" was too well learned when they returned to the "backwardness" of Franco's Spain and was much more important than the "national form." Certainly, the importance of Spanish-language training and cultural performance was essential. Cultural programs helped to define the ethnonational community even as the people within that community resided outside of the nation-state. The continued use of Spanish and courses on Spanish history, geography, and literature reinforced a connection to Spain. Performances of national music or dance, especially for a Soviet audience, helped to further mark, reinforce, and sustain the youngsters' identification as Spanish.[45] These measures kept alive the notion of home and the desire by many to return to Spain someday. Moreover, the constant refrain to study and work hard as preparation to overthrow the fascists who had forced them from their country added another layer of institutional discipline to manufactured consent among the refugees.

Nevertheless, language and literature were not enough to make Spain familiar to returnees. Ways of life and ways of thought had been entrenched to such a degree that many returnees loathed the poverty, unemployment, violence, misogyny, lack of infrastructure, and oppression they experienced in Spain. Manuel Arce remembered the USSR as "much more advanced in technology, teaching, health, and other areas."[46] Isabel Álvarez had heard so much about the maltreatment of returnees that she gave up her ticket and stayed in the USSR.[47] Others recalled that the disturbing and stifling gender roles and discrimination of the Catholic Church, government, and society reinforced their love of the Soviet Union.[48] This casts the USSR in a different light. Rather than comparing the USSR to prosperous Europe, scholars need to consider which Europe they mean and that different Soviet peoples experienced Soviet upbringing differently.

Many returnees could not overcome the clash of world views when they returned to family in Spain. Those refugees who remained in the USSR, however, often seem to have integrated and prospered despite the initial problems in developing independence from Soviet organizations and the PCE. In other words, the "socialist content" aided integration in the Soviet Union but fostered marginalization on refugees' return to Franco's Spain. "National in form" provided familiarity on their return to Spain, yet it also blended well in the multinational performance of Sovietness in the USSR.

What began with a Soviet international defence of the republic and against fascism led to long-term humanitarian assistance for 2,895 Spanish refugee children. As a result of the education and upbringing in the special Soviet boarding schools, most of these Spaniards emerged with a Soviet international mindset that led to participation in events such as Moscow's 1957 World Festival of Youth and Students, efforts to halt imperialism, and work to develop Fidel Castro's revolution in Cuba.[49] The vast state resources expended on the refugee children created many lasting bonds between them and the Soviet Union and its way of life and thinking.

The vast majority of the Spanish refugee children had spent more years in the Soviet Union than they had in Spain, which likely led to some confusion or ambivalence as to which was their rightful homeland. Much of the disenchantment came from the gap between the "imagined Spain" constructed during their times in the Soviet boarding schools and the reality of life upon the return to their first homeland. In fact, they were torn between their two homelands, the values and norms learned in the USSR, and the life of their families and friends in Spain. Many ached to return to Spain and yet were anguished to leave what they had come to know and appreciate in the USSR. Hybridity allowed some to adapt while preventing others from integrating into Spanish life. Whereas Russian-language training and Soviet education allowed mobility for national minorities in the USSR, it hindered (or at least did not help) mobility in Spain.

Stalin's Niños leads to a final caveat: just because a boarding school had international students did not mean that it operated in a way that was fundamentally different than that of the Soviet schools or of modern educational practices generally. We need to distinguish between institutions, based on the relative ethnic and linguistic homogeneity and heterogeneity of the pupils, and place the institutions in context. The making of Hispano-Soviets occurred in a particular place and time and in a modern educational culture that valued the transformation and training of youth for the future, while also acknowledging particularist cultures among the student population. As they were considered little heroes in the fight against fascism and had Soviet and Spanish institutions working on their behalf, the niños de la guerra received better treatment and more resources than did children from "enemy" populations. Understanding their education and upbringing can help us understand better the adults they became, and it can also shed light on Soviet priorities for healthy, numerate, literate, patriotic, disciplined, politically conscious, internationalist children who were ready and prepared to build socialism. These modern Hispano-Soviet adults show that the commitment to "national in form, socialist in content" was a formula to reforge nationalities, foreign and domestic, into a supranational identity by means of national languages and cultures. Reforging is much easier with children who are malleable and spend long hours in state institutions like boarding schools where they can be trained, disciplined, and surveilled. However, the individuality of people and their experiences still divided their outcomes. The transformation into Hispano-Soviets allowed many to become transnational, flowing across cultures and boundaries, but at the same time it hindered others in the transition back to Spain.

Glossary

casa de niños. Boarding school
colonias escolares. School colonies
detskii sovet. Children's council
los enchufados. The connected
hispanidad. Spanishness
internaty. Boarding schools for gifted, troubled, or disabled Soviet children
kruzhok, kruzhki. Study circle(s)
kul'turnost'. Culturedness or acculturation
kul'turnyi. Acculturated
niños. Children
niños de la guerra. Children of the Spanish Civil War
obuchenie. Education
patria. Homeland
puño. Raised-fist salute
shefstvo. Patronage
vospitanie. Upbringing
vospitateli. Educators

Notes

Introduction

1 C.B. Moreno, M. Itkis, and J.P. Felipe, eds, *Dobro pozhalovat' na nash prazdnik* (Moscow: Prosveshchenie, 1974), 95. All translations throughout are mine unless otherwise noted. Mark Aldrich assisted me on this Mateu poem.
2 The institutions were known in Spanish as *las casas de niños* and in Russian as *detskie doma dlia ispanskikh detei*. Both languages recognize the institutions as "homes" or sites of living; however, they were also sites of learning. Therefore, I will use the terms *boarding schools, homes*, and *children's homes* interchangeably. This is not to confuse the reader with *internaty*, which typically were boarding schools for gifted, troubled, or disabled Soviet children.
3 Jacqueline Fear-Segal, *White Man's Club: Schools, Race, and the Struggle for Indian Acculturation* (Lincoln: University of Nebraska Press, 2007), 159–69.
4 My term *Hispano-Soviet* derives from Ché Guevera's *hispanosoviético*. Roger González Martell, "Niños de la guerra en la Unión Soviética, hispanosoviéticos en Cuba," 11, accessed 14 November 2018, www.Scribd.com/doc/68821252/Ninos-de-la-guerra-en-la-Union-Sovietica-Hispanosovieticos-en-Cuba.
5 A. Gudimov, "Gosti iz Ispanii," *Izvestiia*, 8 April 1937, 4; Elena Kononenko, *Malen'kie ispantsy* [Little Spaniards] (Moscow: Detizdat, 1937), 3–12.
6 Centro Documental de la Memoria Histórica, Salamanca, Spain (hereafter cited as CDMH), P.S. Barcelona, 87/17/2.
7 Marie José Devillard et al., eds, *Los niños españoles en la URSS, 1937–1997: Narración y memoria* (Barcelona: Ariel, 2001), 205.
8 Alicia Alted Vigil, Encarna Nicolás Marín, and Roger González Martell, *Los niños de la guerra de España en la Unión Soviética: De la evacuación al retorno (1937–1999)* (Madrid: Fundación Francisco Largo Caballero, 1999), 163.
9 Luis Suárez Fernández, *Franco y la URSS: La diplomacia secreta (1946–1970)* (Madrid: Ediciones Rialp, 1987); Rafael Moreno Izquierdo, *Los niños de Rusia: La verdadera historia de una operación de retorno* (Barcelona: Crítica, 2017).

Moreno has calculated 2,622 returnees, but like other scholars he is unable to disaggregate the children who fled in 1937-8. Other data are found in Devillard et al., *Los niños españoles*, 250; Immaculada Colomina Limonero, *Dos patrias, tres mil destinos: Vida y exilio de los niños de la guerra de España refugiados en la Unión Soviética* (Madrid: Cinca, 2010), 215; Carmen González Martínez, "El retorno a España de los 'niños de la guerra civil,'" *Anales de Historia Contemporánea* 19 (2003): 81-3. Luis Antonio Palacio Pilacés has suggested approximately 2,600 people in the seven expeditions, of whom about 1,500 were former *niños de la guerra* (children of the war). Palacio, *Tal vez el día: Aragoneses en la URSS (1937-1977): El exilio y la Division Azul* (Zaragosa, Spain: Editorial Comuniter S.L., 2013), 1002.

10 Among the best examples are Alted Vigil, Marín, and Martell, *Los niños*; Susana Castillo, *Mis años en la escuela soviética* (Madrid: Catarata, 2009); Colomina Limonero, *Dos patrias*; Devillard et al., *Los niños*; Verónica Sierra Blas, *Palabras huérfanas: Los niños y la Guerra Civil* (Barcelona: Taurus, 2009), ch. 7; Enrique Zafra, Rosalía Crego, and Carmen Heredia, *Los niños españoles evacuados a la URSS (1937)* (Madrid: Ediciones de la Torre, 1989).

11 Jochen Hellbeck has warned of the "risk of reconstructing past subjective life experience on the basis of memoirs." Hellbeck, "Fashioning the Stalinist Soul: The Diary of Stepan Podlubnyi (1931-1939)," *Jahrbücher für Geschichte Osteuropas* 44, no. 3 (1996): 348. Verónica Sierra Blas, "Reconstructing Silences: On the Study and Editing of Private Letters by Spanish Children Evacuated to Russia during the Spanish Civil War," *Variants* 8 (2012): 95-109. Many of the letters are archived in CDMH in Salamanca, and some are reprinted in Zafra, Crego, and Heredia, *Los niños*, 101-28, and Sierra Blas, *Palabras huérfanas*, 192-288. The more helpful of the small memoir literature includes Manuel Arce Porres, *Memorias de Rusia: Vivencias de un niño de la guerra* (Madrid: Editorial Multipress, 2009); Isabel Argentina Álvarez Morán, *Memorias de una niña de la guerra* (Gijón, Spain: Fundación Municipal Cultura, Educación y Universidad Popular, 2003); Bernardo Clemente del Río Salceda, *20,000 días en la URSS: Recuerdos, descubrimientos y reflexiones de un niño de la guerra* (Madrid: Entrelineas Editores, 2004); José Fernández Sánchez, *Memorias de un niño de Moscú: Cuando Salí de Ablaña* (Barcelona: Planeta, 1999); José Fernández Sánchez, *Mi infancia en Moscú: Estampas de una nostalgia* (Madrid: Ediciones El Museo Universal, 1988); Virgilio de los Llanos Más, *¿Te acuerdas, tovarisch ...? Del archivo un "niño de la guerra"* (Valencia, Spain: Institució Alfons el Magnànim, 2002); Carmen Parga, *Antes que sea tarde* (Madrid: Compañía Literaria, 1996); and teacher Alejandra Soler Gilabert, *La vida es un río caudaloso con peligrosos rápidos: Al final de todo ... sigo comunista* (Valencia, Spain: Universitat de Valencia, 2009).

12 Glennys Young also has called for greater attention to archival sources in her "To Russia with 'Spain': Spanish Exiles in the USSR and the *Longue Durée* of Soviet History," *Kritika: Explorations in Russian and Eurasian History* 15, no. 2 (2014):

415; "¿Sujetos peligrosos? Repatriados españoles desde la URSS en la Provincia de Vizcaya, 1956-1963," *Cuadernos de Historia Contemporánea* 38 (2016): 107.

13 María Encarna Nicolás Marín, "La integración de los niños y jóvenes en la emigración de la Guerra civil: El caso de la Unión Soviética," *Anales de Historia Contemporánea*, 19 (2003): 60–73; Natalia Kharitonova, "Sovetskie pedagogicheskie rabotniki detskikh domov dlia ispanskikh detei glazami byvshikh vospitannikov," in *Antropologiia sovetskoi shkoly: Kul'turnye universalii i provintsial'nye praktiki* (Perm, Russia: Permskii gosudarstevennyi universitet, 2010), 175–92.

14 A.V. Elpat'evskii, *Ispanskaia emigratsiia v SSSR: Istoriografiia i istochniki, popytka interpretatsii* (Moscow: GERS, 2002).

15 Daniel Kowalsky, *Stalin and the Spanish Civil War* (New York: Columbia University Press, 2004).

16 Karl Schlögel, *Moscow, 1937* (Malden, MA: Polity, 2012), 2.

17 Michel Foucault, *Security, Territory, Population: Lectures at the Collège de France, 1977–1978*, ed. Michel Senellart, trans. Graham Burchell (Basingstoke, UK: Palgrave Macmillan, 2007), 87–90.

18 On Homi Bhabha's understanding of "third space," see his "Cultural Diversity and Cultural Differences," in *The Post-Colonial Studies Reader*, 2nd ed., ed. Bill Ashcroft, Gareth Griffiths, and Helen Tiffin (New York: Routledge, 2006), 156.

19 Some of the studies that discuss the urge to move groups out of "backwardness" include Ali Igmen, *Speaking Soviet with an Accent: Culture and Power in Kyrgyzstan* (Pittsburgh, PA: University of Pittsburgh Press, 2012); Adeeb Khalid, *Making Uzbekistan: Nation, Empire, and Revolution in the Early USSR* (Ithaca, NY: Cornell University Press, 2015); Paula Michaels, *Curative Powers: Medicine and Empire in Stalin's Central Asia* (Pittsburgh, PA: University of Pittsburgh Press, 2002); Douglas Northrop, *Veiled Empire: Gender and Power in Stalinist Central Asia* (Ithaca, NY: Cornell University Press, 2004); Brigid O'Keeffe, *New Soviet Gypsies: Nationality, Performance, and Selfhood in the Early Soviet Union* (Toronto: University of Toronto Press, 2013); Matthew D. Pauly, *Breaking the Tongue: Language, Power, and Education in Soviet Ukraine, 1923–1934* (Toronto: University of Toronto Press, 2014); Yuri Slezkine, *Arctic Mirrors: Russia and the Small People of the North* (Ithaca, NY: Cornell University Press, 1994). Establishing fixed locations was part of general modern state practices. For just one example see Jane Caplan and John Torpey, eds, *Documenting Individual Identity: The Development of State Practices in the Modern World* (Princeton, NJ: Princeton University Press, 2001).

20 Margaret Barbalet, *Far from a Low Gutter Girl: The Forgotten World of State Wards, South Australia, 1887–1940* (Melbourne: Oxford University Press, 1983); Michael C. Coleman, *American Indians, the Irish, and Government Schooling: A Comparative Study* (Lincoln: University of Nebraska, 2007); Fear-Segal, *White Man's Club*; Sudipa Topdar, "The Corporeal Empire: Physical Education and Politicising Children's Bodies in Late Colonial Bengal," *Gender and History* 29,

no. 1 (2017): 176–97; Clive Whitehead, *Colonial Educators: The British Indian and Colonial Education Service, 1858–1983* (London: I.B. Tauris, 2003).
21 David Hoffmann, *Cultivating the Masses: Modern State Practices and Soviet Socialism, 1914–1939* (Ithaca, NY: Cornell University Press, 2011); Peter Holquist, "'Information Is the Alpha and Omega of Our Work': Bolshevik Surveillance in Its Pan-European Perspective," *Journal of Modern History* 69, no. 3 (1997): 415–50; Terry Martin, *The Affirmative Action Empire: Nations and Nationalism in the USSR, 1923–1939* (Ithaca, NY: Cornell University Press, 2001); Tricia Starks, *The Body Soviet: Hygiene, Propaganda, and the Revolutionary State* (Madison: University of Wisconsin Press, 2008); Amir Weiner, ed., *Landscaping the Human Garden: Twentieth-Century Population Management in a Comparative Framework* (Stanford, CA: Stanford University Press, 2003).
22 On Soviet education see the many works of Larry E. Holmes and E. Thomas Ewing cited throughout this volume, as well as *Narodnoe obrazovanie v SSSR: Obshcheobrazovatel'naia shkola; Sbornik dokumentov, 1917–1973 gg.* (Moscow: Pedagogika, 1973); N.I. Boldyrev, ed., *Klassnyi rokovoditel'* (Moscow: Akademii pedagogiceskih nauk RSFSR, 1955); A.M. Danaev, ed., *Narodnoe obrazovanie: Osnovnaye postanovlennia, prikazy i instruktsii* (Moscow: Minsterstvo prosveshcheniia RSFSR, 1948); John Dunstan, *Soviet Schooling in the Second World War* (London: Palgrave Macmillan, 1997); Lisa A. Kirschenbaum, *Small Comrades: Revolutionizing Childhood in Soviet Russia, 1917–1932* (New York: Routledge, 2001); N.P. Kuzin, M.N. Kolmakova, and Z.I. Ravkin, *Ocherki istorii shkoly i pedagogicheskoi mysli narodov SSSR, 1917–1941 gg.* (Moscow: Pedagogika, 1980); Ann Livschiz, "Growing Up Soviet: Childhood in the Soviet Union, 1917–1958," (PhD diss., Stanford University, 2007). On wayward children see Alan Ball, *And Now My Soul Is Hardened: Abandoned Children in the Soviet Union, 1917–1938* (Berkeley: University of California Press, 1996); Juliane Fürst, "Between Salvation and Liquidation: Homeless and Vagrant Children and the Reconstruction of Soviet Society," *Slavonic and East European Review* 86, no. 2 (2008): 232–58; Rachel Green, "'There Will Not Be Orphans among Us': Soviet Orphanages, Foster Care, and Adoption, 1941–1956" (PhD diss., University of Chicago, 2006); Olga Kucherenko, *Soviet Street Children in the Second World War: Welfare and Social Control under Stalin* (London: Bloomsbury, 2016); A.M. Nechaeva, *Okhrana detei-sirot v Rossii: Istoriia i sovremennost'* (Moscow: Dom Rossiskogo detskogo fonda, 1994); Margaret Stolee, "Homeless Children in the USSR, 1917–1957," *Soviet Studies* 40 (January 1988): 64–83. The best works on mobilized children in war are Julie deGraffenried, *Sacrificing Childhood: Children and the Soviet State in the Great Patriotic War* (Lawrence: University Press of Kansas, 2014); and Olga Kucherenko, *Little Soldiers: How Soviet Children Went to War, 1941–1945* (Oxford: Oxford University Press, 2011).
23 Kate Ferris, "Parents, Children and the Fascist State: The Production and Reception of Children's Magazines in 1930s Italy," in *Parenting and the State*

in Britain and Europe, c. 1870–1950: Raising the Nation, ed. Hester Barron and Claudia Siebrecht (New York: Palgrave Macmillan, 2017), 185.

24 Anna Davin, *Growing Up Poor: Home, School and Street in London, 1870–1914* (London: Rivers Oram Press, 1996); Susannah Wright, "Teachers, Family and Community in the Urban Elementary School: Evidence from English School Log Books," *History of Education* 41, no. 2 (2011): 155–73; Stephen Humphries, *Hooligans or Rebels? An Oral History of Working-Class Childhood and Youth, 1889–1939* (Oxford: Blackwell, 1981).

25 Lisa Kirschenbaum, *International Communism and the Spanish Civil War: Solidarity and Suspicion* (Cambridge: Cambridge University Press, 2015), especially ch. 1; Elizabeth McGuire, *Red at Heart: How Chinese Communists Fell in Love with the Russian Revolution* (Oxford: Oxford University Press, 2018); Magdalena Gross, "Reclaiming the Nation: Polish Schooling in Exile during the Second World War," *History of Education Quarterly* 53, no. 3 (2013): 233–54; Irena Wasilewska, *Suffer Little Children* (London: Maxlove, 1946).

26 Terry Martin, "Modernization or Neo-traditionalism? Ascribed Nationality and Soviet Primordialism," in *Stalinism: New Directions*, ed. Sheila Fitzpatrick (New York: Routledge, 2000), 348–67; Yuri Slezkine, "The USSR as a Communal Apartment, or How a Socialist State Promoted Ethnic Particularism," *Slavic Review* 53, no. 2 (1994): 414–52.

27 See note 20 above.

28 Celia Haig-Brown has shown the agency of children in maintaining their culture that is "built around opposition to the severity of [adults'] rules and regulations guiding their lives." Celia Haig-Brown, *Resistance and Renewal: Surviving the Indian Residential School* (Vancouver, BC: Arsenal Pulp Press, 1988), 98.

29 Oleg Khlevniuk, "The Objectives of the Great Terror, 1937–1938," in *Stalinism: The Essential Readings*, ed. David Hoffmann (Oxford: Blackwell, 2003), 87–104.

30 The importance of the prosaic everyday is most visible in Elizabeth McGuire, "Sino-Soviet Every Day: Chinese Revolutionaries in Moscow Military Schools, 1927–1930," in *Everyday Life in Russia Past and Present*, ed. Choi Chatterjee, David Ransel, Mary Cavender, and Karen Petrone, 329–49 (Bloomington: Indiana University Press, 2015).

31 On national operations see Terry Martin, "The Origins of Soviet Ethnic Cleansing," *Journal of Modern History* 70, no. 4 (1998): 813–61.

32 Edward Shils, "Social and Psychologial Aspects of Displacement and Repatriation," *Journal of Social Issues* 2, no. 3 (1946): 3–18.

33 The children even used the term *los enchufados* (the connected) to describe the most privileged in their ranks. Devillard et al., *Los niños*, 122, 127–9, 140–1.

34 Yaroslav Bilinsky, "Education of the Non-Russian Peoples in the USSR, 1917–1967," *Slavic Review* 27, no. 3 (1968): 411–37; Peter Blitstein, "Nation-Building or Russification? Obligatory Russian Instruction in the Soviet Non-Russian School, 1938–1953," in *A State of Nations: The Soviet State and Its Peoples in the Age of Lenin*

and Stalin, ed. Ronald G. Suny and Terry D. Martin (New York: Oxford University Press, 2001), 253–74; Peter A. Blitstein, "Stalin's Nations: Soviet Nationality Policy between Planning and Primordialism, 1936–1953" (PhD diss., University of California, Berkeley, 1999); E. Thomas Ewing, "Ethnicity at School: 'Non-Russian' Education in the Soviet Union during the 1930s," *History of Education* 35, no. 4–5 (2006): 499–519.

35 Matthew Payne, "The Forge of the Kazakh Proletariat? The Turksib, Nativization, and Industrialization during Stalin's First Five-Year Plan," in *A State of Nations: Empire and Nation-Making in the Age of Lenin and Stalin*, ed. Ronald Grigor Suny and Terry Martin (New York: Oxford University Press, 2001), 235.

36 These terms come from Martin, *Affirmative Action Empire*, and Francine Hirsch, *Empire of Nations: Ethnographic Knowledge and the Making of the Soviet Union* (Ithaca, NY: Cornell, 2005). Hirsch critiques Martin's notion of national minorities benefiting at the expense of majorities.

37 Larry Holmes, "Magic into Hocus-Pocus: The Decline of Labor Education in Soviet Russia's Schools, 1931–1937," *Russian Review* 51, no. 4 (1992): 545–65.

38 Jeffrey Brooks, *Thank You, Comrade Stalin! Soviet Public Culture from Revolution to Cold War* (Princeton, NJ: Princeton University Press, 2001), 83–105; Catriona Kelly, *Children's World: Growing Up in Russia, 1890–1991* (New Haven, CT: Yale University Press, 2007), 93–129; Kirschenbaum, *Small Comrades*, 133–59.

39 On Soviet provisioning, protection, and care of the most vulnerable in society as a way to promote a higher morality than that of their capitalist counterparts, see Maria Cristina Galmarini-Kabala, *The Right to Be Helped: Deviance, Entitlement, and the Soviet Moral Order* (DeKalb, IL: Northern Illinois University Press, 2016).

40 deGraffenried, *Sacrificing Childhood*. See also Kelly, *Children's World*, ch. 7.

41 Liisa Malkki, "National Geographic: The Rooting of Peoples and the Territorialisation of National Identity among Scholars and Refugees," *Cultural Anthropology* 7, no. 1 (1992): 24–44; Valentine Daniel, "The Refugee: A Discourse on Displacement," in *Exotic No More: Anthropology on the Frontlines*, ed. Jeremy MacClancey (Chicago: University of Chicago Press, 2002), 270–86; Tara Zahra, *The Lost Children: Reconstructing Europe's Families after World War II* (Cambridge, MA: Harvard University Press, 2011).

42 On the need for complicating the sometime unitary narratives of the Stalinist 1930s, see Katerina Clark, *Moscow, the Fourth Rome: Stalinism, Cosmopolitanism, and the Evolution of Soviet Culture, 1931–1941* (Cambridge, MA: Harvard University Press, 2011), 1–7; Schlögel, *Moscow*, 7. Michael David-Fox has correctly warned against accepting binaries of Soviet exceptionalism and shared modernity: *Crossing Borders: Modernity, Ideology, and Culture in Russia and the Soviet Union* (Pittsburgh, PA: University of Pittsburgh Press, 2015), particularly chs 1 and 2.

43 Nicholas Timasheff, *The Great Retreat: The Growth and Decline of Communism in Russia* (New York: Dutton, 1946).

44 Payne, "The Forge of the Kazakh Proletariat?" 224.
45 Slezkine, "USSR as Communal Apartment," 414–52.
46 David Brandenberger, *National Bolshevism: Stalinist Mass Culture and the Formation of Modern Russian National Identity, 1931–1956* (Cambridge, MA: Harvard University Press, 2002); Hirsch, *Empire of Nations*, 7–14; Martin, *Affirmative Action Empire*, 429–32.
47 *Segunda patria* is a common phrase found in early letters home; CDMH, P.S. Barcelona, 87/17/6. Children from the Greek Civil War who grew up in Eastern Europe also learned new languages, received an education, and developed connections to their "second homelands." Loring M. Danforth and Riki Van Boeschoten, *Children of the Greek Civil War: Refugees and the Politics of Memory* (Chicago: University of Chicago Press, 2012), ch. 4.
48 Hirsch, *Empire of Nations*, 7–8.
49 Castillo, *Mis años*, 79, includes a table showing the initial ethno-national composition of the homes.
50 Devillard et al., *Los niños*, 83–4; Elpat'evskii, *Ispanskaia emigratsiia v SSSR*, 122; Kharitonova, "Sovetskie pedagogicheskie rabotniki," 189.
51 Dorothy Legaretta, *The Guernica Generation: Basque Refugee Children of the Spanish Civil War* (Reno: University of Nevada Press, 1985), 167.
52 Clemente del Río Salceda, *20,000 días*, 81, 120.
53 *Pravda*, 25 June 1937, 6; A. Ponevezhskii, "Baskskie deti priekhali v Moskvu," *Pravda*, 26 June 1937, 6. Emphasis added.
54 L. Shapiro and A. Finogenov, "Deti Baskonii na novoi rodine," *Pravda*, 24 June 1937, 1. Emphasis added.

1 "Like Reaching Paradise after Being in Hell"

1 Ronald Fraser, *Blood of Spain: The Experience of Civil War, 1936–1939* (London: Allen Lane, 1979), 434.
2 Kononenko, *Malen'kie ispantsy*, 68.
3 CDMH, P.S. Barcelona, 87/17/11, 87/17/1, 87/17/3.
4 Legarreta, *Guernica Generation*, 21.
5 "Rasskaz ispanskoi pionerki," *Pravda*, 4 April 1937, 6.
6 A. Baev, "Deti iz strani baskov," *Pravda*, 28 June 1937, 6.
7 Francisco Espinosa Maestra, *Violencia roja y azul: España, 1936–1950* (Barcelona: Editorial Crítica, 2010); Santos Juliá and Julián Casanova, *Victimas de la Guerra Civil* (Madrid: Ediciones Temas de Hoy, 1999); Mirta Núñez Díaz-Balart et al., *La gran represión: Los años de plomo del franquismo* (Barcelona: Flor del Viento, 2009); Stanley G. Payne and Jesús Palacios, *Franco: A Person and Political Biography* (Madison: University of Wisconsin Press, 2014), ch. 9; Paul Preston, *The Spanish Holocaust: Inquisition and Extermination in Twentieth-Century Spain* (London: Harper Press, 2013).

8 Devillard et al., *Los niños*, 225–58. Most of the data came from the Centro Español in Moscow. As the Centro's data derive primarily from its surveys conducted forty years after the niños' arrival, we need to understand the lack of precision when memory alone is the source.
9 On these progressive educational colonies see "Las colonias escolares durante la Guerra Civil (1936–1939)," *Espacio, tiempo y forma* 5, no. 2 (1989): 299–337; P.L. Moreno Martinez, *Educación, salud y protección a la infancia: Las colonias escolares de Cartagena (1907–1936)* (Cartegena, Spain: Aglaya, 2000); Juan Félix Rodríguez Pérez and Francisco Canes Garrido, *Las colonias escolares municipales madrileñas (1910–1936)* (Madrid: Universidad Complutense de Madrid, 2001); Gregorio Arrien, *La generación del exilio: Génesis de las escuelas vascas y las colonias escolares (1932–1940)* (Bilbao, Spain: ONURA, 1983); Cristina Escrivá and Rafael Maestre Marín, *De las negras bombas a las doradas naranjas: Colonias escolares, 1936–1939* (Tavernes Blanques, Spain: Eixam, 2011); José Ignacio Cruz, *Las colonias escolares valencianas, 1906–1936: Un ejemplo de renovación educativa* (Valencia, Spain: Universidad de Valencia, 2012).
10 Colomina Limonero, *Dos patrias*, 20.
11 Devillard et al., *Los niños*, 234–5.
12 Alted Vigil, Marín, and Martell, *Los niños*, 51–2; Devillard et al., *Los niños*, 234; Milagros Latorre Piquer, "De niña española a mujer en la URSS," in *Nuevas raíces: Testimonios de mujeres españolas en el exilio* (Alicante, Spain: Biblioteca Virtual Miguel de Cervantes, 2002), 69; Zafra, Crego, and Heredia, *Los niños*, 142–3; Verónica Sierra Blas, "Educating the Communists of the Future: Notes on the Educational Life of the Spanish Children Evacuated to the USSR during the Spanish Civil War," *Paedagogica Historica* 51, no. 4 (2015): 498; Fernández Sánchez, *Memorias de un niño de Moscú*, 77.
13 Devillard et al., *Los niños*, 236.
14 These short student biographies are found throughout Gosudarstvennyi arkhiv Rossiiskoi federatsii (State Archive of the Russian Federation, Moscow; hereafter cited as GARF), f. A-307. Russian archival rules do not permit the review of the personal files at this time.
15 Legarreta, *Guernica Generation*, 158.
16 Adrian Shubert, *The Road to Revolution in Spain: The Coal Miners of Asturias, 1860–1934* (Urbana: University of Illinois Press, 1987).
17 A. Gudimov, "Gosti iz Ispanii," *Izvestiia*, 8 April 1937, 4.
18 Castillo, *Mis años*, 57–8.
19 Arce Porres, *Memorias*, 16; Latorre Piquer, "De niña española," 67.
20 Parents often requested a final destination in nearby French Basque territory, the United Kingdom, or the Soviet Union. However, the children often were divided up at a French port and arrived in an unknown destination.
21 Zafra, Crego, and Heredia, *Los niños*, 132.
22 Zafra, Crego, and Heredia, 134.

23 Among other possible sources on non-intervention see Antony Beevor, *The Battle for Spain: The Spanish Civil War, 1936-1939* (New York: Penguin Books, 2006), ch. 13; Enrique Moradiellos, "The Allies and the Spanish Civil War," in *Spain and the Great Powers in the Twentieth Century*, ed. Sebastian Balfour and Paul Preston (New York: Routledge, 1999), ch. 5; Enrique Moradiellos, *El reñidero de Europa: La dimensión internacional de la Guerra Civil española* (Barcelona: Península, 2001); Stanley G. Payne, *The Spanish Civil War, the Soviet Union, and Communism* (New Haven, CT: Yale University Press, 2004), ch. 7; Stanley G. Payne, *The Spanish Civil War* (Cambridge: Cambridge University Press, 2012), ch. 10; Paul Preston, *The Spanish Civil War: Reaction, Revolution, Revenge* (New York: W.W. Norton, 2006), 136-62.

24 N. Tokarev, "Ispanskie deti v Arteke," *Pravda*, 1 April 1937, 6; B. Kamir, "Ispanskie deti na otdykhe v Suuk-Su," *Komsomol'skaia Pravda*, 1 April 1937, 4; "V Artek priekhali ispanskie deti," *Izvestiia*, 2 April 1937, 3. In many countries the summer holiday out of the city was a rather common antidote to the ills of the modern industrial city. Cruz Orozco, *Las colonias escolares valencianas*; Laura Lee Downs, *Childhood in the Promised Land: Working-Class Movements and the Colonies de Vacances in France, 1880-1960* (London: Routledge, 2002); Hester Barron, "'Little Prisoners of City Streets': London Elementary Schools and the School Journey Movement, 1918-1939," *History of Education* 42, no. 2 (2013): 166-81.

25 Suan Breakwell has argued that in the movement from Madrid to the Levante provinces during the Spanish Civil War, "evacuation of children, far from being government driven, was very much in the hands of numerous union, political and workers' groups, as well as humanitarian organizations linked to political parties." Breakwell, "'Knowing How to Be a Mother': Parenting, Emotion and Evacuation Propaganda during the Spanish Civil War, 1936-1939," in *Parenting and the State in Britain and Europe, c. 1870-1950*, ed. Hestor Barron and Claudia Siebrecht (New York: Palgrave Macmillan, 2017), 209.

26 V. Solov'ev, "Baskskie deti u leningradskikh pionerov," *Pravda*, 25 June 1937, 6; "Parakhod 'Santai' priblizhaetsia k beregam SSSR," *Komsomol'skaia Pravda*, 21 June 1937, 4; "Leningrad gotovitsia k priemu baskskikh detei," *Komsomol'skaia Pravda*, 21 June 1937, 4; "Stolitsa zhdet detei geroicheskoi ispanii," *Komsomol'skaia Pravda*, 5 October 1937, 1. There was also one smaller evacuation in 1939. As the Spanish Republic collapsed, children of Spanish Communist Party leaders and military officers evacuated to live with their parents in Moscow.

27 Further details on the expeditions can be found in Zafra, Crego, and Heredia, *Los niños*, 35-50; Devillard et al., *Los niños*, ch. 1; Alted Vigil, Marín, and Martell, *Los niños*, chs 1-2; Castillo, *Mis años*, 31-70; Colomina Limonero, *Dos patrias*, 22-6; and Elpat'evskii, *Ispanskaia emigratsiia v SSSR*, 52-6. To date, most scholars have not mentioned the 12 July 1938 arrival of seventy-four Spanish children. "Ispanskie deti pribyli v Leningrad," *Komsomol'skaia Pravda*, 15 July 1938, 4; "Ispanskie deti na puti v Leningrad," *Izvestiia*, 11 July 1938, 4; "Ispanskie deti v

SSSR," *Izvestiia*, 14 July 1938, 4; "Ispanskie deti v Leningrade," *Pravda*, 13 July 1938, 6. On 30 November 1938, *Izvestiia* also wrote about another "large group of children from Republican Spain" that was set to arrive on 4–5 December 1938 aboard the *Feliks Dzerzhensky*.

28 Eduardo Pons Prades, *Los niños republicanos: El exilio* (Madrid: Oberon, 2005), 119.
29 Colomina Limonero, *Dos patrias*, 20. Adults evacuated with the children also thought that their stay would be brief. Soler Gilabert, *La vida*, 37.
30 Alted Vigil, Marín, and Martell, *Los niños*, 52.
31 Alted Vigil, Marín, and Martell, 80. An August 1937 report showed that 70 per cent (1,053 of 1,498) of children were placed in sanatoria because of illness; GARF, f. 8009, op. 20, d. 45, ll. 14–22.
32 Refugee studies have recently started to replace stories of victimhood with understandings of agency. Peter Gatrell, *Making of the Modern Refugee* (Oxford: Oxford University Press, 2013), shows how governmental and non-governmental agencies have often stripped refugees of their own agency.
33 Colomina Limonero, *Dos patrias*, 24.
34 Castillo, *Mis años*, 59–61.
35 Quotations from Colomina Limonero, *Dos patrias*, 24–5; Zafra, Crego, and Heredia, *Los niños*, 134, 44; Alted Vigil, Marín, and Martell, *Los niños*, 51–2; Devillard et al., *Los niños*, 79–80. In 1938 Franco called for all children to return to Spain and even formed the Extraordinary Delegation for the Repatriation of Minors to seize children from nearby countries. Alicia Alted Vigil, "Le retour en Espagne des enfants évacués pendant la guerre civile espagnole: La délégation extraordinaire au rapatriement des mineurs (1938–1954)," in *Enfants de la guerre civile: Vécus et représentations de la génération née entre 1925 et 1940*, ed. Centre d'histoire de l'Europe du vingtième siècle (Paris: L'Harmattan, 1999), 53; Ricard Vinyes, Montse Armengou, and Ricard Belis, *Los niños perdidos del franquismo* (Barcelona: Random House Mondadori, 2003).
36 Glennys Young coined the term *espanophilia* in her "To Russia with 'Spain,'" 404. Sheila Fitzpatrick has labelled the Spanish Civil War "the international event of the decade for the Soviet public, heavily covered in the newspapers." Sheila Fitzpatrick, *Everyday Stalinism: Ordinary Life in Extraordinary Times; Soviet Russia in the 1930s* (New York: Oxford University Press), 171. Katerina Clark also discusses the fascination with the conflict in *Moscow, the Fourth Rome*, 242–75.
37 On press media coverage of the Spanish Civil War see Kirschenbaum, *International Communism*, 125–31; David E. Allen, "The Soviet Union and the Spanish Civil War" (PhD diss., Stanford University, 1952); Daniel Kowalsky, "The Soviet Cinematic Offensive in the Spanish Civil War," *Film History* 19, no. 1 (2007): 10–19.
38 GARF, f. 8265, op. 3, d. 44; GARF, f. 8265, op. 3, d. 39, l. 12.
39 *Pravda*, 15 September 1936, 1–2; 16 September 1936, 1–2; 17 September 1936, 3; 18 September 1936, 2; 19 September 1936, 2; 20 September 1936, 3.
40 Schlögel, *Moscow*, 97.

41 Fernández Sánchez, *Mi infancia*, 24.
42 Russian State Archive of Socio-political History (hereafter cited as RGASPI), f. 17, op. 120, d. 266, l. 85.
43 V.A. Talashova, "Sovetskii Komsomol: Aktivnyi uchastnik dvizheniia solidarnosti s respublikanskoi Ispaniei v period natsional'no-revliutsionnyoi voiny, 1936–1939" (PhD diss., Vologodskii gosudarstvennyi. pedagogicheskii Institut, 1972), 119.
44 Voroshilov to Stalin, Russian State Military Archive (hereafter cited as RGVA), f. 33987, op. 3, d. 853, l. 72. Cited in Kowalsky, *Stalin and the Spanish Civil War*, ch. 5.
45 RGASPI, f. 17, op. 3, d. 983, l. 67.
46 RGASPI, f. 495, op. 18, d. 1225.
47 Colomina Limonero, *Dos patrias*, 29.
48 Colomina Limonero, 21.
49 Devillard et al., *Los niños*, 78; Alted Vigil, Marín, and Martell, *Los niños*, 52, 80.
50 Fraser, *Blood of Spain*, 434.
51 "Rasskaz ispanskoi pionerki," *Pravda*, 4 April 1937, 6. Charito instead studied rail transport. Encinas, *Fuentes*, 71. Military themes were common in early letters home. See, for example, CDMH, P.S. Bilbao, 5/11/28; 5/12/69.
52 CDMH, P.S. Barcelona, 87/17/6.
53 Kowalsky, *Stalin and the Spanish Civil War*, ch. 5.
54 Kowalsky, "The Soviet Cinematic Offensive," 13.
55 Kononenko, *Malen'kie ispantsy*. It had a print run of 50,300.
56 Glennys Young has argued that two Spanish youth who died fighting for the Soviets in the Second World War – María Pariña Ramos and Dolores Ibárruri's son Rubén Ruiz Ibárruri – were "depicted not only as heroic soldiers, but as leaders whose special capacity to inspire derived from the Spanish Civil War." Young, "To Russia with 'Spain,'" 409–10.
57 Tokarev, "Ispanskie deti v Arteke," *Pravda*, 1 April 1937, 6.
58 "V Artek priekhali ispanskie deti," *Izvestiia*, 2 April 1937, 3.
59 Gross, "Reclaiming the Nation," 244; Wasilewska, *Suffer Little Chidren*, 64–7.
60 Kononenko, *Malen'kie ispantsy*. For a further explication of this book see Karl D. Qualls, "Defining the Ideal Soviet Childhood: Reportage about Child Evacuees from Spain as Didactic Literature," in *War and Childhood in the Era of the Two World Wars*, ed. Mischa Honeck and James Marten (Cambridge: Cambridge University Press, 2019).
61 Kononenko, *Malen'kie ispantsy*, 69.
62 Kononenko, 70. "Saragossa" was likely a child from Zaragoza or one of the Roda Zarabozo children. Soviet writers struggled with transliterating unfamiliar names.
63 Zafra, Crego, and Heredia, *Los niños*, 105.
64 Devillard et al., *Los niños*, 45, 80; Zafra, Crego, and Heredia, *Los niños*, 44, 105, 107; CDMH, P.S. Barcelona, 87/17/2.

65 Zafra, Crego, and Heredia, *Los niños*, 109.
66 Zafra, Crego, and Heredia, 134; Álvarez Morán, *Memorias*, 189; Soler Gilabert, *La vida*, 41.
67 Colomina Limonero, *Dos patrias*, 27.
68 Devillard et al., *Los niños*, 43.
69 Zafra, Crego, and Heredia, *Los niños*, 111.
70 Devillard et al., *Los niños*, 85-6.
71 Clemente del Río Salceda, *20,000 días*, 66.
72 Latorre Piquer, "De niña española," 69.
73 Vicente Ramos, *La Guerra Civil (1936-1939) en la provincia de Alicante* (Alicante, Spain: Ediciones Biblioteca Alicantina, 1973), vol. 2, 231.
74 Fernández Sánchez, *Mi infancia*, 37.
75 Zafra, Crego, and Heredia, *Los niños*, 107; Pons Prades, *Los niños*, 105; Alted Vigil, Marín, and Martell, *Los niños*, 53.
76 Devillard et al., *Los niños*, 86.
77 Although Verónica Sierra, "Reconstructing Silences," notes some censorship of children's letters home, the concurrence of oral testimonies decades later in Spain suggests that effusive letters on arrival were not all manufactured by Soviet or Spanish adults.
78 Kononenko, *Malen'kie ispantsy*, 85.
79 Zafra, Crego, and Heredia, *Los niños*, 107. Enrique Zafra, a Spanish teacher who evacuated with the children, collected letters and oral testimonies for the fiftieth anniversary of their flight from Spain. These sources are archived in CDMH, ES.37274, CDMH/11.82.
80 Zafra, Crego, and Heredia, *Los niños*, 101, 45, 60, 117, 102-7.
81 Kononenko, *Malen'kie ispantsy*, 85.
82 Zafra, Crego, and Heredia, *Los niños*, 107.
83 Zafra, Crego, and Heredia, 101.
84 Pons Prades, *Los niños*, 116.
85 On drawing as a form of therapy and propaganda in the Spanish Civil War see Christian Roith, "Trotz allem zeichnen sie: Der Spanische Bürgerkrieg mit Kinderaugen gesehen," *Paedagogica Historica* 45, no. 1-2 (2009): 191-214.
86 Kononenko, *Malen'kie ispantsy*, 86; drawings, 57, 65. Anthony L. Geist, *They Still Draw Pictures: Children's Art in Wartime from the Spanish Civil War to Kosovo* (Urbana: University of Illinois Press, 2002), 13-75; Aldous Huxley, *They Still Draw Pictures! With 60 Illustrations Made by Spanish Children during the War* (New York: Spanish Child Welfare Association, 1938). Fifth grader Amelia Bernaldo de Quirós from Madrid noted the beauty of the Moscow metro. CDMH, P.S. Barcelona, 87/17/1.
87 Kononenko, *Malen'kie ispantsy*, 87. Francoist propaganda asserted that the Soviet Union had stolen the Spaniards. Eduardo Comín Colomner, *Españoles esclavos en Rusia* (Madrid: Publicaciones Españoles, 1952), 14.

88 *Jauja* refers to a place where one's needs are met effortlessly. Zafra, Crego, and Heredia, *Los niños*, 101.
89 Alted Vigil, Marín, and Martell, *Los niños*, 97.
90 Zafra, Crego, and Heredia, *Los niños*, 119.
91 Alted Vigil, Marín, and Martell, *Los niños*, 54; Zafra, Crego, and Heredia, *Los niños*, 101.
92 Álvarez Morán, *Memorias*, 70.
93 GARF, f. 8009, op. 20, d. 45, l. 6.
94 Castillo, *Mis años*, 63.
95 *Holding On, Fighting Back: The Long Road Home to Spain*, directed by Pedro Carvajal (Princeton, NJ: Films for the Humanities and Sciences, 2002), DVD.
96 Devillard et al., *Los niños*, 94.
97 Devillard et al., 94. Many leftists in Spain were still Catholic, including those in the Basque Communist Party.
98 Devillard et al., 196–9.
99 Zafra, Crego, and Heredia, *Los niños*, 107.
100 Devillard et al., *Los niños*, 95.
101 Devillard et al., 95.
102 Many oral histories give only the interviewee's gender, year of birth, and place of birth.
103 Zafra, Crego, and Heredia, *Los niños*, 134; GARF, f. 8009, op. 20, d. 45, ll. 1–22.
104 GARF, f. 8009, op. 20, d. 45, ll. 1–22.
105 It is quite possible that the number 1,498 refers to the children who arrived in July and does not include the small group of 72 children who arrived a few months earlier at Artek.
106 GARF, f. 8009, op. 20, d. 45, l. 22.
107 Devillard et al., *Los niños*, 95–6.
108 Larry Holmes has shown that even in Kirov oblast', where Narkompros evacuated during the war, Spanish schools received better provisions than those of their Soviet equivalents. Larry E. Holmes, *Stalin's World War II Evacuations: Triumph and Troubles in Kirov* (Lawrence: University of Kansas Press, 2017), 68–9, 83–5.
109 Legarreta, *Guernica Generation*, 51. For a brief comparative overview see Alicia Alted Vigil, "Repatriation or Return? The Difficult Homecoming of the Spanish Civil War Exiles," in *Coming Home?*, vol. 1, *Conflict and Return Migration in the Aftermath of Europe's Twentieth-Century Civil Wars*, ed. Sharif Gemie and Scott Soo (Newcastle-upon-Tyne, UK: Cambridge Scholars Publishing, 2013), 20–6.
110 Jesús J. Alonso Carballés, *1937: Los niños vascos evacuados a Francia y a Bélgica; Historia y memoria de un éxodo infantil, 1936–1940* (Bilbao, Spain: Asociación de Niños Evacuados el '37, 1998); Xavier García Argüello, *El mar de la libertad: Breve crónica de las evacuaciones de niños vascos durante la Guerra del '37* (Bilbao, Spain: Asociación de Jubilados Evacuados de la Guerra Civil y Ayuntamiento de Bilbao, 2002); Legarreta, *Guernica Generation*, ch. 2; Pierre

Marques, *Les enfants espagnols réfugiés en France (1936–1939)* (Paris: self-pub., 1993). Similar anti-Soviet propaganda greeted their return to Spain in the 1950s. Magdalena Garrido Caballero, "Españoles repatriados de la URSS en la propaganda del régimen franquista," in *Actas del VI encuentro de investigadores sobre el franquismo*, ed. Juan José Carerras and Ángela Cenarro (Zaragoza, Spain: Contexto Gráfico, 2006), 117–30.

111 Adrian Bell, *Only for Three Months: The Basque Refugee Children in Exile* (Norwich, UK: Mousehold Press, 2007); Gregorio Arrien, *Niños vascos evacuados a Gran Bretaña* (Bilbao, Spain: Asociación de Niños Evacuados el '37, 1998); Natalia Benjamin, ed., *Recuerdos: Basque Refugee Children in Great Britain* (Norwich, UK: Mousehold Press, 2007); Yvonne Cloud, *The Basque Children in England: An Account of Their Life at North Stoneham Camp* (London: Victor Gollancz, 1937); Hywell Davies, *Fleeing Franco: How Wales Gave Shelter to Refugee Children from the Basque Country during the Spanish Civil War* (Cardiff: University of Wales Press, 2011); Legarreta, *Guernica Generation*, ch. 3.

112 Alonso Carballés, *1937*; Emilia Labajos Pérez and Fernando Vitoria-García, *Los niños españoles refugiados en Bélgica, 1936–1939* (Valencia, Spain: Asociación de los Niños de la Guerra de Namur, 1997); Legarreta, *Guernica Generation*, ch. 4; *L'hebergement des enfants de la guerre d'Espagne en Belgique* (Brussels: Federación de Asociaciones de Enseñanza y Centros Españoles en Bélgica, 1992).

113 Legarreta, *Guernica Generation*, ch. 6; Dolores Pla Brugat, *Los Niños de Morelia* (Mexico City: Instituto Nacional de Antropología e Historia, 1985); Dolores Pla Brugat, "Los niños del exilio español en México," in *El exilio de los niños*, ed. Alicia Alted, Roger González, and María José Millían (Madrid: Fundación Francisco Largo Caballero / Fundación Pablo Iglesias, 2003), 162–77; Immaculada García Lozano and Dolores Moreno Burgos, *Los raíles del exilio: "Niños de Morelia"; Uno éxodo a México* (Madrid: Fundación de los Ferrocarriles Españoles, 2007); Agustín Sánchez Andrés, et al., eds, *Un capitulo de la memoria oral del exilio: Los niños de Morelia* (Morelia and Madrid: Universidad Michoacana de San Nicolás de Hidalgo–Comunidad de Madrid, 2002).

2 "We, the Spanish, Were like an Island"

1 Jaime Camino, *Intimas conversaciones con la Pasionaria* (Barcelona: Dopesa, 1977), 172.
2 Schlögel, *Moscow*, 98.
3 Álvarez Morán, *Memorias*, 73; Clemente del Río Salceda, *20,000 días*, 77; Fernández Sánchez, *Mi infancia*, 59–60. Fernández Sánchez recalls never being without money as an adolescent, because his Soviet friends would loan him what he needed.
4 Larry E. Holmes, "Spain in the Depths of Russia, 1941–1945" (unpublished manuscript); Latorre Piquer, "De niña española," 92. Bernardo del Río, for example, met his wife, Raisa, at the Higher School of Transport Engineers.

5 For a discussion of the return to teacher-centred instruction and the importance of discipline in the classroom, see E. Thomas Ewing, *The Teachers of Stalinism: Policy, Practice and Power in Soviet Schools of the 1930s* (New York: Peter Lang, 2002), chs 5 and 6; Larry Holmes, *Stalin's School: Moscow's Model School No. 25, 1931–1937* (Pittsburgh, PA: University of Pittsburgh Press, 1999), ch. 7.
6 Ann Livschiz, "Pre-revolutionary in Form, Soviet in Content? Wartime Educational Reforms and the Postwar Quest for Normality," *History of Education* 35, no. 4–5 (2006): 541–60.
7 B.G. Anan'ev, "O glavnom 'zakone' pedologii," *Sovetskaia pedagogika*, no. 1 (1937): 14–34; Ewing, *Teachers of Stalinism*, 151–87; Holmes, *Stalin's School*, 137–41.
8 Joseph Stalin, "Report to the Eighteenth Congress of the CPSU(B) on the Work of the Central Committee, March 10, 1939," in *Problems of Leninism* (Moscow: Foreign Languages Publishing House, 1954), 780–9; William Chase, *Enemies within the Gates? The Comintern and the Stalinist Repression, 1934–1939* (New Haven, CT: Yale University Press, 2001); William Chase, "Scapegoating One's Comrades in the USSR, 1934–1937," *Russian History* 38, no. 1 (2011): 23–41; Elena Dundovich, "Le purghe Staliniane e il Komintern: La guerra di Spagna e i suoi riflessi sulla politica interna Sovietica," *Storia delle Relazioni Internazionali* 11, no. 1 (January 1996): 3–35; Kevin McDermott, "Stalinist Terror in the Comintern: New Perspectives," *Journal of Contemporary History* 30 (January 1995): 111–30. Only about two thousand Spanish communists were allowed entry to the USSR in April–May 1939. See David Wingeate Pike, *In the Service of Stalin: The Spanish Communists in Exile, 1939–1945* (Oxford: Clarendon Press, 1993), 17, 36; Elpat'evskii, *Ispanskaia emigratsiia v SSSR*, 38–40; Alicia Alted Vigil, *La voz de los vencidos: El exilio republican de 1939* (Madrid: Aguilar, 2005), 48, 162–3.
9 Ewing, "Ethnicity at School," 504–5. Lisa Kirschenbaum, *International Communism and the Spanish Civil War*, 30–6, makes a similar observation about the Lenin School – a school for older international communists – and its ability to foster long-term connections.
10 Devillard et al., *Los niños*, 114, makes this point clearly in discussing the distinct personalities and methodologies of the various directors. Immaculada Colomina Limonero embedded the variety of experiences in the title of her book *Dos patrias, tres mil destinos* [Two homelands, three thousand destinations].
11 Soler Gilabert, *La vida*, 62.
12 Arxiu Nacional de Catalunya, Barcelona (hereafter cited as ANC), f. 555, d. 254.
13 Devillard et al., *Los niños*, 81.
14 Pons Prades, *Los niños*, 119.
15 Kucherenko, *Soviet Street Children*, passim. José Fernández Sánchez recalled itinerant Soviets, usually intellectuals, coming to his evacuated school, looking for work and food (*Mi infancia*, 137).
16 GARF, f. A-307, op. 2, d. 406, ll. 1–2.

17 This brief experiment ended as the Second World War started in the USSR, and the older children were sent to work or to labour training. See chapter 6 herein.
18 Pons Prades, *Los niños*, 119.
19 A lack of trained cadres, particularly in non-Russian educational institutions, was common and limited teaching effectiveness. Ewing, "Ethnicity at School," 506; Kirschenbaum, *International Communism*, 28–9.
20 Fernández Sánchez, *Memorias*, 153.
21 Devillard et al., *Los niños*, 98.
22 Colomina Limonero, *Dos patrias*, 49; Kharitonova, "Sovetskie pedagogicheskie rabotniki," 178.
23 Arce Porres, *Memorias*, 51.
24 GARF, f. A-307, op. 1, d. 345, ll. 15–32.
25 Devillard et al., *Los niños*, 100.
26 Colomina Limonero, *Dos patrias*, 48–9.
27 I.A. Kairov, *Pedagogika* (Moscow: Uchpedgiz, 1939), 366.
28 Katerina Clark, *The Soviet Novel: History as Ritual* (Bloomington: Indiana University Press, 2000).
29 "Vserossiiskoe soveshchanie po rabote detskikh domov," *Narodnoe obrazovanie*, no. 12 (1948): 72.
30 Latorre Piquer, "De niña española," 86–7.
31 Michel Foucault, "The Subject and Power," *Critical Inquiry* 8, no. 4 (1982): 790; Foucault, *Security, Territory, Population*, 87–90.
32 Michel Foucault, *Discipline and Punish: The Birth of the Prison* (New York: Vintage Books, 1979), 183. For a complex analysis of Foucaultian history of children see Bernadette Baker, "Foucault, Historiography, and Writing a History of the Child: Productive Paradoxes," *History of Education Review* 30, no. 1 (2001): 20–33. Foucault's application to Soviet schooling is most evident in E. Thomas Ewing's discussion of disciplinary strategies; see his *Teachers of Stalinism*, 189–225.
33 Hygiene and sanitation has long been part of the Soviet modernization process. See David L. Hoffmann, *Stalinist Values: The Cultural Norms of Soviet Modernity, 1917–1941* (Ithaca, NY: Cornell University Press, 2003), esp. ch. 1; Northrop, *Veiled Empire*, 60–4; O'Keeffe, *New Soviet Gypsies*, 67–73; Starks, *The Body Soviet*; Slezkine, *Arctic Mirrors*, esp. ch. 7.
34 *Sanitarnye pravila dlia detskikh uchrezhdenii*, 2nd ed. (Leningrad, 1940), 21–6; *Spravochnik sovetskogo rabotnika* (Moscow: Vlast' sovetov, 1937), 816.
35 B. Selikhanovich, "Osnovy vospitaniia kommunisticheskoi morali," *Sovetskaia pedagogika*, no. 7 (1940): 3–17.
36 GARF, f. A-2306, op. 70, d. 5987, l. 8.
37 GARF, f. A-2306, op. 70, d. 6002.
38 GARF, f. 8009, op. 20, d. 45, ll. 17–22.
39 This must refer to Rufino Castaños Martínez who was born in Oviedo in 1885. He joined the Spanish Socialist Workers' Party (PSOE) at age twenty-five and then, six years later, the PCE. Encina, *Fuentes*, 237.

40 Arce Porres, *Memorias*, 27–8.
41 GARF, f. 2306, op. 70, d. 5991, ll. 12–23; GARF, f. A-307, op. 2, d. 200, l. 19. Few students had parents in the USSR, the exceptions being exiled leaders of the PCE and some Republican military officers.
42 Fernández Sánchez, *Memorias*, 140; Arce Porres, *Memorias*, 30.
43 Soler Gilabert, *La vida*, 43–4; RGASPI, f. 533, op. 10, d. 1442, ll. 60–79.
44 Devillard et al., *Los niños*, 105–6.
45 Fernández Sánchez, *Memorias*, 78.
46 The most enduring symbol was Dolores Ibárruri. Kirschenbaum, *International Communism*, 200–5; Lisa Kirschenbaum, "Exile, Gender, and Communist Self-Fashioning: Dolores Ibárruri (La Pasionara) in the Soviet Union," *Slavic Review* 71, no. 3 (Fall 2012): 566–89.
47 Peter Gatrell and Nick Baron, "Violent Peacetime: Reconceptualizing Displacement and Resettlement in the Soviet–East European Borderlands after the Second World War," in *Warlands: Population Resettlement and State Reconstruction in the Soviet–East European Borderlands, 1945–50*, ed. Baron and Gatrell (New York: Palgrave Macmillan, 2009), 259–60.
48 GARF, f. 5451, op. 43, d. 106a, l. 236.
49 Devillard et al., *Los niños*, 105.
50 GARF, f. A-307, op. 2, dd. 1, 4, 156, 162, 240, 407, 409, 460.
51 GARF, f. A-307, op. 1, d. 347, ll. 11–14; GARF, f. A-307, op. 1, d. 349, ll. 1–30; Encinas, *Fuentes*, 463, 198.
52 Clemente del Río Salceda, *20,000 días*, 137–43.
53 Colomina Limonero, *Dos patrias*, 47.
54 Colomina Limonero, 46–7.
55 Camino, *Íntimas conversaciones*, 172–4.
56 Constancia de la Mora, *Vmesto roskoshi* (Moscow: Khudozhestvennaia literatura, 1943), 268. I. Hidalgo de Cisneros, *Meniaiu kurs: Memuary* (Moscow: Izdatel'stvo politicheskoi literatury, 1967), 408–9; Constancia de la Mora, *Doble esplendor: Autobiografía de una aristocrata española republicana y comunista* (Barcelona: Critica, 1977), 310, 375–9.
57 M. Deineko, "Piatiletnii plan razvitiia shkol'nogo obrazovanii," *Narodnoe obrazovanie*, no. 7 (1946): 14–29. On failures in non-Russian schools see P. Glagolev, "Ne russkie shkoly i zadachi ikh ukrepleniia," *Narodnoe obrazovanie*, no. 9 (1947): 18–28. On non-Russian schools more generally see Blitstein, "Nation-Building or Russification?"; Ewing, "Ethnicity at School"; Barbara A. Anderson and Brian D. Silver, "Equality, Efficiency, and Politics in Soviet Bilingual Education Policy, 1934–1980," *American Political Science Review* 78, no. 4 (1984): 1019–39.
58 Elizabeth McGuire has shown that a lack of teachers of Mandarin led many of these children to lose most of their understanding of the language (*Red at Heart*, ch. 13).
59 GARF, f. A-307, op. 1, d. 338, l. 88. This industrial notion of "forging" new people appeared in the earliest days of the new Bolshevik state as seen in the poetry of Vladimir Kirillov ("Iron Messiah") and Aleksei Gastev ("We Grow out of Iron").

60 Homi K. Bhabha, "Signs Taken for Wonders: Questions of Ambivalence and Authority under a Tree outside Delhi, May 1817," *Critical Inquiry* 12, no. 1 (1985): 156; emphasis in the original.
61 Colomina Limonero, *Dos patrias*, 46–7.
62 Evgeny Dobrenko, "The School Tale in Children's Literature of Socialist Realism," in *Russian Children's Literature and Culture*, ed Marina Balina and Larissa Rudova (New York: Routledge, 2008), 58.
63 GARF, f. A-2306, op. 70, d. 5987, ll. 1–3.
64 GARF, f. A-2306, op. 70, d. 5987, l. 1.
65 *Kul'turnost'* refers less to high or low culture but more to one's behaviours and attitudes in daily life. Vadim Volkov, "The Concept of Kul'turnost': Notes on the Stalinist Civilizing Process," in *Stalinism: New Directions*, ed. Sheila Fitzpatrick (New York: Routledge, 2000), 210–30.
66 An edict of the Supreme Soviet published in *Izvestiya* on 27 June 1940 made tardiness and absenteeism crimes. Donald Filtzer, *Soviet Workers and Stalinist Industrialization: The Formation of Modern Soviet Production Relations, 1928–1941* (London: Pluto Press, 1986), 107–15 and ch. 9. For labour edicts targeting adolescents see Olga Kucherenko, "State v. Danila Kuz'mich: Soviet Desertion Laws and Industrial Child Labor during World War II," *Russian Review* 71 (July 2012): 391–412.
67 GARF, f. A-2306, op. 70, d. 5998, l. 1.
68 GARF, f. A-2306, op. 70, d. 5987, l. 2.
69 Spanish Republican propaganda during the civil war also stressed the need to send children away from the front lines, where they could be nurtured and educated to become the "men of tomorrow" who would reconstruct the "New Spain" as "agents of regeneration." Breakwell, "Knowing How to Be a Mother," 214.
70 CDMH, P.S. Santander 0, 51/7; Alted Vigil, Marín, and Martell, *Los niños*, 62.
71 Josef Stalin, *Socheineniia*, vol. 16, 100, translated in Slezkine, "USSR as a Communal Apartment," 449.
72 The best source to date is Catriona Kelly, *Comrade Pavlik: The Rise and Fall of a Soviet Boy Hero* (London: Granata, 2007).
73 Green, "There Will Not Be Orphans among Us," 115–18.
74 Kucherenko, *Little Soldiers*, 26–7; Makarenko, *Pedagogicheskaia poema* [Pedagogical poem] (Moscow, 1964), 127; Joseph Zajda, *Education in the USSR* (Oxford: Pergamon Press, 1980), 15.
75 Calls for increased discipline and disciplinary strategies had been growing throughout the 1930s. Ewing, *Teachers of Stalinism*, ch. 6.
76 Alted Vigil, Marín, and Martell, *Los niños*, 99.
77 GARF, f. A-307, op. 1, d. 122, l. 5ob.
78 Devillard et al., *Los niños*, 103.
79 On street children and crime see Alan Ball, *And Now My Soul Is Hardened*; Green, "There Will Not Be Orphans among Us," 29–80; Livschiz, "Growing Up Soviet," ch. 4; Kucherenko, *Soviet Street Children*.

80 Kharitonova, "Sovetskie pedagogicheskie rabotniki," 188.
81 S. Aleksandrov, "K itogam diskussii o problemakh vospitaniia," *Vozhatyi*, no. 20 (1940): 25–8; A.S. Makarenko, "Metody vospitaniia," *Sovetskaia pedagogika*, no. 5–6 (1943): 10–17 [from a 10 January 1938 lecture]; E.N. Medynskii, "Pedagogicheskoe nasledstvo A.S. Makarenko i ego znachenie v period Velikoi Otechsetvennoi Voiny," *Sovetskaia pedagogika*, no. 8–9 (1943): 1–7. On Makarenko see Götz Hillig and Marianne Krüger-Potratz, "Die 'zweite Geburt' des A.S. Makarenko: Zugleich ein Beitrag zu einem kaum bekannten Kapitel aus der Geschichte der sowjetischen Pädagogik, 1939–1941," in *Vergleichende Bildungsforsschung: DDR, Osteuropa und interkulturelle Perspektiven*, ed. Bernhard Dilger, Friedrich Kübart, and Hans-Peter Schaefer (Berlin: Verlag Arno Spitz, 1986), 318–42; Larry E. Holmes, "School and Schooling under Stalin, 1931–1953," in *Educational Reform in Post-Soviet Russia: Legacies and Prospects*, ed. Ben Eklof, Larry E. Holmes, and Vera Kaplan (London: Frank Cass, 2005), 56–101. For workshops see RGASPI, f. 533, op. 10, d. 2635, l. 66; GARF, f. A-307, op. 1, d. 294, l. 4; GARF, f. A-2306, op. 70, d. 6097, l. 1.
82 Fernández Sánchez, *Memorias*, 128.
83 Devillard et al., *Los niños*, 101–3.
84 Castillo, *Mis años*, 12; Kharitonova, "Sovetskie pedagogicheskie rabotniki," 178–9.
85 Arce Porres, *Memorias*, 51.
86 Jochen Hellbeck, through a study of Soviet autobiographies, has argued that Soviet adults also feared ostracism from the social collective. *Revolution on My Mind: Writing a Diary under Stalin* (Cambridge, MA: Harvard University Press, 2006), 10–11.
87 I.I. Daniushevskii, "Voprosy vospitaniia detei v detskom dome," *Detskii dom*, 1 (1944): 3–11.
88 GARF, f. A-307, op. 1, d. 344, l. 3; f. A-307, op. 1, d. 128, l. 2; f. A-307, op. 1, d. 136, l. 2; f. A-307, op. 1, d. 267, l. 4; f. A-307, op. 1, d. 246, ll. 23–5.
89 Ralph Talcott Fisher, *Pattern for Soviet Youth: A Study of the Congresses of the Komsomol, 1918–1954* (New York: Columbia University Press, 1959), ch. 6; deGraffenried, *Sacrificing Childhood*, 8; Allen Kassof, *The Soviet Youth Program: Regimentation and Rebellion* (Cambridge, MA: Harvard University Press, 1965); Vladimir Kudinov, *Detskoe i molodezhnoe dvizhenie v Rossii v XX veke* (Kostroma, Russia: Kostromskoi gostudarstvennoi universitet, 2000).
90 For more on the role of youth organizations in social upbringing see Fedor Korolev, *Sovetskaia shkola v period industrializatsii* (Moscow: Uchebno-pedagogicheskoe izdatelstvo, 1959), 263.
91 Colomina Limonero, *Dos patrias*, 42.
92 RGASPI, f. 533, op. 6, d. 463, ll. 5–8.
93 GARF, f. A-2306, op. 70, d. 6097, l. 1.
94 The same was true in more inclusive junior cadet schools and Soviet schools in general. Olga Kucherenko, "*In loco parentis*: Junior Cadet Schools in the Soviet

Union during the Second World War," in *Parenting and the State in Britain and Europe, c. 1870-1950*, ed. Hester Barron and Claudia Siebrecht (New York: Palgrave Macmillan, 2017), 239; Igor Kon, "Telesnye nakazaniia deti v Rossii: Proshloe i nastoiashchee," *Istoricheskaia psikhologiia i sotsiologiia istorii* 1 (2011): 83.

95 Devillard et al., *Los niños*, 103.
96 GARF, f. 8009, op. 20, d. 45, ll. 14–22.
97 María Encarna Nicolás Marín, "La integración de los niños y jóvenes en la emigración de la Guerra Civil: El caso de la Unión Soviética," *Anales de Historia Contemporánea* 19 (2003): 62.
98 GARF, f. A-307, op. 1, d. 148, l. 23; f. A-307, op. 1, d. 221, l. 2.
99 RGASPI, f. 533, op. 10, d. 2635, ll. 66, 95.
100 Colomina Limonero, *Dos patrias*, 49–50. The paucity of quality cadres doomed more than one Soviet project. See Daniel Peris, *Storming the Heavens: The Soviet League of the Militant Godless* (Ithaca, NY: Cornell University Press, 1998), ch. 7.
101 Devillard et al., *Los niños*, 104.
102 Makarenko, *Pedagogicheskaia poema*, ch. 1.
103 Daniushevskii, "Voprosy vospitaniia detei v detskom dome," 3–11.
104 F. Lebedev and T.K. Chuguev, "Ob antireligioznom vospitanii v shkole," *Sovetskaia pedagogika*, no. 8 (1940): 3–13; William B. Husband, *"Godless Communists": Atheism and Society in Soviet Russia, 1917-1932* (Dekalb, IL: Northern Illinois University Press, 2000); Peris, *Storming the Heavens*; Richard Stites, *Revolutionary Dreams: Utopian Vision and Experimental Life in the Russian Revolution* (Oxford: Oxford University Press, 1991), ch. 5.
105 GARF, f. 5451, op 43, d. 106a, ll. 97–100.
106 GARF, f. A-2306, op. 70, d. 6009, ll. 1–5. The 1940 data likely include Spaniards who arrived after Franco's 1939 victory, took positions in the schools, and then were removed. It is unclear why this mid-year report lists thirty-three Spaniards removed and the year-end report counted only twenty-nine.
107 GARF, f. A-307, op. 2, d. 3, ll. 1–2.
108 GARF, f. A-307, op. 2, d. 1384, l. 1.
109 Bote was eventually arrested and detained for several years before he repatriated in 1956. Encinas, *Fuentes*, 219.
110 All cases are noted in GARF, f. A-307, op. 2, d. 460, ll. 1–3.
111 Kirschenbaum, *International Communism*, 43.
112 On the ideal Soviet classroom teacher see Ewing, "A Stalinist Celebrity Teacher: Gender, Professional, and Political Identities in Soviet Culture of the 1930s," *Journal of Women's History* 16, no. 4 (Winter 2004): 92–118; Ewing, *Teachers of Stalinism*, chs 5–6.
113 GARF, f. A-307, op. 2, d. 409, ll. 1–2. For characterizations about Spanish adults at the Lenin School in the 1930s see Kirschenbaum, *International Communism*, 144–8.
114 GARF, f. A-2306, op. 70, d. 6009, ll. 3–4; f. A-307, op. 1, d. 15, l. 14. She did not emigrate soon. She worked on a state farm until her repatriation some time later.

115 Report undated, GARF, f. A-307, op. 2, d. 1376, ll. 3–4.
116 GARF, f. A-307, op. 2, d. 407 (January 1939). Encina, *Fuentes*, 197, notes that Bajo died in 1938.
117 Sheila Fitzpatrick, *Tear Off the Masks! Identity and Imposture in Twentieth-Century Russia* (Princeton, NJ: Princeton University Press, 2005), pt. 5.
118 GARF, f. A-2306, op. 70, d. 5987, l. 6.
119 It is not yet clear how widespread such removals were or how aware Spaniards were of what was going on around them. Valentìn González, known as the civil war hero "El Campesino," reported in his memoir that Soviets had liquidated 60 per cent of teachers by the time he arrived in 1939. Jesús Hernández, former minister of education for the republic, stated much the same, that after the Spanish Civil War had ended, teachers were expelled and/or arrested and replaced with Russian teachers and textbooks, and the children were put into labour as well as schooling. The Soviet government expelled both authors in 1939, so there is a strong possibility for bias. Moreover, they were not arrested or killed, which seems to weaken their claim. One archival document from December 1947 shows fifty-eight Spaniards in the Karaganda gulag, but these were sailors and pilots and not the child refugees or teachers. RGASPI, f, 17, op. 130, d. 23, ll. 203–6. See also Luiza Iordache, *Republicanos españoles en el Gulag, 1939–1956* (Barcelona: Institut de Ciències Polítiques i Socials, 2008). There is no documentary evidence supporting claims of a mass liquidation. Valentín González, *Vida y muerte en la URSS* (Buenos Aires: S.A. Editorial Bell, 1951), 190; Jesús Hernández, *El país de la gran mentira* (Madrid: E.G. del Toro, 1974), 222–3. Labour was part of the niños' training, and factory work after education was typical in the USSR during the Second World War.
120 Devillard et al., *Los niños*, 107. The phrase *viva la pepa* also can suggest complete chaos, disorder, and incompetence.
121 Castillo, *Mis años*, 167.
122 ANC, f. 555, d. 254, "Memories dels treballadors que van estar amb els nens espanyols a la casa no. 13 de Kiev."
123 Fernández Sánchez, *Memorias*, 95.
124 Stephen Kotkin, *Magnetic Mountain: Stalinism as a Civilization* (Berkeley: University of California Press, 1995), ch. 5, describes "speaking Bolshevik" as a way to learn and use rhetorical tools both to survive in the Soviet system and to get from it what was desired.
125 A. Ia. Vyshinskii, "Vystuplenie na vserossiiskom soveshchanii aktiva uchitelei i rukovodiashchikh rabotnikov narodnogo obrazovaniia," *Sovetskaia Pedagogika*, no. 10 (1939): 29–34.
126 F. Kozhevnikov, "Opyt samostoiatel'nogo izucheniia istorii VKP(b)," *Sovetskaia pedagogika*, no. 3 (1940): 64–9; "K itogam XVIII partiinoi konferentsii," *Sovetskaia pedagogika*, no. 4 (1941): 3–10; Brandenberger, *National Bolshevism*, 63–74.
127 Katerina Clark, *Moscow*.

3 *Obuchenie*: Classroom Instruction

1. *Pravda*, 17 August 1942.
2. Cited in Colomina Limonero, *Dos patrias,* 35.
3. GARF, f. 2306, op. 7, d. 5993, l. 3. He died in 1938, so his letter likely went unheeded.
4. Martin, *Affirmative Action Empire*, 1–19.
5. Guy Neave, "War and Educational Reconstruction in Belgium, France and the Netherlands, 1940–1947," in *Education and the Second World War: Studies in Schooling and Social Change*, ed. Roy Lowe (London: Falmer Press, 1992), 84.
6. On teaching patriotism and democracy to imprisoned Japanese children in the United States see Thomas James, *Exile Within: The Schooling of Japanese Americans, 1942–1945* (Cambridge, MA: Harvard University Press, 1987), esp. chs 3–4; Yoon K. Pak, *Wherever I Go, I Will Always Be an American: Schooling Seattle's Japanese Americans during World War* (New York: Routledge Falmer, 2002), chs 4–5. For a comparison of Japanese, German, and American schools in the Crystal City, Texas, internment camp, see Karen L. Riley, *Schools behind Barbed Wire: The Untold Story of Wartime Internment and the Children of Arrested Enemy Aliens* (Lanham, MD: Rowman & Littlefield, 2002).
7. Owen Griffiths, "Japanese Children and the Culture of Death, January–August 1945," in *Children and War*, ed. James Marten (New York: New York University Press, 2002), 160–71; Kathleen S. Uno, *Passages to Modernity: Motherhood, Childhood, and Social Reform in Early Twentieth-Century Japan* (Honolulu: University of Hawaii Press, 1999), 8.
8. Michael H. Kater, *Hitler Youth* (Cambridge, MA: Harvard University Press, 2004), 28–69; Lisa Pine, "The Dissemination of Nazi Ideology and Family Values through School Textbooks," *History of Education* 25, no. 1 (1996): 91–109; Nicholas Stargardt, *Witnesses of War: Children's Lives under the Nazis* (New York: Vintage, 2007).
9. Kenny Cupers, "Governing through Nature: Camps and Youth Movements in Interwar Germany and the United States," *Cultural Geographies* 15 (2008): 173–205.
10. Robert William Kirk, *Earning Their Stripes: The Mobilization of American Children in the Second World War* (New York: Peter Lang, 1994); Steven Mintz, *Huck's Raft: A History of American Childhood* (Cambridge, MA: Harvard University Press, 2004), 254–74; Lisa L. Ossian, "'Too Young for a Uniform': Children's War Work on the Iowa Farm Front, 1941–1945," in *Children and War: A Historical Anthology*, ed. James Marten (New York: New York University Press, 2002), 254–65.
11. Dunstan, *Soviet Schooling*, chs 7–8; Ann Livschiz, "Children's Lives after Zoia's Death: Order, Emotions and Heroism in Children's Lives and Literature in the Post-War Soviet Union," in *Late Stalinist Russia: Soviet between Reconstruction and Reinvention*, ed. Juliane Fürst (New York: Routledge, 2006), 204.

12 As scholars investigate policies and reports, however, we need to be cognizant that theory and reality often diverged. "Model schools" with their abundant resources created a stark contrast with the vast majority of schools that had to make do with the pedagogical resources and expertise available. Holmes, *Stalin's School*, 163–4.
13 L.I. Gerchikova, "Rabota detskikh bibliotek v voennoe vremia," *Sovetskaia pedagogika*, 9 (1941): 54.
14 S.M. Rives, "O postanovke vospitatel'noi raboty v shkolnom internate," *Sovetskaia pedagogika* 11, no. 12 (1941): 29; emphasis in original.
15 Moreno, Itkis, and Felipe, *Dobro pozhalovat' na nash prazdnik*, 95.
16 L.L. Grinberg, "Prosveshchenie v revoliutsionnoi Ispanii," *Sovestakaia pedagogika*, no. 2 (1937): 106–8.
17 Christopher Cobb, "The Republican State and Mass Educational-Cultural Initiatives," in *Spanish Cultural Studies: An Introduction: The Struggle for Modernity*, ed. Helen Graham and Jo Labanyi (Oxford: Oxford University Press, 1995), 133–8.
18 José Alvarez Junco, "Education and the Limits of Liberalism," in *Spanish Cultural Studies*, ed. Graham and Labanyi, 42–5, 48.
19 Charles F. Gallagher, *Culture and Education in Spain* (Hanover, NH: American Universities Field Staff, 1979), 13; Antonio Guzmán et al., *Causas y remedio del analfabetismo en España* (Madrid: Publicaciones de la Junta Nacional contra el Analfabetismo, Ministerio de Educación Nacional, 1955), 15–20, 31–49; Antonio Cazorla Sánchez, *Fear and Progress: Ordinary Lives in Franco's Spain, 1939–1975* (Malden, MA: Wiley Blackwell, 2010), 88–94.
20 GARF, f. 5283, op. 7, d. 1015, l. 79; f. A-307, op. 1, d. 1, l. 1.
21 Kowalsky, *Stalin and the Spanish Civil War*, ch. 5, contains an interesting discussion of the attempts of Spanish diplomat Vicente Polo to bring Spanish textbooks to the refugee children.
22 Clemente del Río Salceda, *20,000 días*, 68. We have little demographic information on the bilingual translators, but one press report noted that four of the ten translators sent to help with a new shipload of Basque children were Argentinian Pioneers. "Leningrad gotovitsia k priemu baskskikh detei," *Pravda*, 21 June 1937, 4.
23 While the emphasis on Russifying the homes increased in the war years, it seems like little more than an extension of the russocentric curriculum and culture that had emerged in the late 1930s. Brandenberger, *National Bolshevisim*, chs 4 and 10; Dunstan, *Soviet Schooling* (New York: St Martin's Press, 1997).
24 P.M. Minin, "Georicheskie obrazy narodnogo patriotizma v klassichskoi literature," *Sovetskaia pedagogika*, no. 3–4 (1942): 54–70; N.V. Udina, "K voprosu o vospitanii sovetskogo patriotizma v sovetskoi shkole," *Sovetskaia pedagogika*, no. 5 (1938): 33–46; V.A. Zorin, "Vospitanie sovetskogo patriotizma," *Sovetskaia pedagogika*, no. 4 (1937): 27–31; GARF, f. A-307, op. 1, d. 77, ll. 144–50; f. A-307, op. 1, d. 95, l. 29.
25 "Rech Narodnogo Komissara Prosveshchinaia RSFSR V.P. Potemkina na sobranii aktiva uchitelei," *Sovetskaia pedagogika*, no. 5/6 (1943): 7.

26 P.M. Kuz'min, "Vospitanie sovetskogo patriotism cherez massovye vechera v shkole," *Sovetskaia pedagogika,* no. 10 (1939): 84–90.
27 "Stalinskaia Konstitutsiia i kommunisticheskoe vospitanie podrastaiushchego pokolenia," *Sovetskaia pedagogika,* no. 4 (1937): 6.
28 Kevin M.F. Platt and David Brandenberger, eds, *Epic Revisionism: Russian History and Literature as Stalinist Propaganda* (Madison: University of Wisconsin Press, 2006), 4.
29 N.V. Udina, "K voprosu o vospitanii sovetskogo patriotizma v sovetskoi shkole," *Sovetskaia pedagogika,* no. 5 (1938): 36.
30 E.I. Rudneva, "Kommunistichekoe vospitanie na urokakh istorii v nachalnnoi shkole," *Sovetskaia pedagogika,* no. 8–9 (1939): 88–94. For war-time changes in Soviet history syllabi see Dunstan, *Soviet Schooling,* 134–8.
31 GARF, f. A-307, op. 1, d. 26, l. 10.
32 On the rewriting of Nevsky as hero see Platt and Brandenberger, *Epic Revisionism,* chs 15–16.
33 Álvarez Morán, *Memorias,* 88.
34 The Spanish Civil War's "ethical untouchability" became a moral centrepiece of international communism after the Second World War. Gina Hermann, *Written in Red: The Communist Memoir in Spain* (Urbana: University of Illinois Press, 2010), x–xv.
35 GARF, f. A-307, op. 1, d. 26, l. 49. Some Spaniards claim they were never taught Spanish history. Fernández Sánchez, *Memorias,* 88–9.
36 RGASPI, f. 533, op. 10, d. 1443, ll. 33–79.
37 Dunstan, *Soviet Schooling in the Second World War,* 129–30.
38 A.G. Yezernitskii, "Bolee reshitel'no izmenit' programmy po geografii," *Sovetskaia pedagogika,* no. 4 (1941): 57–60.
39 V.A. Zorin, "Vospitanie sovetskogo patriotizma," *Sovetskaia pedagogika,* no. 4 (1937): 30.
40 RGASPI, f. 533, op. 10, d. 2619, contains about forty pages of such letters.
41 RGASPI, f. 533, op. 10, d. 2619, l. 4.
42 GARF, f. A-307, op. 1, d. 12, ll. 19–19ob.
43 V.M. Vasil'eva, "O politicheskom vospitanii v nachal'noi shkole," *Sovetskaia pedagogika,* no. 4 (1937): 32–9.
44 Fernández Sánchez, *Memorias,* 104.
45 Clemente del Río Salceda, *20,000 días,* 76.
46 B. Dobrinin and J. Maguidovich, *Geografía de España* (Moscow: Ministry of Education, 1940); Clemente del Río Salceda, *20,000 días,* 68.
47 Latorre Piquer, "De niña española," 77.
48 Blitstein, "Nation-Building or Russification?" 253–74.
49 O. Vasil'eva, *Lecturas escogidas* (Moscow: Ediciones Cooperativas de los Obreros Extranjeros, 1938). Cited in Colomina Limonero, *Dos patrias,* 38. A language textbook was printed in the year before by an author of the same name. See

O. Vasil'eva, *Uchebnik ispanskogo iazyka: Nachal'nyi kurs* (Moscow: Izdatel'skoe t-vo inostrannykh rabochikh v SSSR, 1937).
50 GARF, f. A-307, op. 1, d. 122, l. 3.
51 GARF, f. A-307, op. 1, d. 346, l. 1.
52 P. Glagolev, "Ne russkie shkoly i zadachi ikh ukrepleniia," *Narodnoe obrazovanie*, no. 9 (1947): 18-28. Ewing has suggested that the failure of Russian teachers to learn the language of instruction in non-Russian schools limited their personal connections with their students and the effectiveness of their overall instruction. Ewing, "Ethnicity at School," 517.
53 GARF, f. A-2306, op. 70, d. 6009, ll. 1-2. With a lack of Spanish speakers, the use of French to communicate with Spanish cadres was near-standard practice. Kirschenbaum, *International Communism*, 28-9.
54 Kirschenbaum, *International Communism*, 29; Clemente del Río Salceda, *20,000 días*, 79; Fernández Sánchez, *Memorias*, 98, 120, 124.
55 GARF, f. A-307, op. 1, d. 83, l. 7.
56 RGASPI, f. 533, op. 10, d. 1437; f. 533, op. 10, d. 1438; f. 533, op. 10, d. 1442; f. 533, op. 10, d. 2634.
57 Fernández Sánchez, *Memorias*, 89, 94, 131.
58 Álvarez Morán, *Memorias*, 79.
59 *Programmy srednei shkole: Literatura, VIII-X klassy* (Moscow, 1944): 4.
60 *Programmy srednei shkole*, 4.
61 P.M. Minin, "Georicheskie obrazy narodnogo patriotizma v klassichskoi literature," *Sovetskaia pedagogika*, no. 3-4 (1942): 54-70.
62 N.V. Udina, "K voprosu o vospitanii sovetskogo patriotizma v sovetskoi shkole," *Sovetskaia pedagogika*, no. 5, (1938): 38, 43.
63 David Powelstock, "Fashioning 'Our Lermontov': Canonization and Conflict in the Stalinist 1930s," in *Epic Revisionism: Russian History and Literature as Stalinist Propaganda*, ed. Platt and Brandenberger, 283.
64 GARF, f. A-307, op. 1, d. 77, ll. 144-50.
65 GARF, f. A-307, op. 1, d. 83, l. 8.
66 On children's literature of the Second World War and the late Stalin period, see Ben Hellman, *Fairy Tales and True Stories: The History of Russian Literature for Children and Young People (1574-2010)* (Leiden, Netherlands: Brill, 2013), ch. 8.
67 Evgeny Dobrenko, *The Making of the State Reader: Social and Aesthetic Context of the Reception of Soviet Literature*, trans. Jesse Savage (Stanford, CA: Stanford University Press, 1997).
68 GARF, f. A-307, op. 1, d. 63, l. 10ob.
69 GARF, f. A-307, op. 1, d. 111, l. 11.
70 On varied readings of symbolic language between Soviet authors and audiences, see Serhy Yekelchyk, "*Diktat* and Dialogue in Stalinist Culture: Staging Patriotic Historical Opera in Soviet Ukraine, 1936-1954," *Slavic Review* (Fall 2000): 597-624. Republican soldiers often learned proper understandings of films about

the Red Army after "explanatory conversations." Kirschenbaum, *International Communism*, 213. Even an ideological play could leave open numerous possible interpretations for the performer. Gleb Tsipursky, *Socialist Fun: Youth, Consumption, and State-Sponsored Popular Culture in the Soviet Union, 1945–1970* (Pittsburgh, PA: University of Pittsburgh Press, 2015), ch. 2.
71 GARF, f. A-307, op. 1, d. 111, l. 11.
72 GARF, f. A-307, op. 1, d. 95, l. 29.
73 Pine, "Dissemination of Nazi Ideology"; Lisa Pine, *Education in Nazi Germany* (Oxford: Berg, 2010), ch. 4; Alessandro Pes, "Becoming Imperialist: Italian Colonies in Fascist Textbooks for Primary Schools," *Journal of Modern Italian Studies* 18, no. 5 (2013): 599–614; Alessio Ponzio, *Shaping the New Man: Youth Training Regimes in Fascist Italy and Nazi Germany* (Madison: University of Wisconsin Press, 2015); Richard Rubinger, "Education in Wartime Japan, 1937–1945," in *Education and the Second World War*, ed. Roy Lowe (London: Falmer Press, 1992), 59–72; Geoffrey Giles, "Schooling for Little Soldiers: German Education in the Second World War," in *Education and the Second World War*, ed. Roy Lowe, 17–29; Alessandra Tarquini, "Fascist Educational Policy from 1922 to 1943: A Contribution to the Current Debate on Political Religions," *Journal of Contemporary History* 50, no. 2 (2015): 168–87; Richard Wolff, "'Fascistizing' Italian Youth: The Limits of Mussolini's Educational System," *History of Education* 13, no. 4 (1984): 287–98.
74 William M. Tuttle, *"Daddy's Gone to War": The Second World War in the Lives of an American Generation* (New York: Oxford University Press, 1995); Andrew Spaull, "World War II and the Secondary School Curriculum: USA and Australia," in *Education and the Second World War*, ed. Roy Lowe, 159–76.

4 *Vospitanie*: *Kul'turnost'* and *Kruzhki*

1 Volkov, "The Concept of *Kul'turnost'*," 210–30.
2 Devillard's research team found respondents used the word *protección* frequently. Devillard et al., *Los niños*, 90–1.
3 GARF, f. A-2306, op. 70, d. 5987, l. 1
4 GARF, f. A-2306, op. 70, d. 5987, l. 2.
5 Kirschenbaum, *International Communism*, ch. 1.
6 Cited in Colomina Limonero, *Dos patrias*, 35.
7 "Pravila dlia uchashchikhsia," *Sovetskaia pedagogika*, no. 10 (1943): 2.
8 GARF, f. A-307, op. 1, d. 82, ll. 6–6ob.
9 *Holding On, Fighting Back*; Encinas, *Fuentes*, 406.
10 Devillard et al., *Los niños*, 86.
11 Arce Porres, *Memorias*, 70.
12 Fernández Sánchez, *Memorias*, 106.
13 Fernández Sánchez, 93.

14 GARF, f. A-2306, op. 70, d. 5987, l. 3.
15 GARF, f. A-307, op. 1, d. 128, l. 2ob.
16 Gleb Tsipursky has convincingly argued that during the first months after the war, following a period of war-time leniency, Soviet cultural policy appeared to allow for a more pluralistic model. *Socialist Fun*, ch. 1.
17 P.N. Gurzdev, "Voprosy trudovogo vospitaniia v detskom dome i internate," *Sovetskaia pedagogika*, no. 8 (1945): 24.
18 RGASPI, f. 533, op. 10, d. 1442, l. 11; Fernández Sánchez, *Mi infancia*, 57.
19 S.N. Belousov, "Ob otklikakh na stat'iu E. Kononenko – Grubost'," *Sovetskaia pedagogika*, no. 8 (1938): 144–52; E. Kononenko, "Grubost'," *Komsomol'skaia pravda*, 3 January 1938, 1.
20 Fernández Sánchez, *Mi infancia*, 18.
21 A. Kairov, "K voprosu ob ukreplenii ditsipliny v shkole," *Sovetskaia pedagogika*, no. 7 (1943): 21–6.
22 V.P. Potemkin, "Ob uluchshenii kachestva obucheniia i vospitaniia v shkole: Doklad Narodnogo Komissara Prosveshcheniia RSFSR akademika V.P. Potemkina na Vserossiiskom soveshchanii po narodnomu obrazovaniiu (15–19 avgusta 1944 g.)," *Sovetskaia pedagogika*, no. 11–12 (1944): 1–8; E. Thomas Ewing, *Separate Schools: Gender, Policy, and Practice in Postwar Soviet Education* (DeKalb: Northern Illinois University Press, 2010); Livschiz, "Growing Up Soviet," chs 6–7.
23 Ia. B. Reznik, "O znachenii vospitaniia," *Sovetskaia pedagogika*, no. 4–5 (1940): 42–50.
24 M.I. Kalinin, "O kommunisticheskom vospitanie," *Sovetskaia pedagogika*, no. 11–12 (1940): 3–13.
25 Henry Giroux and David Purpel, eds, *The Hidden Curriculum and Moral Education: Deception or Discovery?* (Berkeley, CA: McCutchan, 1983).
26 B.G. Anan'ev, "O glavnom 'zakone' pedologii," *Sovetskaia pedagogika*, no. 1 (1937): 14–34; Ewing, *Teachers of Stalinism*, esp. ch. 5; Holmes, *Stalin's School*, 137–41.
27 GARF, f. A-307, op. 1, d. 128, l. 2ob.
28 GARF, f. A-307, op. 1, d. 77, ll. 14–15 (schedule); f. A-2306, op. 70, d. 5987, l. 4 (sleep mandate). Spaniards recall a slightly different timetable, but the essentials of rising, exercising, washing, eating, class, free time, and then more classes and activities are the same. Latorre Piquer, "De niña española," 70–1; Álvarez Morán, *Memorias*, 71–2.
29 Starks, *Body Soviet*, esp. chs 4 and 6 on the home and the body.
30 For example, GARF, f. A-307, op. 1, d. 83, l. 17; f. A-307, op. 1, d. 346, ll. 83–91; f. A-2306, op. 70, d. 6126, l. 5; f. A-307, op. 1, d. 296, l. 1.
31 GARF, f. A-2306, op. 70, d. 5987, ll. 3–4.
32 Clemente del Río Salceda, *20,000 días*, 73.
33 GARF, f. A-307, op. 1, d. 221, l. 4.

34 Alted Vigil, Marín, and Martell, *Los niños*, 48, 54, 98, 100–1, 106, 129.
35 Zafra, Crego, and Heredia, *Los niños*, 138.
36 Zafra, Crego, and Heredia, 119.
37 Clemente del Río Salceda, *20,000 días*, 70–1, 120.
38 Zafra, Crego, and Heredia, *Los niños*, 101.
39 RGASPI, f. 533, op. 10, d. 1442, l. 69.
40 Fernández Sánchez, *Memorias*, 152.
41 Latorre Piquer, "De niña española," 68.
42 Álvarez Morán, *Memorias*, 18. On the early egalitarianism in Soviet culture see Stites, *Revolutionary Dreams*, ch. 6.
43 Fernández Sánchez, *Memorias*, 104.
44 GARF, f. A-307, op. 2, d. 94, l. 15; Clemente del Río Salceda, *20,000 días*, 71.
45 Clemente del Río Salceda, 71.
46 Cynthia Ruder, *Building Stalinism: The Moscow Canal and the Creation of Soviet Space* (London: I.B. Taurus, 2018); Schlögel, *Moscow*, 274–93; S. Ia. Zhuk, *Kanal Moskva-Volga: Vspomagatel'nye raboty, 1932–1937* (Moscow: Gosudarstvennoe izdatel'stvo stroitel'noi literatury, 1945).
47 Clemente del Río Salceda, *20,000 días*, 73; Fernández Sánchez, *Memorias*, 125.
48 Devillard et al., *Los niños*, 92–3.
49 Latorre Piquer, "De niña española," 75.
50 Clemente del Río Salceda, *20,000 días*, 71.
51 Pons Prades, *Los niños*, 105.
52 Igmen, *Speaking Soviet*, 140–2, passim; Khalid, *Making Uzbekistan*, esp. chs 8 and 9.
53 Zafra, Crego, and Heredia, *Los niños*, 139–40; Clemente del Río Salceda, *20,000 días*, 76.
54 GARF, f. A-2306, op. 70, d. 6125, l. 1.
55 In a rather bizarre incident Isabel Álvarez recalls needing a stray cat to see the effects of gas in her toxicology class. The students gassed one to death before the cat's owner rushed in and called them cat killers. She relates this to Spanish literature, because when the culprit was not exposed, it was "as in *Fuenteovejuna*." Álvarez Morán, *Memorias*, 108.
56 RGASPI, f. 533, op. 10, d. 1436, ll. 14–17, 22–3.
57 Devillard et al., *Los niños*, 111.
58 Clemente del Río Salceda, *20,000 días*, 73; CDMH, P.S. Barcelona, 87/17/2; 87/17/5; 87/17/4.
59 GARF, f. A-307, op. 1, d. 248, l. 8.
60 Kononenko, *Malen'kie ispantsy*, 109–15.
61 GARF, f. A-307, op. 1, d. 345, ll. 7–8; Fernández Sánchez, *Mi infancia*, 84.
62 Kononenko, *Malen'kie ispantsy*, 114.
63 Matthew Bernstein, *Controlling Hollywood: Censorship and Regulation in the Studio Era* (New Brunswick, NJ: Rutgers University Press, 1999); Leonard J. Leff

and Jerold L. Simmons, *The Dame in the Kimono: Hollywood, Censorship, and the Production Code* (Lexington: University of Kentucky Press, 2013); Dmitry Shlapentokh and Vladimir Shlapentokh, *Soviet Cinematography, 1918–1991: Ideological Conflict and Social Reality* (New York: Aldine de Gruyter, 1993), chs 7–9; Richard Taylor, *Film Propaganda: Soviet Russia and Nazi Germany* (London: Croom Helm, 1979).

64 *Spravochnik sovetskogo rabotnika*, 816.
65 N.Z. Uritskii, "Kino vo vneclassnoi rabote," *Sovetskaia pedagogika*, no. 2 (1941): 62–8.
66 In a letter to her family in Spain Julia Sedaño reported seeing Spanish newsreels in 1938, but I have yet to see significant evidence of Spanish feature films in the boarding schools. CDMH, P.S. Santander, O, 51/7/107.
67 GARF, f. A-307, op. 1, d.175, l. 35.
68 Jamie Miller, *Soviet Cinema: Politics and Persuasion under Stalin* (New York: I.B. Tauris, 2010), 13.
69 On this ritual of Stalinist political culture see Alexei Kojevnikov, "Rituals of Stalinist Culture at Work: Science and the Games of Intraparty Democracy circa 1948," *Russian Review* 57 (January 1998): 25–52.
70 See for example, GARF, f. A-307, op. 1, d. 221, l. 5; f. A-307, op. 1, d. 248, l. 8; f. A-307, op. 1, d. 175, l. 35; f. A-307, op. 1, d. 346, 83; f. A-307, op. 1, d. 83, l. 6; f. A-307, op. 1, d. 95, l. 39; f. A-307, op. 1, d. 111, l. 12.
71 Stephen Norris, *Blockbuster History in the New Russia: Movies, Memory, and Patriotism* (Bloomington: Indiana University Press, 2012), 5.
72 Evgenii Dobrenko, *Stalinist Cinema and the Production of History: Museum of the Revolution* (New Haven, CT: Yale University Press, 2008), 2–3.
73 On the refashioning of Ivan the Terrible's reign see Platt and Brandenberger, *Epic Revisionism*, chs 10–11.
74 Erik van Ree, *The Political Thought of Joseph Stalin: A Study in 20th Century Revolutionary Patriotism* (New York: Routledge, 2002), 304.
75 Films mentioned in this section are found in GARF, f. A-307, op. 1, d. 83, l. 6; f. A-307, op. 1, d. 95, l. 39; f. A-307, op. 1, d. 111, l. 12; f. A-307, op. 1, d. 346, ll. 83–91; f. A-307, op. 1, d. 175, l. 35; f. A-307, op. 1, d. 221, l. 5; f. A-307, op. 1, d. 248, l. 8.
76 Dobrenko, "The School Tale," 48.
77 GARF, f. A-307, op. 1, d. 111, l. 12. On attacks against Western influences in the sciences see Ethan Pollock, *Stalin and the Science Wars* (Princeton, NJ: Princeton University Press, 2006), 6–7, passim.
78 GARF, f. A-307, op. 1, d. 95, l. 39; Fernández Sánchez, *Mi infancia*, 55.
79 Clemente del Río Salceda, *20,000 días*, 74–5; *Memorias*, 166.
80 GARF, f. A-307, op. 1, d. 83, l. 5 (quotation); f. A-307, op. 1, d. 248, l. 8; f. A-307, op. 1, d. 95, l. 39. Laurence Senelick and Sergei Ostrovsky, eds, *The Soviet Theater:*

A Documentary History (New Haven, CT: Yale University Press, 2014), esp. chs 7–9.
81 Fernández Sánchez, *Memorias*, 104.
82 M.I. Kalinin, "O kommunisticheskom vospitanie," *Sovetskaia pedagogika*, no. 11–12 (1940): 3–13.
83 GARF, f. A-307, op. 1, d. 175, l. 27.
84 GARF, f. A-307, op. 1, d. 349, l. 15.
85 RGASPI, f. 533, op. 10, d. 2635, l. 12.
86 Clemente del Río Salceda, *20,000 días*, 78; Fernández Sánchez, *Memorias*, 104–8.
87 GARF, f. A-307, op. 1, d. 83, l. 4.
88 GARF, f. A-307, op. 1, d. 128, l. 1ob.
89 GARF, f. A-307, op. 1, d. 153, l. 6.
90 GARF, f. A-307, op. 1, d. 83, l. 11.
91 Arce Porres, *Memorias*, 120, 124–6.
92 Kirschenbaum, "Exile, Gender, and Communist Self-Fashioning," 566–89; Álvarez Morán, *Memorias*, 18.
93 For a similar example among the Soviet Gypsy community see O'Keeffe, *New Soviet Gypsies*, ch. 3.
94 GARF, f. A-307, op. 1, d. 267, l. 1. On gender segregation see Alted Vigil, Marín, and Martell, *Los niños*, ch. 4.
95 GARF, f. A-307, op. 1, d. 95, ll. 54–5.
96 Zafra, Crego, and Heredia, *Los niños*, 55. Álvarez Morán, *Memorias*, 74–9.
97 Clemente del Río Salceda, *20,000 días*, 68; Fernández Sánchez, *Memorias*, 94; Zafra, Crego, and Heredia, *Los niños*, 55, 51.
98 GARF, f. A-307, op. 1, d. 111, l. 13.
99 GARF, f. A-307, op. 1, d. 349, l. 15.
100 GARF, f. A-307, op. 1, d. 95, ll. 41–3. Álvarez Morán, *Memorias*, 81.
101 Zafra, Crego, and Heredia, *Los niños*, 55; CDMH, P.S. Santander, O, 49/3/29.
102 GARF, f. A-307, op. 1, d.175, l. 2.
103 Zafra, Crego, and Heredia, *Los niños*, 55.
104 RGASPI, f. 533, op. 10, d. 2635, l. 12; GARF, f. A-307, op. 1, d. 111, l. 12; f. A-307, op. 1, d. 77, l. 11.
105 GARF, f. A-2306, op. 70, d. 6097, l. 1.
106 K.P. Iagodovskii, "Iunnatskaia rabota v detskom dome," *Detskii dom* 1 (1944): 31–43.
107 RGASPI, f. 533, op. 10, d. 2635, l. 96; GARF, f. A-307, op. 1, d. 346, ll. 48–48ob.
108 GARF, f. A-307, op. 1, d. 128, l.1ob.
109 Fernández Sánchez, *Mi infancia*, 45; Soler Gilabert, 44–53.
110 Devillard et al., *Los niños*, 109.
111 Clemente del Río Salceda, *20,000 días*, 119, Fernández Sánchez, *Memorias*, 121, 125.
112 Latorre Piquer, "De niña española," 113.
113 Igmen, *Speaking Soviet*; O'Keeffe, *New Soviet Gypsies*; Pauly, *Breaking the Tongue*.

5 Becoming Soviet in Traumatic Times

1. Devillard et al., *Los niños*, 115.
2. Arce Porres, *Memorias*, 34–7; Fernández Sánchez, *Memorias*, 131.
3. Alicia Alted Vigil, Roger González, and Maria José Millan, eds, *El exilio de los niños: Catálogo de la exposición* (Madrid: Fundación Pablo Iglesias y Fundación Largo Caballero, 2003); Cloud, *Basque Children in England*; Geneviève Dreyfus-Armand, "L'accueil des enfants espagnols en France pendant la guerre d'Espagne et après la victoire franquiste," *Documents pour l'histoire du français langue étrangère ou seconde* 46 (2011): 1–13; Célia Keren, "Les enfants espagnols réfugiés en France 1939 ou la crise de la solidarité ouvrière," *Les Cahiers du Centre de Recherches Historiques* 44 (2009): 1–13; Pons Prades, *Los niños*.
4. Arce Porres, *Memorias*, 21.
5. GARF, f. A-2306, op. 70, d. 6045, ll. 1–2ob.
6. Encinas, *Fuentes*, 522.
7. Colomina Limonero, *Dos patrias*, 74. This could be the girls Puri and Conchita who are mentioned in Álvarez Morán, *Memorias*, 91.
8. GARF, f. A-307, op. 2, d. 401, ll. 3–3ob. Cited in Elpat'evskii, *Ispanskaia emigratsiia v SSSR*, 81. Mortality was remarkably low given the high rates of disease and malnutrition among the Spaniards when they arrived. This number does not include children killed in combat and must omit the approximately seventy children who died in the siege of Leningrad. Devillard places the total number of deaths at approximately three hundred. Devillard et al., *Los niños*, 12. The most complete list of Spanish war-time deaths is contained in Fundación Nostalgia, *Memoria: En memoria de los combatientes españoles que cayeron luchando contra el fascismo y por la libertad junto al pueblo ruso en la Segunda Guerra Mundial, 1941–1945* (Madrid: Fundación Nostalgia, 2000).
9. Devillard et al., *Los niños*, 115.
10. Latorre Piquer, "De niña española," 80.
11. Natalie Belsky, "Encounters in the East: Evacuees in the Soviet Hinterland during the Second World War" (PhD diss., University of Chicago, 2014); Holmes, *Stalin's World War II Evacuations*; Rebecca Manley, "The Perils of Displacement: The Soviet Evacuee between Refugee and Deportee," *Contemporary European History* 16, no. 4 (2007): 495–509; Rebecca Manley, *To the Tashkent Station: Evacuation and Survival in the Soviet Union at War* (Ithaca, NY: Cornell University Press, 2009); Paul Stronski, *Tashkent: Forging a Soviet City, 1930–1966* (Pittsburgh, PA: University of Pittsburgh Press, 2010), ch. 4.
12. Devillard et al., *Los niños*, 205.
13. Álvarez Morán, *Memorias*, 83–99, 106.
14. Manley, "The Perils of Displacement," 508. Manley also notes an ongoing hierarchy of entitlement in evacuation and a great deal of distrust from local authorities. Manley, *To the Tashkent Station*, 152–3.

15 deGraffenried, *Sacrificing Childhood*, 98–102; Dunstan, *Soviet Schooling*, 52–69; Livschiz, "Growing Up Soviet," chs 3–4.
16 Colomina Limonero, *Dos patrias*, 70. Scholarship on the siege of Leningrad is voluminous. For different approaches see Richard Bidlack and Nikita Lomagin, *The Leningrad Blockade, 1941–1944: A New Documentary History from the Soviet Archives* (New Haven, CT: Yale University Press, 2012); David Glantz, *The Siege of Leningrad, 1941–1944: 900 Days of Terror* (London: Spellmount, 2001); Lisa Kirschenbaum, *The Legacy of the Siege of Leningrad, 1941–1995: Myth, Memories, and Monuments* (New York: Cambridge University Press, 2006); Lisa Kirschenbaum, "Innocent Victims and Heroic Defenders: Children and the Siege of Leningrad," in *Children and War: A Historical Anthology*, ed. James Marten (New York: New York University Press, 2002), 279–90; Cynthia Simmons and Nina Perlina, *Writing the Siege of Leningrad: Women's Diaries, Memoirs, and Documentary Prose* (Pittsburgh, PA: University of Pittsburgh Press, 2005).
17 Colomina Limonero, *Dos patrias*, 71.
18 Colomina Limonero, 77.
19 Soler Gilabert, *La vida*, 57.
20 Colomina Limonero, *Dos patrias*, 73. Soler Gilabert, *La vida*, 53; Arce Porres, *Memorias*, 60.
21 On planning for Soviet evacuations and the disorder in practice see Manley, *To the Tashkent Station*, chs 1–3.
22 GARF, f, A-2306, op. 70, d. 6000, l. 2.
23 For an examination of the tracing of missing children see Kelsey Norris, "World War II-Era Unaccompanied Children and the Politics of Family Reunification" (unpublished manuscript).
24 Colomina Limonero, *Dos patrias*, 78–9. Isabel Álvarez Morán has noted that most of the Georgians with whom she lived and worked had little to no knowledge of Russian. *Memorias*, 104–15.
25 GARF, f. A-307, op. 2, d. 415, ll. 4, 17, 23–5. The latter exchange is most interesting. A Virginia Rosenblueth from Brookline, Massachusetts, wrote to the International Red Cross, seeking two siblings from Bilbao. The result of the inquiry is not clear.
26 Fernández Sánchez, *Memorias*, 128–9.
27 GARF, f. A-307, op. 1, d. 282, ll. 15–25.
28 Colomina Limonero, *Dos patrias*, 74.
29 John Dunstan, *Soviet Schooling in the Second World War* (New York: St Martin's Press, 1997), 42.
30 Soler Gilabert, *La vida*, 52–3.
31 Fernández Sánchez, *Memorias*, 127.
32 Arce Porres, *Memorias*, 38–9.
33 Colomina Limonero, *Dos patrias*, 75.
34 GARF, f. 5451, op. 28, d. 40, l. 15.
35 GARF, f. A-307, op. 1, d. 136, ll. 1–8.

36 GARF, f. A-2306, op. 70, d. 6051; f. A-2306, op. 70, d. 6022, l. 2.
37 Holmes, *Stalin's World War II Evacuations*, 68–9, 83–5.
38 Colomina Limonero, *Dos patrias,* 79–80; GARF, f. A-307, op. 2, d. 32, l. 13; f. A-307, op. 1, d. 136, l. 3.
39 Alted Vigil, Marín, and Martell, *Los niños*, 145–6; GARF, f. A-307, op. 1, d. 141, l. 7; f. A-307, op. 1, d. 221, l. 2ob.
40 GARF, f. A-307, op. 1, d. 141, l. 5; f. A-307, op. 1, d. 189, l. 2; f. A-307, op. 1, d. 274, l. 3. Anna Pavlovna Fernandez-Eres, "Ispanskie 'deti voiny' v 1941–1944 gg.: Opyt evakuatsii v glubokii tyl," *Otechestvennaia istoriia* 16, no. 3 (2014): 505.
41 Latorre Piquer, "De niña española," 83.
42 deGraffenried, *Sacrificing Childhood*, ch. 2; Kucherenko, *Little Soldiers*, pt. 1; Livschiz, "Growing Up Soviet," chs 3–4.
43 Colomina Limonero, *Dos patrias*, 76.
44 Colomina Limonero, 79.
45 Fernández Sánchez, *Memorias*, 125.
46 William Moskoff, *Bread of Affliction: The Food Supply in the USSR during World War II* (Cambridge: Cambridge University Press, 2002), 171–6.
47 Arce Porres, *Memorias*, 25–40.
48 GARF, f. A-307, op. 1, d. 221.
49 Fernandez-Eres, "Ispanskie 'deti voiny' v 1941–1944 gg.," 506; GARF, f. A-307, op. 1, d. 267, l. 2; f. A-307, op. 1, d. 136, l. 3.
50 Álvarez Morán, *Memorias*, 86.
51 Colomina Limonero, *Dos patrias*, 79; Fernández Sánchez, *Memorias*, 133, 146–7. On the necessity of local production as distribution networks collapsed, see Moskoff, *Bread of Affliction*, ch. 5. For an insightful transnational history of gardening in the world wars, and particularly women's crucial role, see Cecilia Gowdy-Wygant, *Cultivating Victory: The Women's Land Army and the Victory Garden Movement* (Pittsburgh, PA: University of Pittsburgh Press, 2013).
52 GARF, f. A-2306, op. 70, d. 6045, ll. 1–2ob.
53 GARF, f. A-307, op. 1, d. 267, l. 1.
54 Soviet orphanages expanded rapidly during the Second World War, and Catriona Kelly has noted that war orphans, as opposed to street children, in those institutions began to receive greater attention than in the pre-war period (*Children's World*, 242–57). Julie deGraffenried has suggested that much was promised, but little done (*Sacrificing Childhood*, 41–4). For a look at orphanages in Kirov during the war see Holmes, *Stalin's World War II Evacuations*, 42–68.
55 For an example from Saratov see GARF, f. A-2306, op. 70, d. 6022, l. 2. This was quite typical east of the Ural Mountains where local officials tried to protect and maximize their resources when evacuees crowded into towns and cities. Manley, *To the Tashkent Station*, ch. 6.
56 Jeffrey W. Jones, *Everyday Life and the "Reconstruction" of Soviet Russia during and after the Great Patriotic War, 1943–1948* (Bloomington, IN: Slavica, 2008), ch. 2; Moskoff, *Bread of Affliction*, 179–80; Sarah Davies, "'Us against Them':

Social Identity in Soviet Russia, 1934–1941," *Russian Review* 56, no. 1 (January 1997): 70–89.
57 Rachel Green, "There Will Not Be Orphans among Us," ch. 3; Livschiz, *Growing Up Soviet*, 469.
58 GARF, A-2306, op. 70, d. 5991, ll. 9–11.
59 GARF, A-2306, op. 70, d. 5991, l. 7.
60 GARF, f. A-2306, op. 70, d. 6027, ll. 1–8.
61 GARF, f. A-2306, op. 70, d. 6022, ll. 3–4.
62 Fernández Sánchez, *Memorias*, 131–3; Colomina Limonero, *Dos patrias*, 79.
63 A report from 1944 noted that after evacuation more students ended up in sanatoria with tuberculosis. GARF, f. 5451, op. 28, d. 40, l. 15.
64 For examples of patronage arrangements see GARF, f. A-307, op. 1, d. 309; f. A-2306, op. 70, d. 6000, l. 9; f. A-2306, op. 70, d. 6061, ll. 5–6; Green, "There Will Not Be Orphans among Us," 109–12; Fernández Sánchez, *Memorias*, 125; Livschiz, "Growing Up Soviet," 479. Catriona Kelly has noted that patronage arrangements also served a surveillance function in children's institutions (*Children's World*, 225).
65 GARF, f. 5451, op 28, d. 40, l. 17.
66 Soler Gilabert, *La vida*, 63.
67 Latorre Piquer, "De niña española," 83; Fernández Sánchez, *Mi infancia*, 145; Arce Porres, *Memorias*, 32–3.
68 GARF, f. A-307, op. 1, d. 238, l. 5. We must be cautious in accepting such metrics. It is important to note that April to September is precisely the time of year when food is most abundant. One could expect smaller gains and possibly losses during the leaner winter months.
69 GARF, f. A-2306, op. 70, d. 6053, l. 2. Although spelled *Pelaes* in Cyrillic, this was likely Álvaro Peláez Antón, a Spanish member of the Comintern.
70 Arce Porres, *Memorias*, 48–9.
71 GARF, f. A-2306, op. 70, d. 6061, ll. 5–6.
72 Arce Porres, *Memorias*, 66.
73 GARF, f. A-307, op. 1, d. 77, ll. 28–33; Encinas, *Fuentes*, 131–5.
74 Manley, "The Perils of Displacement," 497.
75 Moskoff, *Bread of Affliction*, 177–82.
76 Livschiz, "Growing Up Soviet."
77 S.A. Chernik, *Sovetskaia obshcheobrazovatel'naia shkola v gody Velikoi Otechestvennoi voiny* (Moscow: Pedagogika, 1984), 117–18.
78 Dunstan, *Soviet Schooling*, 127–9; Pine, *Education in Nazi Germany*, ch. 3.
79 Fernández Sánchez, *Memorias*, 115. Álvarez noted that she learned shooting, first aid, and anti-gas defence in 1938. *Memorias*, 72.
80 ANC f. 555, d. 254; Fernández Sánchez, *Memorias*, 120.
81 P.M. Kuz'min, "Vospitanie sovetskogo patriotism cherez massovye vechera v shkole," *Sovetskaia pedagogika*, no. 10 (1939): 84–90; V. Tikhonov, "Oboronnaia

rabota v shkole i ee rol' v ukreplenii distsipliny i povyshenii uspevaemosti uchashchikhsia," *Sovetskaia pedagogika*, no. 9 (1940): 62–6; Dunstan, *Soviet Schooling*, 117–30. Ann Livschiz points to the Finnish war as the decisive moment in schools' turning to greater discipline and patriotism ("Growing Up Soviet," 345–7).
82 Latorre Piquer, "De niña española," 79.
83 deGraffenried, *Sacrificing Childhood*, 60–2; Evgeny Dobrenko, "The School Tale"; Alexander Prokhorov, "Arresting Development: A Brief History of Soviet Cinema for Children and Adolescents," in *Russian Children's Literature and Culture*, ed. Marina Balina and Larissa Rudova (New York: Routledge, 2008), 43–66 and 129–52; Kelly, *Children's World*, 477; Kucherenko, *Little Soldiers*, 26–8; Livschiz, "Growing Up Soviet," 406–13.
84 deGraffenried, *Sacrificing Childhood*, ch. 2.
85 GARF, f. A-307, op. 1, d. 221. l. 5; Arce Porres, *Memorias*, 32–3; Latorre Piquer, "De niña española," 79–83; Fernández Sánchez, *Memorias*, 75–8.
86 V. Shkolvskii, "O trudovom vospitanie," *Detskaia literatura* 2 (1941): 13–15; N.A. Mikhailov, "Trudovoe i voennoe vospitanie detei," *Detskaia literatura* 2 (1941): 4–5.
87 Tsentral'nyi gosudarstvennyi arkhiv Sankt-Peterburga, f. 5039, op. 3, d. 503, l. 69; Livschiz, "Growing Up Soviet," 357.
88 P.N. Gurzdev, "Voprosy trudovogo vospitaniia v detskom dome i internate," *Sovetskaia pedagogika*, no. 8 (1945): 24–32; Arce Porres, *Memorias*, 32–3; Fernández Sánchez, *Memorias*, 130, 144; Latorre Piquer, "De niña española," 82.
89 Child labour, especially in agriculture, was also common in democracies during the Second World War. Lisa L. Ossian, "Too Young for a Uniform," 254–65; Penny Elaine Starns and Martin L. Parsons, "Against Their Will: The Use and Abuse of British Children during the Second World War," in *Children and War*, ed. James Martin, 266–78.
90 GARF, f. A-307, op. 1, d. 26, l. 14.
91 GARF, f. A-307, op. 1, d. 26, ll. 14–15; RGASPI, f. 533, op. 10, d. 2635, l. 20.
92 Clemente del Río Salceda, *20,000 días*, 129–30; However, Fernández remembered having only target rifles. *Memorias*, 118–19.
93 Shortages of trainers, spaces, and weapons and other gear were the norm in the Soviet Union during the war. Dunstan, *Soviet Schooling*, 177–80.
94 GARF, f. A-307, op. 1, d. 26, ll. 12, 19.
95 GARF, f. A-307, op. 1, d. 26, l. 14; Arce Porres, *Memorias*, 60; Soler Gilabert, *La vida*, 53.
96 Fernández Sánchez, *Memorias*, 128–9, 156. Manuel Arce Porres shares his understanding. *Memorias*, 24–49.
97 Clemente del Río Salceda, *20,000 días*, 129–34, 156; Fernández Sánchez, *Memorias*, 154.
98 Vinyes, Armengou, and Belis, *Los niños perdidos*, 175. Others who recalled fighting incendiary bombs include Álvarez Morán, *Memorias*, 84; Soler Gilabert,

La vida, 49–50. Children and youth mobilized for war both spontaneously and because of Soviet propaganda. See deGraffenried, *Sacrificing Childhood*, chs 2–3; Kucherenko, *Little Soldiers*, esp. chs 1 and 4.
99 Clemente del Río Salceda, *20,000 días*, 129.
100 GARF, f. A-307, op. 1, d. 19, ll. 29, 89.
101 GARF, f. A-307, op. 1, d. 95, l. 27.
102 GARF, f. A-307, op. 1, d. 346, l. 65; Álvarez Morán, *Memorias*, 77.
103 GARF, f. A-307, op. 1, d. 153.
104 Fernández Sánchez, *Memorias*, 106, 139.
105 GARF, f. A-307, op. 1, d. 346, l. 5.
106 GARF, f. A-307, op. 1, d. 95, l. 21.
107 GARF, f. A-307, op. 1, d. 83, l. 9.
108 GARF, f. A-307, op. 1, d. 77, ll. 11, 39; Anderson and Silver, "Equality, Efficiency, and Politics," 120–1; Blitstein, "Nation-Building or Russification?" 256–61; Ewing, "Ethnicity at School," 517–18.
109 GARF, f. 5451, op. 43, d. 519, l. 417.
110 Iu. Tuishev, "Podgotovka uchitelei russkogo iazyka dlia nerusskikh shkol," *Narodnoe obrazovanie*, no. 8 (1950): 62–6. Peter Blitstein shows that war-time shortages of trained staff and a paucity of textbooks made acquisition of Russian exceptionally difficult for national minorities. Blitstein, "Nation-Building or Russification?" 262.
111 V.P. Potemkin, "Ob uluchshenii kachestva obucheniia i vospitaniia v shkole: Doklad Narodnogo Komissara Prosveshcheniia RSFSR akademika V.P. Potemkina na Vserossiiskom soveshchanii po narodnomu obrazovaniiu (15–19 avgusta 1944 g.)," *Sovetskaia pedagogika*, no. 11–12 (1944): 3.
112 GARF, f. A-2306, op. 70, d. 6094, l. 1.
113 Clemente del Río Salceda, *20,000 días*, 69.
114 Álvarez Morán, *Memorias*, 71, 103–15.
115 GARF, f. A-307, op. 1, d. 95, ll. 24, 28.
116 Fernández Sánchez, *Memorias*, 106. This section comes from GARF, f. A-307, op. 1, d. 26, ll. 1–14, unless otherwise indicated.
117 V.G. Daev, *Ispanskie gosti na rodine Sadko: Itogi zhurnalistskogo poiska* (St Petersburg: Sudarynia, 1997), 23.
118 Clemente del Río Salceda, *20,000 días*, 129–34, 156; Fernández Sánchez, *Memorias*, 154; Soler Gilabert, *La vida*, 48.
119 Larry E. Holmes details a series of inspections of Home No. 10 in early 1942 in his *Stalin's World War II Evacuations*, 64–9, 113–16.
120 GARF, f. A-307, op. 1, d. 284, ll. 1–2.
121 Álvarez Morán, *Memorias*, 79.
122 GARF, f. A-307, op. 1, d. 282, ll. 15–25. For our best understanding of evacuation to Kirov, see Larry E. Holmes, *Stalin's World War II Evacuations*. He also documents the displacement of Kirov's school in *Kirov's School No. 9: Power, Privilege, and Excellence in the Provinces, 1933–1945* (Kirov, Russia: Loban, 2008).

123 GARF, f. A-307, op. 1, d. 282, ll. 15-25. New war-time school rules for disciplining time and the Spanish body came a full year before the 1943 announcement of similar rules for all Soviet schools. The Spanish children's Home No. 10 had evacuated to Kirov, the site of Narkompros's war-time headquarters. One must wonder if the Spanish homes' rules of 1942 had any influence on the union-wide rules of 1943. "Pravila dlia uchashchikhsia," *Sovetskaia pedagogika*, no. 10 (1943): 2.
124 M.P. Malyshev, "Shkola i vospitanie kharaktera," *Sovetskaia pedagogika*, no. 6 (1941): 3-16; Dunstan, *Soviet Schooling*, ch. 8.
125 S. Kamenogradskii, "Vospitanie chestnosti i pravdivosti," *Sovetskaia pedagogika* no. 2 (1941): 48.
126 "Pravila dlia uchashchikhsia," *Sovetskaia pedagogika*, no. 10 (1943): 2.
127 A. Kairov, "Vospitanie pravdivosti," *Sovetskaia pedagogika*, no. 8-9 (1943): 8-12.
128 V.F. Shishkin, "O vospitanii kul'tury povedeniia," *Sovetskaia pedagogika*, no. 5-6 (1944): 51-3. Older Spanish youth were given the latitude to smoke. Clemente del Río Salceda, *20,000 días*, 120.
129 A. Kairov, "Muzhestvo i ego vospitanie v nashi dni," *Sovetskaia pedagogika*, no. 8-9 (1942): 6.
130 Given memories of the vagrancy in the 1920s, children were also a potential threat to order. Elizabeth White, "The Return of Evacuated Children to Leningrad, 1944-6," in *The Disentanglement of Populations: Migration, Expulsion and Displacement in Post-War Europe, 1944-9*, ed. Jessica Reinisch and Elizabeth White (New York: Palgrave Macmillan, 2011), 251-70.
131 Latorre Piquer, "De niña española," 95.
132 Arce Porres, *Memorias*, 29-37.
133 GARF, f. A-307, op. 2, d. 415, l. 35. Serrano died in 1948 in the home at Solnechnogorsk where he worked. Encinas, *Fuentes*, 540.
134 GARF, f. A-307, op. 2, d. 415, ll. 35-6, 47, 70.
135 GARF, f. A-307, op. 2, d. 415, ll. 47, 74. There are many other examples. One wonders if the clothing they "stole" was the clothes on their back. It is possible that authorities considered this a theft of state property. After the war Viana studied ballet in Leningrad and became a dance teacher in Riga. Encinas, *Fuentes*, 568.
136 Clemente del Río Salceda, *20,000 días*, 148-50.
137 Arce Porres, *Memorias*, 43-4; Devillard et al., *Los niños*, 115; Fernández Sánchez, *Memorias*, 166.
138 GARF, f. 5451, op. 43, d. 519, ll. 342, 345. Manley, "The Perils of Displacement," 505-6.
139 Prosecutors and judges often were reluctant to pursue many violations. Holmes, *Stalin's World War II Evacuations*, 79-81; Peter H. Solomon, *Soviet Criminal Justice under Stalin* (Cambridge: Cambridge University Press, 1996), 307-24; Kelly, *Children's World*, 112-13, 232-3.
140 GARF, f, A-2306, op. 70, d. 6000, l. 5.

141 GARF, f. 5451, op. 24, d. 113, ll. 1–2. Livschiz, "Growing Up Soviet," ch. 4, shows similar steep declines in educational personnel during the war, particularly in more male-dominated courses like physical, military, and agricultural education.
142 GARF, f. A-307, op. 2, d. 415, l. 6.
143 GARF, f. A-2306, op. 70, d. 6096, l. 1.
144 Fernández Sánchez, *Memorias*, 150.
145 Clemente del Río Salceda, *20,000 días*, 120.
146 These types of shortages were consistent within the Soviet Union in general. Livschiz, "Growing Up Soviet," 41, 59–147, passim; Dunstan, *Soviet Schooling*, 54–6. The crisis of shortages led to the mass mobilization of children and youth. deGraffenried, *Sacrificing Childhood*, ch. 2.
147 GARF, f. A-307, op. 1, d. 153, ll. 1–7; Colomina Limonero, *Dos patrias*, 34; Fernandez-Eres, "Ispanskie 'deti voiny' v 1941–1944 gg.," 506. Some Spanish adults, seeing the difficulty of learning Russian on their own, took language classes at night. Soler Gilabert, *La vida*, 47.
148 Colomina Limonero, *Dos patrias*, 80.
149 RGASPI, f. 17, op. 130, d. 10, ll. 18–19.
150 RGASPI, f. 17, op. 130, d. 10, ll. 22–3.
151 GARF, f. 5446, op. 1, d. 227, ll. 163–6.
152 GARF, f. A-2306, op. 70, d. 6084, ll. 1–2.
153 GARF, f. A-2306, op. 70, d. 6084, ll. 4–5.
154 Karl D. Qualls, *From Ruins to Reconstruction: Urban Identity in Soviet Sevastopol after World War II* (Ithaca, NY: Cornell University Press, 2009), ch. 3. Rebecca Manley reminds us that "battles over housing became one of the primary sites of conflict in the period of post-war reconstruction." Manley, "'Where Should We Resettle the Comrades Next?' The Adjudication of Housing Claims and the Construction of the Post-War Order," in *Late Stalinist Russia: Soviet between Reconstruction and Reinvention*, ed. Juliane Fürst (New York: Routledge, 2006), 234; Manley, "Perils of Displacement, 495–509. John Dunstan has noted that ministerial confiscation of school properties predated the war and the resultant shortages in supplies and accommodations (*Soviet Schooling*, 53–4).
155 GARF, f. 5451, op. 43, d. 519, l. 414.
156 On the clash between official and peasant cultures see David L. Hoffmann, *Peasant Metropolis: Social Identities in Moscow, 1929–1941* (Ithaca, NY: Cornell University Press, 1994), ch. 6; Starks, *Body Soviet*; Richard Stites, *Revolutionary Dreams*, esp. chs 6 and 10.
157 Donald Filtzer, *Hazards of Urban Life in Late Stalinist Russia: Health, Hygiene, and Living Standards, 1943–1953* (Cambridge: Cambridge University Press, 2010), 127–62.
158 GARF, f. 5451, op. 43, d. 519, ll. 357–64.
159 GARF, f. A-307, op. 1, d. 153, l. 3.
160 GARF, f. 5451, op. 43, d. 519, l. 414.

161 GARF, f. 5451, op. 43, d. 519, l. 412. Holmes, *Stalin's World War II Evacuations*, ch. 4, shows many of the same shortages in Kirov's Russian schools during the war.
162 GARF, f. A-307, op. 1, d. 153, l. 1; f. A-307, op. 1, d. 270, l. 2; f. A-2306, op. 70, d. 6112, ll. 14–15. Although the shortage of teachers, particularly men, was common among most belligerent nations, labour education took a variety of forms. In England, for example, labour education involved one of the few war-time reforms, and it consisted mostly of farming and animal husbandry. Roy Lowe, "Education in England during the Second World War," in *Education and the Second World War: Studies in Schooling and Social Change*, ed. Roy Lowe (London: Falmer Press, 1992), 11.
163 GARF, f. A-307, op. 1, d. 153, l. 3.
164 GARF, f. 5451, op. 43, d. 519, l. 413.
165 GARF, f. A-307, op. 1, d. 153, l. 4.
166 On role modelling see Karl D. Qualls, "From Hooligans to Disciplined Students: Displacement, Resettlement, and Role Modelling of Spanish Civil War Children in the Soviet Union, 1937–1951," in *Displaced Children in Russian and Eastern Europe, 1915–1953: Ideologies, Identities, Experiences*, ed. Nick Baron (Leiden, Netherlands: Brill, 2017), 131–54.
167 GARF, f. A-307, op. 1, d. 153, l. 5ob; Encinas, *Fuentes*, 170.
168 GARF, f. A-307, op. 1, d. 153, 4ob; Encinas, *Fuentes*, 460, 512.
169 GARF, f. 5451, op. 43, d. 519, l. 412. The "additional resources" likely refers to *shefstvo*, or the system in which local institutions, factories, and even collective farms paired with educational institutions to help them financially and/or to provide material goods.
170 Colomina Limonero, *Dos patrias*, 128–36.
171 GARF, f. A-307, op. 1, d. 82, ll. 6–6ob.
172 The medical report from this school year notes that the children who arrived from the Spanish homes in Evpatoriia and Nakhabino were particularly unhealthy. GARF, f. A-307, op. 1, d. 82, l. 14.
173 Legarretta, *Guernica Generation*, 167.
174 Clemente del Río Salceda, *20,000 días*, 66, 81, 120.
175 Karen Petrone, "Between Exploitation and Empowerment: Soviet Women Negotiate Stalinism," in *Gender and Mass Dictatorship*, ed. Jie-Hyun Lim and Karen Petrone, 125–41 (New York: Palgrave Macmillan, 2011), 131.
176 Soler Gilabert, *La vida*, 65.

6 No Longer Children

1 Álvarez Morán, *Memorias*, 115.
2 Livschiz, "Growing Up Soviet," 355.
3 Arce Porres, *Memorias*, 31–44; Devillard et al., *Los niños*, 115; Fernández Sánchez, *Memorias*, 142, 165–8; Latorre Piquer, "De niña española," 105; Clemente del Río Salceda, *20,000 días*, 150–1.

4   Devillard et al., *Los niños*, 141.
5   GARF, f. A-2306, op. 70, d. 6027, ll. 1-8; quotation on l. 4ob.
6   Alan Ball, "State Children: Soviet Russia's *Besprizornye* and the New Socialist Generation," *Russian Review* 52, no. 2 (1993): 230.
7   Alex Inkeles and Raymond Bauer, *The Soviet Citizen: Daily Life in a Totalitarian Society* (Cambridge, MA: Harvard University Press, 1961), 79.
8   Latorre Piquer, "De niña española," 88-9.
9   Livschiz, "Growing Up Soviet," 348-9; on the shift to labour education for children generally see 349-74.
10 deGraffenried, *Sacrificing Childhood*, 53-4; Dunstan, *Soviet Schooling*, 56-7; Donald Filtzer, *Soviet Workers and Late Stalinism: Labour and the Restoration of the Stalinist System after World War II* (Cambridge: Cambridge University Press, 2002), 13-40; Kucherenko, "State v. Danila Kuz'mich," 392-4; Livschiz, "Growing Up Soviet," ch. 3.
11 Colomina Limonero, *Dos patrias*, 110; Álvarez Morán, *Memorias*, 81. The need for discipline among Spanish refugees spread across the seas. One can even see this in *New York Times* articles about unruly Basque children in other countries. "Britain to Return 15 Youths to Spain: 'Incorrigible' Basque Children Responsible for 'Terrorism' in Camp, Official Says," 27 July 1937, 6; "41 Bilbao Children Go Wild in Geneva," 6 August 1937, 2.
12 RGASPI, f. 533, op. 10, d. 2635, l. 101.
13 RGASPI, f. 533, op. 10, d. 2635, l. 101.
14 Livschiz, "Growing Up Soviet," 247.
15 RGASPI, f. 533, op. 10, d. 1436, l. 35.
16 RGASPI, f. 533, op. 10, d. 1436, l. 38.
17 RGASPI, f. 533, op. 10, d. 1436, l. 40.
18 Colomina Limonero, *Dos patrias*, 114.
19 RGASPI, f. 533, op. 10, d. 1436, l. 40.
20 RGASPI, f. 533, op. 10, d. 1436, ll. 33-41. These were possibly children of Republican pilots and others who arrived from Spain in 1939 after Franco's victory and went straight to Soviet factories. A March 1940 review of Spanish youth in factories notes that many came in the last days of the civil war, and several with injuries came straight from the front lines. RGASPI, f. 533, op. 10, d. 2631, ll. 67-76. This report, however, describes them as willing and enthusiastic, though still deficient in their cultural and political knowledge.
21 RGASPI, f. 533, op. 4, d. 405, ll. 10-14.
22 RGASPI, f. 533, op. 10, d. 2635, l. 97. The Spaniards, at age sixteen, could apply for citizenship and thus replace the yellow passport that marked them as foreigners with a Soviet passport that introduced new opportunities for them. Colomina Limonero, *Dos patrias*, 105-7; Elpat'evskii, *Ispanskaia emigratsiia*, ch. 7.
23 Colomina Limonero, *Dos patrias*, 114.
24 RGASPI, f. 533, op. 10, d. 2634, l. 1.

25 Clemente del Río Salceda, *20,000 días*, 122; Latorre Piquer, "De niña española," 73.
26 GARF, f. A-307, op. 1, d. 349, ll. 1–2. The Red Cross was also involved in provisioning, as can be seen in the 1944 letter to Molotov addressing clothing needs among the Spaniards. RGASPI, f. 7, op. 130, d. 10, l. 59, cited in Colomina Limonero, *Dos patrias*, 127.
27 RGASPI, f. 533, op. 10, d. 1442, ll. 10–15.
28 RGASPI, f. 533, op. 10, d. 1442, ll. 60–79.
29 GARF, f. A-307, op. 1, d. 349, ll. 14–15.
30 GARF, f. A-307, op. 1, d. 345, ll. 11–14.
31 GARF, f. A-2306, op. 70, d. 6061, ll. 5–6.
32 GARF, f. A-2306, op. 70, d. 6061, l. 10.
33 GARF, f. A-2306, op. 70, d. 6027, ll. 1–8.
34 GARF, f. A-307, op. 1, d. 26, l. 21; Fernandez-Eres, "Ispanskie 'deti voiny' v 1941–1944 gg.," 505.
35 GARF, f. 5451, op. 28, d. 40, l. 18.
36 Alted Vigil, Marín, and Martell, *Los niños*, 164.
37 GARF, f. 5451, op. 43, d. 519, l. 337.
38 Jesús Hernández, *Le Grande Trahison* (Paris: Fasquelle, 1953), 222–3.
39 Examples are included in GARF, f. A-307, op. 2, d. 312, ll. 1–17; f. A-307, op. 2, d. 255, ll. 1–32.
40 Álvarez Morán, *Memorias*, 79.
41 GARF, f. A-307, op. 2, d. 255, ll. 4, 21.
42 Encinas, *Fuentes*, 403.
43 GARF, f. A-307, op. 2, d. 255, l. 8.
44 GARF, f. A-307, op. 2, d. 255, l. 14.
45 Catriona Kelly has made a similar argument about the educational system as a whole that required "extraordinary levels of self-reliance and initiative in a system that did much to discourage the manifestation of exactly these qualities" (*Children's World*, 284).
46 Kojevnikov, "Rituals of Stalinist Culture at Work," 25–52.
47 Fernández Sánchez, *Memorias*, unpaginated.
48 GARF, f. A-307, op. 2, d. 255, l. 12.
49 Michael Rasell and Elena Iarskaia-Smirnova, eds, *Disability in Eastern Europe and the Former Soviet Union: History, Policy and Everyday Life* (New York: Routledge, 2014), 42–96; William O. McCagg and Lewis Siegelbaum, eds, *People with Disabilities in the Soviet Union: Past and Present, Theory and Practice* (Pittsburgh, PA: University of Pittsburgh Press, 1989); Jim Riordan, ed., *Soviet Education: The Gifted and the Handicapped* (New York: Routledge, 1988); Irina Sandomirskaia, "Skin to Skin: Language in the Soviet Education of Deaf-Blind Children, the 1920s and 1930s," *Studies in East European Thought* 60, no. 4 (2008): 321–37.
50 Arce Porres, *Memorias*, 45.
51 Colomina Limonero, *Dos patrias*, 124; Alted Vigil, Marín, and Martell, *Los niños*, 189.

52 Arce Porres, *Memorias*, 41, 126.
53 Colomina Limonero, *Dos patrias*, 117; Devillard et al., *Los niños*, 120.
54 Devillard et al., 122.
55 Devillard et al., 116. Ann Livschiz, "Growing Up Soviet," shows how Soviet policies created rural-urban and even class divides, thereby protecting and nurturing some children while turning others into adults.
56 Llanos Más, *¿Te acuerdas, tovarisch?*, 14; Arce Porres, *Memorias*, 48–9.
57 Clemente del Río Salceda, *20,000 días*, 180–90.
58 Alicia Alted Vigil, "Education and Political Control," in *Spanish Cultural Studies: An Introduction: The Struggle for Modernity*, ed. Helen Graham and Jo Labanyi (Oxford: Oxford University Press, 1995), 196–201; Cobb, "The Republican State," 133–8; Cazorla Sánchez, *Fear and Progress*, 88–94; Juan Manuel Fernández Soria, *Educación y cultura en la Guerra Civil (España 1936-1939)* (Valencia, Spain: Nau Libres, 1984); Gallagher, *Culture and Education in Spain*, pts. 5–6; Claudio Lozano Seijas, *La educación republicana, 1931-1939* (Barcelona: Universidad de Barcelona, 1980); Antonio Molero Pintado, *La reforma educativa de la Segunda República Española: Primer bienio* (Madrid: Santillana, 1977).
59 GARF, f. 5451, op. 43, d. 519, ll. 405–32.
60 GARF, f. A-307, op. 1, d. 349, l. 10.
61 Arce Porres, *Memorias*, 46–7.
62 GARF, f. 5451, op. 24, d. 113, l. 20. Suspicion of Soviet evacuees was also common. Manley, "The Perils of Displacement," 498–500.
63 Those children who voluntarily entered the Red Army – like Emiliano Aza, Julián Balaguero, José Gallego, and Manuel Renovales – and trade schools may have recognized the shift from the indulgent "happy childhood" narrative to the more socially conscious "sacrificing childhood" narrative described in deGraffenried, *Sacrificing Childhood*.
64 GARF, f. 5451, op. 43, d. 519, ll. 420–1. A month later, in December 1945, the numbers changed slightly, with 2,150 now living "independent lives" and 804 still in homes. The key addition is a notation that twelve Spanish youth were in corrective labour colonies. GARF, f. 5451, op. 43, d. 519, ll. 357–64. This was a common problem in the war years when nearly 170,000 children were convicted. In 1944 just over 81 per cent of inmates in juvenile labour colonies were held for theft. Kucherenko, *Soviet Street Children*, ch. 2.
65 GARF, f. 5451, op. 43, d. 519, l. 421.
66 GARF, f. 5451, op. 43, d. 519, ll. 195–6; f. 5451, op. 43, d. 601, ll. 6–7.
67 GARF, f. 5451, op. 43, d. 519, l. 171.
68 GARF, f. 5451, op. 43, d. 519, ll. 358–61.
69 Colomina Limonero, *Dos patrias*, 126.
70 GARF, f. 5451, op. 43, d. 519, l. 431.
71 GARF, f. 5451, op. 43, d. 519, ll. 424, 429. The Spaniards were between sixteen and twenty-one years of age, and the Soviet characterizations show all of them

working and possessing "good behaviour." All but one was in the Komsomol, and they joined their parents in exile. Archivo General de la Administración, SGM 237, cited in Alted Vigil, "Repatriation or Return?" 24; Alted Vigil, Marín, and Martell, *Los niños*, 181. Milagros Latorre Piquer noted that this was the first time she had received shoes that fit. Latorre Piquer, "De niña española, 106, 113.

72 With low real wages during and after the Second World War, material support in the form of workplace-allocated rations and housing was essential to the survival strategies of most Soviet citizens. Jones, *Everyday Life*, ch. 2; Elena Zubkova, *Russia after the War: Hopes, Illusions, and Disappointments, 1945–1957* (Armonk, NY: M.E. Sharpe, 1998), chs 3–5.
73 GARF, f. 5451, op. 43, d. 519, l. 339.
74 GARF, f. 5451, op. 43, d. 519, l. 419.
75 Devillard et al., *Los niños*, 141.
76 On the process of "escalating negativity," see Larry E. Holmes, "Ascent into Darkness: Escalating Negativity in the Administration of Schools in the Kirov Region, 1931–1941," *History of Education*, 35, no. 4–5 (2006): 521–40.
77 Devillard et al., *Los niños*, 115.
78 GARF, f. 5451, op. 43, d. 519, l. 419. A Spanish metalworker, for example, would receive an average month salary of 400–700 rubles. GARF, f. 5451, op. 43, d. 519, l. 339.
79 GARF, f. 5451, op. 43, d. 519, l. 419. *Narodnoe khoziaistvo SSSR v Velikoi Otechestvennoi Voine, 1941–45 gg.: Statisticheskii sbornik* (Moscow: Informatsionno-izdatel'skii tsentr, 1990), 215. Data on wages are notoriously elusive. For the 1930s see Lewis Siegelbaum, *Stakhanovism and the Politics of Productivity in the USSR, 1935–1941* (Cambridge: Cambridge University Press, 1988), 214–23; Sarah Davies, *Popular Opinion in Stalin's Russia: Terror, Propaganda and Dissent, 1934–1941* (Cambridge: Cambridge University Press, 1997), 24; Jane Chapman, *Real Wages in Soviet Russia since 1928* (Cambridge, MA: Harvard University Press, 1963), ch. 9. All these scholars recognize that real wages remained below 1928 levels, and, as Donald Filtzer notes, the "arbitrary and spurious" setting of wages and bonuses throughout 1930s makes it impossible to know what the average wages were. Filtzer, *Soviet Workers and Stalinist Industrialization*, 214.
80 GARF, f. 5451, op. 43, d. 519, ll. 417–18.
81 Devillard et al., *Los niños*, 118.
82 GARF, f. A-307, op. 1, d. 349, ll. 2, 8.
83 GARF, f. A-2306, op. 70, d. 5991, ll. 9–11. While all this might appear remarkable, we should be cognizant that the folder (GARF, f. 5451, op. 43, d. 519) containing most of these reports encompasses a tremendous number of secret documents inquiring into the condition of Soviet workers in general. Much of the material is devoted to the working of libraries, kindergartens, nurseries, and factory clubs. At this point in 1945 the regime was simply trying to understand the scale of destruction and disrepair and to begin to plan for reconstruction of daily life.

84 Pons Prades, *Los niños*, 119.
85 Nicolás Marín, "La integración de los niños," 63.
86 Arce Porres, *Memorias*, 69–70.
87 Devillard et al., *Los niños*, 122, 127–9, 140–1.
88 Colomina Limonero, *Dos patrias*, 134–5.
89 RGASPI, f. 533, op. 10, d. 533, l. 480.
90 Alted Vigil, Marín, and Martell, *Los niños*, 148–9. On theft in Soviet cadet schools see Kucherenko, "*In loco parentis*," 238–9.
91 GARF, f. A-307, op. 1, d. 345, ll. 15–32.
92 Latorre Piquer, "De niña española," 105, 98–9.
93 Arce Porres, *Memorias*, 72; Alted Vigil, Marín, and Martell, *Los niños*, 165.
94 Alted Vigil, Marín, and Martell, 163.
95 GARF, f. A-307, op. 1, d. 175, ll. 6, 11.
96 Kelly, *Children's World*, 142, 153.
97 It is important to note that many of the Spaniards became prize-winning workers. See, for example, Colomina Limonero, *Dos patrias*, 136; Devillard et al., *Los niños*, 140–1.
98 Kucherenko, "State v. Danila Kuz'mich," 400–2.
99 GARF, f. 5451, op. 43, d. 519, l. 417.
100 GARF, f. 5451, op. 43, d. 601, ll. 6–7; f. 5451, op. 43, d. 519, ll. 195–6.
101 Nick Baron and Peter Gatrell, "Population Displacement, State Building, and Social Identity in the Lands of the Former Russian Empire, 1917–23," *Kritika: Explorations in Russian and Eurasian History* 4, no. 1 (Winter 2003): 62.
102 Zafra, Crego, and Heredia, *Los niños*, 76. Valery Chkalov, pilot and hero of the Soviet Union, visited the Tarasovka boarding school for Spaniards several times in 1938. Colomina Limonero, *Dos patrias*, 183.
103 GARF, f. 5451, op. 43, d. 519, l. 416; Colomina Limonero, *Dos patrias*, 188.
104 Alted Vigil, Marín, and Martell, *Los niños*, 172; Colomina Limonero, *Dos patrias*, 184; Manuel Aznar Soler, "Teatro, literatura y cultura del exilio republicano español en la Unión Soviética (1939–1949)," *Exils et migrations ibériques au XXéme siècle*, no. 6 (1999): 61–76.
105 Colomina Limonero, *Dos patrias*, 184–7. The chronology of Colomina Limonero's statement about Spanish film is unclear, but because she referenced only films from the mid-1950s, these viewings likely only started after Stalin's death in 1953 as relations with Spain started to normalize.
106 GARF, f. 5451, op. 43, d. 519, ll. 359–61.
107 Zafra, Crego, and Heredia, *Los niños*, 90. Several scholars have noted the importance of clubs like Chkalov. See Igmen, *Speaking Soviet*, 37–69; O'Keeffe, *New Soviet Gypsies*, 108–34.
108 A photograph of the performance can be found in Sierra, "Educating the Communists of the Future," 514.
109 Arce Porres, *Memorias*, 93.
110 GARF, f. 5451, op. 43c, d. 601, l. 74.

111 As with many clubs for "outsiders" in the Soviet Union, these clubs sought to overcome "backwardness" and serve as a place for entertainment, education, and social connection. See O'Keeffe, *New Soviet Gypsies*, 108–42. The Chkalov Club was provisioned better than the Red Star Gypsie club of the 1920s.
112 Nick Baron, "Remaking Soviet Society: The Filtration of Returnees from Nazi Germany, 1944–49," in *Warlands: Population Resettlement and State Reconstruction in the Soviet-East European Borderlands, 1945–50*, ed. Peter Gatrell and Nick Baron (New York: Palgrave Macmillan, 2009), 90, 105.
113 Siobhan Peeling, "Dirt, Disease and Disorder: Population Re-placement in Post-War Leningrad and the 'Danger' of Soviet Contamination," in *Warlands*, ed. Gatrell and Baron, 117–39; O'Keeffe, *New Soviet Gypsies*, 71–3.

Conclusion: Life after Stalin

1 Devillard et al., *Los niños*, 139.
2 *Holding On, Fighting Back*.
3 Devillard et al., *Los niños*, 244. For slightly different data see Zafra, Crego, and Heredia, *Los niños*, 74–6.
4 Devillard et al., 245.
5 On the importance of Spanish medical specialists see Miguel Marco Igual, *Los médicos republicanos españoles en la Unión Soviética* (Barcelona: Flor de Viento Ediciones, 2010).
6 In all, approximately two hundred Spanish engineers and other specialists left the USSR to assist Fidel Castro. Gonzáles Martell, "Niños de la guerra"; Young, "To Russia with 'Spain,'" 395–6; Zafra, Crego, and Heredia, *Los niños*, 93.
7 Colomina Limonero, *Dos patrias*, 128–38.
8 Colomina Limonero, 59–63; Eduardo Pons Prades, *Republicanos españoles en la Segunda Guerra Mundial* (Madrid: La Esfera de los Libros, 2003); Sierra Blas, *Palabras huérfanas*, 322. Estimates of Spaniards in the Red Army vary widely from approximately six to eight hundred, but these numbers include more than the young refugees of 1937–8. Fundación Nostalgia, *Memoria*, is the most complete list of Spaniards who died in the USSR.
9 Iordache, *Republicanos españoles en el Gulag*, 61–80, 136–42; Elpat'evskii, *Ispanskaia emigratsiia v SSSR*, 280–4; Colomina Limonero, *Dos patrias*, 92–103; Secundino Serrano, *Españoles en el GULAG: Republicanos bajo el estalinismo* (Madrid: Península, 2011).
10 Devillard et al., *Los niños*, 253–4.
11 Colomina Limonero, *Dos patrias*, 217–20; González Martínez, "El retorno a España," 84; Young, "¿Sujetos peligrosos?" 115–17.
12 Colomina Limonero, *Dos patrias*, 201–3; Elpat'evskii, *Ispanskaia emigratsiia v SSSR*, 248; Latorre Piquer, "De niña española," 102–12; Manuel Tourne, *Las dos guerras de mi infancia* (Mexico City: Centro Gráfico Industrial, 2006), 450–4.

13 On the negotiations see Suárez Fernández, *Franco y la URSS*; Elpat'evskii, *Ispanskaia emigratsiia v SSSR*, 245–8; Moreno Izquierdo, *Los niños de Rusia*.
14 The PCE, wanting to avoid "the defamation" of the USSR, fought against repatriation throughout the early 1950s. Iordache, *Republicanos españoles en el Gulag*, 61.
15 Colomina Limonero, *Dos patrias*, 204–5.
16 Alted Vigil, "Repatriation or Return?" 25; Colomina Limonero, *Dos patrias*, 215, 232–5; Devillard et al., *Los niños*, 247–8; Zafra, Crego, and Heredia, *Los niños*, 79–84. Colomina Limonero cites a Soviet Red Cross and Red Crescent report showing the higher totals of 2,000 adults and 900 children returning to Spain in 1956–9, but the report does not distinguish between niños de la guerra and other Spaniards. Citing Spanish Red Cross data, Carmen González Martínez suggests that in 1956 alone 1,673 Spaniards, 87 Russian women, and 667 children went to Spain ("El retorno a España," 81–3).
17 Devillard et al., *Los niños*, 250.
18 Colomina Limonero, *Dos patrias*, 233. Another estimate suggests that 1,899 Spaniards – not all niños de la guerra – returned to Spain between 1956 and 1959 and that about 400 went back to the USSR. *Novoe vremia*, no. 12 (1960): 27, 36.
19 González Martínez, "El retorno a España," 82–3.
20 Devillard et al., *Los niños*, 251; Alted Vigil, "Repatriation or Return?" 25. The collapse of the Soviet Union led to further repatriation: 47 (1991), 53 (1992), 44 (1993), and 17 (1994). González Martínez, "El retorno a España," 83.
21 Cazorla Sánchez, *Fear and Progress*, 17–56; Payne and Palacios, *Franco*, ch. 9; Stanley Payne, *The Franco Regime, 1936–1975* (Madison: University of Wisconsin Press, 1987), ch. 16; Preston, *The Spanish Holocaust*, 471–518.
22 Cazorla Sánchez, *Fear and Progress*, 40; Young, "¿Sujetos peligrosos?" 122.
23 Young, 103–27. She is writing against the common victim narrative that is dominant in Spanish scholarship, such as in Magdalena Garrido Caballero, "Fracturas de guerra: Los niños de la guerra Civil española en el Reino Unido y la Unión Soviética," *Bulletin of Spanish Studies* 89, no. 7–8 (2012): 254. See also Colomina Limonero, *Dos patrias*, 227–33.
24 Young, "¿Sujetos peligrosos?" 122.
25 Cazorla Sánchez, *Fear and Progress*, 90–2.
26 Vinyes, Armengou, and Belis, *Los niños perdidos del franquismo*, 178.
27 Colomina Limonero, *Dos patrias*, 220–1.
28 González Martínez, "El retorno a España," 91.
29 Colomina Limonero, *Dos patrias*, 139. These are all imprecise categories that belie the level of training and skill of the Spaniards.
30 Arce Porres, *Memorias*, 127.
31 Alted Vigil, "Repatriation or Return?," 16–34; Colomina Limonero, *Dos patrias*, 223–5; Zafra, Crego, and Heredia, *Los niños*, 89.
32 Colomina Limonero, *Dos patrias*, 225.
33 Arce Porres, *Memorias*, 128–33.

34 Arce Porres, 100; Colomina Limonero, *Dos patrias*, 226.
35 Colomina Limonero, "El Rusiñol."
36 Garrido Caballero, "Fracturas de guerra," 249.
37 González Martínez, "El retorno a España," 89–98.
38 Colomina Limonero, *Dos patrias*, 217–36; Sierra Blas, *Palabras huérfanas*, 329. Discrimination and vigilantism increased because of Francoist propaganda about the "communist hell" in which the returnees had been raised. Garrido Caballero, "Fracturas de guerra," 253; Garrido Caballero, "Españoles repatriados de la URSS," 117–30; Garrido Caballero, "Las relaciones hispano-soviéticas en la propaganda e informes diplomáticos del franquismo," in *Actas del VII encuentro de investigadores sobre el franquismo* (Santiago de Compostela, Spain: Universidad de Santiago de Compostella, 2010). Franco had blamed the Spanish Republic for following "Kremlin orders" to "wrench" the children from Spain. Jesús J. Alonso Carballés, "En torno a la tutela de los niños republicanos expatriados durante la guerra civil: Disposiciones legales y conflictos internos, 1936–1938," in *L'exili republicá: Actes del Vé Colloqui Republica, Guerra Civil i Franquisme* (Barberá del Vallés, Spain: Ajuntament de Barberá del Vallés, 2002), 80.
39 On the CIA's "Project Children" see Lawrence E. Rogers, "Project Children," *Studies in Intelligence* 7 (1963), cited in Young, "¿Sujetos peligrosos?" 104; Colomina Limonero, *Dos patrias*, 218; Zafra, Crego, and Heredia, *Los niños*, 84.
40 Colomina Limonero, *Dos patrias*, 217–36; Devillard et al., *Los niños*, 246–58; Elpat'evskii, *Ispanskaia emigratsiia v SSSR*, 268–84; Zafra, Crego, and Heredia, *Los niños*, 88–94.
41 Glennys Young adapted Alexei Yurchak's notion of an "imaginary west" to coin the term *imagined Spain*. Alexei Yurchak, *Everything Was Forever, Until It Was No More: The Last Soviet Generation* (Princeton, NJ: Princeton University Press, 2005), 158–206; Young, "¿Sujetos peligrosos?" 111–13.
42 Gatrell and Baron, "Violent Peacetime," 262.
43 In a 2012 BBC interview the son of a Spanish child refugee in the United Kingdom stated that his mother never felt at home in the United Kingdom or in Spain, because she lived in a sort of "limbo" between the two. http://www.basquechildren.org/video/bbcsouth (accessed 2 November 2018).
44 Slezkine, "USSR as Communal Apartment," 451.
45 Examples of this type of performance for non-Spaniards can be found in GARF, f. A-307, op. 1, d. 18, l. 15; Fernández Sánchez, *Memorias*, 150–2.
46 Arce Porres, *Memorias*, 100.
47 Álvarez Morán, *Memorias*, 209.
48 Colomina Limonero, *Dos patrias*, 219–20, 226.
49 Gonzáles Martell, "Niños de la guerra," 4; Young, "To Russia with 'Spain,'" 395–6; Zafra, Crego, and Heredia, *Los niños*, 93.

Bibliography

Archival Sources

Archivo Histórico del Partido Comunista de España (AHPCE) [Historical Archive of the Spanish Communist Party], Madrid

Dirigentes PCE [PCE Leaders]

Arxiu Nacional de Catalunya (ANC) [National Archive of Catalonia], Barcelona

Fondo 555, Centro Español de Moscú [Spanish Centre of Moscow]

Centro Documental de la Memoria Histórica (CDMH) [Documentary Centre of HIstorical Memory], Salamanca

ES.37274.CDMH/10.8, Delegación Nacional de Servicios Documentales de la Presidencia del Gobierno [National Delegation of Documentary Services of the Presidency of the Government] (P.S. Bilbao, P.S. Fotografías, P.S. Santander)
ES.37274.CDMH/11.82, Zafra García, Enrique
ES.37274.CDMH/12.47, Colección de documentación del Archivo Estatal de Rusia de Historia Sociopolítica [Documentation Collection of the Russian State Archive of Socio-political History]

Fundación Francisco Largo Caballero (FFLG) [Foundation Francisco Largo Caballero], Alcalá de Henares (Madrid)

Gosudarstvennyi Arkhiv Rossiiskoi Federatsii (GARF) [State Archive of the Russian Federation], Moscow

F. A-307, Detskie doma ispanskikh detei i Dom dlia ispanskoi molodezhi pri Ministerstve prosvesheniia RSFSR (1937–1951) [Children's Homes for Spanish Children and Home for Spanish Youth under the Ministry of Education RSFSR (1937–1951)]

F. A-2306, Ministerstvo prosveshcheniia RSFSR [Ministry of Education, RSFSR]
F. 5283, Vsesoiuznyi obshchestvo kul'turnykh sviazei s zagranitsei (VOKS) [All-Union Society of Cultural Relations Abroad]
F. 5446, Soveta Ministrov SSSR [USSR Council of Ministers]
F. 5451, Vsesoiuznyi tsentral'nyi sovet professional'nykh soiuzov (VTsSPS) [All-Union Central Council of Professional Unions]
F. 8009, Ministerstvo zdravookhraneniia SSSR [Ministry of Health, USSR]
F. 8265, Mezhdunarodnaia organizatsiia pomoshchi bortsam revoliutsii (MOPR) [International Organization of Aid to Fighters of the Revolution]

Rossiiskii Gosudarstvennyi Arkhiv Sotsial'no-Politicheskoi Istroii (RGASPI) [Russian State Archive of Socio-political History], Moscow

F. 17, Tsentral'nyi Komitet KPSS [Central Committee]
F. 495, Komintern [Communist International]
F. 533, Kommunisticheskii internatsional molodezhi [Communist International of Youth]

Published Primary Sources

Newspapers

Izvestiia
Komsomol'skaia pravda
New York Times
Pravda

Journals

Detskaia literatura
Detskii dom
Narodnoe obrazovanie
Sovetskaia pedagogika
Vozhatyi

Articles, Books, Document Collections

Álvarez Morán, Isabel Argentina. *Memorias de una niña de la guerra.* Gijón, Spain: Fundación Municipal Cultura, Educación y Universidad Popular, 2003.
Arce Porres, Manuel. *Memorias de Rusia: Vivencias de un niño de la guerra.* Madrid: Editorial Multipress, 2009.
Camino, Jaime. *Intimas conversaciones con la Pasionaria.* Barcelona: Dopesa, 1977.

Clemente del Río Salceda, Bernardo. *20,000 días en la URSS: Recuerdos, descubrimientos y reflexiones de un niño de la guerra*. Madrid: Entrelineas Editores, 2004.
Daev, V.G. *Ispanskie gosti na rodine Sadko: Itogi zhurnalistskogo poiska*. St Petersburg, Russia: Sudarynia, 1997.
Danaev, A.M., ed. *Narodnoe obrazovanie: Osnovanye postanovlennia, prikazy i instruktsii*. Moscow: Minsterstvo Prosveshcheniia RSFSR, 1948.
Dobrinin, B., and J. Maguidovich. *Geografía de España*. Moscow: Ministry of Education, 1940.
Fernández Sánchez, José. *Memorias de un niño de Moscú: Cuando salí de Ablaña*. Barcelona: Planeta, 1999.
- *Mi infancia en Moscú: Estampas de una nostalgia*. Madrid: Ediciones El Museo Universal, 1988.
Hidalgo de Cisneros, I. *Meniaiu kurs: Memuary*. Moscow: Izdatel'stvo politicheskoi literatury, 1967.
Huxley, Aldous. *They Still Draw Pictures! With 60 Illustrations Made by Spanish Children during the War*. New York: Spanish Child Welfare Association, 1938.
Kairov, I.A. *Pedagogika*. Moscow: Uchpedgiz, 1939.
Kononenko, Elena. *Malen'kie ispantsy* [Little Spaniards]. Moscow: Detizdat, 1937.
Latorre Piquer, Milagros. "De niña española a mujer en la URSS." In *Nuevas raíces: Testimonios de mujeres españolas en el exilio*, edited by Blanca Bravo, 61–113. Alicante, Spain: Biblioteca Virtual Miguel de Cervantes, 2002.
Llanos Más, Virgilio de los. *¿Te acuerdas, tovarisch ...? Del archivo un "niño de la guerra."* Valencia, Spain: Institució Alfons el Magnànim, 2002.
Makarenko, Anton. *Pedagogicheskaia poema* [Pedagogical poem]. Moscow, 1964.
Mora, Constancia de la. *Doble esplendor: Autobiografía de una aristócrata española republicana y comunista*. Barcelona: Critica, 1977.
- *Vmesto roskoshi*. Moscow: Khudozhestvennaia literatura, 1943.
Narodnoe khoziaistvo SSSR v Velikoi Otechestvennoi Voine, 1941–45 gg.: Statisticheskii sbornik. Moscow: Informatsionno-izdatel'skii tsentr, 1990.
Narodnoe obrazovanie v SSSR: Obshcheobrazovatel'naia shkola; Sbornik dokumentov, 1917–1973 gg. Moscow: Pedagogika, 1973.
Parga, Carmen. *Antes que sea tarde*. Madrid: Compañía Literaria, 1996.
Programmy srednei shkole: Literatura, VIII–X klassy. Moscow, 1944.
Sanitarnye pravila dlia detskikh uchrezhdenii. 2nd ed. Leningrad, 1940.
Soler Gilabert, Alejandra. *La vida es un río caudaloso con peligrosos rápidos: Al final de todo ... sigo comunista*. Valencia, Spain: Universitat de Valencia, 2009.
Spravochnik sovetskogo rabotnika. Moscow: Vlast' sovetov, 1937.
Stalin, Joseph. "Report to the Eighteenth Congress of the CPSU(B) on the Work of the Central Committee, March 10, 1939." In *Problems of Leninism*, 780–9. Moscow: Foreign Languages Publishing House, 1954.
Tourne, Manuel. *Las dos guerras de mi infancia*. Mexico City: Centro Gráfico Industrial, 2006.

Vasil'eva, O. *Lecturas escogidas*. Moscow: Ediciones Cooperativas de los Obreros Extranjeros, 1938.
- *Uchebnik ispanskogo iazyka: Nachal'nyi kurs*. Moscow: Izdatel'skoe t-vo inostrannykh rabochikh v SSSR, 1937.

Secondary Sources

Allen, David E. "The Soviet Union and the Spanish Civil War." PhD diss., Stanford University, 1952.

Alonso Carballés, Jesús J. "En torno a la tutela de los niños republicanos expatriados durante la guerra civil: Disposiciones legales y conflictos internos, 1936–1938." In *L'exili republicá: Actes del Vé Colloqui Republica, Guerra Civil i Franquisme*, edited by F. Bonamusa and J. Puy. Barberá del Vallés, Spain: Ajuntament de Barberá del Vallés, 2002.

- *1937: Los niños vascos evacuados a Francia y a Bélgica; Historia y memoria de un éxodo infantil, 1936–1940*. Bilbao, Spain: Asociación de Niños Evacuados el '37, 1998.

Alted Vigil, Alicia. "Education and Political Control." In *Spanish Cultural Studies: An Introduction; The Struggle for Modernity*, edited by Helen Graham and Jo Labanyi, 196–201. Oxford: Oxford University Press, 1995.

- "Repatriation or Return? The Difficult Homecoming of the Spanish Civil War Exiles." In *Coming Home?*, vol. 1, *Conflict and Return Migration in the Aftermath of Europe's Twentieth-Century Civil Wars*, edited by Sharif Gemie and Scott Soo, 16–34. Newcastle-upon-Tyne, UK: Cambridge Scholars Publishing, 2013.

- "Le retour en Espagne des enfants évacués pendant la guerre civile espagnole: La délégation extraordinaire au rapatriement des mineurs (1938–1954)." In *Enfants de la guerre civile: Vécus et représentations de la génération née entre 1925 et 1940*, edited by Centre d'histoire de l'Europe du vingtième siècle, 47–59. Paris: L'Harmattan, 1999.

- *La voz de los vencidos: El exilio republican de 1939*. Madrid: Aguilar, 2005.

Alted Vigil, Alicia, Roger González, and Maria José Millan, eds. *El exilio de los niños: Catálogo de la exposición*. Madrid: Fundación Pablo Iglesias y Fundación Largo Caballero, 2003.

Alted Vigil, Alicia, Encarna Nicolás Marín, and Roger González Martell. *Los niños de la guerra de España en la Unión Soviética: De la evacuación al retorno (1937–1999)*. Madrid: Fundación Francisco Largo Caballero, 1999.

Álvarez Junco, José. "Education and the Limits of Liberalism." In *Spanish Cultural Studies: The Struggle for Modernity*, edited by Helen Graham and Jo Labanyi, 45–52. Oxford: Oxford University Press, 1995.

Anderson, Barbara A., and Brian D. Silver. "Equality, Efficiency, and Politics in Soviet Bilingual Education Policy, 1934–1980." *American Political Science Review* 78, no. 4 (1984): 1019–39.

Arrien, Gregorio. *La generación del exilio: Génesis de las escuelas vascas y las colonias escolares (1932-1940)*. Bilbao, Spain: ONURA, 1983.
- *Niños vascos evacuados a Gran Bretaña*. Bilbao, Spain: Asociación de Niños Evacuados el '37, 1998.

Aznar Soler, Manuel. "Teatro, literatura y cultura del exilio republicano español en la Unión Soviética (1939-1949)." *Exils et migrations ibériques au XXéme siècle*, no. 6 (1999): 61-76.

Baker, Bernadette. "Foucault, Historiography, and Writing a History of the Child: Productive Paradoxes." *History of Education Review* 30, no. 1 (2001): 20-33.

Ball, Alan. *And Now My Soul Is Hardened: Abandoned Children in the Soviet Union, 1917-1938*. Berkeley: University of California Press, 1996.
- "State Children: Soviet Russia's *Besprizornye* and the New Socialist Generation." *Russian Review* 52, no. 2 (1993): 230.

Barbalet, Margaret. *Far from a Low Gutter Girl: The Forgotten World of State Wards, South Australia, 1887-1940*. Melbourne, Australia: Oxford University Press, 1983.

Baron, Nick. "Remaking Soviet Society: The Filtration of Returnees from Nazi Germany, 1944-49." In *Warlands: Population Resettlement and State Reconstruction in the Soviet-East European Borderlands, 1945-50*, edited by Peter Gatrell and Nick Baron, 89-116. New York: Palgrave Macmillan, 2009.

Baron, Nick, and Peter Gatrell. "Population Displacement, State Building, and Social Identity in the Lands of the Former Russian Empire, 1917-23." *Kritika: Explorations in Russian and Eurasian History* 4, no. 1 (Winter 2003): 51-100.

Barron, Hester. "'Little Prisoners of City Streets': London Elementary Schools and the School Journey Movement, 1918-1939." *History of Education* 42, no. 2 (2013): 166-81.

Beevor, Antony. *The Battle for Spain: The Spanish Civil War, 1936-1939*. New York: Penguin Books, 2006.

Bell, Adrian. *Only for Three Months: The Basque Refugee Children in Exile*. Norwich, UK: Mousehold Press, 2007.

Belsky, Natalie. "Encounters in the East: Evacuees in the Soviet Hinterland during the Second World War." PhD diss., University of Chicago, 2014.

Benjamin, Natalia, ed. *Recuerdos: Basque Refugee Children in Great Britain*. Norwich, UK: Mousehold Press, 2007.

Bernstein, Matthew. *Controlling Hollywood: Censorship and Regulation in the Studio Era*. New Brunswick, NJ: Rutgers University Press, 1999.

Bhabha, Homi K. "Cultural Diversity and Cultural Differences." In *The Post-Colonial Studies Reader*, 2nd ed., edited by Bill Ashcroft, Gareth Griffiths, and Helen Tiffin, 55-7. New York: Routledge, 2006.
- "Signs Taken for Wonders: Questions of Ambivalence and Authority under a Tree outside Delhi, May 1817." *Critical Inquiry* 12, no. 1 (1985): 144-65.

Bidlack, Richard, and Nikita Lomagin. *The Leningrad Blockade, 1941-1944: A New Documentary History from the Soviet Archives*. New Haven, CT: Yale University Press, 2012.

Bilinsky, Yaroslav. "Education of the Non-Russian Peoples in the USSR, 1917-1967." *Slavic Review* 27, no. 3 (1968): 411-37.
Blitstein, Peter. "Nation-Building or Russification? Obligatory Russian Instruction in the Soviet Non-Russian School, 1938-1953." In *A State of Nations: The Soviet State and Its Peoples in the Age of Lenin and Stalin*, edited by Ronald G. Suny and Terry D. Martin, 253-74. New York: Oxford University Press, 2001.
- "Stalin's Nations: Soviet Nationality Policy between Planning and Primordialism, 1936-1953." PhD diss., University of California, Berkeley, 1999.
Boldyrev, N.I., ed. *Klassnyi rokovoditel'*. Moscow: Akademii pedagogicheskih nauk RSFSR, 1955.
Brandenberger, David. *National Bolshevism: Stalinist Mass Culture and the Formation of Modern Russian National Identity, 1931-1956*. Cambridge, MA: Harvard University Press, 2002.
Breakwell, Suan. "'Knowing How to Be a Mother': Parenting, Emotion and Evacuation Propaganda during the Spanish Civil War, 1936-1939." In *Parenting and the State in Britain and Europe, c. 1870-1950: Raising the Nation*, edited by Hestor Barron and Claudia Siebrecht, 207-30. New York: Palgrave Macmillan, 2017.
Brooks, Jeffrey. *Thank You, Comrade Stalin! Soviet Public Culture from Revolution to Cold War*. Princeton, NJ: Princeton University Press, 2001.
Caplan, Jane, and John Torpey, eds. *Documenting Individual Identity: The Development of State Practices in the Modern World*. Princeton, NJ: Princeton University Press, 2001.
Castillo, Susana. *Mis años en la escuela soviética*. Madrid: Catarata, 2009.
Cazorla Sánchez, Antonio. *Fear and Progress: Ordinary Lives in Franco's Spain, 1939-1975*. Malden, MA: Wiley Blackwell, 2010.
Chapman, Jane. *Real Wages in Soviet Russia since 1928*. Cambridge, MA: Harvard University Press, 1963.
Chase, William. *Enemies within the Gates? The Comintern and the Stalinist Repression, 1934-1939*. New Haven, CT: Yale University Press, 2001.
- "Scapegoating One's Comrades in the USSR, 1934-1937." *Russian History* 38, no. 1 (2011): 23-41.
Chernik, S.A. *Sovetskaia obshcheobrazovatel'naia shkola v gody Velikoi Otechestvennoi voiny*. Moscow: Pedagogika, 1984.
Clark, Katerina. *Moscow, the Fourth Rome: Stalinism, Cosmopolitanism, and the Evolution of Soviet Culture, 1931-1941*. Cambridge, MA: Harvard University Press, 2011.
- *The Soviet Novel: History as Ritual*. Bloomington: Indiana University Press, 2000.
Cloud, Yvonne. *The Basque Children in England: An Account of Their Life at North Stoneham Camp*. London: Victor Gollancz, 1937.
Cobb, Christopher. "The Republican State and Mass Educational-Cultural Initiatives." In *Spanish Cultural Studies: An Introduction; The Struggle for Modernity*, edited by Helen Graham and Jo Labanyi, 133-8. Oxford: Oxford University Press, 1995.

Coleman, Michael C. *American Indians, the Irish, and Government Schooling: A Comparative Study*. Lincoln: University of Nebraska, 2007.
Colomina Limonero, Immaculada. *Dos patrias, tres mil destinos: Vida y exilio de los niños de la guerra de España refugiados en la Unión Soviética*. Madrid: Cinca, 2010.
– "El Rusiñol: Adaptación cultural y lingüística de los exiliados españoles en la antigua Unión Soviética." In *La Guerra Civil Española, 1936-1939: Actas Congreso Internacional*, edited by Juliá Santos. Madrid: Sociedad Estatal de Conmemoraciones Culturales, 2007.
Comín Colomner, Eduardo. *Españoles esclavos en Rusia*. Madrid: Publicaciones Españoles, 1952.
Crego Navarro, Rosalía. "La colonias escolares durante la Guerra Civil (1936-1939)." *Espacio, tiempo y forma* 5, no. 2 (1989): 299-328.
Cruz Orozco, José Ignacio. *Las colonias escolares valencianas (1906-1936): Un ejemplo de renovación educativa*. Valencia, Spain: Universitat de Valencia, 2012.
Cupers, Kenny. "Governing through Nature: Camps and Youth Movements in Interwar Germany and the United States." *Cultural Geographies* 15 (2008): 173-205.
Danforth, Loring M., and Riki Van Boeschoten. *Children of the Greek Civil War: Refugees and the Politics of Memory*. Chicago: University of Chicago Press, 2012.
Daniel, Valentine. "The Refugee: A Discourse on Displacement." In *Exotic No More: Anthropology on the Frontlines*, edited by Jeremy MacClancey, 270-86. Chicago: University of Chicago Press, 2002.
Daniushevskii, I.I. "Voprosy vospitaniia detei v detskom dome." *Detskii dom*, no. 1 (1944): 3-11.
David-Fox, Michael. *Crossing Borders: Modernity, Ideology, and Culture in Russia and the Soviet Union*. Pittsburgh, PA: University of Pittsburgh Press, 2015.
Davies, Hywell. *Fleeing Franco: How Wales Gave Shelter to Refugee Children from the Basque Country during the Spanish Civil War*. Cardiff: University of Wales Press, 2011.
Davies, Sarah. *Popular Opinion in Stalin's Russia: Terror, Propaganda and Dissent, 1934-1941*. Cambridge: Cambridge University Press, 1997.
– "'Us against Them': Social Identity in Soviet Russia, 1934-1941." *Russian Review* 56, no. 1 (January 1997): 70-89.
Davin, Anna. *Growing Up Poor: Home, School and Street in London, 1870-1914*. London: Rivers Oram Press, 1996.
deGraffenried, Julie K. *Sacrificing Childhood: Children and the Soviet State in the Great Patriotic War*. Lawrence: University Press of Kansas, 2014.
Devillard, Marie José, Álvaro Pazos, Susana Castillo, and Nuria Medina, eds. *Los niños españoles en la URSS, 1937-1997: Narración y memoria*. Barcelona: Ariel, 2001.
Dobrenko, Evgeny. *The Making of the State Reader: Social and Aesthetic Context of the Reception of Soviet Literature*. Translated by Jesse Savage. Stanford, CA: Stanford University Press, 1997.
– "The School Tale in Children's Literature of Socialist Realism." In *Russian Children's Literature and Culture*, edited by Marina Balina and Larissa Rudova, 43-66. New York: Routledge, 2008.

- *Stalinist Cinema and the Production of History: Museum of the Revolution*. New Haven, CT: Yale University Press, 2008.
Downs, Laura Lee. *Childhood in the Promised Land: Working-Class Movements and the Colonies de Vacances in France, 1880–1960*. London: Routledge, 2002.
Dreyfus-Armand, Geneviève. "L'accueil des enfants espagnols en France pendant la guerre d'Espagne et après la victoire franquiste." *Documents pour l'histoire du français langue étrangère ou seconde* 46 (2011): 1–13.
Dundovich, Elena. "Le purghe Staliniane e il Komintern: La guerra di Spagna e i suoi riflessi sulla política interna Sovietica." *Storia delle Relazioni Internazionali* 11, no. 1 (January 1996): 3–35.
Dunstan, John. *Soviet Schooling in the Second World War*. New York: St Martin's Press, 1997.
Elpat'evskii, A.V. *Ispanskaia emigratsiia v SSSR: Istoriografiia i istochniki, popytka interpretatsii*. Moscow: GERS, 2002.
Encinas Moral, Ángel Luis. *Fuentes históricas para el estudio de la emigración Española a la U.R.S.S. (1936–2007)*. Madrid: Exterior XXI, 2008.
Escrivá, Cristina, and Rafael Maestre Marín. *De las negras bombas a las doradas naranjas: Colonias escolares, 1936–1939*. Tavernes Blanques, Spain: Eixam, 2011.
Espinosa Maestra, Francisco. *Violencia roja y azul: España, 1936–1950*. Barcelona: Editorial Crítica, 2010.
Ewing, E. Thomas. "Ethnicity at School: 'Non-Russian' Education in the Soviet Union during the 1930s." *History of Education* 35, no. 4–5 (2006): 499–519.
- *Separate Schools: Gender, Policy, and Practice in Postwar Soviet Education*. DeKalb: Northern Illinois University Press, 2010.
- "A Stalinist Celebrity Teacher: Gender, Professional, and Political Identities in Soviet Culture of the 1930s." *Journal of Women's History* 16, no. 4 (Winter 2004): 92–118.
- *The Teachers of Stalinism: Policy, Practice and Power in Soviet Schools of the 1930s*. New York: Peter Lang, 2002.
Fear-Segal, Jacqueline. *White Man's Club: Schools, Race, and the Struggle for Indian Acculturation*. Lincoln: University of Nebraska Press, 2007.
Fernandez-Eres, Anna Pavlovna. "Ispanskie 'deti voiny' v 1941–1944 gg.: Opyt evakuatsii v glubokii tyl." *Otechestvennaia istoriia* 16, no. 3 (2014): 503–8.
Fernández Soria, Juan Manuel. *Educación y cultura en la Guerra Civil (España 1936–1939)*. Valencia, Spain: Nau Libres, 1984.
Ferris, Kate. "Parents, Children and the Fascist State: The Production and Reception of Children's Magazines in 1930s Italy." In *Parenting and the State in Britain and Europe, c. 1870–1950: Raising the Nation*, edited by Hester Barron and Claudia Siebrecht, 183–206. New York: Palgrave Macmillan, 2017.
Filtzer, Donald. *Hazards of Urban Life in Late Stalinist Russia: Health, Hygiene, and Living Standards, 1943–1953*. Cambridge: Cambridge University Press, 2010.
- *Soviet Workers and Late Stalinism: Labour and the Restoration of the Stalinist System after World War II*. Cambridge: Cambridge University Press, 2002.

- *Soviet Workers and Stalinist Industrialization: The Formation of Modern Soviet Production Relations, 1928–1941*. London: Pluto Press, 1986.
Fisher, Ralph Talcott. *Pattern for Soviet Youth: A Study of the Congresses of the Komsomol, 1918–1954*. New York: Columbia University Press, 1959.
Fitzpatrick, Sheila. *Everyday Stalinism: Ordinary Life in Extraordinary Times: Soviet Russia in the 1930s*. New York: Oxford University Press, 1999.
- *Tear Off the Masks! Identity and Imposture in Twentieth-Century Russia*. Princeton, NJ: Princeton University Press, 2005.
Foucault, Michel. *Discipline and Punish: The Birth of the Prison*. New York: Vintage Books, 1979.
- *Security, Territory, Population: Lectures at the Collège de France, 1977–1978*. Edited by Michel Senellart. Translated by Graham Burchell. Basingstoke, UK: Palgrave Macmillan, 2007.
- "The Subject and Power." *Critical Inquiry* 8, no. 4 (1982): 777–95.
Fraser, Ronald. *Blood of Spain: The Experience of Civil War, 1936–1939*. London: Allen Lane, 1979.
Fundación Nostalgia. *Memoria: En memoria de los combatientes españoles que cayeron luchando contra el fascismo y por la libertad junto al pueblo ruso en la Segunda Guerra Mundial, 1941–1945*. Madrid: Fundación Nostalgia, 2000.
Fürst, Juliane. "Between Salvation and Liquidation: Homeless and Vagrant Children and the Reconstruction of Soviet Society." *Slavonic and East European Review* 86, no. 2 (2008): 232–58.
Gallagher, Charles F. *Culture and Education in Spain*. Hanover, NH: American Universities Field Staff, 1979.
Galmarini-Kabala, Maria Cristina. *The Right to Be Helped: Deviance, Entitlement, and the Soviet Moral Order*. DeKalb: Northern Illinois University Press, 2016.
García Argüello, Xavier. *El mar de la libertad: Breve crónica de las evacuaciones de niños vascos durante la Guerra del '37*. Bilbao, Spain: Asociación de Jubilados Evacuados de la Guerra Civil y Ayuntamiento de Bilbao, 2002.
García Lozano, Immaculada, and Dolores Moreno Burgos. *Los raíles del exilio: "Niños de Morelia"; Uno éxodo a México*. Madrid: Fundación de los Ferrocarriles Españoles, 2007.
Garrido Caballero, Magdalena. "Españoles repatriados de la URSS en la propaganda del régimen franquista." In *Actas del VI encuentro de investigadores sobre el franquismo*, edited by Juan José Carerras and Ángela Cenarro, 117–30. Zaragoza, Spain: Contexto Gráfico, 2006.
- "Fracturas de guerra: Los niños de la guerra Civil española en el Reino Unido y la Unión Soviética." *Bulletin of Spanish Studies* 89, no. 7–8 (2012): 241–54.
- "Las relaciones hispano-soviéticas en la propaganda e informes diplomáticos del franquismo." In *Actas del VII encuentro de investigadores sobre el franquismo*. Santiago de Compostela, Spain: Universidad de Santiago de Conpostella, 2010.

Gatrell, Peter. *Making of the Modern Refugee.* Oxford: Oxford University Press, 2013.
Gatrell, Peter, and Nick Baron. "Violent Peacetime: Reconceptualizing Displacement and Resettlement in the Soviet-East European Borderlands after the Second World War." In *Warlands: Population Resettlement and State Reconstruction in the Soviet–East European Borderlands, 1945–50*, edited by Nick Baron and Peter Gatrell, 255–68. New York: Palgrave Macmillan, 2009.
Geist, Anthony L. *They Still Draw Pictures: Children's Art in Wartime from the Spanish Civil War to Kosovo.* Urbana: University of Illinois Press, 2002.
Giles, Geoffrey. "Schooling for Little Soldiers: German Education in the Second World War." In *Education and the Second World War: Studies in Schooling and Social Change*, edited by Roy Lowe, 17–29. London: Falmer Press, 1992.
Giroux, Henry, and David Purpel, eds. *The Hidden Curriculum and Moral Education: Deception or Discovery?* Berkeley, CA: McCutchan, 1983.
Glantz, David. *The Siege of Leningrad, 1941–1944: 900 Days of Terror.* London: Spellmount, 2001.
González, Valentín. *Vida y muerte en la URSS.* Buenos Aires: S.A. Editorial Bell, 1951.
González Martell, Roger. "Niños de la guerra en la Unión Soviética, hispanosoviéticos en Cuba." http://www.Scribd.com/doc/68821252/Ninos-de-la-guerra-en-la-Union-Sovietica-Hispanosovieticos-en-Cuba
González Martínez, Carmen. "El retorno a España de los 'niños de la guerra civil.'" *Anales de Historia Contemporánea* 19 (2003): 75–100.
Gowdy-Wygant, Cecilia. *Cultivating Victory: The Women's Land Army and the Victory Garden Movement.* Pittsburgh, PA: University of Pittsburgh Press, 2013.
Green, Rachel. "'There Will Not Be Orphans among Us': Soviet Orphanages, Foster Care, and Adoption, 1941–1956." PhD diss., University of Chicago, 2006.
Griffiths, Owen. "Japanese Children and the Culture of Death, January–August 1945." In *Children and War: A Historical Anthology*, edited by James Marten, 160–71. New York: New York University Press, 2002.
Gross, Magdalena. "Reclaiming the Nation: Polish Schooling in Exile during the Second World War." *History of Education Quarterly* 53, no. 3 (2013): 233–54.
Guzmán Reina, Antonio. *Causas y remedio del analfabetismo en España.* Madrid: Publicaciones de la Junta Nacional contra el Analfabetismo, Ministerio de Educación Nacional, 1955.
Haig-Brown, Celia. *Resistance and Renewal: Surviving the Indian Residential School.* Vancouver, BC: Arsenal Pulp Press, 1988.
L'hebergement des enfants de la guerre d'Espagne en Belgique. Brussels: Federación de Asociaciones de Enseñanza y Centros Españoles en Bélgica, 1992.
Hellbeck, Jochen. "Fashioning the Stalinist Soul: The Diary of Stepan Podlubnyi (1931–1939)." *Jahrbücher für Geschichte Osteuropas* 44, no. 3 (1996): 344–73.
– *Revolution on My Mind: Writing a Diary under Stalin.* Cambridge, MA: Harvard University Press, 2006.

Hellman, Ben. *Fairy Tales and True Stories: The History of Russian Literature for Children and Young People (1574–2010)*. Leiden, Netherlands: Brill, 2013.
Hermann, Gina. *Written in Red: The Communist Memoir in Spain*. Urbana: University of Illinois Press, 2010.
Hernández, Jesús. *Le Grande Trahison*. Paris: Fasquelle, 1953.
– *El país de la gran mentira*. Madrid: E.G. del Toro, 1974.
Hillig, Götz, and Marianne Krüger-Potratz. "Die 'zweite Geburt' des A.S. Makarenko: Zugleich ein Beitrag zu einem kaum bekannten Kapitel aus der Geschichte der sowjetischen Pädagogik, 1939–1941." In *Vergleichende Bildungsforsschung: DDR, Osteuropa und interkulturelle Perspektiven*, edited by Bernhard Dilger, Friedrich Kübart, and Hans-Peter Schaefer, 318–42. Berlin: Verlag Arno Spitz, 1986.
Hirsch, Francine. *Empire of Nations: Ethnographic Knowledge and the Making of the Soviet Union*. Ithaca, NY: Cornell, 2005.
Hoffmann, David L. *Cultivating the Masses: Modern State Practices and Soviet Socialism, 1914–1939*. Ithaca, NY: Cornell University Press, 2011.
– *Peasant Metropolis: Social Identities in Moscow, 1929–1941*. Ithaca, NY: Cornell University Press, 1994.
– *Stalinist Values: The Cultural Norms of Soviet Modernity, 1917–1941*. Ithaca, NY: Cornell University Press, 2003.
Holding On, Fighting Back: The Long Road Home to Spain. Directed by Pedro Carvajal. Princeton, NJ: Films for the Humanities and Sciences, 2002. DVD.
Holmes, Larry E. "Ascent into Darkness: Escalating Negativity in the Administration of Schools in the Kirov Region, 1931–1941." *History of Education*, 35, no. 4–5 (2006): 521–40.
– *Kirov's School No. 9: Power, Privilege, and Excellence in the Provinces, 1933–1945*. Kirov, Russia: Loban, 2008.
– "Magic into Hocus-Pocus: The Decline of Labor Education in Soviet Russia's Schools, 1931–1937." *Russian Review* 51, no. 4 (1992): 545–65.
– "School and Schooling under Stalin, 1931–1953." In *Educational Reform in Post-Soviet Russia: Legacies and Prospects*, edited by Ben Eklof, Larry E. Holmes, and Vera Kaplan, 56–101. London: Frank Cass, 2005.
– "Spain in the Depths of Russia, 1941–1945." Unpublished manuscript.
– *Stalin's School: Moscow's Model School No. 25, 1931–1937*. Pittsburgh, PA: University of Pittsburgh Press, 1999.
– *Stalin's World War II Evacuations: Triumph and Troubles in Kirov*. Lawrence: University of Kansas Press, 2017.
Holquist, Peter. "'Information Is the Alpha and Omega of Our Work': Bolshevik Surveillance in Its Pan-European Perspective." *Journal of Modern History* 69, no. 3 (1997): 415–50.
Humphries, Stephen. *Hooligans or Rebels? An Oral History of Working-Class Childhood and Youth, 1889–1939*. Oxford: Blackwell, 1981.

Husband, William B. *"Godless Communists": Atheism and Society in Soviet Russia, 1917–1932*. Dekalb: Northern Illinois University Press, 2000.
Igmen, Ali. *Speaking Soviet with an Accent: Culture and Power in Kyrgyzstan*. Pittsburgh, PA: University of Pittsburgh Press, 2012.
Ignacio Cruz, José. *Las colonias escolares valencianas, 1906–1936: Un ejemplo de renovación educativa*. Valencia, Spain: Universidad de Valencia, 2012.
Inkeles, Alex, and Raymond Bauer. *The Soviet Citizen: Daily Life in a Totalitarian Society*. Cambridge, MA: Harvard University Press, 1961.
Iordache, Luiza. *Republicanos españoles en el Gulag, 1939–1956*. Barcelona: Institut de Ciències Polítiques i Socials, 2008.
James, Thomas. *Exile Within: The Schooling of Japanese Americans, 1942–1945*. Cambridge, MA: Harvard University Press, 1987.
Jones, Jeffrey W. *Everyday Life and the "Reconstruction" of Soviet Russia during and after the Great Patriotic War, 1943–1948*. Bloomington, IN: Slavica, 2008.
Juliá, Santos, and Julián Casanova. *Victimas de la Guerra Civil*. Madrid: Ediciones Temas de Hoy, 1999.
Kassof, Allen. *The Soviet Youth Program: Regimentation and Rebellion*. Cambridge, MA: Harvard University Press, 1965.
Kater, Michael H. *Hitler Youth*. Cambridge, MA: Harvard University Press, 2004.
Kelly, Catriona. *Children's World: Growing Up in Russia, 1890–1991*. New Haven, CT: Yale University Press, 2007.
– *Comrade Pavlik: The Rise and Fall of a Soviet Boy Hero*. London: Granata, 2007.
Keren, Célia. "Les enfants espagnols réfugiés en France 1939 ou la crise de la solidarité ouvrière." *Les Cahiers du Centre de Recherches Historiques* 44 (2009): 1–13.
Khalid, Adeeb. *Making Uzbekistan: Nation, Empire, and Revolution in the Early USSR*. Ithaca, NY: Cornell University Press, 2015.
Kharitonova, Natalia. "Sovetskie pedagogicheskie rabotniki detskikh domov dlia ispanskikh detei glazami byvshikh vospitannikov." In *Antropologiia sovetskoi shkoly: Kul'turnye universalii i provintsial'nye praktiki*, 175–92. Perm, Russia: Permskii gosudarstevennyi universitet, 2010.
Khlevniuk, Oleg. "The Objectives of the Great Terror, 1937–1938." In *Stalinism: The Essential Readings*, edited by David Hoffmann, 87–104. Oxford: Blackwell, 2003.
Kirk, Robert William. *Earning Their Stripes: The Mobilization of American Children in the Second World War*. New York: Peter Lang, 1994.
Kirschenbaum, Lisa. "Exile, Gender, and Communist Self-Fashioning: Dolores Ibárruri (La Pasionaria) in the Soviet Union." *Slavic Review* 71, no. 3 (Fall 2012): 566–89.
– "Innocent Victims and Heroic Defenders: Children and the Siege of Leningrad." In *Children and War: A Historical Anthology*, edited by James Marten, 279–90. New York: New York University Press, 2002.
– *International Communism and the Spanish Civil War: Solidarity and Suspicion*. Cambridge: Cambridge University Press, 2015.

- *The Legacy of the Siege of Leningrad, 1941-1995: Myth, Memories, and Monuments.* New York: Cambridge University Press, 2006.
- *Small Comrades: Revolutionizing Childhood in Soviet Russia, 1917-1932.* New York: Routledge, 2001.

Kojevnikov, Alexei. "Rituals of Stalinist Culture at Work: Science and the Games of Intraparty Democracy circa 1948." *Russian Review* 57 (January 1998): 25-52.

Kon, Igor. "Telesnye nakazaniia deti v Rossii: Proshloe i nastoiashchee." *Istoricheskaia psikhologiia i sotsiologiia istorii* 1 (2011): 83.

Korolev, Fedor. *Sovetskaia shkola v period industrializatsii.* Moscow: Uchebno-pedagogicheskoe izdatelstvo, 1959.

Kotkin, Stephen. *Magnetic Mountain: Stalinism as a Civilization.* Berkeley: University of California Press, 1995.

Kowalsky, Daniel. "The Soviet Cinematic Offensive in the Spanish Civil War." *Film History* 19, no. 1 (2007): 10-19.
- *Stalin and the Spanish Civil War.* New York: Columbia University Press, 2004.

Kucherenko, Olga. "*In loco parentis*: Junior Cadet Schools in the Soviet Union during the Second World War." In *Parenting and the State in Britain and Europe c. 1870-1950: Raising the Nation*, edited by Hester Barron and Claudia Siebrecht, 231-54. New York: Palgrave Macmillan, 2017.
- *Little Soldiers: How Soviet Children Went to War, 1941-1945.* Oxford: Oxford University Press, 2011.
- *Soviet Street Children in the Second World War: Welfare and Social Control under Stalin.* London: Bloomsbury, 2016.
- "State v. Danila Kuz'mich: Soviet Desertion Laws and Industrial Child Labor during World War II." *Russian Review* 71 (July 2012): 391-412.

Kudinov, Vladimir. *Detskoe i molodezhnoe dvizhenie v Rossii v XX veke.* Kostroma, Russia: Kostromskoi gostudarstvennoi universitet, 2000.

Kuzin, N.P., M.N. Kolmakova, and Z.I. Ravkin. *Ocherki istorii shkoly i pedagogicheskoi mysli narodov SSSR, 1917-1941 gg.* Moscow: Pedagogika, 1980.

Labajos Pérez, Emilia, and Fernando Vitoria-García. *Los niños españoles refugiados en Bélgica, 1936-1939.* Valencia, Spain: Asociación de los Niños de la Guerra de Namur, 1997.

Leff, Leonard J., and Jerold L. Simmons. *The Dame in the Kimono: Hollywood, Censorship, and the Production Code.* Lexington: University of Kentucky Press, 2013.

Legarreta, Dorothy. *The Guernica Generation: Basque Refugee Children of the Spanish Civil War.* Reno: University of Nevada Press, 1985.

Livschiz, Ann. "Children's Lives after Zoia's Death: Order, Emotions and Heroism in Children's Lives and Literature in the Post-War Soviet Union." In *Late Stalinist Russia: Soviet between Reconstruction and Reinvention*, edited by Juliane Fürst, 192-208. New York: Routledge, 2006.
- "Growing Up Soviet: Childhood in the Soviet Union, 1917-1958." PhD diss., Stanford University, 2007.

- "Pre-revolutionary in Form, Soviet in Content? Wartime Educational Reforms and the Postwar Quest for Normality." *History of Education* 35, no. 4–5 (2006): 541–60.
Lowe, Roy. "Education in England during the Second World War." In *Education and the Second World War: Studies in Schooling and Social Change*, edited by Roy Lowe, 4–16. London: Falmer Press, 1992.
Lozano Seijas, Claudio. *La educación republicana, 1931–1939*. Barcelona: Universidad de Barcelona, 1980.
Malkki, Liisa. "National Geographic: The Rooting of Peoples and the Territorialisation of National Identity among Scholars and Refugees." *Cultural Anthropology* 7, no. 1 (1992): 24–44.
Manley, Rebecca. "The Perils of Displacement: The Soviet Evacuee between Refugee and Deportee." *Contemporary European History* 16, no. 4 (2007): 495–509.
- *To the Tashkent Station: Evacuation and Survival in the Soviet Union at War*. Ithaca, NY: Cornell University Press, 2009.
- "'Where Should We Resettle the Comrades Next?' The Adjudication of Housing Claims and the Construction of the Post-War Order." In *Late Stalinist Russia: Soviet between Reconstruction and Reinvention*, edited by Juliane Fürst, 233–46. New York: Routledge, 2006.
Marco Igual, Miguel. *Los médicos republicanos españoles en la Unión Soviética*. Barcelona: Flor de Viento Ediciones, 2010.
Marques, Pierre. *Les enfants espagnols réfugiés en France (1936–1939)*. Paris: self-published, 1993.
Martin, Terry. *The Affirmative Action Empire: Nations and Nationalism in the USSR, 1923–1939*. Ithaca, NY: Cornell University Press, 2001.
- "Modernization or Neo-traditionalism? Ascribed Nationality and Soviet Primordialism." In *Stalinism: New Directions*, edited by Sheila Fitzpatrick, 348–67. New York: Routledge, 2000.
- "The Origins of Soviet Ethnic Cleansing." *Journal of Modern History* 70, no. 4 (1998): 813–61.
Mateu, Julio. *Olivos y abedules: Poesías escogidas*. Moscow: Progress, 1977.
McCagg, William O., and Lewis Siegelbaum, eds. *People with Disabilities in the Soviet Union: Past and Present, Theory and Practice*. Pittsburgh, PA: University of Pittsburgh Press, 1989.
McDermott, Kevin. "Stalinist Terror in the Comintern: New Perspectives." *Journal of Contemporary History* 30 (January 1995): 111–30.
McGuire, Elizabeth. *Red at Heart: How Chinese Communists Fell in Love with the Russian Revolution*. Oxford: Oxford University Press, 2018.
- "Sino-Soviet Every Day: Chinese Revolutionaries in Moscow Military Schools, 1927–1930." In *Everyday Life in Russia Past and Present*, edited by Choi Chatterjee, David Ransel, Mary Cavender, and Karen Petrone, 329–49. Bloomington: Indiana University Press, 2015.
Michaels, Paula. *Curative Powers: Medicine and Empire in Stalin's Central Asia*. Pittsburgh, PA: University of Pittsburgh Press, 2002.

Miller, Jamie. *Soviet Cinema: Politics and Persuasion under Stalin*. New York: I.B. Tauris, 2010.
Mintz, Steven. *Huck's Raft: A History of American Childhood*. Cambridge, MA: Harvard University Press, 2004.
Molero Pintado, Antonio. *La reforma educativa de la Segunda República Española: Primer bienio*. Madrid: Santillana, 1977.
Moradiellos, Enrique. "The Allies and the Spanish Civil War." In *Spain and the Great Powers in the Twentieth Century*, edited by Sebastian Balfour and Paul Preston, 96–126. New York: Routledge, 1999.
– *El reñidero de Europa: La dimensión internacional de la Guerra Civil española*. Barcelona: Península, 2001.
Moreno, C.B., M. Itkis, and J.P. Felipe, eds. *Dobro pozhalovat' na nash prazdnik*. Moscow: Prosveshchenie, 1974.
Moreno Izquierdo, Rafael. *Los niños de Rusia: La verdadera historia de una operación de retorno*. Barcelona: Crítica, 2017.
Moreno Martinez, P.L. *Educación, salud y protección a la infancia: Las colonias escolares de Cartagena (1907–1936)*. Cartagena, Spain: Aglaya, 2000.
Moskoff, William. *Bread of Affliction: The Food Supply in the USSR during World War II*. Cambridge: Cambridge University Press, 2002.
Neave, Guy. "War and Educational Reconstruction in Belgium, France and the Netherlands, 1940–1947." In *Education and the Second World War: Studies in Schooling and Social Change*, edited by Roy Lowe, 84–127. London: Falmer Press, 1992.
Nechaeva A.M. *Okhrana detei-sirot v Rossii: Istoriia i sovremennost'*. Moscow: Dom Rossiskogo detskogo fonda, 1994.
Nicolás Marín, María Encarna. "La integración de los niños y jóvenes en la emigración de la Guerra Civil: El caso de la Unión Soviética." *Anales de Historia Contemporánea*, 19 (2003): 60–73.
Norris, Kelsey. "World War II-Era Unaccompanied Children and the Politics of Family Reunification." Unpublished manuscript.
Norris, Stephen. *Blockbuster History in the New Russia: Movies, Memory, and Patriotism*. Bloomington: Indiana University Press, 2012.
Northrop, Douglas. *Veiled Empire: Gender and Power in Stalinist Central Asia*. Ithaca, NY: Cornell University Press, 2004.
Núñez Díaz-Balart, Mirta, Manuel Álvaro Dueñas, Francisco Espinosa Maestre, and José María García Márquez. *La gran represión: Los años de plomo del franquismo*. Barcelona: Flor del Viento, 2009.
O'Keeffe, Brigid. *New Soviet Gypsies: Nationality, Performance, and Selfhood in the Early Soviet Union*. Toronto: University of Toronto Press, 2013.
Ossian, Lisa L. "'Too Young for a Uniform': Children's War Work on the Iowa Farm Front, 1941–1945." In *Children and War: A Historical Anthology*, edited by James Marten, 254–65. New York: New York University Press, 2002.
Pak, Yoon K. *Wherever I Go, I Will Always Be an American: Schooling Seattle's Japanese Americans during World War*. New York: Routledge Falmer, 2002.

Palacio Pilacés, Luis Antonio. *Tal vez el día: Aragoneses en la URSS (1937–1977); El exilio y la Division Azul*. Zaragosa, Spain: Editorial Comuniter S.L, 2013.

Pauly, Matthew D. *Breaking the Tongue: Language, Power, and Education in Soviet Ukraine, 1923–1934*. Toronto: University of Toronto Press, 2014.

Payne, Matthew. "The Forge of the Kazakh Proletariat? The Turksib, Nativization, and Industrialization during Stalin's First Five-Year Plan." In *A State of Nations: Empire and Nation-Making in the Age of Lenin and Stalin*, edited by Ronald Grigor Suny and Terry Martin, 223–52. Oxford University Press, 2001.

Payne, Stanley G. *The Franco Regime, 1936–1975*. Madison: University of Wisconsin Press, 1987.

– *The Spanish Civil War*. Cambridge: Cambridge University Press, 2012.

– *The Spanish Civil War, the Soviet Union, and Communism*. New Haven, CT: Yale University Press, 2004.

Payne, Stanley G., and Jesús Palacios. *Franco: A Person and Political Biography*. Madison: University of Wisconsin Press, 2014.

Peeling, Siobhan. "Dirt, Disease and Disorder: Population Re-placement in Post-War Leningrad and the 'Danger' of Soviet Contamination." In *Warlands: Population Resettlement and State Reconstruction in the Soviet–East European Borderlands, 1945–50*, edited by Peter Gatrell and Nick Baron, 117–39. New York: Palgrave Macmillan, 2009.

Peris, Daniel. *Storming the Heavens: The Soviet League of the Militant Godless*. Ithaca, NY: Cornell University Press, 1998.

Pes, Alessandro. "Becoming Imperialist: Italian Colonies in Fascist Textbooks for Primary Schools." *Journal of Modern Italian Studies* 18, no. 5 (2013): 599–614.

Petrone, Karen. "Between Exploitation and Empowerment: Soviet Women Negotiate Stalinism." In *Gender and Mass Dictatorship*, edited by Jie-Hyun Lim and Karen Petrone, 125–41. New York: Palgrave Macmillan, 2011.

Pike, David Wingeate. *In the Service of Stalin: The Spanish Communists in Exile, 1939–1945*. Oxford: Clarendon Press, 1993.

Pine, Lisa. "The Dissemination of Nazi Ideology and Family Values through School Textbooks." *History of Education* 25, no. 1 (1996): 91–109.

– *Education in Nazi Germany*. Oxford: Berg, 2010.

Pla Brugat, Dolores. "Los niños del exilio español en México." In *El exilio de los niños*, edited by Alicia Alted, Roger González, and María José Millían, 162–77. Madrid: Fundación Francisco Largo Caballero / Fundación Pablo Iglesias, 2003.

– *Los niños de Morelia*. Mexico City: Instituto Nacional de Antropología e Historia, 1985.

Platt, Kevin M.F., and David Brandenberger, eds. *Epic Revisionism: Russian History and Literature as Stalinist Propaganda*. Madison: University of Wisconsin Press, 2006.

Pollock, Ethan. *Stalin and the Science Wars*. Princeton, NJ: Princeton University Press, 2006.

Pons Prades, Eduardo. *Los niños republicanos: El exilio*. Madrid: Oberon, 2005.

– *Republicanos españoles en la Segunda Guerra Mundial*. Madrid: La Esfera de los Libros, 2003.

Ponzio, Alessio. *Shaping the New Man: Youth Training Regimes in Fascist Italy and Nazi Germany*. Madison: University of Wisconsin Press, 2015.

Powelstock, David. "Fashioning 'Our Lermontov': Canonization and Conflict in the Stalinist 1930s." In *Epic Revisionism: Russian History and Literature as Stalinist Propaganda*, edited by Kevin Platt and David Brandenberger, 283–307. Madison: University of Wisconsin Press, 2006.

Preston, Paul. *The Spanish Civil War: Reaction, Revolution, Revenge*. New York: W.W. Norton, 2006.

– *The Spanish Holocaust: Inquisition and Extermination in Twentieth-Century Spain*. London: Harper Press, 2013.

Prokhorov, Alexander. "Arresting Development: A Brief History of Soviet Cinema for Children and Adolescents." In *Russian Children's Literature and Culture*, edited by Marina Balina and Larissa Rudova, 129–52. New York: Routledge, 2008.

Qualls, Karl D. "Defining the Ideal Soviet Childhood: Reportage about Child Evacuees from Spain as Didactic Literature." In *War and Childhood in the Era of the World Wars*, edited by Mischa Honeck and James Marten, 71–86. Cambridge: Cambridge University Press, 2019.

– "From Hooligans to Disciplined Students: Displacement, Resettlement, and Role Modelling of Spanish Civil War Children in the Soviet Union, 1937–1951." In *Displaced Children in Russia and Eastern Europe, 1915–1953: Ideologies, Identities, Experiences*, edited by Nick Baron, 131–54. Leiden, Netherlands: Brill, 2017.

– *From Ruins to Reconstruction: Urban Identity in Soviet Sevastopol after World War II*. Ithaca, NY: Cornell University Press, 2009.

Ramos, Vicente. *La Guerra Civil (1936–1939) en la provincia de Alicante*. Alicante, Spain: Ediciones Biblioteca Alicantina, 1973.

Rasell, Michael, and Elena Iarskaia-Smirnova, eds. *Disability in Eastern Europe and the Former Soviet Union: History, Policy and Everyday Life*. New York: Routledge, 2014.

Riley, Karen L. *Schools behind Barbed Wire: The Untold Story of Wartime Internment and the Children of Arrested Enemy Aliens*. Lanham, MD: Rowman & Littlefield, 2002.

Riordan, Jim, ed. *Soviet Education: The Gifted and the Handicapped*. New York: Routledge, 1988.

Rodríguez Pérez, Juan Félix, and Francisco Canes Garrido. *Las colonias escolares municipales madrileñas (1910–1936)*. Madrid: Universidad Complutense de Madrid, 2001.

Roith, Christian. "Trotz allem zeichnen sie: Der Spanische Bürgerkrieg mit Kinderaugen gesehen." *Paedagogica Historica* 45, no. 1–2 (2009): 191–214.

Rubinger, Richard. "Education in Wartime Japan, 1937–1945." In *Education and the Second World War: Studies in Schooling and Social Change*, edited by Roy Lowe, 59–72. London: Falmer Press, 1992.

Ruder, Cynthia. *Building Stalinism: The Moscow Canal and the Creation of Soviet Space*. London: I.B. Taurus, 2018.

Sánchez Andrés, Agustín, Silvia Figueroa, Eduarado Mateo Gambarte, Beatriz Morán Gortari, and Graciela Sánchez Almanza, eds. *Un capítulo de la memoria oral del exilio: Los niños de Morelia*. Morelia and Madrid: Universidad Michoacana de San Nicolás de Hidalgo–Comunidad de Madrid, 2002.

Sandomirskaia, Irina. "Skin to Skin: Language in the Soviet Education of Deaf-Blind Children, the 1920s and 1930s." *Studies in East European Thought* 60, no. 4 (2008): 321–37.

Schlögel, Karl. *Moscow, 1937*. Malden, MA: Polity, 2012.

Senelick, Laurence, and Sergei Ostrovsky, eds. *The Soviet Theater: A Documentary History*. New Haven, CT: Yale University Press, 2014.

Serrano, Secundino. *Españoles en el GULAG: Republicanos bajo el estalinismo*. Madrid: Península, 2011.

Shils, Edward. "Social and Psychologial Aspects of Displacement and Repatriation." *Journal of Social Issues* 2, no. 3 (1946): 3–18.

Shlapentokh, Dmitry, and Vladimir Shlapentokh. *Soviet Cinematography, 1918–1991: Ideological Conflict and Social Reality*. New York: Aldine de Gruyter, 1993.

Shubert, Adrian. *The Road to Revolution in Spain: The Coal Miners of Asturias, 1860–1934*. Urbana: University of Illinois Press, 1987.

Siegelbaum, Lewis. *Stakhanovism and the Politics of Productivity in the USSR, 1935–1941*. Cambridge: Cambridge University Press, 1988.

Sierra Blas, Verónica. "Educating the Communists of the Future: Notes on the Educational Life of the Spanish Children Evacuated to the USSR during the Spanish Civil War." *Paedagogica Historica* 51, no. 4 (2015): 496–519.

– *Palabras huérfanas: Los niños y la Guerra Civil*. Barcelona: I.B. Taurus, 2009.

– "Reconstructing Silences: On the Study and Editing of Private Letters by Spanish Children Evacuated to Russia during the Spanish Civil War." *Variants* 8 (2012): 95–109.

Simmons, Cynthia, and Nina Perlina. *Writing the Siege of Leningrad: Women's Diaries, Memoirs, and Documentary Prose*. Pittsburgh, PA: University of Pittsburgh Press, 2005.

Slezkine, Yuri. *Arctic Mirrors: Russia and the Small People of the North*. Ithaca, NY: Cornell University Press, 1994.

– "The USSR as a Communal Apartment, or How a Socialist State Promoted Ethnic Particularism." *Slavic Review* 53, no. 2 (1994): 414–52.

Solomon, Peter H. *Soviet Criminal Justice under Stalin*. Cambridge: Cambridge University Press, 1996.

Spaull, Andrew. "World War II and the Secondary School Curriculum: USA and Australia." In *Education and the Second World War: Studies in Schooling and Social Change*, edited by Roy Lowe, 159–76. London: Falmer Press, 1992.

Stargardt, Nicholas. *Witnesses of War: Children's Lives under the Nazis*. New York: Vintage, 2007.

Starks, Tricia. *The Body Soviet: Hygiene, Propaganda, and the Revolutionary State*. Madison: University of Wisconsin Press, 2008.

Starns, Penny Elaine, and Martin L. Parsons. "Against Their Will: The Use and Abuse of British Children during the Second World War." In *Children and War: A Historical Anthology*, edited by James Marten, 266–78. New York: New York University Press, 2002.

Stites, Richard. *Revolutionary Dreams: Utopian Vision and Experimental Life in the Russian Revolution*. Oxford: Oxford University Press, 1991.

Stolee, Margaret K. "Homeless Children in the USSR, 1917–1957." *Soviet Studies* 40 (January 1988): 64–83.

Stronski, Paul. *Tashkent: Forging a Soviet City, 1930–1966*. Pittsburgh, PA: University of Pittsburgh Press, 2010.

Suárez Fernández, Luis. *Franco y la URSS: La diplomacia secreta (1946–1970)*. Madrid: Ediciones Rialp, 1987.

Talashova, V.A. "Sovetskii Komsomol: Aktivnyi uchastnik dvizheniia solidarnosti s respublikanskoi Ispaniei v period natsional'no-revliutsionnyoi voiny, 1936–1939." PhD diss., Vologodskii gosudarstvennyi pedagogicheskii institut, 1972.

Tarquini, Alessandra. "Fascist Educational Policy from 1922 to 1943: A Contribution to the Current Debate on Political Religions." *Journal of Contemporary History* 50, no. 2 (2015): 168–87.

Taylor, Richard. *Film Propaganda: Soviet Russia and Nazi Germany*. London: Croom Helm, 1979.

Timasheff, Nicholas. *The Great Retreat: The Growth and Decline of Communism in Russia*. New York: Dutton, 1946.

Topdar, Sudipa. "The Corporeal Empire: Physical Education and Politicising Children's Bodies in Late Colonial Bengal." *Gender and History* 29, no. 1 (2017): 176–97.

Tsipursky, Gleb. *Socialist Fun: Youth, Consumption, and State-Sponsored Popular Culture in the Soviet Union, 1945–1970*. Pittsburgh, PA: University of Pittsburgh Press, 2015.

Tuttle, William M. *"Daddy's Gone to War": The Second World War in the Lives of an American Generation*. New York: Oxford University Press, 1995.

Uno, Kathleen S. *Passages to Modernity: Motherhood, Childhood, and Social Reform in Early Twentieth-Century Japan*. Honolulu: University of Hawaii Press, 1999.

van Ree, Erik. *The Political Thought of Joseph Stalin: A Study in 20th Century Revolutionary Patriotism*. New York: Routledge, 2002.

Vinyes, Ricard, Montse Armengou, and Ricard Belis. *Los niños perdidos del franquismo*. Barcelona: Random House Mondadori, 2003.

Volkov, Vadim. "The Concept of Kul'turnost': Notes on the Stalinist Civilizing Process." In *Stalinism: New Directions*, edited by Sheila Fitzpatrick, 210–30. New York: Routledge, 2000.

Wasilewska, Irena. *Suffer Little Children*. London: Maxlove, 1946.

Weiner, Amir, ed. *Landscaping the Human Garden: Twentieth-Century Population Management in a Comparative Framework*. Stanford, CA: Stanford University Press, 2003.

White, Elizabeth. "The Return of Evacuated Children to Leningrad, 1944–6." In *The Disentanglement of Populations: Migration, Expulsion and Displacement in Post-War Europe, 1944–9*, edited by Jessica Reinisch and Elizabeth White, 251–70. New York: Palgrave Macmillan, 2011.

Whitehead, Clive. *Colonial Educators: The British Indian and Colonial Education Service, 1858–1983*. London: I.B. Tauris, 2003.

Wollf, Richard. "'Fascistizing' Italian Youth: The Limits of Mussolini's Educational System." *History of Education* 13, no. 4 (1984): 287–98.

Wright, Susannah. "Teachers, Family and Community in the Urban Elementary School: Evidence from English School Log Books." *History of Education* 41, no. 2 (2011): 155–73.

Yekelchyk, Serhy. "*Diktat* and Dialogue in Stalinist Culture: Staging Patriotic Historical Opera in Soviet Ukraine, 1936–1954." *Slavic Review* (Fall 2000): 597–624.

Young, Glennys. "¿Sujetos peligrosos? Repatriados españoles desde la URSS en la Provincia de Vizcaya, 1956–1963." *Cuadernos de Historia Contemporánea* 38 (2016): 103–27.

– "To Russia with 'Spain': Spanish Exiles in the USSR and the *Longue Durée* of Soviet History." *Kritika: Explorations in Russian and Eurasian History* 15, no. 2 (2014): 395–420.

Yurchak, Alexei. *Everything Was Forever, Until It Was No More: The Last Soviet Generation*. Princeton, NJ: Princeton University Press, 2005.

Zafra, Enrique, Rosalía Crego, and Carmen Heredia. *Los niños españoles evacuados a la URSS (1937)*. Madrid: Ediciones de la Torre, 1989.

Zahra, Tara. *The Lost Children: Reconstructing Europe's Families after World War II*. Cambridge, MA: Harvard University Press, 2011.

Zajda, Joseph. *Education in the USSR*. Oxford: Pergamon Press, 1980.

Zhuk, S. Ia. *Kanal Moskva-Volga: Vspomagatel'nye raboty, 1932–1937*. Moscow: Gosudarstvennoe izdatel'stvo stroitel'noi literatury, 1945.

Zubkova, Elena. *Russia after the War: Hopes, Illusions, and Disappointments, 1945–1957*. Armonk, NY: M.E. Sharpe, 1998.

Index

Note: Italicized page numbers refer to illustrations.

acculturation. See *kul'turnost'*
Alberti, Rafael, 98
Alcorta, Carmen, 158
All-Union Central Council of Trade Unions (VTsSPS), 127, 131, 138, 145–9, 151
All-Union Society for Cultural Relations with Foreign Countries (VOKS), 66
Álvarez, Esther, 127, 160
Álvarez, Segis, 138
Álvarez Morán, Isabel Argentina, 39, 69, 73, 135; on returning to Spain, 165; during the Second World War, 102–3, 150; on transitioning to workforce, 132
Arce, Manuel, 43, 54, 144, 145; medical career of, 162; during the Second World War, 106, 107, 110, 120, 150
Argüelles, Anita, 110
Argüelles Fernández, José, 159
Arrizabalaga Arana, Paulino, 159
Artek Pioneer camp, 11, 20, 85–90, *86*
assimilation, 7–8, 42, 132; "double," 12–13. See also *kul'turnost'*
Avelairas, Joaquín, 158
Aza Ocaña, Emiliano, 52

Bajo, Elías, 60, 63
Balaguer, Luis, 48, 49, 151
Baron, Nick, 153
Bartolomé, Luciano, 143, 144

Bash, Iakov, 74
Basurto, Paco, 110
Belanguero brothers, 159
bilingual education, 42, 48–52, 62, 156, 162–5; literature and, 71–7, 152–3; Narkompros policies for, 141; during the Second World War, 115–17. See also Russian language instruction
boarding schools (*casas de niños*), 9, 34–49; administrators at, 43–5; as disciplinary institution, 41–9; educators at, 46–9; medical staff at, 45–6; Soviet regulations for, 51–2, 60–1, 123; staff dismissals at, 58–61, 121, 127, 157
Bolotnikov, Ivan, 68
Borodin, Aleksandr, 94
Bosque Arin, Ana del, 21
Bote, Juan, 58
Boy Scouts of America, 64–5
Brandenberger, David, 12
Bruno, Charito, 24–5
Budennyi, Semen, 113

Caballero, Juan José, 120
Calderón de la Barca, Pedro, 98, 152
Camino, Jaime, 39
Campoamor, Ramón de, 73
Carazo Pereda family, 30
Cárdenas, Lázaro, 37–8
Carrillo, Santiago, 87–9

Castaños, Rufino, 46
Castro, Fidel, 13, 158, 165
Catholicism, 10, 37, 65–6, 161, 163–5
Cenitagoya, Adolfo, 20, 28, 115
Centro Español de Moscú, 62, 159
Cervantes, Miguel de, 73, 76, 89, 98, 152
Chao, Lina, 59–60
Chapaev, Vasilii, 113
Chapí, Ruperto, 152
Chekhov, Anton, 73, 74, 75
Chernyshevskii, Nikolai, 74
Chervinskii, Petr, 74
children's councils, 3, 44, 54–5, 105, 119
Chinese students, 8, 9
Chkalov, Valery, 22, 68, 70, 71, 95
Chkalov Club, 5, 151–2, 157
Chukovskii, Nikolai, 75
Cisneros, Hidalgo de, 49–50, 52–3
"civilizing mission," 11
Clark, Katerina, 44, 62
cold war, 92–3, 131, 160
Colomina Limonero, Immaculada, 6, 132
colonias escolares (school colonies), 18
Communist International (Comintern), 9, 23, 105, 138; PCE and, 39, 73, 130, 138; purge of 1939 in, 40, 61, 72, 111; Red Cross and, 20
Communist Youth International, 89, 110
Communist Youth League. *See* Komsomol
Cooper, James Fenimore, 75
Cruz Arjona, Gonzalo, 160
Cuba, 13, 80, 158, 165

Darío, Rubén, 73
Defoe, Daniel, 75
Delgado, Vincente, 115
delinquency, 53–4, 151, 156; Makarenko on, 44; punishment of, 56–7; during the Second World War, 108, 118, 120. *See also* discipline
Derzhavin, Gavrila, 116

Devillard, Marie José, 17, 18, 78
Díaz, Florentina, 158
Díaz, José, 80, 95, 96, 116, 136
Díez, Antonio, 135
Dimitrov, Georgi, 110
diphtheria, 85
discipline, 43–9, 79–84; Foucault on, 44–5; punishment and, 56–60; responsibility and, 53–4; *vospitanie* and, 118–22. *See also* delinquency
displaced-persons camps, 47
Dobrenko, Evgeny, 92
Dostoevskii, Fyodor, 73
Dumas, Alexandre, 75
Dunstan, John, 106

education, 40–1, 65–6, 156, 163–4; extracurricular activities and, 47, 78–87; films and, 90–4; Franco's policies of, 46–7, 66; of Marxism-Leninism, 8, 40, 50, 55–6, 129, 156–9; physical, 83–4, 120; political, 59, 61–2, 94–9; theatre and, 93–4, 97; vocational, 144, 147, 157. *See also* bilingual education; *obuchenie*
Egorov, Aleksandr, 29
Ehrenburg, Il'a, 74
Elpat'evskii, A.V., 6
Estévez, Leonor, 122

Fadeev, Alexander, 74, 75
Fernández, Jacinta, 96
Fernández, María, 142
Fernández, Pilar, 4–5, 28, 30
Fernández Sánchez, José, 22, 28–30, 47, 182n3; on films, 93; during the Second World War, 105–7, 114, 121
Ferris, Kate, 8
Ferro, Amor, 110
films, 25, 55, 90–3, 112, 117
Finland, USSR's war with, 65, 79, 112, 133, 135, 139
Foucault, Michel, 44–5

Frades, Mariano, 160
Franco, Francisco, 17–19, 69, 72, 146; Catholicism and, 37, 161; death of, 162; educational policies of, 46–7, 66; Hitler and, 19, 26; persecution of leftists by, 5, 36, 161–3; resistance against, 80; on returning children from USSR, 101; during the Second World War, 116; victory of, 27, 52, 79, 157; Western support of, 129, 160
Frunze, Mikhail, 113
Fund for Aid to the Women and Children of Spain, 152

Gaidar, Arkady, 112
García, Divina, 30
García, Dolores, 59
García, José, 158
García Lorca, Federico, 73, 76, 98
gender roles, 84, 97, 130, 157, 159, 165
Girgor'ev, Sergei, 75
Glazunov, Aleksandr, 94
Gogol, Nikolai, 74, 116
Gómez, Agustín, 84, 159
González, América, 59
González Martínez, Carmen, 155
Gorbachev, Mikhail, 164
Gorky, Maksim, 73, 74, 75
Gounod, Charles François, 81–2, 98
Great Terror (1936–8), 16, 40, 60, 111; groups targeted during, 9; *kul'turnost'* and, 78
Grizodubova, Valentina, 68
Gromov, Mikhail, 68
Guernica, 3, 17, 19
Gulag prisoners, 61, 85, 159
Gutiérrez, Ángel, 87
Gypsies, 7

Hirsch, Francine, 12–13, 64
hispanidad (Spanishness), 14, 69, 155, 156
Hitler, Adolf, 19, 26, 146

Hitler Youth, 64–5
Huete, Tomás, 110
Hugo, Victor, 74, 75
hygiene, 45, 54–5; classes on, 83, 111; infectious diseases and, 34–6, 45–6, 83, 106, 109, 125; during the Second World War, 79–80, 106–9

Ibárruri, Dolores, 49–53, 63, 69, 73, 136, 142; on cadre development, 79; at civil war commemorations, 95; family of, 19, 115, 159; as role model, 96; on war-time evacuations, 122–3
Igmen, Ali, 99–100
indigenization (*korenizatsiia*) policy, 12, 13
International Children's Home, 8, 50, 155
International Organization for Aid to Revolutionary Fighters (MOPR), 22
International Red Aid, 3–4, 20
internationalism, 11–12, 62, 69, 156–8; patriotism and, 64, 76, 81, 157, 163; russocentrism and, 12, 16, 64–8
Italy, fascist, 19, 26, 77

Japan, nationalism in, 77
JSU. *See* Unified Socialist Youth
juvenile delinquency. *See* delinquency

Kalinin, Mikhail I., 82
Kataev, Valentin, 75
Komsomol (Communist Youth League), 15, 47, 89, 110; Central Committee of, 133, 135, 157; literary programs of, 76; political education and, 81, 96; on Russian language instruction, 117; on Spanish culture instruction, 136; Young Pioneers and, 54, 55
Konchalovsky, Petr, 95
Koniakhina, E.V., 109
Kononenko, Elena, 26–31, 89–90
Korchagin, Pavel, 74
Koshevaia, Elena, 74, 75

Koshevoi, Oleg, 74
Kosygin, Aleksei, 123
Kotovskii, Grigorii, 113
Kowalsky, Daniel, 6, 25
kruzhki (study circles), 15, 81, 83, 152; on Bolshevik Party, 139; films for, 90–1; holiday celebrations of, 89; as political work, 95–7
kul'turnost' (acculturation), 17, 51–2, 59, 83, 94; films about, 91; phases of, 78; during the Second World War, 120–2, 126–9; *vospitanie* and, 151. *See also* assimilation
Kutuzov, Mikhail, 68

Labour Reserve system, 132, 135, 157
Lagos, Alfonso, 116
Landa, Rubén, 73
Latin American movements, 10, 64, 121, 158, 160
Latorre Piquer, Milagros, 28, 85–7, 99; brother of, 138; in Mexico, 160; on transition to workforce, 135; during the Second World War, 101, 102, 110, 120
Leningrad, siege of, 69, 103, 104, 150
Levterova, K., 41
literature lessons, 47, 71–7, 92, 116, 152–3
Livschiz, Ann, 111
Llanos, Virgilio, 145
Lomonosov, Mikhail, 116
London, Jack, 74, 75

Machado, Antonio, 98, 115, 116
Makarenko, Anton, 40, 47; methods of, 54, 61; *Pedagogical Poem*, 44, 57
Maklai, Milukho, 92
Maksimova, N.G., 68–70
Malea, José, 110
Malenkov, Georgii, 122–3, 142
Manley, Rebeccah, 103
Manuilskii, Dmitrii, 22
Mares'ev, Aleksei, 75

Marinero, Celestina, 142–3
Marinero, Pedro, 143
marriage statistics, 159
Marti, Andre, 95
Martin, Terry, 12, 64
Martínez, António, 32, 53, 80, 158
Marxism-Leninism, 64, 67, 81; educational policies and, 8, 40, 50, 55–6, 129, 156–9; Gorbachev and, 164; literary criticism and, 98; religion and, 10, 57, 163. *See also* internationalism
Mateu, Julio, 3, 4, 65
May Day celebrations, 89–90
Mayakovsky, Vladimir, 74
Meseguer Ramos, José María, 136, 137
Mexico, Spanish immigrants of, 37–8, 127, 147–8, 160
Miller, Jamie, 91
Minin, Kuzma, 68
Mola, Emilio, 17
Molinas family, 4, 19, 20, 24, 160
Molotov, Vyacheslav, 95, 134, 147
Monzó Carbonell, Daniel, 28–9
Mora, Constancia de la, 49–50, 52–3
Morozov, Pavlik, 53
Moscow-Volga Canal, 16, 85
Muñoz, Ventura, 158
Mussolini, Benito, 19, 26, 77

Napoleon Bonaparte, 68, 69, 74
Narkompros (People's Commissariat of Enlightenment), 23–4, 42–3, 48, 81, 133–4; All-Union Society for Cultural Relations with Foreign Countries and, 66; priorities of, 53; on Russian language skills, 141; during the Second World War, 107, 115, 117, 123–4, 146; vocational training by, 147
Narkomzdrav (health ministry), 34–5, *124*
Naumov, I., 124
Navalón, Ángel, 158
Navarro, Francisco, 115

Naves, Fausto, 120
Neave, Guy, 64
Nekrasov, Nikolai, 74
Nevsky, Aleksandr, 68, 74, 92
New Year's celebrations, 87, *88*
Nicolás Marín, María Encarna, 56
NKVD (People's Commissariat for Internal Affairs), 34–5, 107, 139
Norris, Stephen, 92
Novodevichii Cemetery, 85

obuchenie (education), 63–4; *vospitanie* versus, 52, 79–82, 130–1. *See also* education
O'Keeffe, Brigid, 99–100
opera, 81–2, 94
Orlova, Lyubov, 22
Oyarzábal, Jesús, 31, 84

paedology, 40, 61, 81–2, 84
Papanin, Ivan, 68, 70, 95
París, Mercedes, 127
patriotism, 65; films about, 92–3; internationalism and, 64, 76, 81, 157, 163; lessons on, 56, 67–71, *71*, 115, 120–2, 129; literature and, 73–7
Pauly, Matthew, 99–100
Pavlov, Ivan, 67
PCE. *See* Spanish Communist Party
pedagogy, 44–5, 116–17; child-centred, 40, 61; teacher-centred, 57, 81–2, 84. *See also* Russian language instruction
Peláez, Álvaro, 48, 110
Peluso, Edmund, 72
People's Commissariat for Internal Affairs (NKVD), 34–5, 107, 139
People's Commissariat of Enlightenment. *See* Narkompros
Pérez, Ángeles, 28
Pérez, María, 158
Peter the Great, 68, 92
physical education, 83–4, 120, 157

Picasso, Pablo, 17
Pioneers. *See* Young Pioneers
Pita, Federico, 136–9
Polevoi, Boris, 74, 75
Polish students, 8, 9, 26
Potemkin, Vladimir, 67, 109, 110, 123
Pozharsky, Dmitry, 68
Pugachev, Emilian, 68
Pushkin, Aleksandr, 16, 74, 76, 94

Ramón Jiménez, Juan, 98
Razin, Stenka, 68, 98
Recarey, Manuel, 138
Red Cross/Red Crescent, 3–4, 105, 160
Reid, Thomas Mayne, 75
reintegration in Spain, 159–66
Remedios family, 19
Ricardo, Juan, 104, 105
Rimsky-Korsakov, Nikolai, 94
Rincón, Ramiro, 158
Río, Bernardo del, 49, 70, 83; during the Second World War, 115, 121, 138; teaching career of, 158
Rivas, Luis, 160
Rodríguez, Ángel, 20
Rodríguez, Juan, 16
Rodríguez, Teresa, 59
Roldán brothers, 21, 29, 34
Rolland, Romain, 74
Romanov dynasty, 68
Roure, Carmen, 127
Rozenfel'd, Semen, 74
Ruiz Ibárruri, Rubén, 115, 159
Russian Civil War, 44, 83, 91–2
Russian language instruction, 10, 42, 105, 156–7; Narkompros policies for, 141; during the Second World War, 115–17, 128–9, 138. *See also* bilingual education
Russian Revolution, 89, 91–2, 95
Russian Soviet Federative Socialist Republic (RSFSR), 42, 104–5, 123

Russification policies, 117–18, 134. *See also* Soviet values
Russo-Finnish War (1939), 65, 79, 112, 133, 135, 139
Russo-Turkish wars, 68
russocentrism, 12, 16, 64–8, 92

Saakadze, Georgi, 92
Sagasti, Ruperto, 159
Sáinz Castillo, Marcelino, 102
Sáiz, Jesús, 151
San Baudelio, Isidro, 30
Sánchez, Alberto, 97
Sánchez Urquijo, Araceli, 30, 41, 149–50
Schlögel, Karl, 7
Scott, Walter, 47, 75
Second World War, 47, 101–31; evacuations during, 36–7, 104–26, *124*, 139–42; hygiene lessons during, 79–80, 106, 108, 109; *kul'turnost'* during, 120–2, 126–9; Narkompros during, 107, 115, 117, 123–4; reconstruction after, 132–54; Russian language instruction during, 115–17, 128–9, 138
Serrano, Francisco, 120
sexual misconduct, by staff, 59–61
Shaps, Aleksandr, 97
Sierra, Aya, 120
Sierra, Verónica, 6
Slezkine, Yuri, 164
socialist realism, 90
Soler, Alejandra, 46, 106
Solo Rodríguez, Ángel, 144
Soviet values, 13, 48–9, 151, 156–7; films and, 90–3, 113; indigenization policy and, 12, 13; literature and, 73–7; political work and, 94–9; role models of, 49–61, 82–4, 118–23, 127; Russification policies and, 117–18, 134; during the Second World War, 112–26; *vospitanie* and, 79–81

Sovnarkom (Council of People's Commissars), 106, 140
Spanish Civil War commemorations, 87–9, 95
Spanish Communist Party (PCE), 5, 9, 34, 47–8; Comintern and, 39, 73, 130, 138; newspaper of, 115; on repatriation, 160; on returnees to Spain, 101; Soviet boarding homes and, 51–2, 59, 64, 80, 122–3, 157; on vocational training, 144
Spanish language instruction. *See* bilingual education
Stalin, Joseph, 11, 40, 118, 156, 160; on cadres, 57, 61, 62; Constitution of, 56, 67, 129; on history of Communist Party, 95; nationalism of, 12, 62, 92, 158; reforms of, 150; show trials of, 16
Stalingrad, battle of, 122
Stowe, Harriet Beacher, 75
study circles. See *kruzhki*
Suárez, Meri, 72, 160
Suvorov, Aleksandr, 68, 92
Sviatoslavych, Igor, 94

Talón, Vicente, 110, 139
theatre excursions, 93–4, 97
Timoshenko, Semen, 113
Tolstoy, Lev, 47, 69, 74, 75, 116
Tourne family, 160
Tseretelli, Akaki, 98
Tsintsadze, Sulkhan, 98
Turgenev, Ivan, 47, 74, 75, 116
Turkey, 9, 68
Twain, Mark, 75

Ukraine, 14, 104, 163; boarding schools in, 42, 122; Nazi invasion of, 69, 75
Undiano, Enrique, 30
Unified Socialist Party (Catalonia), 127
Unified Socialist Youth (JSU), 55, 70, 136, 139

USSR, 5; Constitution of, 56, 67, 129; Finnish War of, 65, 79, 112, 133, 135, 139; Volga Germans of, 9, 102, 106–8, 146. *See also* Soviet values

Val, Delfin, 84, 87
Valverde, Josefina, 160
Varela, Jesús, 159
Vasnetsov, Viktor, 74
Vázquez, Enrique, 160
Vega, Lope de, 73, 89, 98, 152
Verne, Jules, 75
Vertov, Dziga, 90
Viana, Gerardo, 120
Vidal, José Luis, 135
Vincente, Esther, 158
vocational training, 144, 147, 157
VOKS (All-Union Society for Cultural Relations with Foreign Countries), 66
Volga Germans, 9, 102, 106–8, 146
Volkov, Vadim, 78
Volma, Abraham, 61
Voroshilov, Kliment, 22–3, 113
vospitanie (upbringing), 50, 59, 77, 133, 151, 161–5; discipline and, 118–22; goals of, 79; Kalinin on, 82; *obuchenie* versus, 52, 79–82, 130–1
vospitateli (non-classroom educators), 42
VTsSPS. *See* All-Union Central Council of Trade Unions

workforce, transitioning to, 132, 135, 142–54, 157
World Festival of Youth and Students (Moscow, 1957), 165
World War II. *See* Second World War

Young, Glennys, 161
Young Pioneers, 24–5, 54–5; Black Sea camp of, 11, 20, 85–90, *86*; political education of, 81; Spanish children greeted by, 14, *23*, 27–9, *29*; uniforms of, 44
youth homes, 133–42, 150, 157

Zafra, Enrique, 97, 151
Zapatero, Isabel, 110
Zaragoza, José, 115
Zemliachka, Rosalia, 109
Zhdanov, Andrei, 94

www.ingramcontent.com/pod-product-compliance
Lightning Source LLC
Chambersburg PA
CBHW030312080526
44584CB00012B/545